PETER WITHE

ALL FOR THE LOVE OF THE GAME

PETER WITHE

ALL FOR THE LOVE OF THE GAME

With

Simon Goodyear

Foreword by

Ray Clemence

Published in 2017 by Goodyear Publications
www.goodyearpublications.com

ISBN (Hardback): 978-1-909811-38-6
ISBN (Paperback): 978-1-909811-37-9
ISBN (ePub): 978-1-909811-39-3
ISBN (ePDF): 978-1-909811-40-9

Trinity Mirror, The Nottingham Evening Post, Roy Peters and Getty Images have given permission to use photographs within this book. Every effort has been made to trace all other photographers. Some photographs were sourced from Peter's personal collection.

A full CIP record for this book is available from the British Library.

Design and Typesetting by Riverside Publishing Solutions, Salisbury

Printed and bound in the UK by Jellyfish Solutions, Swanmore

Dedication

This book is dedicated to my beautiful wife and soulmate, Kathy and to our children Jason, Gareth and Stephen.

Contents

Also by the Author

The Gerry Hitchens Story – From Mine to Milan

La Storia di Gerry Hitchens (Italian version)

The Bobby Thomson Story – The Real Bobby Dazzler

The Harry Moseley Story – Making it Happen

Memories Made in Aston

A Note from the Author

"I remember this big, burly giant with a beard who could play a bit and, more importantly, had a proven goal-scoring record."

****

This is more than a story about someone who has been in love with football all his life; it is also about a love affair with a lady called Kathy, who has stayed with Peter since the age of 13 and has lived the life of a footballer's wife ever since. I knew Peter would have a million stories to tell and could fill a book or three, and he took little convincing to let me record them for him. It was a pleasure to sit and listen to them all.

A biography of Peter Withe has been a long time in the making; long before I got in touch with Ian Seddon, Peter's advisor, via Twitter in the late summer of 2012. It may have seemed a random request at the time, but it turned out to be the opportune moment to pose such a cheeky question as Ian just happened to be looking for a ghost writer to help Peter pen his (many) memories. I had a pre-existing connection with Peter as my late father, David Goodyear, had known him from his days as the secretary of the Aston Villa Former Players' Association in the 1980s and 1990s. It was that connection that Peter remembered with fondness and in some ways, I guess, helped me secure the job of putting into writing the memories of one of my all-time footballing heroes.

The name Peter Withe is surely etched in the memory of every Aston Villa fan of a certain age. Even if you don't support the 'Villans', who can ever forget that famous line by the late (and great) ITV commentator Brian Moore, during the 1982 European Cup Final ... 'Shaw, Williams, prepared to adventure down the left. There's a good ball played in for Tony Morley. Oh, it must be! It is! Peter Withe!'

My own personal memories of Peter begin when I was a teenager in the early 1980s. Watching Villa play week in, week out, I remember this big, burly giant with a beard who could play a bit and, more importantly, had a proven goal-scoring record. I knew Peter had scored goals at his previous clubs, including Brian Clough's Nottingham Forest. He seemed like a larger than life character, totally committed to the cause and a tireless worker on the field of play. He always led the line fearlessly and scored his share of goals. I seem to remember Peter was the last piece of the jigsaw for Ron Saunders when he signed from Newcastle in the summer of 1980. He had turned down his boyhood club Everton to come to Villa Park and that, to me, suggested he wanted success.

Peter was a 'showman' if you like, not flash or fancy but always running towards the Holte End terraces after each home game to collect a bag of sweets from one of his adoring fans, often throwing a claret and blue sweat-band into the crowd.

It goes without saying that without the time, effort and patience of Peter (and Kathy) over the last five years we probably wouldn't have a book to print. I would also like to thank Stephen Withe for all his help during this journey and for his continued support with the publication and marketing of the book. I am truly privileged and proud to have written this book for Peter (and his family), a man who not only is a true football legend but one of the nicest guys you could ever meet.

Simon Goodyear
www.goodyearpublications.com

Foreword

By Ray Clemence

****

My impression of Peter was that of a whole-hearted player who was physically strong and gave everything for the cause. He was good in the air, would never give less than 100 per cent and expected the same from everyone who played alongside him, whether with Villa or playing for England. Peter was the ultimate team-player — even when he wasn't in the England team and was training with the squad, he'd be 100 per cent behind the lads who were playing.

I first remember playing against Peter when I made my debut for Spurs against Villa in the 1981 Charity Shield at Wembley. I dropped a cross and it fell to Peter, who buried the ball into the net. We later became good friends off the pitch, mainly through our coaching careers, and we spent some time together out in Thailand when he was their national coach.

We share a passion for golf and played in several pro-celebrity tournaments during our playing days. I'd say Peter is slightly better than me, although he has been around the world a lot in recent years so we haven't played for a while. I'd probably bet I play more than he does now, even though he lives on a golf course out in Australia!

Although we don't see much of each other now, we still keep in regular contact on social media and remain good friends.

Ray Clemence

Former England, Liverpool and Tottenham Hotspur goalkeeper

Prologue

Being A Footballer's Wife

****

By Kathy Withe

Being a footballer's wife in the 1970s and 1980s was completely different to the WAG experience today. It was not a glamorous life of big houses, designer clothes and flash cars. I didn't like it if I'm honest. I didn't like the way the footballers' wives were always in the public eye. I didn't want to be in the newspapers or on TV, although some clearly did and loved it. Being a private person, it just wasn't the way I wanted to live my life, but I put up with it for Peter. It had been his dream to be a professional footballer from a very early age.

To me there seemed to be a pecking order for the wives to follow; if your husband wasn't playing in the first team nobody wanted to talk to you, which I found odd but if he was in the first team, everyone was interested in you all of a sudden. I found that side of it very difficult to comprehend.

I had no idea back in the early 1970s, when Peter was a part-time footballer, that he was destined to hit the big time and we'd travel up and down the country (and around the world) just for him to kick a ball around. In fact, Peter was also a part-time electrician at the time because he didn't earn enough from football. My idea of Peter being a footballer was that it was 'just a job' even though he moved from club to club and town to town. However, once Peter signed for Wolves things changed (for the better) and we started to get our life together. The club found us a new house to live in and things were looking good.

The down side of being a footballer's wife is that your husband (or boyfriend) is always away, either training, playing in matches or travelling to games. In the early days, I didn't have anyone around me to talk to or to help me with our young baby. I was on my own and lonely for long periods of time while Peter was 'doing his job.' I found that side of it very difficult to handle.

When we lived in the US for the 12 months that Peter played for Portland Timbers life was amazing. It was a total contrast to when he was at Wolves, more like being on holiday than working. Peter was around a lot more; I saw him most days and he'd be home at a set time every day, except when the Timbers played away games. I attended all the games and the atmosphere was fantastic. We were in the public eye but there wasn't that pecking order because everyone was on the same level. It was such good fun but reality kicked in and the 'holiday' ended after his contract expired and he signed for Birmingham City. All of a sudden things were back to how they had been before – and I was back living the life of a footballer's wife.

Peter's pedigree and profile became higher with every club he moved to. From Birmingham we moved to Nottingham and we settled in immediately – we liked Nottingham and wanted to make a life there. Our second son, Stephen was born while Peter was at Nottingham Forest and I was ready to settle there long term, but Brian Clough put paid to that and we were off to Newcastle after only two years. That's football for you, I guess.

The biggest step up was when Peter signed for Aston Villa and his profile increased to sky-high proportions. It was there he was first selected to play for England and that brought its own issues. Being on England duty meant players would be away for days on end and the wives and girlfriends would become even lonelier. Even though I hated football I went to watch all of his appearances for England because it was important for me to support my husband, especially in playing for his country, of which he was immensely proud.

Certainly, in the early years, Peter wasn't earning a lot of money, and would supplement his income by doing TV work on the odd occasion. In later years, the money increased and we steadily bettered ourselves in terms of living in bigger and better homes and being able to have nice family holidays. Obviously, the money wasn't anything like modern footballers' wages, but we had a good life from football. Peter wasn't (and still isn't) a gambler so we didn't get into any financial problems like some players did – and still do.

The one thing I hated though was speaking to the media. When Peter was at Forest, reporters would phone quite regularly for him and if I answered I would ask why they wanted to do an interview and what the article was about before they could even talk to Peter. Once, while Peter was at Villa, we were asked to do an interview for a football magazine. The article was supposed to be about Peter's life and the crew took pictures of the house and the kids. Although I went along with it I was a bit suspicious for some reason. My suspicion was well founded once I read the article. The title read: 'Peter Withe' (on one page) and 'Peter Without' (on the opposite page). While Peter Withe had everything in life, the 'Peter Without' was some other footballer (called Peter) who wasn't doing so well in his career – he may have been in the fourth division or something, while Peter was playing in the first division with Villa. The article compared the two Peters' careers. We had no idea the magazine was going to do that comparison otherwise we wouldn't have done the interview – I was furious and I felt really bad for the other Peter.

Being a footballer requires maximum dedication but being a footballer's wife requires a lot of tolerance (as well as dedication). My husband always came first – sometimes even before the kids – all because he was a footballer. When Peter was at the top of his profession a typical day consisted of early morning training followed by an afternoon round of golf. Some days, the boys would go out for the evening after the golf and it was the same the next day and the day after that. The golf seemed to take Peter away from his family and on to another level in a way. There were times when I felt pressured to go out with him to club social events, but that required careful planning because we had three kids and I had to get babysitters in to look after them for a few hours. In fact, I didn't have one babysitter but several at any one time, just so I could go and support Peter. I did make the effort to be by his side on many occasions; if I had had the choice I'd have been with my kids, but being a footballer's wife dictated otherwise.

If I was lonely when Peter was a player, him being a football manager was even worse, and there was a time when I wanted it no more. After Peter hung up his boots in 1989 he got his first managerial job at Huddersfield and of course we moved up there. It was as though I was just dumped there and neglected in a three-bedroomed house in the middle of nowhere. Every day was the same: Peter would leave the house in the early hours and return late at night only to get up and do it all again the next day. I got so bored on my own and that's when it suddenly hit me that I didn't want to live like that any more. It was a very difficult time of our lives. We didn't have any family in Huddersfield and there was no one to talk to or to help us with the kids – I knew no one there. I don't know how, but we lasted two years in Yorkshire before moving back to Birmingham.

Moving back to Birmingham was a good move because my life was there. I had a job at the NEC and I played some squash with friends. It was a totally different experience to the previous two years because I felt I had my life back. However, jobs in football don't last long and his job changed when the management at Villa changed. He was asked to do some scouting for Brian Little, a job he told me he'd never do. I never wanted him to do it because we knew someone whose marriage had broken down as a result of him being a football scout. Her husband was away for days on end and they hardly ever saw each other. I didn't want that with our marriage; however, Peter accepted the job. He found himself away a lot, up and down the UK and abroad. Although he enjoyed it, it took its toll and we eventually had to talk about how it was affecting our relationship. I gave Peter the choice and he thankfully chose to save our marriage.

When the Thailand job came up in 1998 our lives changed yet again. I had no choice really in going to Thailand – it was either that or end our marriage. However, being in a different country we were together, even more so, and it was different to when Peter was a player or a manager back home. It was exciting and there didn't seem the same intense pressure that there was back in England.

When Peter finished football for good we moved to Perth, Western Australia for five years just to get away from it all. It was really strange being together at home for long periods of time. I am a homely person but Peter is the opposite and would rather be out playing golf or watching sports with his mates. Peter had been used to people doing things for him for most of his life, but I found myself telling Peter to do things like put the bins out, lock the door when he came in at night, wash up the dishes, even things like putting water in the car – all those things most people take for granted and do all the time. It used to make me laugh, him not being used to doing those silly little things. However, it was good to have him there with me. Still to this day, I love Peter being at home with me, even though he still likes to spend time out playing golf or going out with his mates. Don't get me wrong, if he got another job somewhere else I'd be 100 per cent behind him and would never stop him doing anything he wanted to do – I never stopped him going anywhere in his football career and always backed him.

All-in-all, being a footballer's wife has had its ups and downs, but the positives far outweigh the negatives we've encountered. Our dreams came true when we travelled to South Africa at the age of 20, way back in 1971. We had never travelled far out of Liverpool let alone abroad, and found ourselves 8,000 miles away, in the sun. It was a far cry from the post-war Liverpool we had grown up in. We hadn't been brought up with money in our family and we had it hard for so long, unlike most modern footballers who think money grows on trees. Peter always had to fight for every last penny he brought into the family but I can honestly say he earned every last penny of it.

Would I do it all again? 100 per cent, yes, I would and all for Peter. Because it was all he ever wanted – to be a professional footballer.

Kathy Withe

1

From Signing Autographs to Signing On

"...ten years previously, I'd scored the winning goal in the European Cup final... Now I was on the dole."

****

For the first time in 20 years, I was faced with having no money, no job and no prospects. It was hard but I was determined to get through whatever life chucked at me – for the sake of my family.

You don't expect to find too many ex-professional footballers standing in the dole queue waiting to sign on but that was the reality I faced in October 1992. I'd just been sacked by Wimbledon and things were getting nasty as I'd raised a case against the club for unfair dismissal. All of a sudden I had no income (apart from the unemployment benefit) and an increasing family to feed. To top it all, my son, Jason, was thinking of getting married, but that was just the start of it.

For me, the hardest part of being jobless was having to go to the Unemployment Benefit Office in Solihull to sign on. Only ten years previously, I'd scored the winning goal in the European Cup Final, yet I found myself on the dole. That didn't seem right to me. It was strange that I was sitting in the interview room in the dole office and was asked what my profession was. The look on the interviewer's face when I gave my response was a picture. It was kind of funny at the time because I don't think they had too many ex-professional football players or managers go through their doors, especially in Solihull. I hated signing on (who doesn't) but it wasn't like I had to sign on and then wait for something to happen – I was trying to find a job. I had to! It was as simple as that.

I only had to make the trip to queue up and sign on once a fortnight, but even that was too often for me. Of course, my presence set tongues wagging, but I tried to be oblivious to the attention I was creating. A few people who recognised me asked me to sign autographs (something I've always obliged in doing) but on the whole most people didn't bother me (or didn't recognise me). I was just a 'normal' person who had bills to pay and a family to support, so the money had to come from somewhere. It was bad enough that we contemplated selling our house in Dorridge, but I was adamant things wouldn't get to that stage and always hopeful that something would crop up.

For me, the Wimbledon compensation saga was dragging on far too long and with other things going on in my life at that time, the stress was piling up. I was trying to keep my family together the best I could, but faced difficult situations from all sides, not least a family dispute. Things were desperate but I was adamant that I was going to find work and keep my family together. Kathy had urged me to sell the house to raise some capital at one stage, but I didn't want to go down that road. I was desperate not to show my outward emotion and stress to my family – I'm not that type of person anyway but it was important to me to appear capable. Inwardly, I felt under pressure, and it was hard to focus on anything else; but throughout that period I always tried to stay optimistic. I was out of work and broke, but there were people far worse off than me. I still had my family and a roof over my head. Things weren't too bad if you looked at it that way.

I received a pay-off from Wimbledon some months later, but soon after was faced with a bill for solicitors' fees for the Wimbledon saga, followed by a bill from the taxman, so there wasn't anything much left of the money from the Wimbledon pay-off.

It was a time of my life I wouldn't want to go through ever again and wouldn't wish on anyone, but that I now put down to experience, I suppose. Those experiences made me very wary of everything I do in my life, every decision I make and everything and anyone I get involved with.

2

Born to Be a Winner

"One day, I'm going to play at Wembley."

****

My dream to be a footballer began at 43 Almond Street, Speke, Liverpool on the 30 August 1951. According to my mother, I arrived kicking and screaming, so was meant to be a footballer from day one, it seemed.

Looking back on my life then, it was so cosy and carefree, with families enjoying the peacetime that followed the end of the Second World War. It was like opening a window on an exciting period of optimism after years of doom and gloom: anything and everything seemed possible. We didn't have much but we were happy; we had peace, freedom and a sense of wanting to move on from the bleak years that our parents had just suffered. Liverpool's traditional sense of community, strengthened by the war years, provided a secure background from which children and teenagers could welcome a second Elizabethan era.

If you lived in Liverpool in those days, you were either a red (Liverpool) family or a blue (Everton) family. The club you supported sometimes divided families, and even your marriage options were limited by your allegiance to the reds or the blues – very rarely did the two meet, let alone marry, God forbid! For many years, and certainly until the Shankly era, the rivalry between the clubs was relatively benign. This was particularly the case from the end of the Second World War until the early 1960s, when Liverpool were pretty poor, it has to be said. During most of the 1950s it was difficult for Evertonians to maintain much of a rivalry as our neighbours were languishing in Division Two (or the Championship as it's now known to our younger readers).

I was born into an Evertonian family and I certainly got my Everton influence from my father's side; his brothers and sisters were all Evertonians. I had an aunt on my father's side who was Everton crazy. Her son, Harold, used to sell programmes at Goodison Park on match days, helped by my father. Harold was a bit of a comedian, and I always remember people congregating around him while he was selling his programmes, stood there telling jokes all afternoon, a real personality. Then there was my aunt Madge. She was what we called a 'groupie Evertonian' because she got kitted out on match days in every piece of blue and white clothing she could find, and she had dozens of badges attached to numerous scarves which were wrapped around her neck and wrists. She was a real character as well and you'd often read about her in the local papers. She was one of those ladies who everyone knew at Goodison Park and had followed Everton for many years. By comparison, my sister Rose wasn't into football at all (as most women weren't in those days) and so went wherever my mother went on a Saturday afternoon – usually into town, shopping.

I was barely out of nappies when I was introduced to a football, but my first experience of going to watch Everton was with my father around age 4 or 5. Before every home game at Goodison Park, we would go to my grandmother's house and she would always make a thick barley soup. It was lovely; that boiling hot soup warmed our hearts and lined our stomachs before we all went to the game. They lived only a stone's throw from Goodison Park, and as soon as the match had finished, we'd go back to my grandmother's for another bowl of thick, hearty soup. When I look back at my early life, I think I must have taken it in turns to visit either grandparents on a Saturday and it must have coincided with Everton playing at home.

I had always hung around the street corners with a group of scallies including my mates, Ron Smith and Tommy McNally, with whom I did the paper round. When we finished our round we would traipse off to the nearest local school and climb over the fence to play football in the playground, even though the gates were locked. Sometimes we would be chased away by the caretaker for being on the school grounds. There were usually around ten of us playing football, sometimes other kids would join us so ten became fifteen or twenty. We'd spend hours and hours playing there every day, and we loved it. I think we played football anywhere we could: in the street, in the park, in the school playground and sometimes we didn't even have a football to kick and made do with a can or a bottle – whatever we could find. Whatever it was we ended up kicking it and I would always try to 'hog' the ball (or can) as I considered myself to be the best player in the group, dribbling past ten or twenty lads at a time. I was that confident as a footballer that I once said to my mates, 'One day I'm going to play at Goodison Park.'

Of course, my mates didn't want to believe me, 'Nah, you'll never play at Goodison.'

I replied, 'I tell you, I'm going to play for Everton at Goodison Park and one day I'm going to play at Wembley.' I always said I'd prove my mates wrong and I did just that.

At the age of 13 or 14 I started to help young Harold selling his programmes before home games. During the 1966 World Cup, Brazil were based in the north west and three Group 3 matches were played at Goodison Park, which had a capacity back then of 70,000. In 1966 Brazil weren't the great team they became years later, and only won one out of three games in their group, failing to qualify for the next stages. In other words, the European teams had kicked Pele out of the tournament. Anyway, Harold and I, together with my brothers, Paul and Gerard, and my father, all sold programmes during the World Cup games and we couldn't sell them fast enough; they literally sold like hot cakes. Pile after pile sold almost as quickly as we could pick them up with people stopping us to buy them before we even got back to our pitch. It was a kind of ferry service coming and going back and forth to where the programmes were stored. The programmes were collectable because they were not specific to the game; as a tournament brochure they covered all 8 venues used in the World Cup. That was a summer I'll never forget and we all know what happened on Saturday, 30 July 1966!

My father was a semi-professional footballer at a young age and it was only the war that stopped him from playing at a higher level. Of course, he was a centre-forward (I wonder where I got that from?) and he carried on after the war, playing for his works' teams. From a really young age, we all used to go and watch Dad play on a Saturday and sometimes on a Sunday for his works' team, Metal Box. That really cemented my love for football. My first proper football boots were a pair of huge, orange toe-capped leather boots. They were real 'old school' boots and they were hard and stiff, unlike the soft, plastic boots today's players wear. I remember hitting them with a hammer to try to soften the ends up but they were solid.

My father was the one who taught me how to kick a ball properly, not to toe-poke it like you were taught at school, but to kick it with the inside of your foot. I was the only one in the family who could kick with both feet, unlike my father and my brothers who were all right-footed.

When we discovered we were actually quite good at football, Dad encouraged us all to play for the school teams, and not just football; we got involved in football, rugby, cricket and indoor sports such as table tennis. Not only did we all play for the school teams, we also got involved with Saturday and Sunday league adult teams from an early age, even joining the Wednesday team so we could play for three different teams during the week. At the end of the day we just wanted to play football, no matter who it was for.

In those days you could play in teams above your own age group and as I was one of the better players in my school I was picked to play in a more senior team against a school in Childwall. I remember getting there and seeing a pair of massive-looking goalposts which had nets, something we weren't used to. We made the most of those nets, and I scored a hat-trick playing as a striker. Someone asked me how I scored three goals and I replied, 'It was the first time I've played with nets. It was nice to hear the ball hit the back of the net.' It was also the first time I got my name in the papers. Looking back, that hat-trick gave me the incentive to carry on pursuing my dream to one day play at Goodison Park, but my brothers became a bit disillusioned with football and never really had the same ambition as I did, although they were good. Seeing my name in the paper gave me a big lift and for a 12-year-old it was a big deal indeed.

Towards the end of our schooling my brothers and I wrote off to a lot of football clubs asking for trials – because that's what you had to do in those days to get yourself noticed. I thought I was good enough to play football for a living; it seemed easy enough and I didn't know what else to do – what better way to earn a living than to play football? One day we were invited to play for South Liverpool, a non-league team based in Garston, which was the next village to where we lived. Paul played centre-back and Gerard and I played upfront (although I could play in various positions really). In our mind we thought we were quite good at the time but when we went for the trial, none of us got a look-in. There was a big clique at the club and everyone else knew each other. We played in a practice match and no one passed the ball to us. It was a major disappointment but in a way, it probably only encouraged me even more to make it as a professional.

I was the youngest person in my class at school as I was born on 30 August so I was able to leave school in the July at the age of 14, whereas most of my peers left school at 15. I could have stayed on for another year and I did consider it but to be perfectly honest I needed to go out to work to help 'pay my way' as we were a working-class family and, well, we needed the money. One of the jobs I had included helping the milkman before going to school, which meant getting up at 5am to earn about 2 shillings a week. I also helped the bread man, did a paper round and I had an order round for the local fruit and veg shop. If you wanted money in those days you had to find the jobs and work for it. It was the only way you could survive because you didn't get pocket money back then, unless your parents were wealthy. Basically, if you wanted it, you'd have to go out and get it. However, for all those jobs, I still had to help the family out and gave some of it to my mother to help with paying for the gas or the electric meter. We didn't have a TV in those days; my grandfather, who was a little bit better off than my parents had a TV and we used to go there to watch it. In fact at one stage he had two TVs, one on top each other and they had a meter at the back of each. As there were only two channels in those days, he used to watch them both at the same time. The TVs in the late 1950s and early 1960s were huge, weighed a ton and he had one on top another. Amazing!

As children we never wanted for anything and never went without anything, and when I look back at what my parents tried to do for us I am truly grateful to them, although there were times when it must have been hard, such as when my father lost his job. He wasn't out of work for very long, and I remember when he wasn't working, it was doubly hard for my parents to keep the four of us. They were tough times and many people were in the same boat, struggling to keep their families fed. My eldest brother, Paul, always wanted to be a butcher and worked full-time in a butcher's shop. Gerard always wanted to be a mechanic and he had a job working on the buses. With my schooling behind me, it was my turn to be thrown out into the big, wide world to search for work, not really knowing what I wanted to do, unlike my brothers who knew what they wanted. Well, I say I didn't know what I wanted to do, I did – I wanted to be a footballer, pure and simple. But I was a million miles away from that and couldn't see it happening at the age of 14. The idea of being a professional footballer seemed pie in the sky to everyone who knew me, so I had to get on with it and try to find something I was suited to in the meantime.

As we approached the time we were able to leave school, a careers officer was on hand to help direct us into the type of job or career which would be best suited to our talents and capabilities. These would include apprenticeships for electricians, plumbers, carpenters, fitters and all other forms of skilled work. They were well sought after and were considered careers for life – not just jobs. Everyone kept telling me, 'You've got to get a trade,' so I applied for several jobs in those fields. I had a few interviews after leaving school, including an interview to be a carpenter at a company called A. E. Smith-Coggins in Bootle, but didn't get the job. Undeterred, I applied for a couple of other positions including a job as a mechanic. I was interviewed on the Friday but found out while I was completing the application form that the job was for the same company that had just turned me down (A. E. Smith-Coggins) and as fate would have it I got the job as an apprentice mechanic there. When the manager asked me when I could start I replied without hesitation that I could start on Monday. It was only mid-August so technically I was still 14 years old when I started (illegally) at A. E. Smith-Coggins. I think if they had realised I was underage I probably wouldn't have got the job but I didn't say anything and neither did they!

My first day at work arrived and the first person I remember meeting was a guy called David Copeland who was the senior apprentice – which basically meant he had been there the longest.

The first thing he said to me was, 'Are you Everton or Liverpool?'

I replied, 'I'm an Evertonian.'

He then asked, 'Are you left-footed or right-footed?' I had to pause then because I was a natural left-footer but could also kick right-footed so I replied:

'I'm a left-footer.'

It was only in the years that followed did I realise the significance of those questions. I don't know if it was some local myth, but apparently, left-footers were historically associated with being Catholics and right-footers were seen as being Protestants.

There's another misunderstanding surrounding Evertonians being mainly Catholic borne of the association with St Domingo's Methodist Church, which was situated near to Goodison Park. It's a fact that many local clubs around the world were (and still are) bred with a religious, political or socio-economic divide, as Scotland where Celtic and Rangers have always had a clear demarcation in terms of fans, origin and growth. For the rivalry between Everton and Liverpool, it may have been like that in the distant past, when the two clubs were formed but it's not like that so much in the city today (or indeed when I was growing up in the city) although the strong Catholic backing was further accentuated during the 1950s, when the likes of Peter Farrell, Tommy Eglington and a few other Irish players became fan favourites at Goodison Park. Yes, it was probably apparent that, historically, Everton Football Club had largely rested on a Catholic support base; however, some supporters were biased towards Everton's close ties with Celtic and believed that Liverpool shared similar relations with Rangers, a Protestant-driven side. Families have always been divided when it came to club loyalty but in reality, being a Protestant or a Catholic had nothing to do with it in my case. Catholic families remained divided with red and blue supporters and the same applied to the Protestants. Whatever the historical background of the club was, in reality the rivalry was now purely to do with football and nothing else. As I've mentioned before, in Liverpool, you were either Liverpool or Everton, red or blue – pure and simple.

Looking into my family tree, I have recently discovered that my mother's side of the family were Irish and had the surname of McEvoy. The odd thing is that my father's side of the family originated from Denmark. If I was playing today I could have qualified to play for England, the Republic of Ireland or Denmark but your parents' background didn't count in those days – it was all about where you were born, and I was English. Since the early 20th Century there has been a big Irish population living in Liverpool and as early as 1909, there was sectarian violence on the streets, but by the 1960s the regeneration of the city effectively saw an end to that division. Religion, though, was a serious thing when I was growing up. My parents and their parents before them, being Catholic, never mixed with Protestants and you were frowned upon if, God forbid, you married a Protestant. It was something you never even contemplated. It was strange really because both my brothers ended up marrying Protestant ladies later on in life. Those marriages were still frowned upon but the difference was it was at least accepted. The unwritten rule was that you had to get married in the Protestant church of your future wife, but again, that was frowned upon. Things started to change from the 1960s onwards and it became quite common for that kind of mixing of religions to happen. Even my mother now gladly goes to either church on a regular basis, even though years before she would never have set foot (or be allowed to set foot) in a Protestant church.

Away from religion, my first wage packet at A. E. Smith-Coggins was about £3.25s and I couldn't wait to get home to give some money to Mum. But when I got home, Mum told me to keep it all as it was my first proper wage packet, for which I was grateful.

I can't really recall what I spent that first wage packet on, but looking back I was a bit of a record collector so it was probably something music related. Liverpool has a lengthy tradition of music, both classical and pop and not just The Beatles. Its pop and rock music scene was important in the development of a number of bands and artists since the 1950s, and to the development of 'Merseybeat' in the 1960s, popularised by artists such as Gerry & the Pacemakers. Even before 'Merseybeat' Liverpool fostered successful acts such as Frankie Vaughan, Lita Roza and Billy Fury.

As a youngster growing up in the city, I loved my music and was a member of a record club. I used to visit my uncle Harold quite a lot as he was a keen collector, and I started to become interested in records because he had a big collection. We used to listen to records together, artists like Frankie Vaughan and Billy Fury. Another friend I had was Tommy Smith (not *the* Tommy Smith!) and he liked The Beatles (as the whole world did) and later on, T-Rex and bands like that; I liked The Beatles but I didn't want to listen to that sort of music for some reason so I went off and listened to The Beach Boys, Stevie Wonder, Marvin Gaye, The Temptations, The Four Tops and Motown. As I settled into my job, I remember eventually saving enough money to buy my first record and my first record player. The first record I bought was in fact a Smokey Robinson & The Miracles single as he wrote a lot of his own music so while the rest of Liverpool (and the world) were in love with John, Paul, George and Ringo, I was on a completely different musical planet.

There were loads of groups being formed in Liverpool in the 1960s on the back of the success of the 'Merseybeat' bands and on the back of my love for music, me and some of my mates decided to form a group, even though we didn't have any instruments and were basically pretty crap! It must have been one of those crazy decisions you make when you're young; we ended up making our own instruments or borrowing from friends. My father borrowed a guitar from a friend, and although I started to learn to play it, I didn't think it would take me anywhere; After all, nothing could replace football, which was a big distraction anyway. We'd be playing in the band, rehearsing and someone would always knock on the door asking if we wanted to play footie so we'd always drop our instruments and go down the road to kick a ball around. For me, it was always football, football and more football. I kept the music to just listening, and the band soon disbanded.

Of course, it wasn't just football and music I was interested in when I was a 15-year-old boy; around that time I discovered the opposite sex and one girl in particular. It was common for groups of lads to hang around street corners in Liverpool, and indeed I suspect every town and city in the country during the late 1960s. Most kids of that age smoked and I used to hang around the street corner with a group of five or six other lads and we'd always see a particular girl walking past on her way to her friend's house down the road. It was a long time before I made an effort to talk to her and the typical cocky teenager as I was, I broke the ice one day when I felt I had enough confidence with words to the effect 'Evening Kathy ... How yer doing?'

Kathy Bell only lived six doors away but I didn't really know anything about her as I was sort of seeing a girl who lived in Halewood, which wasn't a million miles away, even though our friendship wasn't anything serious.

I really liked the look of Kathy and all the lads were trying to chat her up – but I tried a bit harder. I soon found out that Kathy had an older sister called Eileen so I used to go with my brothers to knock on their parents' door and ask Kathy if Eileen wanted to come out and see my brothers. I remember Kathy saying to Eileen one day, 'It's that bloody Withe family again.'

I replied by saying, 'Does your Eileen want to come out and see our Paul?' which was met with a reply in the negative! It was obvious Kathy didn't like me or my brother very much at first but as time went on we got to know each other. However, it was slow going and a bit of a struggle at the start: at one point she even denied to her friends that she was even slightly interested in me!

After a few months Kathy started talking to me and we struck up some good conversations, and the more we chatted the more she got to like me. I don't know what it was about Kathy but I knew from the first time I saw her that there was something about her. My pursuit of Kathy had taken three years and I wasn't about to give up. In those days I used to get a bus home from work in Bootle which stopped near where Kathy worked in Woolton. She worked for a hosiery manufacturer called Bear Brand. However, if you're thinking we'd have a good old chat on the bus you'd be wrong; I was that knackered after finishing work, what with all the football matches and training on top of that, I'd always end up sleeping on the bus journey from Bootle to Speke. It's a wonder I even knew Kathy had got on the bus sometimes! The bus would drop me off near home and I would end up walking the rest of the way on my own, as Kathy was quite shy and didn't want anyone gossiping about us. She didn't really want to be involved with my group of mates at first either, but once one of her friends became close to one of mine she started to mingle. By that time I'd finished with the girl from Halewood so that left me open to get to know Kathy a bit more, even though we weren't really dating each other (or even talking much for that matter!).

The start of our relationship was more like a 'dare' than anything else, which doesn't sound very romantic at all, does it? I had some cigarettes and she asked me for one and I said to her:

'I'll tell you what; I'll give you a cigarette if you give me a kiss.' It was a bit of a light-hearted joke but she agreed, so I gave her a cigarette and she gave me a kiss. Always the charmer, I asked her, 'Is that what you call a kiss?'

Kathy was a bit bemused by my wit and said, 'What do you mean?' which was met with a reply of:

'That's not a kiss! This is a kiss ...' as I got hold of her and gave her a proper kiss on the lips. That was it – I was in love. I knew there and then that we would be together forever. I don't know why, but that was the strength of my feelings for her. It seemed like the longest courtship in the world but to me it was all worth it and after another few weeks had passed we were never out of each other's company.

Kathy was just as smitten as I was and we ended up arranging a date. It was a hard courtship at first, probably because I wanted to play football all the time; in hindsight I made it hard for her but she didn't question why I was making things so difficult. We were too involved with each other by that time – teenagers shouldn't be attached to each other like we were at that young age but we were in love.

I was babysitting one evening for our next-door neighbour and Kathy called round to see me but I gave her one of those looks that suggested there was a problem. Kathy asked what the matter was and I replied:

'I think we're too young. I need to have a life. I'm finishing it.'

It must have sounded a bit harsh and Kathy stared at me with a blank look and just walked away. It occurred to me that even though she only lived six doors away, I'd probably never see her again – Kathy must have thought the same. I knew I'd hurt her as soon as I told her we were finished, and I also knew I'd made a huge mistake. However, about three weeks passed by, and every day I hung around the street trying to see her. I suspect she was trying to avoid me (and who would have blamed her), until one day I finally managed to catch her attention.

'Can I talk to you?' I said. Kathy again refused to talk to me – she must have been hurting and I saw it in her eyes. As she walked away, I chased after her and repeated, 'Can I talk to you? We need to talk.' I wasn't about to give up easily and was adamant I was going to say my piece. 'I'm sorry. I made a mistake. I've fallen in love with you and I can't forget you.' Kathy wanted confirmation of what I meant and I told her, 'I need to be with you. I want to be with you for the rest of my life.'

That was it. Within minutes, Kathy and I were back together. I think Kathy wanted reassurances that I felt the same as her – and I did.

It didn't take me long to find out that A. E. Smith-Coggins had a football team, as most large companies did back then. The coach wasn't convinced that I would get into the team as I was only 5ft 7in tall as a 15-year-old, and he even tried to steer me away from playing for them, so I decided I'd just turn up for the game. I'm not sure why I was smaller than my two brothers at that time, who were both over 6ft as 15-year-olds. Even my father was over 6ft so I had a lot of growing to do. Incidentally, within 15 months I had shot up to 6ft 2in tall – my current height. Anyway, I arrived at the ground and the coach asked me if I could play left-back, so I agreed. I had played mostly on the left wing, although I preferred being a striker and I had never played as a left-back before, but I wasn't going to argue. As it turned out, I ended up playing in goal for A. E. Smith-Coggins every Saturday. Come Sunday, I'd play as a left-winger or in midfield for another team. It didn't matter to me where I played or who I played for, just as long as I was playing. I hated not playing football.

On one occasion I was playing for a Sunday team and someone approached me and asked who I played for on Saturdays. I said I played for the works' team and he told me about a team called Lockheed, who were an aerospace manufacturing company and they had a team virtually over the road from home. They had a fabulous set-up there; first-class pitches and an excellent social club. Now, for me to play for A. E. Smith-Coggins every Saturday involved a journey of around ten miles and it was a bit of a pain and cost me money for bus fares, so, when asked if I wanted to play on a first-class pitch and virtually over the road from my house I didn't take much persuading!

The coach at Lockheed wanted me to come along to the next match so I could meet all the players and look at the facilities they offered. The club was years ahead of A. E. Smith-Coggins in terms of facilities; they even had a proper minibus so all the team could travel together to away games, or if they went further afield they'd use a coach. It would have meant going up a level in terms of professionalism and Lockheed were also in a higher league than A. E. Smith-Coggins so I had nothing to lose by joining them and ended up signing for them – I'd have been crazy to have turned them down!

By that time, my other two brothers had virtually stopped playing football but continued to go to Goodison Park to support Everton; for me it was the reverse. I had stopped going to watch Everton because I was playing more football than ever. My appetite for the game intensified and it became such an ambition for me to fulfil my dream and make it as a professional footballer. My elder brother Gerard was always seen as the most talented player in the family – and he probably was if I'm honest. He was faster, a good athlete and generally a better all-round player but because our school wasn't one of Liverpool's 'elite schools' we never got noticed by any of the scouts. Gerard did have trials with the Liverpool Boys team at one stage but never really got any further.

Being an apprentice mechanic at A. E. Smith-Coggins was hard work, especially for a youngster just out of school. I had to do a year in the storeroom to learn all about the specialist equipment, before I even could step foot on to the shop floor. Although I was an apprentice learning how to become a proper mechanic and going to technical college during the week, I wasn't sure whether I wanted to continue after my spell in the stores. Towards the end of that 12-month period, four jobs came up on the noticeboard: a carpenter, a welder, a mechanic and an electrician. As I was already employed there, I could choose which job I wanted to apply for. Everyone advised me to apply for the electrician job, probably because it paid better and was a cleaner job so I took their advice. I became an electrician as soon as I had finished my stint in the stores. Being a mechanic was a dirty job at the best of times and I hated it in a way, so becoming an electrician did me a favour big time.

If I look back on that time it was probably a turning point in my life and, in hindsight, was the best decision I'd made in my short life up until then. I'd been working at A. E. Smith-Coggins for over 12 months and studied to become a mechanic but I had to go to a different college to study to be an electrician. The strangest thing was that the college was situated right in the middle of Stanley Park – the famous park that separates Liverpool FC from Everton FC. The location couldn't have been better for me as every lunchtime during my day release at college me and my mates could put our coats (and jumpers) down to use as goalposts and spend an hour playing football. I will always remember one lad called Peter Duffy who played with us. He was also an electrician studying at the same college and quite a good player as it happened. He said to me once, 'Have you had trials with anyone? I can see you can play a bit. Why don't you go and ask for a trial with one of the local clubs?' So I told him the story about writing off to clubs and being turned down. Peter told me he played for Southport, who at the time were in the fourth division. I later found out that Peter was once on the books at Everton, which I thought was quite impressive, but they released him and he ended up serving his apprenticeship as an electrician instead. One day, Peter encouraged me to go to Southport with him, 'Ah, I don't know ...' I gave the impression I wasn't sure but deep down I wanted the chance to prove I was a decent player. I wrote to the club knowing that Peter had recommended me to the management and I subsequently got invited for a trial at the start of the next season.

I ended up going to Southport one summer's evening with my father and met the manager, Alex Parker. I had the first trial – along with another 99 lads. Fortunately, I managed to get through that one and it was followed by another trial, this time of 50. The next trial was with 40 potentials, and then it went down to 30. The final trial would see the best players from those who were left. They didn't know how many players they were going to take, if any – it could have been fifteen, five or two players. So, ten minutes into the game I went up for the ball and got butted in the head and my eye just closed up; I couldn't see a bloody thing out of one eye. I thought to myself, 'I'm not going off. I'll never get picked if I go off now.' So I carried on playing, even though I couldn't see out of one eye. In the end, the referee, who was also the coach for Southport, stopped the game, called me over and ordered me off.

'Nah, it's alright. I'm OK,' I said but the referee ordered me off the field.

'You can't play like that, lad. You're going to have to go off.'

I begrudgingly trudged off the pitch thinking to myself, 'Well that's the end of that.' I met my dad as I came off the pitch, watched a bit more of the game out of one eye and as the game finished we started to walk out of Haig Avenue only to be met by Alex Parker who was running after us.

He said, 'Where you going, lad?'

I replied, squinting at Alex, 'Well, you don't want me. I've only played ten minutes.'

Alex shook his head and gestured to me to come back and said, 'We need to speak to you, Peter. We like what we've seen tonight and want you to come back. Get your eye sorted out and we'll keep in touch.'

I thought, 'That's it. I'm in here.'

Needless to say my trial was a success and they called me up again to train with the reserves.

That was the start of my football career and it was all thanks to Peter Duffy, who persuaded me to go for a trial at Southport. We (not surprisingly) became good friends. The funny thing was, if I hadn't changed my job at A. E. Smith-Coggins from being a mechanic to an electrician, I probably wouldn't have become a professional footballer as I was 17 years old and time was running out for me. To start your football career at 17 these days would be nigh on impossible but if you were half good enough back then, you'd get a chance – and I welcomed my chance with open arms.

I was still working at A. E. Smith-Coggins during the day as normal but my schedule changed so I had to travel to Southport on a Tuesday and Thursday to train with the lads. In those days we didn't have much money as it was, and on the odd occasion I had to ask some of the lads at work if I could borrow the bus fare to Southport to train in the evening. One time I wasn't able to borrow money so I ran to the training ground, nearly ten miles away from where I worked in Bootle. I eventually got there at 6pm, trained for two hours and then ran the ten miles back home to Speke. I think I got home around midnight and then had to get up at 7am the following morning to start work all over again. There are always times in your life when you do what you need to in order to get where you want to get to. I just had to improvise. I had to get to the training ground somehow as I didn't want to miss training, so I had to run all that way even if it killed me. In fact, it happened a few times that I can remember, but I was fit in those days and it was the time in my life when I discovered I was a decent runner with stamina: so it wasn't really a problem and I loved it.

Those were the days!

It must have been more than a coincidence that Alex Parker used to play for Everton before he became Southport coach. I actually remember watching him play at Goodison Park with my father. He was a Scottish international right-back who moved to Merseyside in 1958 when Everton paid £18,000 for his transfer, although his 'Toffees' debut was delayed by his requirement to fulfil National Service in Cyprus. He eventually became a stalwart of the side, and they won the 1962/63 Division One championship. So to have Alex as my first proper football manager was a great honour.

There's a saying by Friedrich Schiller that goes something like, 'There is no such thing as chance; and what seems to us as a merest accident springs from the deepest source of destiny.' Now, if Alex being my manager wasn't a coincidence in itself, there was a guy at the club called Ben Seddon, who was a centre-half in the team. We were both from Liverpool and we travelled to Southport together, usually by bus, and became good friends. Years later, I found out (by chance) that Ben had a son called Ian Seddon who later became my advisor. (More about that later in the book.) I really believe that life is all about coincidences like that – there are some things that are just meant to be.

I started my football career at Southport in the reserves and scored goals whenever I played. One day, Alex called me into the office and asked me if I could get some time off work to train full-time. He must have seen the potential in me but as I only trained twice a week I was short of match fitness and wasn't up to speed with some of the other lads who were training every day. He wanted me to improve my sharpness and my skill level and thought if I could train more often I could develop my game. Being a typical teenager, I said I could get time off, not really thinking how I would manage it. It wasn't a question of going up to my boss and asking him outright for time off to train with my football team – he would have probably laughed in my face if I had done that. The only alternative I could see was to get a doctor's note and pull a 'sickie' for a few days. So, I went to the doctor's with a spluttering cough and he wrote me out a sick-note for a week off work. Yes, I know it wasn't an honest thing to do, but to me it was a win-win situation, as I received sick pay from A. E. Smith-Coggins *and* I got to train at Southport all week (even though I was apparently off sick). During that week I didn't really think about what I'd do the following week but, as it happened, Alex asked me if I could get another week off, not knowing I was pulling a fast one with work, so I had to go back to the doctor's again and he duly obliged and wrote me out another sick-note. Oh the innocence of youth!

During that second week of training full-time (while off sick from work) Alex called me into the office and said we were playing away at Oldham Athletic on the Saturday and that I was going to get a game in the first team. I was made up and thought I'd hit the big-time already. I'd only had a handful of Lancashire League and Northern Floodlit League appearances so it was like a dream come true. In one of those Floodlit games, I scored a wonderful goal, a diving header five minutes from the end and that game got me noticed by Alex and the coach, Alan Spence.

It then dawned on me that a report of the Oldham game might appear in the newspapers and that I was making my first-team debut so I asked Alex and he replied, 'You're 18 years old, an amateur player and you're playing in the first team of Southport FC in the fourth division. It WILL be in the papers, son. They will want to interview you.' My mind started to wander and I began to think that if the bosses at A. E. Smith-Coggins read the articles in the papers over the weekend I'd be in for it. A lot of people at work knew I played for Southport part-time so that wasn't a big secret but the fact that I was playing while I was supposed to be off sick was another matter and it occurred to me that I'd get the sack if they found out.

In my favour was the fact that I wasn't disillusioned by the game, like so many youngsters who were trying to break into the first team. I would always give 100 per cent endeavour, no question. It wasn't common for amateur players to be picked for the first team of a league side so my full debut for the Southport first team as an 18-year-old was away at Oldham and I hadn't even signed professional papers. We were told to report to Haig Avenue on the Saturday of the game and I remember sitting in the changing room, listening to the lads winding me up: 'Are you nervous lad?' 'How did you sleep last night?' I WAS nervous and I DID sleep OK and I took the banter in good spirit. Someone then came into the changing room and asked me to go into the manager's office for a chat.

I was thinking he wanted to give me last minute instructions or something but as I walked into his office he had his head down and looked up to me and said, 'You can't play.'

I asked, 'What do you mean I can't play?' As it turned out, the secretary hadn't registered me to play in the first team and hadn't paid the £250 fee. The club was hard up and lingering in the bottom tier of English football so they couldn't afford to pay the fee to register me with the FA. I remember thinking to myself, 'Is he winding me up or something? Is this a joke?' The tears started to roll down my face as I saw my first (and maybe only) opportunity to play first-team football was slipping from my reach. Alex said it wasn't my fault and kindly suggested I travelled to Oldham with the team anyway but I had other ideas.

'I'd rather not go boss if you don't mind. I'd rather play in the reserves.'

He thought for a few minutes then said, 'Whatever happens today, you'll play on Tuesday.'

I thought, 'Yeah right...'

So, I stayed behind and played for the reserves. In those days if the first team played away, the reserves always played at home so at least my travelling to Southport wasn't wasted. As it happened, I scored a hat-trick in that game and we won 3–1 so it wasn't all bad. Incidentally, the first team ended up beating Oldham 4–2, so I was certain Alex wouldn't change the side for Tuesday as he'd promised – no way!

On the following Monday morning I was called into the manager's office again and he told me that I was playing on the Tuesday evening.

I asked Alex, 'Why would you want to change a winning team, boss?'

Alex replied, 'I told you on Saturday that you're playing on Tuesday and you're going to play. You scored a hat-trick on Saturday and that showed me the character you have.'

So, I made my debut on the Tuesday at home against Scunthorpe United. We won the game 5–1 and I had a hand in three of the goals but didn't score, although I played centre-forward, which had become my permanent position by then. I was substituted with about ten minutes to go to a standing ovation.

As it happened, a certain (unknown) player called Kevin Keegan scored the goal for Scunthorpe. Kevin was virtually the same age as me but little did I know then that Kevin would sign for Liverpool the next season and start his illustrious career with the 'Reds'.

I later made an appearance in the quarter-final of the Lancashire Senior Cup against Liverpool Reserves and the local media started calling me 'the new Joe Royle.' We had a full-strength team out against Liverpool and Bill Shankly was there, watching the youngsters play. However, that debut game against Scunthorpe was the real platform that lifted my own career from being an unknown 18-year-old from Speke into the heady heights of the fourth division of English football.

My first experience of playing away from home was in the very next game that Saturday. We travelled to Exeter City, but lost the game. I think I made one more appearance for Southport, and at the end of that 1970/71 season Alex said to me, 'You've only got a year of your apprenticeship left, don't give that up, keep playing for us and get time off work when you can. When you've finished your apprenticeship you can come and sign for us as a full-time pro.'

I thought, 'Great, this is what I really want to do.'

Alex also said that the more games I played in, the better I would get, which was only common sense really. He then mentioned that a non-league club called Skelmersdale United had been in touch and were keen on taking me on loan.

The next thing I knew I was playing for Skelmersdale United first team rather than playing for Southport reserves as it was a higher level. While I was there, I played in a few rounds of the Northern Floodlit Cup and we eventually got to the final, which was played at Wigan, and won 3–1. It was my first ever taste of victory and my first winner's medal. As it turned out, Alex got the sack in the summer of 1971, to be replaced by Jimmy Meadows and I returned to Southport after the final.

With Alex gone I didn't know where I stood with Southport so I ended up writing to other clubs to see if I could have a trial with them. I think

Barrow wanted to sign me but I decided to go for a trial at Preston North End as they showed more interest in me. I played in a practice match for them and then went to play in another match for someone else, but Preston contacted me saying they wanted to sign me. In those days, Preston had a decent side and were in Division Two, so I went to Deepdale ready to sign the paperwork, but they told me to go back to Southport to check if I had been released by them. When I went back to Southport, Jimmy Meadows surprisingly offered me a three-month trial at £25 per week with a view to be taken on full-time. Taking into account it was going to cost me about £15 a week to get there I wasn't going to make a fortune out of playing for Southport. Nevertheless, they wouldn't release me, so although I wanted to sign for Preston I ended up doing a full pre-season training at Southport instead.

The training included a lot of running because they had a part-time fitness coach called Joe Lancaster, who I later found out was a top runner who broke the world marathon record in 1954 and was a hopeful to represent Britain in the Olympics before he sadly contracted TB and ended up in an isolation clinic. The amazing thing about Joe was that he smoked – in fact he smoked for 72 years, right up until his death at the age of 92. You'd never have known it because he was just so fit. In the 1960s, Joe was a key member of the Manchester City coaching staff when the twin brilliance of coach Malcolm Allison and manager Joe Mercer guided them to glory. Even considering his background, Joe wasn't a fitness coach at Southport as such, but someone who had been called in to help improve the fitness of the players during pre-season. I found the training quite easy and I was the fittest player in the club by far. I was a bit of a fitness fanatic and could run and run forever – I just loved it. The training started at the ground in Haig Avenue, and then we'd run to the beach to train. We'd do all our training on the beach and then run in the sand dunes before we ran back to the ground. It was the time that people realised that Peter Withe could run – centre-forwards who could score goals were plentiful in supply but a centre-forward who could run and score goals was a rare specimen indeed.

****

I'd been going out with Kathy for several years but it was in early 1971 that we received the news that Kathy was pregnant (with our first boy, Jason).

Kathy told me first and I just said, 'Well, we'll have to get married then won't we?' I didn't tell my mother at the time but someone else had told her, and in truth she already suspected as she knew that Kathy had been feeling sick a lot at work.

Then the shit well and truly hit the fan!

We were both living at our parents' houses at the time – Kathy only being six doors away, and you could say the news didn't go down too well in my household. The idea of a girl being pregnant out of wedlock was frowned upon in Catholic families. I think her mother and father were fine with the news but my parents were livid and we ended up having a bit of a bust up. Despite this, my parents insisted we didn't have to get married; they didn't want us to get married, in fact, as we were so young. But marry we did, and fairly quickly as it happened. We were in love and no one was stopping us getting married. At the time, my elder brother, Paul, was already married and my other brother, Gerard, was planning a wedding so my news came at the wrong time – particularly as we were planning to get married before Gerard.

I was a young man and was worried to death about what was happening to my life. I'd just got my girlfriend pregnant and had fallen out with my parents over it. We'd moved into a house-share together but had nothing — It was a small Victorian house in Lesseps Road, just off Smithdown Road, Liverpool 8, not a million miles away from where I was born, but it was far from the best arrangement, you can imagine – we shared the bathroom and the tiny kitchen with several other couples. To top it all we were about to get married against everyone's better judgement.

I recall one of the Southport players, a lad called Arthur Peet, one of the senior players, saying to me, 'You look a bit worried, Peter. What are you worried about? What's going on?'

I replied, 'Well, I've got to tell the boss I'm getting married.'

We needed somewhere else to live and pretty quickly. I was dreading telling him because we had planned to get married on the Friday before the game on the Saturday afternoon, 'I don't know how to tell him.'

Arthur was straight with me. 'Tell him the truth – he'll be made up for you, believe me. All managers would be made up for you because once you get married you'll be settled down. If they think you're young, free and single you'll be gallivanting around the world. The manager wants players to be settled down.'

I'd never thought of it in that way but I guess it made sense. Arthur had actually put my mind at ease a little bit and I owed him for that.

We got married on 26 February 1971 in a registry office in Brome Terrace, Liverpool attended by about ten people. Not surprisingly, my parents refused to attend, which disappointed me and I can only remember one of my brothers attending as it was on a Friday and everyone else was at work. Our reception was a low-key affair at The Pegasus pub in Speke, attended by a dozen or so people.

At the end of the three-month trial and only having played one pre-season match, Jimmy Meadows didn't sign me up because he didn't think I was good enough. The way the club informed me I wasn't going to be signed up was pretty poor. The manager didn't have the balls to say it to my face and got the club to call me into the office to see the secretary. He told me the news I hadn't been signed, even though I'd worked my socks off for the last three months. It was a shock to the system and a big setback. I was back to square one.

I didn't know where to turn to and started writing to clubs again. About a week after leaving Southport, I phoned Preston to see if they remembered me from pre-season. I told them I had been released from Southport and it happened that they had a practice game that day and advised me that if I could get to the training ground by 12 noon, I could join in. At that time I had an old Ford Anglia so I drove to the Preston training ground from my home in Toxteth. When I arrived I saw a team bus parked outside and, low and behold, it belonged to Southport! You can imagine how I felt seeing their team bus. It couldn't have been any more coincidental – you couldn't have made it up really but, all the same, it was another chance for me to shine.

When I walked into the Preston changing room I spotted Jimmy Meadows and he saw me but we didn't speak. The Preston manager at the time was

Alan Ball senior and his coach was Arthur Cox. I went into the Preston changing room, got my kit and was told by the manager that I'd get a game as soon as he could get me on. Alan kept his word and I got a game and scored two goals in a 3–1 victory. They were obviously pleased with my contribution and they invited me back twice after that practice game. I started playing in reserve games and after a few weeks the club offered me a contract but the financial package would hardly have covered the journey from Liverpool to Preston every day. Money was tight for the club, and unfortunately that was all they could afford to offer me – I think it was around £35 per week. In the end I didn't sign for Preston.

I was out of work again but I'd had a couple of phone calls from clubs including one from Barrow. I went along there and liked the set up and they offered me a two-month trial, but they'd put me up in digs during the week, and I'd travel back to Liverpool after the weekend game. I only played one game for Barrow, who were in the fourth division and, incidentally, my debut for them was against Southport at Haig Avenue. It seemed I couldn't escape Southport FC. When the subject of money was brought up in the contract negotiations the same thing happened as at Preston: they couldn't afford to pay me much of a wage. The travelling was a problem again and there was no way I was going to move to the Lake District, a journey of around 2 hours 30 minutes each way. Kathy didn't want to move to Barrow anyway, mainly because we had only just moved into a council flat on a new estate in Liverpool, 20 minutes from Speke. The estate we lived on later got the nickname 'the concrete jungle' for obvious reasons. While I was away with Barrow for most of the week she was stuck at home on her own. To make matters worse, it was Christmas time, and I missed most of the festive period as I was living and playing in Barrow.

It wasn't the best of times back then. The early 1970s was a time of high unemployment, sky-high inflation, and the period of lurid wallpaper, silly hairstyles and strikes. The era was lampooned and despised as the worst era modern Britain has ever witnessed. On a personal note, I was in and out of clubs, and at the age of 20 or 21, I was desperate to secure a full-time contract. Time was running out for me to fulfil my dream to play at Goodison Park (and for England). Kathy and I had just got married and she was about six months pregnant at the time and we were just settling into our new flat.

I'd previously played with a guy called Billy Haydock, who was a full-back at Southport and I remember he mentioned to me that he was planning to take a coaching job in South Africa. One day, out of the blue, he asked me if I fancied joining him there as a player. I'd hardly been outside of Merseyside, let alone abroad and he was asking me to fly to a foreign country to go and play football. To some it would have seemed like a dream come true but I initially turned him down, mainly due to the fact that we were still trying to settle down in our new place and, after all, Kathy was looking after our first son, Jason, who had been born by then.

You could say the timing wasn't great, however appealing it sounded at the time. If I had been single I'd have gone in an instant, no question, but I had commitments. However, when I went home to tell Kathy the news I got the surprise of my life because she would have packed her bags there and then if she had the chance – she was so excited at the prospect and couldn't wait for us to leave. Kathy saw it as a way out of the concrete jungle we were living in and had no hesitation in saying she wanted to go–and as quickly as possible.

Life has a habit of springing little surprises now and again and that was one of them.

After spending two of the three-month trial period at Barrow and playing one game for the first team, I was getting a bit frustrated with my footballing life and decided to contact Billy Haydock after all to see if the offer of going to South Africa was still on. We had nothing – or very little at least – to keep us in Liverpool, other than our families so we had nothing to lose. It wasn't an ideal situation but it was one of those offers of a lifetime that you rarely get, so it was hard to turn down. The hardest task for us was to tell our parents. How do you tell your parents that you are going to live more than 8,000 miles away?

'What do you mean you're going to South Africa? What, you're leaving Liverpool? Does that mean you won't be going down the pub on a Sunday any more?'

My family couldn't get their heads round it at first. The furthest I'd travelled was North Wales on holiday, or maybe Exeter to play football but South Africa seemed like a world away – I didn't even know where it was if I was honest. I was basically pursuing a career in South Africa because I was desperate to continue my football career, which hadn't really taken off and I was at an age where it was make or break. If nothing else came out of it, it was an opportunity to explore life and to get some sun. It all happened so quickly but we had made a decision and we were going to live by it for better or for worse.

It's still a big thing now when people emigrate to foreign climes to pursue their dreams, but it was a massive thing in the early 1970s. Neither of us were working; I had left my apprenticeship at A. E. Smith-Coggins and had finished playing at Barrow, and Kathy had just become a mother so we had no income and we had rent to pay for the flat, even though it wasn't a lot to pay – and still somehow find money for food. The only way we could get some extra money was to sign on on the dole and I remember that day very clearly.

There were around three weeks to wait until we were due to leave for South Africa so we both went to the unemployment office to sign on. Initially they said I hadn't been out of work long enough to qualify for benefit, and the same was true the following week, and the week after. We had nothing to live on and the dole office was making things harder for us. With about a week to go before we were due to fly out to Port Elizabeth, I had had enough; I thought I'd like to go down to the dole office and tell them to stick their money up their arses. When I arrived, I told them (politely) that they 'wouldn't be seeing me ever again because I'm bleeding leaving to go to South Africa.' The woman behind the counter quizzed me and didn't really get what I was saying but asked me to sign a form of some description. I signed the form and handed it back to her and she went away for a few minutes. When she returned she handed me £25.

'What's this for?' I said.

'You can have this now because you're leaving.'

I couldn't get my head round it (although I didn't complain). We had to live off nothing for three weeks and now we were leaving the country they decided to give us £25? It didn't make sense to me but it was money all the same and it was all we had to take to South Africa.

I remember Kathy telling me one day that when she was nine years old she had a vivid dream about moving far away from Liverpool. It was like she'd had an epiphany because she felt very strongly about it and she even said a prayer to God, thanking him for it. Not only that, the number 9 featured in her dream. So, when the opportunity to go to South Africa came up, the dream came back to Kathy and funnily enough, being a striker, I had taken the number 9 shirt that followed me throughout my domestic football career.

3

Our African Adventure

"How do you tell your parents that you are going to move more than 8,000 miles away to a foreign country?"

****

Immigration from the UK to South Africa in the early 1970s reached a peak. The country offered new opportunities to the skilled British labour force and the chance of a new life in the sun. For Kathy and me it was a case of venturing into the unknown with a new team, hoping I'd get a game of football here or there in order to follow my dream and become a professional footballer. At the very least, it was a chance to get some sun on our backs.

Fortunately, Billy Haydock had arranged everything for us; the flights had been paid for and the accommodation had been booked. If Billy had expected us to pay for the flights we just wouldn't have had enough money to go, full stop. There was no way we could have afforded it, so we were grateful to Billy for that at least.

Arrangements had been made for us to collect the tickets a few days before we flew out. The journey would take us from Manchester to Amsterdam, on to Johannesburg and then to Port Elizabeth. Neither of us had been on an aeroplane before and we were suddenly faced with a three-leg journey. I remember my mum and dad took us to the airport but Kathy's parents didn't come to see her off, which was a bit disappointing. My parents were quite upset at the fact we were leaving home and taking their new grandson away, not just leaving Liverpool but leaving the country. Deep down they were gutted but they didn't show their true feelings when we left them at

Manchester Airport. Or perhaps it hadn't actually sunk in with them that we weren't just moving round the corner and they couldn't just pop in for a cup of tea. Either way, after saying our goodbyes, we were left on our own to make our way to the gate and wait for our flight to be announced.

I'll always remember the first leg of the journey. We were booked on an Aer Lingus flight – an Irish airline flying to Amsterdam – then we had to change to a KLM flight to South Africa. Not being hardened travellers we had no idea where to go when we got off the plane in Amsterdam. We had a three-hour wait until our next flight, so we just wandered around the brand new terminal at Schiphol airport. There were dozens of prams parked up inside the terminal building and as we hadn't brought our pram from home we sort of 'acquired' one.

Kathy put Jason into the pram and said to me, 'Come on Peter, we'll rob the pram.'

I took looked at Kathy and then at the pram and replied, 'How can we rob this pram? It's got Schiphol Airport written all over it!'

I then spotted a really posh-looking baby-changing room, kitted out with everything you could want: nappies, tables, washing facilities – you name it, that airport had the lot. It was unbelievable and it was empty. Kathy took the baby into the changing room and by the time she came out, being a typical Scouser, she'd filled the baby bag with nappies and baby cream, as we hadn't brought anything like that with us. The rest of our waiting time was spent walking around the airport terminal, window-shopping. Even though we had £25 in our pocket, we didn't spend any of it because it had to last us.

When we finally landed in Johannesburg, we were starving. We hadn't spent any of the money we had from the dole office and we hadn't realised the food and drink on board was free. As our departure time to Port Elizabeth approached we heard our names being announced over the PA system to tell us that our connecting flight was late arriving but was waiting for us to board. We would have had to stay overnight in Johannesburg if we had missed it, so we rushed to board the plane. We were immediately taken from the KLM flight across the tarmac to board the connecting flight. It was autumn in Britain and we had our winter clothes on and as we dashed through the airport doors onto the tarmac to meet the connecting flight, we were hit by the blazing hot sun. As we climbed aboard, we realised we were the last to board, so we didn't get to sit together. Kathy was nervous about flying anyway, and not being able to sit next to me made her even more uncomfortable. We eventually settled though and arrived safely in Port Elizabeth in late afternoon. We made our way through customs and entered the Arrivals terminal.

Our African adventure was about to begin.

We didn't have a clue who was supposed to be meeting us so we waited in the terminal building for over half an hour. Eventually, some guy came up to us and asked if I was Graham Birks. He quickly found out I wasn't and he walked off looking for the right person. Another half an hour went by and still no one came to our rescue.

Another guy came up to me after an hour and asked, 'You wouldn't be Peter White would you?'

I chose to ignore the fact he said, 'White' and replied, 'Yeah, I'm Peter Withe.' The guy looked a bit shocked and said we weren't meant to be there until the next day. He then said he'd take us to the hotel where we'd be staying. We later found out that he was one of the directors of Port Elizabeth City FC.

I asked him why Billy (Haydock) wasn't there to meet us and he looked at me, then looked up to the sky and said, 'He's on a plane and he's taken all the money. He's left.' Billy hadn't paid the director his wages and had apparently done a runner. I was assured everything would be fine and I'd get paid, but I wasn't convinced of that.

The guy who met us at the airport in Port Elizabeth didn't tell us at the time that there were two ways to go from the airport to the hotel; one way involved driving through 'The Red Location' (a township where all the black people lived) and the other way was to drive through a place called Summer Sands which was a luxurious part of the city. So, our guy decided to take us down the scenic route, via The Red Location. Sitting in the back of the car, I was amazed at the state of the place and saw literally hundreds and hundreds of black people sitting on the roadside. I'd never seen anything like it and I was thinking, 'What the hell have we come to?' It wasn't very nice to say the least! We finally arrived at the hotel safe and sound; well, it was hardly a hotel – it was not even a 1-star bed and breakfast. It was dark by the time we arrived and we were knackered through all the travelling and waiting around. We were also starving hungry. To top it all, the area looked bleak and dreary and we really didn't fancy the accommodation.

We eventually checked into this so-called hotel and went up to our room to find there was only one single bed in it. I pointed this out to the hotel manager who explained it was the only room he had left. I remarked that there were two of us plus a baby so he agreed to bring us a cot. When we were left alone I looked around the room, opened the cupboards and checked out the bathroom, as you always seem to do when you arrive in a hotel. I remember looking in the wardrobe and saw a huge critter sitting there – it was the size of my hand. I looked at it and it looked back at me and I shut the door quickly. Kathy hated creepy-crawlies so I made sure she didn't see it otherwise she'd go into hysterics. I then suggested we go downstairs and have a look around the place. As soon as we got downstairs I made some excuse that I'd forgotten something and went back upstairs. I bumped into another lad standing on the stairs by our room and asked him:

'There's a bloody great big creature in the wardrobe. What do I do with it?'

The lad replied in his African accent, 'Hit him hard as you can with your shoe, mate.'

I went back into the room, took my shoe off, opened the wardrobe door and then whacked this critter as hard as I could. I looked at it again and it looked straight back at me, as if to say, 'Was that your best shot, mate?' I hit the bloody thing about ten times more but it lived. To this day, I have no idea what that creature was.

The first night in any new place is always daunting but lying in a (single) bed with Kathy that night I started wondering what the bloody hell we were doing in this place. However, we woke up the following morning to bright sunshine and thought perhaps it wasn't so bad after all. We must have had a good sleep, despite the conditions we found ourselves in.

The original deal that Billy Haydock had agreed with me was to play for Port Elizabeth City; they'd find me a paid job during the week and they'd also place us in a suitable furnished apartment so I wouldn't have to worry about anything. As it turned out, there was no job and they had placed us in a very poor quality hotel. Food at the hotel wasn't included so we ended up borrowing money to pay for food. We had left Liverpool with nothing and arrived in South Africa with nothing. It wasn't a great start and not what we had been promised.

With our 25 quid in our pocket and the exchange rate of 2 Rand to the Pound we had to buy a new pram on the first day, which cost 40 Rand, leaving us with 10 Rand left to survive on. It wasn't so bad for me as I got picked up and taken to training every day but Kathy was bored stiff. The hotel was specifically for new immigrants and wasn't equipped for long-term guests. It wasn't exactly suitable for families either as there was only one high-chair and we had to share that with another couple who also had a baby, so mealtimes became a race to get the high-chair first. As it happened, we became friends with the couple, John and Marie, and we keep in touch to this day. There were a few other footballers, including some English guys, staying in the hotel, so we got to know them and their families too. From that perspective at least we weren't alone, after all.

After a few weeks things improved substantially. We moved into an apartment about a mile and half outside the city, up on the hills overlooking Port Elizabeth and not that far from the beach, and I managed to find a job at Ford as an electrician, which actually worked out quite well. I later found out that Port Elizabeth City were sponsored by Ford until 1971 but finding a job there was purely coincidental. Even though we had a lot more money than we had had back in Liverpool we didn't buy any furniture for the apartment for several months and we even used old white sheets with hooks on the ends for curtains. The routine I had was simple. I'd get up at 6am, go to work at Ford until 4.30pm, get changed and see Kathy and Jason for an hour, go to training, and then come home for about 10pm. At the weekend, it was good if we played at home but South Africa being a huge country, if we played away we had to fly everywhere and the distances were hundreds and hundreds of miles.

Not having a car was a bind. If you didn't have a car in South Africa you were stuck and had to rely on other people all the time, which was what we did at first. It was OK for me as I was jetting off here, there and everywhere for free, but it was hard for Kathy as not only did she have a young baby to look after, she had no transportation (not that she could drive anyway). To make matters worse, she didn't know many people so she was basically stuck at home all day on her own with little Jason. Luckily we had kept in touch with John and Marie Jones, the couple we met at the hotel and they had a car and offered to take us out for day trips, which was a nice escape, especially for Kathy. We would also take it in turns to babysit so that gave us some time on our own.

Another friend of mine, Den also offered to take us out in the car. On one occasion we used the coastal route out of Port Elizabeth and we came across some huge sand dunes so we parked the car up. We noticed the beach was packed on this particular day but only at one end. We thought it was a bit strange that the other end of the beach was deserted but we decided to walk to that end and found a suitable place to sit on the beach. Kathy looked after Jason while Den and I headed for the water. We didn't have any surfboards so we used to just bodysurf the waves and generally mess about in the sea. We'd been out for about 15 or 20 minutes and I went to stand up thinking I could touch the seabed, but I suddenly plummeted and went underwater. I managed to get back to the surface but it frightened the life out of me. Then Den went to put his feet on the seabed and he went under as well. We both looked back towards the beach, which must have been about a mile away – I could just make out Kathy in the distance.

I shouted to Den, 'This doesn't seem right to me. Come on Den, we got to start swimming back now!' I was a decent swimmer but Den wasn't that confident, but we both started swimming for dear life back towards the beach. After a few minutes, we realised we hadn't got anywhere and Den started to tire and began to panic. I was still wondering what the hell was going on, so I shouted to Den not to panic and told him we'd try to tread water a little bit in the hope we would be dragged back to shore. We waited for the next big wave to come towards us and I calculated that at certain times there was a bigger wave than normal. When that wave came we body-surfed the wave and it took us a bit closer to the beach. After about half an hour of this we eventually got to the beach, by which time we were both knackered and scared to death.

When we got back I asked Kathy if she saw us out at sea and of course she was oblivious to what we had just gone through as she was relaxing with a book, while Jason was fast asleep. Anyway, when I got my breath back I noticed a signpost on the beach which someone had knocked down, and I turned it over so I could read it:

Deep under-currents –
Don't swim in this area!

I thought, 'Bloody Norah, if only we'd seen the sign before we got dragged out to sea!' It was a lesson learned, I suppose, but that fatal mistake could have cost us our lives.

When Jason was about a year old we had an incident one night while we were playing cards with some friends. All of a sudden I heard Jason choking and we all stopped what we were doing to find Jason in some discomfort. He'd apparently picked a coin up off the floor, near to where we were playing cards, put it in his mouth and it must have got stuck in the back of his tiny throat. Kathy was panicking and I got hold of Jason and started to hit him on his back, trying to dislodge the coin from his throat, while my two friends sat there helpless. After a few minutes I started to wonder how the hell I could save his life, and it was at that point I decided to do something you're not supposed to do, according to the parenting manuals. I put my fingers down his throat. I could feel the coin with the tips of my fingers, grabbed hold of it and it popped out. I was in a cold sweat as it was touch and go whether he would survive. I put him down and breathed out a big sigh of relief. My friends sighed along with us as they were as concerned as we were. However, almost immediately he started choking again so I did the same thing again, putting my fingers in his throat for a second time. Again, everyone panicked. I managed to feel another coin and tilted it in his mouth. All of a sudden, the coin flew out of his mouth and hit the wall. Jason gasped for air once more and Kathy picked him up to give him a big hug. I don't know how it happened, but I assume one of my friends dropped a couple of coins on the floor and, being an inquisitive baby, he just picked them up and put them in his mouth. We made sure after that that we were more conscious of what we left out on the floor when Jason was around.

When we moved from Port Elizabeth to Pretoria another frightening incident happened to Jason when one of our friends, a photographer for the club, took us back to his studio to show off some of the pictures he'd taken of me playing in a match. Jason had just started to walk and my friend was showing us round his studio and all the equipment in it. We then went into another room and I asked my friend if Jason would be alright in the drying room alone. After a few minutes we heard him screaming. Jason had apparently discovered a drying machine, which was the size of a modern-day washing machine with a huge chain that was partly uncovered. He obviously wasn't as tall as the machine and on seeing the chain moving round had decided to grab it, as any kid would I suppose. His hand had got caught up in the chain as it moved around the cogs. My friend immediately stopped the machine and the chain stopped moving, but Jason's fingers were well and truly stuck in the cogs. I asked him if the machine could go into reverse but it couldn't. By now I had started panicking but then remembered I had my toolbox in the car, so I rushed out and grabbed it. I had a hacksaw and started to cut the chain while Jason grabbed hold of me with his other hand, crying. I was terrified that I'd cut Jason's hand off at the same time as cutting the chain, but in the end I got his hand out of the machine without hurting him any further. His fingers had been lodged in-between the cogs of the chain so luckily they hadn't actually cut him. We immediately bathed his poor little fingers in some ice and after a few hours he was right as rain. It just goes to show that if you turn your back on a child for a few seconds anything can happen, and we learned to keep our eyes on him at all times after that.

South Africa turned out to be a bit of a nightmare on the footballing front too. My first manager was Billy Haydock and he left on the same day as we had arrived in the city, so that wasn't a great start. The next manager who took over was a fella called Hughie Maxwell who was a player/manager. Results weren't going too well, in fact, we were bottom of the league (the equivalent of the then English first division) and from a personal perspective, I wasn't scoring goals. I wasn't particularly happy to say the least, except when I was training – I always loved training.

The training sessions were hard under Hughie and always included running. Sometimes he'd bring in a 'ringer'; someone who he knew was a good runner, who would be introduced as a new player on trial. On one occasion, we had a training session on the beach. Hughie's routine was to send the best runners off last and that included me. The ringer was asked to go in with the middle pack. Once I was let off the leash I began to pick off the slower runners and overtake them. By the time I could see the ringer all I could think was, 'How the hell did he get that far ahead?' I eventually caught up with him ten yards from the finishing line. Little did we know at the time, the ringer was a professional athlete and I still managed to beat him.

Hughie came up to me after the race and said, 'You didn't win then?' and I replied, smugly:

'I did actually!' Hughie was taken aback, thinking his ringer would beat me every time. 'Yeah, I beat him in the last ten yards.' I went on. Just as back in Southport, I loved running: even though I probably wasn't the fastest I could run all day long.

There were loads of ex-pros playing in the South African league in the early 1970s. I was the youngest in my team; I was fit and could run all day long, but as a team we weren't making many chances. I wasn't scoring goals, even though I was playing up front and playing regularly.

Hughie said to me one day, 'You can run all day, you can. Why don't you play in midfield?'

I never got the chance to play in midfield for Hughie as he got sacked pretty soon afterwards and they brought in another manager, a Scottish guy called Matt Crowe. Matt was a former footballer who played as a wing-half and had previously played at Norwich City and Brentford. He'd also played for Port Elizabeth City for two seasons in the late 1960s so he was familiar with the South African football scene. He also saw my potential as a midfielder.

Just after Matt took over, we played a game against Durban City, who were one of the top teams in South Africa and we were drawing 0–0 and I was playing in my new position of midfield. I was on the ball and was trying to knock it over this guy who was just about to slide into me, but I lost it. All I could hear was Matt screaming from the touchline. I could hardly hear what he was shouting about but I got the gist of it and I assumed he was shouting at me because I'd lost the ball in the tackle. Not happy with what he was telling me, I duly shouted something back at him equally offensive.

At half-time, we were pleased to be at 0–0 but Matt pointed his finger at me and shouted, 'Don't you dare swear at me again. You, you haven't even played for 'anyone' in the UK.'

In other words, I wasn't a 'star player' and I should keep my mouth shut. Well, that was like a red rag to a bull saying that to me.

'So, to play for you, you have had to have played for a big club, then?' At that point I took my shirt off and was ready to storm out of the dressing room. I was angry as hell but one of my teammates spoke up for me.

'We need you Peter. Don't walk out on us now.'

I took a deep breath and decided to carry on for the second half and we managed to hold on to the draw. After that game I decided I'd had enough and I wouldn't be hanging around Port Elizabeth City much longer if I had anything to do with it. I didn't want to play for Matt Crowe any more, it was as simple as that but I had to bide my time as I had nothing in the UK to go back to. I thought to myself, 'You have to have played for a "big" team to be included in his side. I'll prove him wrong.' There were players like Danny Campbell who had played for West Bromwich Albion in the 1966 League Cup Final; Bernie Marsden had played for Cardiff City and a few others. Most of the lads in the side had played in the UK at some decent level and there were a few decent South African lads.

Some of the lads were pretty good cricketers as well, Danny Campbell included, which went down well in Port Elizabeth as they love their cricket there. It was our friend John Jones's birthday and it was also Kathy's 21st, so John and Marie decided that we would have a joint party at their house. We heard that cricket legend Basil D'Oliveira was in the area coaching youngsters, so we decided to invite him along too. The next-door neighbours, who had also been invited, heard about Basil and swiftly declined the invite simply because he was black, and promptly informed the police. When the party started, the police duly arrived and we hustled Basil into the kitchen while we tried to convince the police there were no black people in the apartment. It worked and we all heaved a sigh of relief. However, that was only the tip of the racial iceberg.

Apartheid was a system of racial segregation under which the rights of the majority black inhabitants of South Africa were curtailed and white supremacy and Afrikaner minority rule was maintained. Everything was segregated: education, medical care, beaches, and other public services, and the government provided black people with services inferior to those of white people. Football in South Africa at the time was no different and was plagued by racism. South Africa was banned by FIFA and other major sporting bodies, so was off the international sporting map. Multi-racial sport remained outlawed and black football fans were even segregated during football matches. I didn't know anything about South African football or the political system there when I arrived but I found out pretty soon that the football side was pretty different to our game back home.

The National Football League (NFL) was the first professional association football league in South Africa, established in 1959. Initially, only two areas of South Africa were represented, Transvaal and Durban, but gradually the league became more geographically representative. Even though black South Africans loved football they weren't allowed to watch us in the main stands where the white people were located. There was a small section where black people were allowed, but it was probably the best-supported section and made more noise than the rest of the crowd! There were black teams in South Africa at the time and they played in the 'Location' but there weren't any black players allowed to play in the African league teams. We went to a game in the 'Location' once and we had to 'sign in' to enter the area. We must have been the safest people there as we were treated like stars by the black people and they all recognised us. I remember watching a game when we were there and they played on what can only be described as a clay surface. It was the worst pitch I'd ever seen and the locals were kicking the ball around in their bare feet, but these lads had great skill and technique, especially playing on the rocky surface.

In the early 1970s apartheid was still very much prevalent and we noticed it particularly where we lived. Some of the residents employed black workers as gardeners, labourers or cleaners and they were 'shipped' into the white areas and taken back to the 'Locations' when they had finished their shifts. Coming from a totally different background and from a country where Apartheid didn't exist (although racism still existed in 1970s Britain) we generally tended to treat everyone the same, black or white. This was difficult when we tried to get to know the black people as they were a bit wary of us (as non-Afrikaners). We found it a bit strange that they seemed to know where they stood with a white Afrikaner (they would often be treated as slaves or beaten) so for a white person to be nice to them was unexpected, and they therefore thought we must have a hidden agenda. It was a sad indictment of the country really, and something we weren't used to.

After being in Port Elizabeth for about six months we were starting to get on our feet and had settled into life in South Africa. However, I started to notice my pay cheques were bouncing. The club were only paying me about £20 or £25 a week as it was, so it wasn't a fortune, but when you can't cash a cheque just when you need the money to live on it hits you hard. I didn't cash the cheques every week – I used to wait a few weeks and we would walk into the city at the weekend to the bank to cash three or four cheques at a time. When it came to cashing the cheques the cashier went away and after a few minutes she came back and said the cheques had bounced. It turned out that there was no money in the Port Elizabeth FC account.

The following week during one of the training sessions, I asked a few of the lads whether they'd had problems cashing their cheques and they obviously knew about the problems the club were facing and said to me that I should have cashed the cheques as I received them. The club were apparently renowned for it but when I took it up with the club they knew what had happened and gave me some flannel about the money situation at the club. That happened a few times but eventually I got my money even though I had to go back to the bank the following week to cash the cheques. I knew by then that the club was on its knees. We were bottom of the league and I still wasn't scoring goals so times were not good for me, or the club. Kathy hated it as well so it was time to move on.

One afternoon we were all called into a meeting after training and told to go to a particular hotel in the city. It was a meeting about the club and the vice-chairman stood up and announced that they had found two buyers to save us. They assured us all that the future was going to be bright. The two buyers were announced and they walked into the room. The guy who was next to me sat there with his mouth wide open and almost wet himself when he saw the new owners walk in. I asked him, 'Do you know who these two blokes are?' He told me the two buyers of the club were Graeme and Peter

Pollock, two of the best South African cricketers in the world at the time. They both walked on to the stage and gave a speech to us. I was thinking to myself there must be a sting in the tail coming soon. I may have been the youngest player at the club and was probably naïve but I turned out to be spot on.

In their speech, the Pollocks said, '... Now we're going to try to save the club but what we'd like you to do is play for nothing.' As soon as he said that my mind started to work overtime and I was ready to say something I'd probably regret. I looked around at the faces in the room and no one was prepared to say anything. I was thinking, 'Are they serious or what?' Then they asked if anyone had any questions and not surprisingly I was first to put my hand up. Everyone else turned to look at me, wondering what I was going to say.

'I ain't playing for nothing!!'

The Pollocks were a bit taken aback with my comment. I explained my position.

'I've come all the way from England to play football. I've got a young family to support. I haven't come here to play for free! I'm sorry.' Some of the other lads were giving me a bit of grief and I said, 'I don't give a monkey's – I ain't playing for free. I may as well go back home rather than play for nothing for you.' To that they told me, in no uncertain terms, that I could do just that!

My friend Graham Birks, who incidentally arrived in Port Elizabeth on the same day as we did, also stood up and said, 'I ain't playing for nothing, either.'

There was no hesitation from the officials and they agreed to let me go – and Graham followed me out of the door too. There were only the two of us who were unwilling to play unpaid and we were both heading for the exit door. It was all the excuse I needed to get the hell out of South Africa – or so I thought.

I found myself yet again without a club and had another decision to make about my football future. In the meantime, Graham and I discussed our options during the car journey back home and decided we'd get a boat back to England. We went as far as working out the cost of it and it turned out to be cheaper than getting a flight back, although it would take two weeks to get home.

The next day I went into work at Ford, Port Elizabeth as normal and spoke to a friend of mine who was a foreman there. He asked me straight out of the blue how the football was going. I thought he must have known something but as it turned out he didn't.

I replied, 'Not very well at the moment. We had a meeting last night and the club wants us all to play for nothing.' I told him I walked out on the club and was thinking about going back to England. 'I told my wife and she's made up that we're going back home.'

The foreman then disappeared for a while and came back a few minutes later and said, 'I've got someone on the phone who wants to speak to you, Peter.'

I looked surprised, 'What do you mean someone wants to speak to me? Who? What's it about?' The foreman originated from Pretoria and apparently he knew the manager of a club called Arcadia Shepherds. His name was Kai Johansen. I took the phone call and heard what he had to say:

'I believe you're leaving Port Elizabeth? Well, I'd like you to come and play for me and I don't want you to play as midfield or full-back. I'll be playing you as a centre-forward.' It was music to my ears. He must have known about the situation at Port Elizabeth and obviously had heard of me as a player so I was pleased we'd spoken. He went on and talked about money and left it at that. I had, in effect, agreed in principal to play for Arcadia Shepherds in Pretoria.

When I returned to Port Elizabeth FC to pick up my belongings, I went into the office and spoke to the chairman and told him I was going to play for Arcadia Shepherds in Pretoria.

He said, 'No you're not! You either go back home to England or we'll demand a fee for you.' I told him they hadn't paid me any wages for a few weeks so how could they claim a fee for me if I went to another club? It was a disgrace and the dispute went on for a while.

A few days later, I spoke to Kai Johansen again and he said he wanted to offer me a three-year contract. Kathy and I spoke about our future and agreed when we left Port Elizabeth we would give it another year, at best, in South Africa as we had nothing to go back to. If we went back to Liverpool we'd have to live with our parents so it was worth giving it another 12 months, particularly as we were beginning to settle down in the country. I said to Kai that I'd play for a year tops. Kai immediately replied and said the deal was off.

'We're not doing the deal for a year. I'm offering you a three-year contract here.'

I went back home and told Kathy that the deal was off as he refused to give me a year's contract.

The next day, Kai contacted me again and agreed to take me for the 12 months after all. I don't know what had changed his mind but he effectively stopped us going back home. In the end, Arcadia had to pay something like 5,000 Rand (around £2,500) to Port Elizabeth to release me from my contract. The club were fairly wealthy so they weren't worried about that sort of money, but the principle of the deal was wrong in my opinion.

As it turned out, Graham and his wife caught that boat and went back to England and he signed for non-league Fleetwood. Most of the lads who I played with at Port Elizabeth stayed at the club; some went to other clubs and the Pollocks took over the finances and the running of the club.

With the deal now confirmed, Kathy, Jason and I flew up to Pretoria to join Kai Johansen's Arcadia Shepherds. We arrived in Port Elizabeth with nothing and we travelled to Pretoria with not much more, except for a pram and a suitcase each. The whole experience of joining Arcadia was in stark contrast to when we arrived in Port Elizabeth only six months previously. Kai personally picked us up in his Mercedes at Johannesburg airport, which was only about 30 miles from Pretoria and took us to a nice hotel where we were to stay until they found us an apartment. We checked into the hotel, dropped our stuff off and Kai wasted no time in taking us out for breakfast to explain what he wanted from me as a player and how I would fit into the team. I had no idea at the time who the hell Kai Johansen was except that he was the player/manager of the club and must have been a fairly wealthy guy. I later found out he was in fact an ex-professional from Denmark who had played for Rangers in Scotland before moving to Cape Town City in 1972 and then on to Arcadia.

It was the start of a new season and I had a good feeling about the set up at Arcadia and was happy that Kai wanted me to play the way I wanted to play; he wanted a target man and I fitted the bill. A few weeks later, one of the owners of Arcadia (who also ran Pepsi Cola in South Africa) gave me a job as an electrician so I could still play football for Arcadia on a semi-professional, part-time basis. Because he was the owner of the company, he would allow me time off to go and train with the lads whenever I wanted. Kai was a forward-thinking person and always made suggestions about how I could improve my game and one day I remember he suggested I changed my goal celebration of all things. He actually suggested I do a somersault when I scored a goal. Those of you who watched football in the 1970s would think that was a crazy idea; I thought it was crazy back then but of course players of today do all sorts of spectacular goal celebrations. He had a vision of the future and was generally ahead of his time and a real character; however, I wasn't about to do somersaults for anyone!

Pretoria, being over 4,000 feet above sea level took some getting used to but I expected it to be hard to train in those conditions. As a player on the opposing side for Port Elizabeth I remembered we couldn't breathe when we played Johannesburg or Arcadia but it only took me a few weeks before I got acclimatised. Whenever we went down to the coast to train it was a doddle – we were so fit and training at altitude was amazing.

All of a sudden everything started to fit into place; I started to score goals for Arcadia and became something of a cult figure for them as some of the goals I scored were pretty spectacular. I even played against my old team, Port Elizabeth, and scored the winning goal so that was especially sweet.

When we lived in Speke, we had an old Ford Anglia van which just about got us around. We didn't have a car the whole time we were in Port Elizabeth, but one of the perks of playing for Arcadia Shepherds was that they had a scheme which gave the staff an option to bid for club cars when they became available – which was every time one of the directors fancied a change. Such a scheme didn't even exist in the UK back then, so I thought it was a pretty great idea! Of course, only the white people could afford cars in South Africa – and probably only football players at that. I put in a bid for a nice sporty car and won, so that was our first car in South Africa. I have always enjoyed driving and was made up that we were finally able to get about the country and no longer had to rely on friends to take us here and there – it was our turn to take our friends out.

Within two months of being in Pretoria, Kathy told me she was homesick and wanted to go back to the UK; she'd had enough of Africa. Although she didn't miss her parents, she missed Liverpool. Kathy wanted us to make a new life back in Liverpool but I was drawn to South Africa. We sat down and discussed the situation that evening and she again showed her intention of going back home after nearly a year of being away.

'I just can't live here any more,' she said. I was taken aback as I'd only signed for the club a couple of months previously, and signed a year's contract. I was just starting to enjoy my football again and I didn't want to turn my back on the club as they'd been really good to me.

After a few minutes thought I said, 'Right, you go back and live with my brother. I have seven months of the season left and that time will go quickly and then I'll come back home.'

The next day I went to see Kai and told him that Kathy was going home. He began to panic, thinking I was going to follow her.

'I'm not leaving, don't worry,' I reassured him. 'Kathy's going back and I'm serving the term of my contract. I've signed the contract so I'm staying.'

I don't know what he was thinking when he heard that news but if I was the manager and a player had told me that, I'd be thinking he wouldn't be 100 per cent focused on the game because his wife and child were thousands of miles away. Kai tried everything to get Kathy to change her mind but she was adamant she wanted to go back.

We were still finding our feet financially so I had to borrow the money from the club to pay £300 for her flight back to Liverpool. We hadn't been home for over a year and she was desperately homesick. It wasn't like it is now where if you play abroad you can get back and forth easily and fairly often, and back then there were no mobile phones, email or FaceTime to keep in touch with the folks back home, let alone regular flights. Back then there was nothing – sometimes there wasn't even a landline phone so we ended up having to hand-write letters that took a week to reach the recipient.

Kathy eventually flew back home with Jason a few days later and I stayed initially with my teammate, Barry Ansell, a former Aston Villa player who had joined Arcadia back in 1968. A few weeks later I moved in with Eric Abreu who had just got married. They'd just bought a new house and asked me and Dave Herald, who was also looking for somewhere to live, if we wanted to rent out a couple of bedrooms as they had a couple of spare rooms in their four-bedroomed house. We jumped at the chance as it was only going to be for six months.

A few weeks after Kathy got back to Liverpool, I received a letter from her and what was in it came as a bit of a shock. I had expected Kathy to say everything was well and she was staying with her parents. After reading the first paragraph I began to panic.

'You'd better get me and Jason back as soon as you possibly can ...'

Kathy and Jason had only been away from me for probably four weeks but she wanted to come back because Jason was missing his dad so much. He had apparently changed since going back to the UK – he was fretting, he had conjunctivitis and was sad all the time. He used to go everywhere with us when we were together in South Africa and he hadn't seen me for weeks.

Kathy had realised she'd made a big mistake as soon as she'd arrived at Speke Airport and saw the rain as she looked out of the window on the plane. She really thought it was the right decision at the time, but just being back in Liverpool made her realise it was a mistake. Maybe she wanted to see what it was like, being back home. It's ironic that she thought she'd made the wrong decision when she flew back to the UK because she (we) said the same thing when we arrived in South Africa a year before; we hated South Africa in the early days. But a lot had happened in those twelve months to change our minds about the country, enough to admit she'd rather be thousands of miles from home with her husband.

I didn't know what either of our families thought of the situation when she returned home – I think my parents must have thought Kathy had left me when they saw her back in Liverpool – but it was our decision after all, and we stuck by it.

The first thing I did after reading the letter from Kathy was to go see Kai Johansen and explain the situation. He again got the wrong end of the stick and thought I'd end up going back to the UK.

'No, actually. She's coming back to South Africa.'

Kai perked up after hearing that news.

'I need to get her on a flight back to Pretoria as soon as possible.'

Kai was delighted: 'Brilliant, brilliant,' he said. He was a charismatic guy and someone who cared about his players and he was genuinely pleased I was going to be seeing out my contract. He offered to sort out another flight for Kathy and Jason, for which I was very grateful, and he also let me use the club minibus so I could pick them up from Jan Smuts Airport in Johannesburg (now called Oliver Tambo International Airport). It was funny when Jason spotted me at the airport because he ignored me and wouldn't come to me at first. He hadn't seen me for six weeks and I suppose that's a long time for a small child, but after a while he was OK. I guess he thought his father had deserted him.

Once Kathy and Jason had arrived back in Pretoria it was a case of finding another place to live that could accommodate all three of us. I was staying with Eric but obviously that wasn't convenient for a family. Luckily, another friend of mine was going away for a month so he let us stay at his place while he was away.

Things started to get back to how they were before Kathy left; the football couldn't have been any better and everyone seemed happy with life – and the sun was still shining. It was a great climate and we had just enough money to live on. One thing that will stick in my memory for ever was the view we had from the apartment we lived in for some of the time we stayed in Pretoria. Looking down some of the avenues, all you'd see was the most amazing Jacaranda trees lining the streets, and when they were in full bloom it was a spectacular sight indeed, with their purple-blue corolla. The food was so different to what we were used to back home. The one thing I remember most is that we always bought prickly pears; you'd never see prickly pears in Liverpool in the 1970s but we'd buy a sack of them at a time – they were moreish and I couldn't get enough of them, and they were cheap. Avocados were the same; I'd buy a sack of them for 2 Rand from a seller on the side of the road.

Pretoria was very different to Port Elizabeth. The city had a different feel about it, we were becoming more sociable and had started to get invited to lots of club functions. The social scene was new to us and we had no experience of it before, so that side of our life was blossoming. I was becoming quite successful on the pitch too, and things were looking up in general. That was, until the club made the announcement that Wolves legend Derek Dougan was coming over to 'guest' for the club. The announcement raised a few eyebrows to say the least. At that time, it is fair to say that Derek was coming to the end of his career; he must have been about 36 years old but still a useful player and fit enough to play competitive games on a regular basis. Derek was the Professional Footballers' Association (PFA) chairman and was instrumental in the establishment of players' rights and free agency, so he was a key figure in the football world back home.

Derek came over to Pretoria with his German wife, Jutta Maria. I think he was asked to come over by the club's sponsors, Pepsi Cola. Malcolm Allison was also due to come over to do some coaching but that was even more secretive than the arrival of Dougan. Foreign clubs were banned from playing in South Africa in the 1970s so to get round that they had organised a host of players to come and had placed them into different teams so that every team in the league had a player from England. The plan was for these guys to play in separate teams at first but then they would come together to play in an international XI against a South Africa XI. Players included the likes of Francis Lee, who went to Port Elizabeth, and we ended up with Rodney Marsh, as well as Derek Dougan. Other players included Geoff Hurst and Tony Coleman (Durban City), Frank McLintock and George

Eastham (Hellenic) and even Johnny Haynes (also Durban City). Most, if not all the teams in South Africa at that time had several players of that stature in their side. They were all, to be fair, at the twilight of their careers back in England, even though they were all top-class players in their day.

The set-up at Arcadia was pretty basic, even compared to the English league of the 1970s. We had to wear our own kit for training and I wore a shirt with a big letter W on the back.

When Kai saw it he said to me, 'What does the W on the back of your shirt stand for?' I thought he was being deadly serious so I told him that all the players had a vote for the worst trainer of the week and he had to wear the shirt with the W on; however, I told him the W stood for 'wanker of the week'. I said it in a serious tone, even though I was only joking but Kai took it literally and actually wrote it in the programme for the next home game.

We were all big lads, and one of the headlines in the local sports magazine said we had a forward line measuring 18ft 7in; I was 6ft 2in, Derek was 6ft 3in and Rodney was over 6ft 2in. Even though we only played one game together it created such a stir that the headline in the paper following the game with a team called Pietermaritzburg in which I scored the winner in a 1–0 victory read:

WITHE OUTSHINES THE TWO STARS

After the game I was asking Rodney about how I'd get back to the UK as I was coming to the end of my contract at Arcadia and he told me that Derek was the man to speak to as he was the chairman of the PFA. I'd already asked Derek a couple of times previously but he didn't really inspire me that he was going to help me, so I put that to the back of my mind.

Kathy and Jason had been back for about six or seven months by now, but there was something niggling in the back of my mind, and my head was telling me it was time go home. Kai was so desperate to keep me at Arcadia and he wanted me to sign another contract – I was that important to the club. When he called me into his office to discuss the terms of a new contract I was beginning to get itchy feet myself and had already spoken to a few people, including Rodney Marsh and Derek Dougan about moving back to the UK. Kai told me he wanted me to sign for another three years and when I refused he went ballistic.

'Don't do this to me now, Peter,' he shouted.

I stressed my point of view once more, 'I'm not signing.'

Kai carried on, 'Why do you have problem after problem?'

I was adamant I wasn't going to sign any contract simply because the club saw me as a commodity not as a person. I had become a success scoring goals left, right and centre and was a cult figure among the fans and I saw the club was just using me as a bargaining tool. Footballers in those days didn't have agents like every footballer does now so I was fighting my own cause against Kai. I stood up for myself because all I was interested in was looking after my family. I told Kai I wasn't signing again and he turned round and said in that case he wouldn't play me.

Just as in Port Elizabeth when they wanted us to play for nothing, I remained cool and collected and said, 'Do as you please, I ain't signing.' It did bother me if I'm honest because all I wanted to do was play football but it was time to move on.

The next game came up and Kai kept his word and left me out of the team. You can probably guess the result – we lost the game. Speculation was rife in the local papers the following morning so he backed down for the next game and brought me back into the team. I duly obliged by scoring two goals and I think he realised there and then that he was on to a loser and he came back and spoke to me in his broad Danish accent:

'I realise that you are a brilliant player, brilliant. I want you to stay. We try and accommodate.'

Again, I was standing firm, 'Whatever you decide I ain't signing that contract, that's for sure.'

We had secured a semi-final place in the championship but I told him I was leaving after that game. He eventually came back to me and said, 'I know you want to go back to the UK so you sign this contract and we'll arrange for you to go for a trial to a club in the UK.' He didn't say to me that Derek Dougan had done this for me but he just said, 'We're arranging this for you.' I had a feeling there and then that Derek must have had something to do with it but couldn't be sure at the time. He also said he'd pay for the flights (which he didn't in the end, but that's another story).

What had actually happened, and I only found this out months later, was that Dougan had a conversation with Wolves manager, Bill McGarry, stating that he'd found his own replacement at Wolves as he was coming to the end of his career. That replacement was yours truly. The arrangement was that I went back to the UK for a three-month trial at Wolves but I'd be under contract with Arcadia.

I ended up being leading scorer for Arcadia that season with 16 goals in 26 appearances, and I received a trophy at the end-of-season awards night for being the foreign player of the year. My room-mate and our centre-back, Dave Herholdt expected to receive a trophy too and was gutted to learn that an older player, Stan Lapot won the club's player of the year award. In my mind Dave should have won it really, and he was absolutely distraught to have lost. I've never seen a player so upset at not winning an award – he even thought it was fixed. That's the way it goes sometimes, I guess. One of the fans, a lady called Ida, who had been befriending us for a while beforehand, put up a prize for being leading scorer, which was an Omega gold watch, at the time valued at about 250 South African Rand (I've still got the watch to this day). Ida was a rich lady and came across as slightly overpowering at times, but it was a lovely gesture all the same. I think she fancied Kai and saw us as a way to get close to him. You could go so far as to say that she used us, but as we were a bit naïve at the time we just saw it as someone being friendly.

Ida looked after us for several months while we were in Pretoria and she actually took us to a restaurant for the first time. We'd never had much in our lives and definitely didn't frequent restaurants back home, apart from the local chippy, so when Ida took us to a restaurant in Pretoria it was a whole new and exciting experience. We hadn't got a clue what to order, so Kathy chose the soup as an easy option. As I looked up and down the menu I noticed the word prawn and it brought me back to the time I was a kid in Liverpool. I remember an older lad who lived by us always bought a bag of prawns to eat in front of us and he would tease us by saying, 'When you get a job you'll be able to afford to buy prawns.' We asked him once if he'd give us one to taste as we hadn't eaten them before and he eventually gave us one of the tiniest prawns you could imagine as a taster. When we asked for another one he'd say, 'Nah, go and get a job.' That was the last time I'd eaten a prawn so I instinctively thought I'd have the prawns for a starter that evening; however, when the waitress came to take my order she asked me how many prawns I'd like, five, seven or nine. I immediately replied nine, thinking that all prawns were as small as the one we tried all those years ago back home. The waitress couldn't believe I would manage nine prawns by myself so she asked me if I was sure. 'Yes, I'm sure. I'll have nine prawns.'

When she came back to bring the food out my prawns were served on a huge plate and she put it in front of me. Well, my eyes nearly popped out when I saw the size of these things – they were massive. I'm not sure if they were prawns because they looked more like langoustine. Both Ida and Kathy stared at the plate of prawns and couldn't believe the size of them. By the time I'd got through three of them, I was beginning to struggle and found them a bit tough to be honest.

Ida leant across the table and said, 'You're supposed to take the shells off the prawns before you eat them.'

I felt so embarrassed. I'd just eaten three huge prawns together with their shells and heads on. I made sure I de-shelled the next one I ate, though.

I eventually signed that new contract with Arcadia in the November of 1973 on the understanding that I was going to Wolves for a trial at the end of the South African season. That meant we'd have been in the country for two years; one year longer than I originally anticipated but it had proved I was a lethal goal-scorer and I was desperate to prove that in the English league as well. It was effectively a 'loan' deal, which was unheard of in English football in the 1970s, but it was approved by the FA nonetheless. I was approaching the peak of my career and it was an important decision for me to make. It was a big move, but I always thought if I didn't make it at Wolves I could always come back to Pretoria as I was under contract with them – although that would be the last resort.

I didn't really want to go back to South Africa – but I didn't tell Kai that.

4

The Wanderer Returns

"I'm sorry we're not going to sign you, but we've had four or five lower league clubs enquire about you."
Bill McGarry

****

No more than six or seven months after Kathy and Jason returned to Pretoria we found ourselves thrown back into another English winter and yet another new place to get used to. This time it was Wolverhampton, which wasn't exactly as glamorous or exotic as Pretoria, but offered a route back into the English game through a top Division One club with a long and illustrious history. Kathy was happy to be back in the UK, although she wasn't going to be living with her parents, so I was happy as well, and looking forward to the new challenge.

Wolves had apparently paid for the flights from South Africa and they looked after us from day one – they were so good to us. When we arrived back in the UK we were picked up at Heathrow Airport and driven up to Wolverhampton. Initially the club found us a hotel until we had settled in, but they later found us a nice place to rent instead.

I started training the very next day, so there was no time for jet lag and little time to settle in at all. I was picked up and taken to the training ground, which was nice. I hadn't met the manager or any of the players and didn't know a lot about Wolves, other than that they were a strong first division side with a big squad.

In those days I had quite long hair – down to my shoulders in fact, as was the trend in the early 1970s. When I walked into the changing room for the first time all the lads had a bit of a laugh at my expense about the state of my hair. I dropped my kit down and Derek Dougan walked in and asked me to come with him to see the manager, Bill McGarry. Derek introduced me to Bill and I shook hands with him. He then told Bill that the lads were taking the mickey out of my hair and Bill started laughing too, and we all had a bit of a joke about it, all light-hearted fun. He went on to tell me I was on trial for three months and wished me well. I was beginning to like the feel of the club and what the manager was saying and as I put my hand on the door to open it, Bill yelled out, 'And by the way, get your effing hair cut before you come back tomorrow!' I said OK and laughed as I went to get changed. That very afternoon after training I found the nearest barbers and got my hair cut. It must have been a big thing at the club that you had to have your hair short, or at least tidy, as the manager was a bit of a stickler for it. Phil Parkes, the goalkeeper, had long hair but he managed to keep it immaculate so he got away with it – but mine was scruffy, long and curly so I had no chance.

Bill had been at Wolves since the 1968/69 season and had taken the club to the 1972 UEFA Cup Final. The only way to describe Bill McGarry was as a 'fearsome character when crossed' and he was a 'hard taskmaster'. He instigated rules on players' diets (and hair), long before the trend became standard practice within the footballing world. There seemed to be a fear factor under Bill. If you were walking down the corridor and you saw Bill walking the other way you'd normally go and hide somewhere, otherwise he'd make some comment like, 'Get your haircut, son,' or 'Get fit'.

I was the new kid on the block when I went to Wolves: no one knew of me, apart from Derek Dougan. Most of the lads probably thought I came from South Africa until I opened my mouth and they heard my broad Scouse accent, at which point they would say, 'You don't sound South African!' Derek had informed everyone that he had found his successor at Wolves, and that had created a bit of interest in the local and national media, so I was asked to do some interviews at the training ground on the Thursday following my introduction to the club. On the Friday, I saw the manager and asked him if the interviews I'd done the day before were going to go out to the national press.

He said, 'Yeah, the interviews will go out to the nationals. Why?' I told Bill the reason why: I hadn't told my parents or any of my family I was back in the country and playing for Wolves. I'd kept the whole thing secret – even Kathy hadn't told her family about our return. Bill was concerned and immediately told me to take the weekend off and sort myself out.

I took Bill's advice and we took the train from Wolverhampton to Liverpool Lime Street and then got a taxi to Speke. We were never able to afford a taxi before so that was something of a novelty. I remember pulling into my parents' street and I saw my mother walking up the road. She was looking at the black cab coming towards the house, and by the time it got to the house she had just arrived at the front door. Black cabs never, ever came up our street, so she was staring at it intently. I opened the door of the taxi with my head bowed low and as I showed my face she almost fell over with shock.

'What are you doing here?'

I told mum that I had come back because I had a three-month trial for Wolves.

'Your dad's going to go barmy when he sees you,' she said.

As a kid I used to go to meet my father from work at the Metal Box factory. I would stand outside waiting for him to pass the wages out on a Thursday night so my mother could go and get some shopping. Now I was back paying my parents a rare visit and it was like going back in time as mum said to me, 'Go and see your dad and tell him you're home.' I was 21 years old and I still had to meet my father from work, but I did as my mum told me and waited for him outside this same window trying to attract someone's attention.

People in the factory knew me from years ago and I heard some of the workers shouting, 'Gerry, Gerry your lad's standing outside again.'

He had no idea I was even back in the country, let alone back in Speke, so he replied, 'What do you mean he's outside?' He came to the window and opened it. 'What you doing here, son?' I told him why I was home and he told me he would finish work early and would see me at home. It was like the old days all over again.

After spending the weekend in Liverpool we returned to Wolverhampton on the Sunday, ready for training the next day. There seemed to be a good, healthy atmosphere in the camp and some very fit players; then there was this guy who'd just arrived from South Africa who was 6ft 2in and weighed about 12 stone (me). I was pretty lean to be honest, but fit, and I was certain I could outrun anyone in that dressing room as I'd been training at altitude for a few months. As it was well into the season I had to report to the reserve-team coach, Norman Bodell, as I had no chance of breaking into the first team straight away. Although Wolves were perceived to be a big club at that time, they had no permanent training facilities so we had to use the local racecourse during the week. There were loads of football pitches in the middle of the racecourse, but come Monday morning they were in a right state as they'd all been used over the weekend. So the first team tended to train in the club gym and we had to go by coach with the youth team to a place called Brocton, on Cannock Chase. In those days, I would say more than half of the training was physical training rather than improving football skills. When we arrived at Brocton it was a case of the youth team going one way, and the reserves running another. It was basic endurance training of stop-start then fast-slow runs and it lasted well over an hour. It was easy for me and Norman couldn't believe my fitness levels or the speed I could run. I used to race with another Scouse lad called John McCauly and we were always first to finish. To fill the time until the others had finished Norman used to get me to practise sprinting.

After a few of these training sessions, word got round that I was some sort of 'superhuman' as I'd always finish training first. Sometimes, the first team would come out to train with us, and I think it was just to see how fit I was. On one occasion, John McCauly, myself and a few others had finished first as usual, and we were waiting for everyone else by the coach. We decided to start running back to Wolverhampton rather than wait for everyone else, just to see how far we could get before the bus caught us up. So, there we were running down a road in the middle of nowhere, but the other lads couldn't keep up.

'Aren't you bloody knackered?'

Some of the lads dropped out and waited for the bus to eventually pick them up but it was nothing to me, I could run all day so I carried on. I was left on my own and I didn't entirely know where I was; I was just running, knowing that John and the other lads had been picked up and were already on the bus looking for me. I had it in mind where I was going, and it was a junction where the coach would turn. Eventually, the bus driver found me about four miles from Brocton, and the lads were all saying, 'How did you get this far?' That happened on several occasions. I think the fitness side of training at Wolves stemmed from Bill McGarry, who was a fitness fanatic himself. Bill liked his golf and was a good squash player and his regimes on the training ground obviously rubbed off on his coaches.

Bill had a golf handicap in single figures. He loved his golf so much, he used to take some of us out on occasions to play at different courses around the area, including to Beau Desert near Cannock, Staffordshire. It was a beautiful course. Even better, it was all paid for and always included lunch, and there were prizes as well to make the game a bit more interesting. If you didn't play golf, unfortunately you had to train. I loved training but I also wanted to learn to play golf, so I made the most of the golf days. I think it was John McCauly who first got me interested in golf, as he was selling all his stuff as he'd had enough of the game. I bought it all from him – clubs, bag, tees, balls, shoes, rainwear, and all for £100. I really wanted to learn because I was pretty poor when I first started out.

Kenny Hibbitt also had a single-figure handicap and after watching me play one day he said, 'Have you read anything about how to play golf?'

Not surprisingly, I said no, and Kenny gave me a Hale Irwin golf book so I could learn. I took it home and read it, and soon realised I was doing everything wrong. I then really tried to learn to play golf properly, rather than just assuming I was doing the right thing. Now there's a lesson for everyone to heed!

I had settled into life at Wolves quite well but I did realise there was huge competition for places, especially up front. I was nearing the end of the loan spell and after one particular training session, Norman took me to one side to tell me the manager may not be signing me permanently. I'd been at Wolves for nearly three months; I'd only played a handful of reserve games and hadn't broken into the first team, so I was gutted. The next morning, Bill called me into the office before training and told me the news I was half expecting.

'I'm sorry; we're not going to sign you. BUT we've had four or five lower-league clubs enquire about you.' The clubs included Mansfield Town and Oxford United and they wanted to sign me on a permanent deal.

I could see the problem Bill had with making that decision. The squad they had at that time was incredible and included the likes of John Richards, Alan Sunderland, Peter Eastoe, Steve Kindon, Steve Daley, Barry Powell, Kenny Hibbitt and Dave Wagstaffe. There were probably about seven strikers to choose from and they were all competing for a first-team place. It was a massive squad and a good one at that, so deciding whether they could give me a contract or not was a hard one. Bill asked me what I wanted to do – stay a bit longer at Wolves, sign for one of the lower-league clubs or go back to Pretoria. I told Bill I had set my heart on staying at Wolves and definitely didn't want to go back to South Africa.

Bill thought for a minute or so and said to me, 'Train this morning and we're going to have a practice match this afternoon, then I'll speak to the coaches afterwards and I'll let you know.' He asked me if I had a preference which club I'd like to go to and I replied that I hadn't thought about it yet. In the meantime, Bill told me there was a stumbling block on the South African side. 'They want £20,000 for you.'

I said to Bill it was a ludicrous amount of money and unheard of in South Africa. 'The most expensive player in South African football history was signed for 20,000 Rand (£10,000). No! That's ridiculous.'

I was so furious I ended up contacting Arcadia Shepherds myself and asked for Kai Johansen to ring me as soon as possible. Kai called me back at home after training.

'What the hell are you playing at?' I demanded. I was furious. He gave me some flannel about me being worth the money. 'I cost you only £5,000 and you now want £20,000?' I then spoke to the chairman at Pretoria, Ken Fulton, who said they wanted me to come back to Pretoria.

'We don't want you to sign for anyone else, Peter.'

I stood my ground, 'Ken, I'm telling you now, I ain't coming back! I'd rather pack the game in. I don't care what you do, if you stop me from doing this, coming back to the UK, I will never play football again. I don't give a monkey's – I ain't coming back!'

He said to me there and then, 'We won't stop you from playing. We wanted you to come back and play for us. We'll give you [this and that].'

I told him again that I wasn't going back. Looking back, I see just what a sneaky bastard Kai had been; he had got me to sign a contract when I went to Wolves on loan under the assumption that I would be signed up, but in hindsight, I wouldn't have signed it and would have come back to the UK at my own expense if I had known a fee would have been asked for.

I went back to see Bill McGarry that same morning and told him what Ken had said. Bill assured me I wasn't going to be sent back to Pretoria and advised me to play in the practice match for the reserves against the first team at the racecourse. I must have been so pumped up for that match because we won the game and I scored all three goals – and I got the feeling the manager didn't expect that result! When I returned to Molineux after the game, Derek Dougan stopped me and said the manager wanted to see me. Although I really thought he still didn't want to sign me and I was expecting the worst, Bill surprised me.

'Well done today. You did very well. Here's a contract.'

I didn't hesitate and signed a contract for Wolverhampton Wanderers at £65 per week. It didn't really matter how much it was for, I just wanted to sign for Wolves, but more to the point, I didn't want to go back to South Africa. There was no mention of a fee being paid at the time but I think Wolves paid around £10,000 to Pretoria (to this day I can't confirm that). I think Bill must have had second thoughts about me after that game; if someone scores three goals against your first team then they must surely be worth a contract? Bill also told me I could have a club house to live in (which worked out at £3 a week for a four-bedroomed detached house). It was a big decision for Bill to make, especially after saying just the day before that I could leave. I guess he decided he'd regret it if he had let me go to another club and I ended up scoring goals there.

After that eventful January day, I went home to Kathy and told her I'd signed for Wolves and we were staying in the UK. Kathy was made up because she didn't want to go back to South Africa either. She had settled down in Wolverhampton and was relieved that the news was good. It was a stroke of luck that we were staying in Wolverhampton but in reality, if things had gone the other way, I don't know – maybe I'd have signed for one of the four lower-league clubs interested in signing me. In the end I was just happy that Wolves had signed me up so quickly and my immediate future had been settled.

Looking back, it was that practice match which clearly changed the direction my career was heading in, even though I thought I'd done enough to earn myself a contract before. I trained most days and even did extra training with the ball in the gym. Sammy Chung and Norman Bodell were brilliant as they both helped me with my skills, particularly how to kick a ball 'properly', and worked on my control. I couldn't get enough of training

I'd scored eight goals in my 13 reserve-team appearances for Wolves so I was ready for the step up into first division football. I made my Wolves debut in a home league match against Bill McGarry's old club, Ipswich Town on 9 March 1974. John Richards had succumbed to injury a week after scoring his famous winner in the League Cup Final against Manchester City just a few days earlier, and I got the nod. Steve Daley was also awarded his debut and we both ended up scoring in a 3–1 win, but I only played for the first team twice more that season. Steve and I became good mates after that game, and towards the end of the season I told him I was going to speak to Bill about going back to South Africa during the summer to play. Steve became excited himself, and I asked him if he fancied coming as well.

'Yeah, we'll have a nice holiday out there and have a good time.'

I told him I could probably get back to Arcadia and promised I'd go and see Bill McGarry.

I picked my moment to speak to Bill and told him of my idea.

'No!' he exclaimed, 'I don't want you to go anywhere! You're in my plans for the future. I don't want you to go to South Africa.' I left it at that and told Steve that Bill didn't want me to go. Steve wasn't happy but that was that.

The team weren't really setting the world alight in the league, but Bill still picked his favourites week in, week out while he had an abundance of young talent waiting in the wings with the likes of myself, Alan Sunderland and Steve Kindon. I confronted Bill one day and asked him why he kept picking the same faces and he responded by saying, 'Because I keep thinking that today's the day that he's going to hit it off.' Years later I asked Bill the same question and he admitted he was wrong to have picked Derek Dougan every match and he should have dropped him out of the team and put the youngsters in. That told me Bill had learned a lesson from his time at Wolves, which to me was the sign of a good manager.

We used to have a sauna in the shower room at Molineux, and one day after a game, Bill randomly walked in and sat next to me. After a few minutes of silence he asked me a question right out of the blue.

'Do you remember you asked me if you could go and play in South Africa? Well, do you fancy going to America?'

I was a little taken aback. 'Why's that then?'

Bill went on, 'Someone's actually asked for you to go and play in America. There's a new franchise started over there and a friend of mine called Vic Crowe is managing it.'

Vic Crowe had been sacked in 1974 after his Villa side finished 14th in Division Two and had taken over a new franchise called Portland Timbers who played in the North American Soccer League (NASL). Professional teams in all major sports operated as franchises within a league and the NASL was no different. Bill continued to sell the idea to me.

'Yeah, he's asked for certain players to go over there and one of them he's asked for is you. Go home and ask Kathy what she thinks and let me know in a few days what you decide?'

I was more than a little spooked by the conversation I'd just had with Bill, as I had had a dream a few years beforehand that I would one day play for Aston Villa under Vic Crowe. I must have had the dream while I was playing in South Africa, when Vic was the manager of Villa. As soon as the name

'Vic Crowe' was mentioned by Bill, the dream I had come back to me. Although, I wouldn't be playing for Villa it seemed fated that I'd be playing for Vic Crowe.

So Kathy and I had another decision to make; whether to stay at Wolves and fight for my place or go to yet another new country and once more into the unknown.

When I saw Steve Daley minutes later in the dressing room, I told him about the bizarre conversation I'd just had with Bill.

Steve just said, 'Bloody hell, I'll do that!' I didn't tell Steve that Vic had asked for me specifically and hadn't asked for him to go.

When I got home, I said to Kathy, 'How do you fancy going to America?' She seemed open to the idea, so the next day, I went to see Bill in his office and agreed to go to Portland Timbers on loan for a season. Bill said he'd try to get me a bit more money in with the deal, which was even better.

Word had obviously got round pretty quickly because about three of the lads including Steve Daley and Phil Parkes came over and asked if I could put a word in with Bill.

'Ask him your bleeding self! I can't do your bleeding asking for you,' I told them. So, I think a few of the lads went to see Bill and asked if they could go as well. In the end, Bill allowed several of us to go, including Barry Powell, Chris Dangerfield and Jimmy Kelly. Unfortunately for Steve Daley, he didn't get his 'holiday' because Bill McGarry wouldn't release him from Wolves.

5

Portland – Soccer City USA

"You're on how much? The guys who collect the garbage get paid more than that!"

****

Portland is known as the City of Roses, and is the second largest city in the Pacific Northwest. We knew nothing about America, let alone Portland, Oregon; we'd only ever been to one foreign country and that was South Africa, so we were venturing into the unknown yet again. Football (or soccer, as the Americans call it) has been the great leveller over the years, the international language which speaks across countries, class and gender. But it didn't really exist in Portland until the early 1970s, when the Timbers franchise was inaugurated into the NASL and I, and the fifteen other British lads who travelled over there in the spring of 1975, made history for football in the US.

The original NASL started in 1968 but hadn't really got going until around 1975 when we travelled over to 'kick-start' a new chapter in the league's history. The British cohort arrived in Portland in dribs and drabs; it was a 6,000-mile journey and a long way in those days. We were all very jet-lagged when we arrived in the city and were transported on to a place called Beaverton, about seven miles west of Portland. Our 'digs' was actually a condo-style accommodation with a swimming pool in the middle of the complex. It was a brand of luxury we hadn't really experienced before. As we arrived in the US, we were greeted by a host – which was typical of American hospitality. What the organisers had actually done was to allocate a family to look after each player (and his family if they had one) and welcome us to the country and to Portland. They were essentially there to assist us with anything we wanted – any problem we had, they would help us with. We were allocated to the Harper family, a couple, a few years older than Kathy and I who had two sons and a daughter. We couldn't believe it – we were being treated like superstars.

The Harpers lived close to the complex and they had a huge, beautiful house with a pool. On our first day we were invited to a family meal at their house.

'We're having salmon, and we'd love you to join us.'

I looked at Kathy and I was thinking, 'What's so special about a tin of salmon?'

We arrived at their house and they showed us around, and we were in awe – it was amazing. When we got to the lounge, Don showed me the 'trap door' in the floor, hidden by a carpet, which led to a cellar where he kept his wine. He moved the carpet to uncover the cellar door and invited me to come and choose some wine. So, off we went into the basement to pick the wine for the meal. When I saw the cellar, it was stacked full, top to bottom with wine. I looked around at all the wine but I hadn't a clue and didn't know which one to pick until I spotted two rows of champagne and, pretending I knew something about wines, said to Don, 'I see you've got a bit of champagne, then?'

Don replied with surprise, 'You like champagne, Peter?' He then picked up two bottles of champagne and handed them to me to take up for dinner while he picked up a couple of bottles of red and white wine. Don was obviously a connoisseur and seemed quite impressed that I liked champagne. Little did he know I had never even tried it before, and knew nothing about wine or champagne whatsoever. He followed me up the stairs and shouted to his wife, 'Norma, they like champagne!!'

We ate the starter, which was a soup and Norma left the table and went into the kitchen.

'Norma's just gone to get the salmon,' Don explained.

As she walked in with this almighty whole salmon, Norma was telling us about it and how it was caught, 'Don went out with his brother this morning and caught this beautiful salmon especially for dinner tonight.'

The last time I had salmon was out of a tin and I was thinking, 'He's actually caught the salmon?' Norma placed the plate of salmon in the middle of the table and I said to Kathy, 'That's definitely not a tin of salmon.' It was our first introduction to fresh salmon.

As Don started to cut the fish off the bone he said, 'Of course we won't eat all this salmon.'

I was salivating and thought to myself, 'I bloody could!'

We just sat there, around the table all night, eating, drinking wine and champagne and chewing the fat for hours. It was an amazing first night in Portland.

That first night spent with the Harpers was followed by our first training session with the Timbers. We trained in the Civic Stadium (now called Jeld-Wen Field). It was actually a baseball stadium and wasn't built for soccer, so the groundsmen had to flatten the mounds where the baseball diamonds were. The ground wasn't grass as we were used to, but some sort of artificial turf, a bit like AstroTurf. They managed to find a pair of goalposts from somewhere and put them out on to the field so we could use them during the training session. Because it was the start of a new franchise, we had attracted some local media attention and I noticed there was a TV camera crew walking around the stadium watching us train. The camera crew hadn't a clue about soccer and they were walking around looking for something to film, probably wondering when this bunch of Limeys were going to show off their skills. I watched two guys filming behind the makeshift goalposts and I said to my Wolves teammate, Jimmy Kelly, 'Pump half a dozen crosses over and let's see what these goals are like?' The goalposts weren't actually in their correct position but they were to the side of the pitch, so Jimmy went to the left wing and Willie Anderson went to the right, with the camera crew standing next to the goalposts. Jimmy then pumped a ball into the area, I jumped up to meet it and headed it beautifully and the guy holding the camera shat himself and almost dropped the camera as the ball came straight towards him at speed.

The crew looked at each other in amazement and one of the guys said to the other, 'Jesus, did you see that? I've never seen anyone head the ball like that before!' He then turned to me and asked, 'Doesn't the ball hurt your head?'

The other guy then shouted over to me, 'Buddy, buddy can you do that again?'

Both Willie and Jimmy then spent the next ten minutes crossing balls into my path from both wings while these two guys filmed us.

Before the opening game of the new campaign, I don't remember getting too much media attention, probably due to soccer being a minority sport in Portland (and in the US). The first game of the new campaign was against Seattle Sounders, our local rivals even though the two cities were over 170 miles apart. It was apparently a sporting tradition in the US that the home team played in white and the opposition always played in a different colour but on that occasion both teams came out wearing white. The Seattle players were asking us why we were wearing white as they thought we would turn up in our traditional green kit. One of our players explained that our away kit was green and our home kit was white. Seattle said they did not have another kit, so management decided we should wear our green kit even though we were the home side. It was all very bizarre and very confusing.

Soccer was pretty much a novelty sport in the US in the 1970s, so everyone was amazed that 7,500 locals turned up in pouring rain to watch a bunch of (mainly) Limeys play their native sport. Ten minutes into the game, the PA announcer broadcast over the tannoy, 'Ladies and gentlemen, please can you stop booing the team in green – it's the home team!' It was a bit like a comedy sketch with the home supporters booing the team in the coloured kit, thinking they were the opposition. We lost that game 1–0, a bad start to the campaign but hardly surprising as we hadn't trained together for very long.

Right at the start of our stay in Portland, we had been allocated four cars between the fifteen of us, but Kathy and I have always liked to do our own thing so I knew we'd really need a car of our own. The one thing I was good at was closing a good deal, so I took it upon myself to go round all the car dealerships in the area, sourcing the best offer. It was during the period when we were just becoming well known, and I remember walking into this particular dealership and spotting a certain car in the showroom. I briefly mentioned who I was to the nearby salesman and he stepped back and looked at me.

'You're Peter Withe, the soccer player?' I explained to him the type of car I wanted and almost immediately he had an idea. 'No problem. I'll get you a car. Leave it with me.' He offered me a Plymouth Gran Fury but he said he would only do the deal if they had the dealership's logo stickers on the side. 'We don't want you driving around with these on the side when you're not working but when you're playing or training, could you put the stickers on the side to advertise the dealership?' We struck a deal and I ended up driving this huge Plymouth Fury around for a few months. It was great because it meant we didn't have to share with the other guys.

During the course of the season we always trained at the baseball stadium, as we didn't have any training facilities of our own. One day, the Portland American football team (Portland Storm) were training there at the same time on the other half of the pitch. During the training sessions, I somehow got hold of an American football while one of their lads got hold of one of our soccer balls. The ball was pretty huge, but I started to throw it, imitating their guys, while they were doing the same with our ball, trying to kick it. One of their guys came over to me and gave me a practice-ball, much smaller than the other ball, which just sat in my hand nicely.

He said to me, 'Do you think you can throw this one, buddy?' The American went on, pointing at a teammate down field, 'You see that fella over there – you think you can pick him out with the ball?'

I thought, 'No problem.' So, I threw the ball with my left hand and it travelled through the air like a missile and landed in the hands of his teammate.

My new mate stood back in total disbelief and said, 'You don't fancy coming for a trial with us do you?' I thought he was joking but the guy was deadly serious, 'No, man, you got a real feel for the ball.' My hand-to-eye coordination was pretty good, being a decent golfer, so I must have been a natural and I continued to ping these balls to the runners and after a while they asked me again to come for a trial. I didn't go after all – I don't know why but I suppose I felt I had a job to do with the Timbers.

Just like most American sports, soccer games could never be draws; Americans hate not seeing a team win so the NASL followed suit in the early days by playing 'overtime' (or extra time as we call it) to see the game to a conclusion. After our first defeat at the start of the season, we enjoyed a nice little run of victories and we became known as the 'overtime kings' because we kept winning in extra time. Inevitably, I scored most of the winning goals. The crowds started to increase as well and 7,500 quickly became 15,000, 20,000 and more. All of a sudden, the home games became sell-outs where 30,000 fans were the norm. The team became increasingly popular and we were asked to go into schools to coach the kids in ball skills. We were very personable and very often we went out into the city to meet our new-found fans. After each game, we'd go to the same hotel in the city and were given free drink vouchers so that we would be there to meet the fans. Hundreds of fans would turn up to meet the 'celebrity players' from England. The Portland fans had a few nicknames for me, including 'the wizard of nod' and 'the mad header' because of my heading ability. The local fans couldn't believe how friendly and hospitable we were and they wanted to have a drink and chat with us.

'Those baseball and basketball players wouldn't give us the time of day but you guys come to meet us every week. You're just "normal" people!'

We had quickly become local celebrities and got invited to appear at several local organisations. On one of these appearances we were invited to a local Portland brewery called Henry Weinhard, located in the city, not far from the training ground. The local brew was called Blitz-Weinhard. I don't think they knew what they had let themselves in for, inviting 15 English football players on a tour of the brewery. The first place we went into was the hospitality room and they put out all their brews on a table for us to try. It was meant to be a tour of the factory and we were supposed to see how the beer was made but there were so many bottles of beer that we didn't vacate the hospitality room. At the end of the day, the bosses said to us, 'As we're so close to the training ground, any time you want to visit, just knock on my door.' It was like an open-ended invite so we took them up on their offer and, after every training session, we knocked on his door and we were welcomed with open arms. Not only that, we ended up having a keg of beer delivered to the complex in Beaverton whenever we wanted one – they placed it at the side of the swimming pool, all fixed up with a tap. It was unbelievable! Happy days!

Match day tickets started to become prized possessions, and people would queue right around the stadium for tickets. This gave us another opportunity to meet our fans after training sessions while they stood in line. We even had people come into the stadium to watch us train. It was unheard of; nothing of the sort had ever happened in Portland before, and us Brits, we loved it. To us, it felt like a holiday but for Vic Crowe and his assistant Leo Crowther, it was quite serious. Their job was to get Portland Timbers to the top of the league. We were all getting paid, obviously; I was getting a lot more than I was at Wolves, probably around £110 per week, and on top of that we had our luxury accommodation. However, some of the younger guys weren't on so much, maybe £70 a week. When we got talking to the fans they were under the impression we were on big money and when we told them how much we were paid, the reply was usually something like, 'And you're on how much? The guys who collect the garbage get paid more than that!' They couldn't believe how little we were being paid, even though it was more than most of us were being paid by our own clubs back home.

At the other end of the football spectrum in the NASL were the New York Cosmos. It was during the 1975 season that the Cosmos acquired the Brazilian superstar Pelé, whom they had been attempting to sign since the team was created back in 1971. The Pelé deal was described as 'the transfer coup of the century' even though the club president had apparently not heard of him before getting involved in soccer, but agreed to finance the transfer when the Cosmos's general manager compared the Brazilian's popularity to that of the Pope. Pelé joined the Cosmos on a salary of US$1.4 million per year, an enormous wage for an athlete at that time and about 1,000 times more than my salary. Pelé's debut was made into a huge event and was broadcast to 22 countries worldwide.

By the time the Timbers visited New York it was well into the season and, as with every away game, it meant lots of travelling and staying overnight in a hotel. We had a guy called Ron Culp who was the physio (or 'coach' as the Americans described him) but also acted as our American mentor, so he was the guy who gave us the lowdown on every city we visited when we were on the team bus. He'd say things like, 'Guys, guys, you're in St Louis, the gateway to the West and famous for ...'

Typical of us Brits at the time, we'd all shout out to him from the back, 'Sit down you asshole, get outta here.'

We had played a game the day before in Boston so it wasn't such a long trip, and when we arrived in New York, after giving us the usual local information about the city, Ron stood at the front of the bus and laid down the law to us, 'Guys, guys, now you better listen to me and you better listen up because if you go off 5th Avenue, 6th Avenue, 7th Avenue or Broadway, we'll find you dead in a gutter!'

The lads stopped what they were doing and listened to Ron for once and couldn't believe what he'd just said. 'What the heck did he just say? Did he say dead?'

Ron carried on, 'If you walk around here in New York City and if a policeman stops you and you start giving him what you give me, he'll hit you with his 'Billy club' (truncheon) so hard and it will take us three days to get you out of jail.' He went on to say the city wasn't safe to walk alone at night and it was run by the local mafia.

The lads soon shut up, 'What the hell have we come to here?'

We arrived at the hotel, The Holiday Inn, shitting ourselves and not really looking forward to our experience in the Big Apple after Ron had talked it down. The hotel wasn't right in the centre of Manhattan, not far off the tourist area but on the wrong side of town. On that occasion I wasn't sharing a room with anyone and when I went to shut the door and then turned to face it, I saw lock after lock on the door. There must have been ten locks on the door – and that was just my hotel room door. I was thinking 'This doesn't feel right to me.' It was more like a prison cell than a hotel room. When I went downstairs I saw the club manager who'd organised the trip.

'You'll have to find another hotel; I'm not staying here!' I told him.

We ended up relocating to 5th Avenue, right in the heart of Manhattan, just across the road from Central Park. It was a bit better – but it wasn't exactly five-star luxury.

The city had become notorious the world over for high crime-rates and other social disorders in the 1970s. Prostitutes and pimps frequented Times Square, while Central Park became feared as the site of muggings and rapes. None of us had been to New York before so we didn't really know what to expect. We had only seen things about New York on TV back home, so what we witnessed one morning in Central Park opened our eyes. As we had nowhere to train and we were staying near Central Park, we decided to try to find a pitch or a big open space where we could train there. While we were walking through the park, we noticed a couple on a park bench in an uncompromising position. We had to look twice and on the second glance we noticed they were blatantly having sex on the bench: they even waved at us and carried on as we walked past. It was something you'd never see in Calderstones Park in Liverpool, that's for sure.

The high volume of crime made sure the three emergency services were kept busy, so all you could hear in New York were sirens whining, every second of the day. There was no let-up and we had to try to train for a couple of hours in that environment. It was something we had never experienced before but we had to get on with it. We eventually found some land and Vic had decided we could only score with our heads as there were no nets to shoot into. One of our players was Tony Betts, who came from Villa and was my 'understudy' for the Timbers (although he always thought he was good enough to be in the team ahead of me – which is how all good players should think). There was a bit of rivalry between us but there was no conflict; I was in the team because I was scoring goals, simple as that. During the course of the training session, a cross came in and it just so happened that Tony was in front of me. As I went up to head the ball, the momentum took me into the back of Tony's head and he fell to the floor. As I got up, I looked at Tony and saw he was struggling – he was spark out. I couldn't believe it and I said to Vic, 'I only went up for the ball and caught his head.' One of the other lads said something like, 'Yeah, you caught him alright,' as if I did it on purpose. What do you do when something like that happens in the middle of Central Park? Well, we had to carry Tony through the park until we reached the nearest street.

A police car just happened to be passing and stopped to see what was up, 'Hey you guys, what's going on here?' The cop said it as though we had just killed Tony.

I replied, 'He's not dead. He's had an accident and he's unconscious.' The cop asked me if an ambulance was required and Ron Culp declined the offer.

'No, no, it's OK we'll get him through.' We managed to get him to the nearest hospital in the end, and apart from having really bad concussion,

Tony lived to see another day. But he missed his chance to play against the Cosmos the next day; in fact he was out for a fortnight.

I think the same thing happened to me a few times in later life, where players came in to challenge and they ended up unconscious. I don't know whether I had a hard head or what but I recall Dave Watson (while playing for Norwich, I think) challenged me once and ended up on the deck, even though he was hard as nails.

After a few days in the Big Apple, we all thought New York was crazy, but brilliant at the same time. We were staying in a huge hotel and our rooms were on the 20th floor. It was around the time that the 'pay as you go' movie was first introduced into hotels so I suggested to the lads that we all get a few beers in and watch a movie. The movie we chose was, of all things, *The Towering Inferno*, the hottest movie of the year. I paid for it and everyone gathered in my room. Every so often, someone would say, 'Bloody hell. We're in a high-rise building in New York and we're on the 20th floor, here,' and we'd be looking out of the window to see if the building was still standing. The movie frightened us to death – 15 grown football players frightened by a movie.

The next day, we all walked from our hotel on 5th Avenue to the Empire State Building and, as usual, the sirens were going off all over the place and when we turned the corner on 5th Avenue into 34th Street we saw probably 20 fire engines outside the Empire State Building. Fresh from watching the movie the night before, we all looked at one another, hesitated and decided we'd risk it, 'It's just like *The Towering Inferno*,' one of the lads joked. So we queued up to pay to go up the Empire State Building and we asked the girl in the kiosk what was going on with the fire engines.

'We have a slight fire in the basement,' she replied.

As soon as she said that, we all turned away, 'Well, I'm not going up there now, that's for sure. A fire in the basement, that's what happened in *The Towering Inferno* and look what happened there! Sod that.'

That was that, and we ended up going back to the hotel, I think. That bloody movie had put us all off going up the most famous building in the world.

Instead of exploring the sights of the city, we returned to the hotel and sneaked into the bar area – we'd all be safe in there. There were only a handful of people there at the time, maybe five or six guys sitting at the bar having a drink. One of them must have heard us talking and recognised our accents, and he walked over to us in a very friendly manner.

'Hey you guys, you from the UK?' He started to strike up a conversation so we told him we were in New York to play soccer against the Cosmos.

One of the guys must have heard something about the game so enquired, 'Is this against the boy, Pelé, or whatever his name is?' He went on about something or other then asked us all if we wanted a drink. We all said we'd have a beer so he duly obliged and asked the barman to serve us beers and we carried on chatting to him for five minutes or so until he went back to his buddies at the bar.

Five minutes later, he glanced over, raised his glass and we called out that our drinks hadn't arrived yet. The guy came over and asked, 'You've a problem guys?'

I repeated to him, 'We haven't got any drinks.'

His mates turned round to the barman, shouted and pointed to the barman, 'Hey, asshole!'

The barman appeared nervous and jumpy and shrugged his shoulders, 'What?'

Our friend shouted at him again, pointed and asked for the barman to come over to him.

'You, you asshole! I told you to get my buddies a drink and you haven't given them their drinks yet.' Our new friend then grabbed the barman by the collar and while he was yelling at him he pointed at his mate at the bar, 'I'm fucking telling yer, you see that guy over there ...? You sort my buddies out with a drink ...' and he then opened his coat to show off a gun. When he'd finished his warning, he let go of the barman who scuttled back to the bar to prepare the drinks. He brought the drinks to the table and quickly went back to the bar just as our friend came over to check on us.

'You guys OK now – you all got drinks?'

A few minutes later, Ray Martin saw us talking to our new friend and came across to join us, put his hand on my shoulder and his other hand on our new friend's shoulder. Our friend not knowing who Ray was, stepped back and pulled out a huge knife and pointed it at Ray. We were all shocked and someone mumbled something like, 'He's one of our players. He's OK.'

Our friend looked over his shoulder in a shifty manner and said quietly, 'You can't be too careful in this city, guys,' and put his blade away in his pocket.

After that kerfuffle, we soon settled down to our drinks. After about 20 minutes our friend came back over to join us again and I asked him if he wanted to come to the game the next day. He replied, 'Nah, I'd love to but I got "business" to attend to, you know what I mean, man? I'll tell you what I'll do though. I'll meet you all in the bar here after your game finishes and we'll have a good time, eh? I'll look after you all.'

The lads looked at each other and we all shook our heads in agreement. We'd met this guy only a matter of hours and didn't know who the hell he was but one of the lads apparently asked him and he said he was 'on "business" from Miami.' He offered an invitation to us to come to Miami and to look him up. One of the lads asked him for a business card.

'Nah, you ask anyone in Miami, in any bar they know me. Just ask for Rocky. They'll make a phone call and I'll come and get yer. I don't give my number out to anyone.'

We later found out this guy, Rocky was the Miami mafia.

After the game the following day, the lads gathered in the bar, where we met Rocky and he took some of our lads into the city, as promised. I didn't go but apparently they all shit themselves with what they encountered. One of the lads who went told me:

'You wouldn't believe it. Rocky drove us up this dimly lit back alley and we pulled up outside this place, got out of the car and Rocky knocked on the door. Someone opened the door and questioned who it was, and Rocky replied, "Just tell Joe it's Rocky," to which the doorman replied, "Fuck off!"

Rocky apparently got angry and threatened the doorman, who then let them all in. Down in the cellar they had seen everything from drugs to illegal booze, and all sorts of weapons. The lads couldn't believe it – it was like a scene from a movie, they said. The lads eventually got back to the hotel at 5am. They wanted to come home after ten minutes, they were that frightened, but Rocky wouldn't let them leave. It sounded like a hell of an evening!

****

Towards the end of the season, Vic Crowe told me that Peter Taylor, the manager at third division Brighton, had agreed a fee with Wolves and was given permission to talk to me. They had apparently shown interest in signing me, but he didn't fly out to the US. We did speak over the phone, however, and he really wanted to sign me. It had been reported in the British press that my transfer fee was £40,000. Peter Taylor even went as far as saying he'd make sure he would find a house in the area, but we left it at that and I agreed to get back in contact with him when the American season had finished. When I reported back to Vic how the telephone conversation had played out, Vic advised me not to do anything just yet. 'Just keep it in the pipeline if nothing else comes up.' I'm sure, looking back now, that Vic must have tipped off Freddie Goodwin at Birmingham, because the next thing I knew he'd flown out to Portland to come and see me play. The talk was that Vic wanted to sell me for no less than £50,000 and for that much Freddie wanted a decent player!

Freddie came to watch me play at home to St Louis and I scored two goals. After the game, I met Freddie in a local hotel to talk over the contract. By the end of that evening I still hadn't signed, and went back to see Vic in the morning. He urged me not to let the contract fall through. I took Vic's advice and the next day I signed for Birmingham City for £50,000. Freddie then asked Vic when I could start at Birmingham: as the season in America was almost over, I'd end up going back to pre-season training in the UK. Vic assured him I'd be back in the UK within the next three or four weeks, but we had some games left to finish first. The American league got wind that there were three or four players, including myself, that were being forced out of their American contract by English clubs, and they wanted them back as contracts had been signed. A statement was soon released by the NASL which said that we couldn't, under any circumstance, leave our club until the competition was over.

The shit well and truly hit the fan following that statement, because the English clubs were demanding their players back but the American league weren't allowing us to leave until the season was officially over – or at least until that player's club had been knocked out of the play-offs. In fact, it was the league's commissioner, ex-Aston Villa player Phil Woosnam, who had made that decision. Birmingham, among other clubs, wanted their money's worth as they had just agreed to pay Portland £50,000 for me, but couldn't yet make use of my services. Among the other guys who had signed for other clubs were Barry Powell, who had signed for Coventry City; Graham Brown, who was wanted to play in goal at Mansfield; Brian Godfrey who was wanted back by Bristol Rovers; and Willie Anderson, who was wanted back by Cardiff City. It was frankly a bit of a mess.

The American league season ended with a play-off situation, and we had to play the Seattle Sounders at home. The game was a 35,000 sell-out and I scored the winner. That meant we would have to play another game and it extended our stay in the US, so the English clubs still weren't happy. After the game, Freddie Goodwin called me and I told him the news that we had won the game. He began to panic like hell and told me I needed to sort it out. I remember Vic called the five of us into the office and said there was nothing he could do to release us while we were still winning. Although he didn't actually tell us to throw the game, he said something like, 'Your destiny is in your own hands. If you need to go home soon, do what you have to do,' and he walked out of the room. I think that the clubs back in England were putting him under pressure – I don't think there was any other explanation for his comments.

I thought to myself, 'Did he just tell us to lose the game?' I looked at the other lads and said, 'Well I ain't losing the bloody game. He virtually said if we get knocked out of the competition we can fly back home.' It has never been in my nature to do anything like that and I wasn't about to start. I told the lads, 'If we make the final, that's what I was brought here for. I'm here to finish the job.'

All four of the other guys then said, 'You're right, we're going out there to win.'

It annoyed us a little bit that we were making thousands of dollars for the club but being paid next to nothing. They had probably budgeted for around 10,000 fans and all of a sudden they were getting 35,000 fans, and there were thousands more who couldn't get into the stadium every week. 'Timbermania' was spreading across the city, and the club were cashing in – big time. We were being paid peanuts based on their budget – the club was making money and we didn't see any of it! We had made the club a success and were making the club a fortune by winning football matches, but we didn't receive any bonuses and, to make it worse, there was nothing we could do about it. Having said that, we all had the attitude 'it's what we do,' and we all loved it.

Just before that semi-final game, Kathy, Jason and I went back to the Harpers' for another beautiful meal and endless bottles of wine and champagne. It just so happened that Don was the accountant for the Timbers, and after the wine had been flowing for a few hours we got into a heated discussion over the finances of the club. My argument was based only on the money we, as players, were making for the club, which had not been anticipated by the club's financial gurus. In hindsight, I think the club would have paid us more but in the end, I recall, they bought each of us expensive gold watches as a thank you gift and they also bought the wives gifts as a gesture. There was never anything written into our contracts that we could have had an option to stay there – it was purely a 'one-off' deal. On the plus side, I had become a cult football figure and the most recognisable commodity for the Timbers, just as I had for Arcadia.

The discussion with Don was a friendly argument; Don at one end of the table and me at the other, with Kathy, Norma and their kids in-between having their own discussion. It went on for some time, well into the early morning and with an enormous amount of beer, wine and champagne consumed, but towards the end I was in full flow and still talking about the club and finances. However, all of a sudden, Don's head dropped right into his dessert. The conversation between the ladies came to a sudden halt and Norma said, 'I've been married to Don for 20 years but I've never, ever seen him that drunk before.'

I'd had as much as Don but I was fine – sober as a judge in fact. Norma offered to put us up for the night, saying I couldn't possibly drive home after having that much alcohol.

'Nah, I'm fine. I'll get a taxi home – but thanks anyway.' I said.

We got into a taxi and went home. The next day, I phoned Norma to see how Don was and he wasn't good; in fact he didn't go into work for three days after that evening, but I was right as rain!

One of the worst stadiums I had ever played in was in San Jose, California. They had an awful stadium and to make matters worse they also had a well-known mascot called Krazy George Henderson who used to run up and down the terraces banging a big drum and would always incite the crowd and the opponents by shouting, 'Kill, kill, kill.' When we played there against the San Jose Earthquakes in a league match, there was a little crowd trouble in the stadium and it was the very first time it had been reported during a NASL game. There were a few naughty tackles flying in on both sides and when I went to tackle one of their guys in the middle of the park the referee blew up for a free kick as the player stayed down, rolling around as if he'd been shot. I went to see how he was and out of the corner of my eye I saw someone running towards me. As I turned to see who it was, a fist came flying towards my face, and I just managed to step away from it. I then went to throw a punch back, connected with my assailant and knocked him flying. After the event, I found out that the supporter who had run on to the pitch and tried to punch me was, in fact, the brother of the player who I had tackled and injured. There was a bit of a melee on and off the field for a few minutes after the incident, and eventually the stewards managed to get the guy off the pitch. The stadium announcer pleaded for calm and eventually the game got back under way. We won 2–1 and I scored one of the goals, but when we had got changed and were ready to get back on the bus, we found we were surrounded by local supporters and they were trying to get into the dressing room. The stewards locked us in the dressing room for a while as a precautionary matter because the fans were trying to break the doors down. It was absolute mayhem and something unheard of in American sports at the time.

The Timbers won the division and we went to the championship game, the Soccer Bowl, but lost to the Tampa Bay Rowdies 2–0. Tampa had Rodney Marsh in their team, and the only reason we lost was because the NASL had picked the location of the final; it was held in San Jose, in front of around 17,000 local fans who booed us throughout the game remembering the last time we had played there. We had two wingers in Jimmy Kelly and Willie Anderson, and we had a fit team – we could run anyone off the park. But they had picked a stadium which was only 55 yards wide. Our stadium in Portland was 75 yards wide and that allowed for wide play. This meant we couldn't play our normal game and Tampa man-marked our two wide players to kill our game. The front men, including myself, didn't get any service because all the play was in the middle of the park. Had the game been played on our normal-sized pitch we would have beaten them, no doubt about that.

The time we spent in Portland was incredible and we crammed so much into that period, it was really amazing. We did so much and made so many friends while we were over there. It was during that season that the Timbers endeared themselves to the city and Portland became known as Soccer City USA. Not only had we put Portland on the map geographically, we had also put Portland Timbers on the US footballing map. In 1967 there were 100,000 people playing soccer in the US, but by the time we left Portland, it was reported that one million kids were playing soccer in US schools, partly because of the British players and world superstars who helped re-form the NASL. We went there in their inaugural season where crowds of 5,000 were not uncommon but by time we left, attendances had grown to 30,000 and thousands more were locked out for our home games. It was an amazing season, but everything in this life comes to an end, and we found ourselves heading back home once more; this time to Birmingham.

6

I've Got the Blues

"Get up there. If they don't want you here then you've got to go to Forest. That Brian Clough – he wins things."
Howard Kendall, former Everton and Birmingham City midfielder

****

The contract to play for Birmingham City was signed and we were excited to be back on English soil. The money wasn't bad; I was on around £65 at Wolves but Freddie had offered me nearly double that plus bonuses. As with every transfer, I received 5 per cent of the £50,000 transfer fee, around £2,500. The move to Birmingham City meant Kathy and I could return to Wolverhampton, which was within reasonable distance for training, so from a personal point of view it was a good move for my family. We did look at a house in Solihull and quickly realised we couldn't afford it so we decided to buy a nice place in the Codsall area, where my mate Ray Martin lived so that we could travel to training together.

Because I had to stay in Portland to play the final in San Jose, I missed the first four games of the 1975/76 season. Birmingham were in the top tier of English football, just like my previous English club, Wolves, and again they had an old-fashioned stadium – St Andrews. However, unlike Wolves, Blues had their own training ground located near Birmingham Airport, albeit rather out-dated, to say the least. The changing rooms looked as though they had been there since the war; they were corrugated buildings that looked like a converted air-raid shelter. Inside wasn't much better and I remember the kit always got dumped in the centre of the changing room so the players could help themselves. It was disorganised chaos, and not what you'd expect from a first division club; but that didn't matter to me because all I wanted to do was to play football.

Freddie Goodwin had been the manager at Blues since taking over from the great Stan Cullis in 1970 and had some success in his second season in getting the team promoted back to Division One as runners-up. Although he was perceived as an old-school manager, he was a forward-thinker who gave a new meaning to training at St Andrews by bringing in a yoga expert, something unheard of in the early 1970s. He was also acclaimed for bringing the legendary Trevor Francis into league football as a 16-year-old. He was a thoroughly nice guy but something wasn't quite right at Blues, even though we had players like Trevor, Bob Hatton, Kenny Burns, Roger Hynd and 'Big Joe' Gallagher in the squad. They had a huge squad and it seemed that when Freddie sold one player he'd bring in two or three as replacements. Birmingham in those days attracted fairly big crowds at St Andrews and any home game averaged over 30,000. It was just as well I missed the start of the season because we lost three out of the first four games and had only one point by the time I made my debut against Ipswich at Portman Road, which we lost as well. My first taste of victory was in my fifth game, against Burnley, where I also scored my first goal in a 4–0 home win. I scored against Newcastle in the following game too, so on a personal note I made a fairly good start to my Birmingham career, even though the team didn't.

The poor start to the season culminated in Freddie's departure in late September 1975 with only two wins from the first eleven games of the season. It was déjà vu. It felt as though whenever I was brought into a club, the manager inevitably got the sack a few weeks later. I suppose that's the way it goes in football sometimes. Incidentally, the next time I saw Freddie was at his house in Tanworth-in-Arden at his leaving party. He actually lived on a golf course called the Ladbroke Park Golf Club and it was a lovely setting. He only invited a select few from the club and I was lucky enough to be one of them, even though I had only known him for a few months.

Yet again, I was at a new club and working for a manager who hadn't recruited me. Willie Bell had been a coach at Blues and had been Freddie's assistant. He'd been at Blues for three or four years and it was his first job as a manager. Willie was a very lovely guy, quietly spoken and never raised his voice – in fact he was probably too nice to be a football manager if I'm perfectly honest. It seemed as though he had been thrown in at the deep end and his task was to rejuvenate a team who had lost some of their confidence. It was a difficult task and I had reservations as to whether he was the man for the job. The club hadn't recovered from the loss of their star striker, Bob Latchford, who had been sold in exchange for Howard Kendall and Archie Styles from Everton a couple of years previously for a record £350,000. Howard Kendall (God rest his soul) was another big character. He was the club captain, a fabulous footballer and probably one of the most talented midfield players NEVER to be capped by England (although he played at all other levels).

We had plenty of strikers at the club, including myself, Trevor, Roger and Kenny but it was obvious something had been wrong because for the previous two seasons, the club had been fighting relegation.

Willie's first meeting with the players was hilarious. I remember he said to us, 'Now that I'm manager, I think it's best you stop calling me "Willie" and you call me "boss" from now on.' All the players agreed so we went out for the first training session under his reign and played a practice game with the youth team. Willie decided to mix the teams up so each team had a mixture of youth- and first-team players. It turned out quite farcical because, bearing in mind he'd just asked the first-team players to call him boss, the youth-team players were still calling him Willie.

One of the first-team players accused him of being contradictory and said, 'Hang on a minute, why are they calling you Willie when you asked us to call you boss? He immediately stopped the game and explained to the youth-team players that they should call him boss as well. Generally, all football players will give a new manager time to settle into his role, but if the manager doesn't know what he's doing or doesn't know what he's talking about then he won't command the respect of the players. He's always going to have a hard job to get them back on side if that's the case. I really think from that moment on, Willie never gained the respect of the team.

That group of players had undoubted talent, and there were some big characters, but that also made for unrest in the camp. Willie soon brought back the former Blues defender, Sid Owen, as senior coach to rekindle their missing fire. Sid had also been at Leeds with Willie, so the two had a close working relationship and knew what each other wanted. Sid was used to coaching top players like Billy Bremner, Johnny Giles and Norman Hunter at Leeds and he came to Blues expecting the players to respond in the same way and do the same things as those players did at Elland Road. Unfortunately for Sid, the players we had at Birmingham just weren't in the same class as they were at Leeds.

Sid Owen was probably the biggest moaner I have ever met in my life. In fact, he was a bigger moaner than Kenny Burns, and that was saying something because Burnsy moaned all the time about absolutely everything. Sid would even moan when someone mis-controlled the ball and would shout out, 'You players, you can't play. You're a disgrace!'

During one training session, Sid told us we were going to play shadow-play. In typical style, Burnsy shouted back, 'There's no sun out today, boss. How can you play shadow-play when there's no sun?' Sid's bright idea was to try to play with no ball – yes, that's right, play football with no ball. Everyone looked at each other when Sid announced that and it turned out to be the funniest training session I'd ever had in my life. What you had to do was pretend to play a game (on a full-sized pitch) but you had no ball to play with. We were chasing shadows, hence the name, 'shadow-play'. We had no idea what was going on or where the ball was supposed to be. We just treated it as a piss-take and it was a complete farce.

Most mornings I'd get to the training ground really early as I had to commute from Wolverhampton. I'd travel in by train with Ray Martin, our full-back (who was also at Portland with me). We'd both get picked up by one of the other players at New Street Station to be taken to the training ground at Elmdon, near Solihull, about 7 miles away. On one particular day I wanted to practise with a ball to kill some time, but there was no one around apart from a couple of apprentices and I couldn't find any balls anywhere. I shouted to a few of the young lads, 'Where's the balls?' but no one knew where the balls were.

A few minutes later, Sid Owen came over so I asked him the same question and he replied pretty matter-of-factly, 'I've hidden them. I've put them away so you can't practise.'

I questioned him, 'What do you mean you've hidden them? I just want to take a ball out and practise.'

He told me in no uncertain terms, 'No! You're not touching the ball all week. I'm going to make you hungry for the ball.'

I looked at him and thought he'd lost the plot. How can a footballer train without the ball, I thought? His theory was basically to starve us of the ball so we would be hungry for it come match-day. I told him again I wanted to practise my skills but he wouldn't have any of it. I'd never experienced anything like it in my playing career; training for a whole week without a ball – it was ridiculous! It was in total contrast to my time at Wolves, where the coaches would go out of their way to help you with anything you wanted extra training on. I would kick a ball against a wall in that freezing cold gym while being taught how to kick the ball properly by Norman Bodell: but at Blues I couldn't even practise with a bloody football! No wonder they struggled in the league. Unbelievable!

Another character at the club was Roger Hynd (who sadly passed away in 2017), a 'man-mountain' of about the same height as me. He was the player who the fans expected to sort things out on the pitch – the senior player at the club. If anything kicked off, Roger would be right in the middle of it, trying to sort it out. He took no prisoners and on one occasion I remember Trevor Francis got kicked on the ankle right on the edge of the box. After a bit of a melee, big Roger strode down the pitch to where Trevor was and someone intervened and tried to wave Roger away, 'It's OK Rog, it's all sorted out now.'

Roger wasn't having any of it and replied in his broad Scottish accent, 'Sorted out? These people [the fans] expect it of me. I've got to do something.'

I remember one time when we were on tour, we were on the beach and the sea was crystal clear. One of the lads said the water was so clear you could see the seabed, so he challenged everyone to swim down to the bottom of the sea. One of the lads asked for volunteers to swim to the seabed and get a handful of sand to prove it could be done. A few of the lads tried but failed and I think it was Mike Kelly who said he'd have a go and fair play to him, he came up to the surface with a handful of sand.

Then Roger had a go because he would always have a go at anything. If you did 50 push-ups, Roger would go one better and do 51, just to prove a point so Roger dived into the sea. While he was trying to reach the bottom of the sea, I asked Mike how he managed to get the sand and he replied, 'I got it from that pot behind you,' pointing to a plant pot situated near me on the path. I said to Mike that Roger wouldn't give up and would probably drown trying to reach the bottom. Low and behold, Roger resurfaced, lungs bursting, and told Mike he was a better man than him. For once he was defeated.

When we played Leeds United, who were renowned at the time for being a decent football side but also had a hard-man reputation, I was always played up against the hardest of them all, Norman Hunter. Norman didn't suffer fools lightly. On one occasion the ball was played up the channel and I jumped to chest it down. Norman hit me as I played the ball, I remember landing on my side and Norman landed on top of me, making sure his full bodyweight rested on my shoulder. I wasn't one for staying down when I was injured so when I remained grounded everyone knew the injury was serious and an ambulance was called. I was taken to Heartlands Hospital (it was called East Birmingham back then) and Kathy and my parents, who were watching from the stands, left the ground and followed the ambulance in the car. When we reached the hospital, I recall being put on to a trolley, still dressed in my Blues kit, and being left in a large waiting room to see the doctor. When the doctor popped his head round the corner he told me he'd found another doctor who wanted to examine me. However, rather than the one doctor I'd expected, 16 student doctors appeared from nowhere. His opening question to me was, 'Well, what have you been doing, Mr Withe?'

Considering I was still dressed in my football kit I thought I'd use my Scouse sense of humour and replied with a straight face, 'I've been shopping on the high street, doc.'

The students found my reply hilarious but the doctor ignored it and started to study my chart before stating the obvious: 'It looks like you've dislocated your shoulder, Mr Withe.' He then asked the students what the treatment for that was and they all replied with their suggestions. The doctor then said, looking at me, 'If this was a big, brave footballer I'd pull his arm out of its socket and push it back in. Can I do that?'

I agreed and said, '... but make sure you put your balls in my other hand.' With that, the students fell about laughing, but the doctor didn't see the funny side and left the room quickly in embarrassment.

Considering the talent and the characters we had in the side we had played poorly and were in a relegation battle for most of that first season, only winning 13 games. The last game of the season was away at Sheffield United and we needed a single point to stay in the division. It had been reported before the game that around 15,000 Blues fans were going to be making the trip north to Sheffield and Willie prepared us as if it was a cup final. We managed a 1–1 draw with Terry Hibbitt scoring our goal, and in the dressing room after the game the champagne was flowing because the draw meant we had stayed in the first division, even if it was by the skin of our teeth. We had a massive squad of players, and if I remember rightly, we fielded no fewer than 26 different players during that long, hard season as we couldn't field a settled side from one week to the next.

Right at the end of that first season at Blues I picked up a knee injury. I remember Howard Kendall ringing me when I was in hospital to say they had some charity event going on. He asked me if I wanted to join in but he wasn't aware I was injured.

'What do you mean you're in hospital?' Howard was the club captain but he'd obviously not been told by the club I'd picked up an injury during the last match of the season at Sheffield United.

'I'm about to have a cartilage operation, Howard.'

He was furious at not being told I was injured, 'This bloody club – they tell you nothing!'

Unfortunately, Howard was right.

The surgeon who operated on my knee was a guy called Mr Pearson and he did a lot of the operations for the local football clubs; in fact he later operated on me when I was at Villa. It was common at that time to give players cortisone injections and of course it was great for surgeons because it effectively meant they wouldn't have to operate as the injection suppressed the immune system and reduced inflammation, easing pain and swelling at the site of the injury. In severe cases they would have to operate and in my case it was a really serious injury, but the doctor decided to err on the side of caution at first, gave me a shot and told me to see how I got on. After a few days it didn't feel any better so I had to go into hospital for the operation.

I was admitted to Birmingham General Hospital (which is now Birmingham Children's Hospital) and was given a side ward, which they described as a 'private ward', but wasn't what I would have called a 'private ward' because it was full of patients! I must have been the youngest person in that ward except for one guy I met called Dennis Collett. Dennis was a Blues fan and obviously knew who I was, so we got chatting about football. When the time arrived for the chap next to me to vacate his bed, Dennis came to join me and quickly occupied the bed next to me. The first night I was in there I remember an almighty racket going on at the end of the ward at 3am. I woke up and looked down the ward. It was an elderly Asian fellow kneeling down and praying; he had his prayer mat out, the lot and at 3am! That was all I needed: my operation was scheduled for the morning and I needed my sleep.

Funnily enough, Dennis was having the same operation as me. In those days, the operation left a huge scar, unlike today's keyhole surgery, and the recovery time was a lot longer. The following morning, after a disturbed night, we both went down to theatre at the same time and had our operations. After our operation, we were wheeled back on to the ward and we were told by the morning nurses that we were due some physio in the afternoon. We both thought it was a bit too soon after the operation and we were both feeling a bit groggy but we left it to the nurses' better judgment. When the physios came over that afternoon, we both almost fell off our beds: one of them looked like a German boxer and the other one was the total opposite, petite and good looking. Dennis looked at them both, turned to me and said, 'Which one have you got then, eh?'

In the end, the 'German boxer' went to Dennis and the petite one came to me. My physio, even though she was small, was every bit as scary as Dennis's physio and she instructed me to lift my leg up while I sat on the bed. As I was fit and young, I could just about manage to lift my leg halfway but Dennis struggled and his physio shouted in her German accent, 'You WILL lift your leg up, Mr Collett.'

Dennis tried but he couldn't lift his leg very far, if at all.

'I can't lift my leg. There's no way I can lift my leg,' he said through gritted teeth.

Dennis's physio then said to us both, 'Right, I'll be back tomorrow morning and I want you both to lift your leg fully.'

To me, that was like a red rag to a bull, and all that day I practised lifting my leg up and down, but Dennis had no chance. The following day when they came back and asked me to lift my leg up I had no problem, but poor old Dennis still couldn't do it. After that, I was up, out of bed and on crutches, all within a few days. Dennis couldn't get out of bed at all for days. I tried to encourage and help him but he just couldn't manage it.

A few days after the operation I asked Kathy to bring me some beer into the hospital as I used to brew my own beer back then. It was obviously not the done thing, but I thought it would be nice if Dennis and I could have a drink while we watched the match that Sunday afternoon. There was a TV room at the end of the corridor, so that afternoon we sneaked out of the ward with a couple of beers in our dressing gown pockets and turned the TV on ready for *The Big Match*. There were a few other guys in the room already, but then another old guy called Geoff walked into the room. Geoff was apparently in hospital because he had problems with his 'waterworks' (he couldn't pass water) and he spotted us drinking our beers.

He looked at us and shouted over, 'What you doing, lads?'

Dennis shouted back, 'We're having a few beers.'

The old boy's eyes lit up as if it was Christmas. 'Give us a beer, give us a beer, lads?' he asked in anticipation.

'You can't have beer – you've got waterworks problems,' I told him.

The old boy shrugged. 'Nah, come on, give us a beer. It's OK. I'll be OK. The nurses won't find out.'

I warned him it was strong beer but he still insisted he wanted to try it and so Dennis gave him a beer. The old boy guzzled half a pint of my home brew down as if he'd never had a beer before in his life.

About three hours later the nurses came over to our beds and asked, 'What have you done to Geoff?'

Dennis and I looked at each other and shrugged our shoulders.

'What do you mean what have WE done to Geoff? We haven't done anything to him.'

The nurses kept quizzing us, 'You must have done something to him because he can't pass water. If I find out you have ...'

The following morning I passed Geoff's bed and said to him, 'Are you alright, Geoff?'

He looked shattered. 'Agh, I'm terrible. You won't believe it.' I asked him what was wrong with him and he suddenly flung his sheets off his bed and took his pyjama bottoms down. I'm not kidding when I say his balls were bloody massive – they were as big as tennis balls. I stared at them with eyes wide open in amazement. I couldn't believe the size of them. I asked him again what was wrong with him.

'I can't pass water can I? My balls swell up when I drink so they're doing everything to try to get the water out of me.' Geoff could barely speak he was in so much pain.

The doctors refused to let us leave hospital until we could walk, or at least walk on crutches, and after about a week I strolled out of the hospital. But poor old Dennis just about managed to leave on crutches, and still in a lot of pain. Luckily, my operation and subsequent recovery didn't affect me playing for Blues, as I had the operation between seasons.

Our pre-season tour was to Holland and I was just getting back to full fitness, probably well into July, although I was still nowhere near match-fit. The plan was for me to play about 20 minutes in each of the pre-season games to increase my fitness levels. Before the first game, I recall Willie Bell saying we could go out into the town for a few beers and relax a bit.

On one particular night we split into groups and went to several different bars, and I was with four or five of the lads having a quiet chat in a local bar. Kenny Burns and Gary Jones went off on their own, but managed to find us sitting quietly in the corner of the bar. Soon afterwards, Trevor Francis, Tony Want, Joe Gallagher and what seemed like the whole of the Blues party came in one by one and joined us. There was a pool table in the middle of the bar and Burnsy and Jonesy took on two of the locals. All I remember was that Jonesy must have touched the backside of one of the local ladies who was watching the game. I don't think he was trying it on or anything – he may even have done it unintentionally – but within minutes I noticed a guy pointing at Gary and speaking in Dutch to him from across the bar. This guy must have been the girl's husband or partner, because he walked over to Jonesy and slapped him. Suddenly mayhem broke out. It was like a scene from the Keystone Cops as one slap escalated into a full-scale riot, with punches flung left, right and centre. Burnsy hit someone with a cue and chairs were thrown all over the place. We managed to find a way out of the bar somehow and we ran out into the street, but the locals started following us. As I wasn't fully fit I was the last one to leave the bar, so I ended up chasing after the locals who were chasing Burnsy, Jonesy and the other lads. After a few minutes, the local lads gave up the chase but I was still behind everyone else. One of the guys spotted me and gave me a kick that floored me. My eye was cut, and all of his mates joined in beating the crap out of me while I was on the ground. When they decided to quit they all ran off, and as I began to run the other way I twisted my ankle. We found out the following day that these guys were Dutch travellers and they came to the same bar the following day looking for us with knives and guns, probably to 'finish the job'. I'm not saying Burnsy started the fight, but he was renowned for getting into trouble, and trouble seemed to follow him around. When Gary Jones joined the club from Everton before the pre-season tour he was warned not to mix with Kenny, so what did Gary Jones do? He latched on to Burnsy and they became very good friends.

So, I went to Holland full of hope for the upcoming season after recovering from a cartilage operation, but ended up with a bloody ankle injury and wasn't able to play a single game on the tour. I also missed the first couple of games of the 1976/77 season, and started the next three or four games but didn't get on the scoresheet. I really believe Willie never thought I was good enough to play in his side. He kept playing Kenny Burns, Bob Hatton and Trevor Francis, and I suppose he had enough firepower up front without me. In any case, Willie had lost the dressing room early into his managerial career with Birmingham, and Sid Owen had also lost the players with his hilarious training methods and his 'you aren't good enough to lace his boots' attitude. Players don't take kindly to coaches saying things like that; they didn't in my day and probably don't now.

I will always remember what turned out to be my last game for Birmingham, a local derby against West Bromwich Albion at St Andrews early on in the 1976/77 season. Willie asked me to play wide on the left – a position I'd never played before – and he wanted Trevor to play down the middle. I didn't have a clue what his thinking was and it clearly didn't work as we lost that game 1–0. The next game was another local derby against Aston Villa and on the Friday before the game, Willie took me to one side and out of the blue said, in a really quiet voice, almost whispering to me in fact, 'Peter, I've had an agreement from Nottingham Forest.' I couldn't hear the rest of what he was saying (and I wasn't taking much notice if I'm honest) as all I was focused on was preparing for the game against Villa the next day. I looked at him and asked him to repeat what he'd just whispered to me but again he spoke to me so quietly I didn't get the gist of what he had said.

I think he said it three times and I ended up shouting to him, 'What is it you're saying?'

He then spoke in his normal tone. 'I've agreed with Nottingham Forest that you can sign for them. I've sold you. You can go and talk to Brian Clough now.'

I managed to hear the last bit and I was gobsmacked. He was obviously embarrassed to tell me the news so I said to him, 'But we're playing tomorrow against Villa – a local derby.'

In no uncertain terms, Willie replied, 'Oh no, you're not. You're not involved. I need you to go to Nottingham and speak to Brian Clough.'

It was obvious that Forest had offered an amount of money that Blues couldn't turn down for me and Willie had agreed to sell me behind my back. The fee I was led to believe was a similar amount to what Blues had paid for me, which was around £50,000. In hindsight, Willie showed me in the time I worked with him how NOT to be a football manager.

I went back into the changing room and bumped into Howard Kendall who asked me what I was doing.

'He's just told me I'm going to Nottingham Forest.'

Howard replied, 'Get up there. If they don't want you here then you've got to go to Forest. That Brian Clough, he wins things.'

That was that. I got changed, phoned Kathy and told her what had happened and drove myself to Nottingham.

I had a blue Ford Escort at the time, and not knowing where I was going I had to try to find the City Ground. All the way to Nottingham I was thinking about what had happened on the training ground earlier that morning. I was also wondering whether I really wanted to join a Division Two club.

But then again, it was Brian Clough – bloody hell, Brian Clough! I'd have been mad not to have joined his team.

7

The Life of Brian

"Right, Lloyd, you're a centre-back – head the bloody ball.
Burns, don't keep giving them the ball.
Withe, you're a striker – score us a goal."
Brian Clough, former Nottingham Forest manager

****

Peter Taylor had been chasing me for a few years, as it happened, so he was no stranger to my talents. While I was at Portland Timbers we spoke about a proposed move to Brighton, a club he was managing in the summer of 1975. Peter wanted to pair me with Peter Ward and said we would have made the best scoring partnership in the country. For some reason, the move fell through and I signed for Birmingham City. I had that in my mind while I was driving up to meet with Peter Taylor and Brian Clough for the first time on that Friday afternoon in mid-September 1976, shortly after being told by Willie Bell that he'd sold me behind my back.

I don't think Brian had even seen me play before, so he had gone on the instincts of Peter Taylor, his assistant manager and right-hand man. I say assistant manager; Peter was more like the chief scout. It was apparent to me that what Brian wanted, Peter delivered. Brian wanted a striker and I was the one he wanted. Peter would have done his homework on me, and in some detail – there would have been a document full of things he'd found out about me, he was that thorough.

When I arrived at the City Ground for my interview I was greeted by Peter Taylor.

'I've been chasing you for nearly three years. I've been sitting in the stands at Wolves and Birmingham with a cloth cap on so I didn't get noticed. I watched you and you did things that other players didn't do – you wanted to play football. When the ball went into the stands you jumped over the fence and ran into the stand to retrieve the ball whereas other players would just have left it. I liked what I saw.'

It was refreshing, what he said to me.

Peter then led me into the ground and we went into an empty boardroom and I was thinking to myself, 'Where's this Brian Clough fella?' I must have been sitting there for 20 minutes just talking football with Peter when the chairman popped in to say hello and all of a sudden the door burst open and in walked Brian, wearing his legendary green tracksuit and holding a squash racket, of all things. He approached me, leaned over and put his squash racket in front of me on the table, looked me in the eyes and said:

'Can you play, young man?'

I looked back at him and said instinctively, 'No!'

Brian looked at Peter Taylor and said, 'I thought you said he could play?' Peter told Brian I could play so Brian looked at me again and said, 'I'll ask you again, young man. Can you play?'

I responded in a serious manner. 'Nope, I've never played squash in my life.'

Peter started giggling and Brian explained himself.

'I'm not talking about squash!'

Brian must have thought I was being funny or clever and looking back it was hilarious the way it happened but I don't think Brian found it that amusing.

Once that confusion had been sorted out, we began to talk about their vision for Forest; that they wanted to get to Division One as quickly as possible. Then Brian said to me, 'I haven't seen you play so I'm going on his (pointing at Peter) recommendation.' Brian ran the football club from top to bottom so he must have trusted Peter's recommendation without actually seeing me play before. Brian didn't have to ask the committee if he could sign players – the ultimate decision was his. He knew the type of players he wanted and he told me I was one of his first signings and he had others in mind.

The next thing we talked about was my current wage at Birmingham.

'I can't believe how much you're on at Birmingham. You earn £125 a week and you get appearance money. We can't afford that here.' By this point I was thinking this must be a wind-up; they want me to step down a division *and* they want me to take less money? Brian continued, 'Look, we'd like to invite you and your wife to the game tomorrow. Come to Nottingham and then we'll get the train to Southampton. Can you sort it out?'

It was short notice and Kathy would have to arrange a babysitter to look after Jason for the whole of Saturday, but I just couldn't miss this chance.

Everything had happened so quickly, I needed time to think about the move and returned home to talk it over with Kathy. I wasn't keen on stepping down a division unless I was joining an ambitious club, but that was just what Forest were – they were on the up.

And it was bloody Brian Clough – how could I say no to him?

Our friends Dennis and Sheila Collett agreed to look after Jason, and we set out to Nottingham early in the morning and left the car at the ground. We travelled to Southampton with Brian and the rest of the lads and watched the game from the stands as guests of the club. I still hadn't signed for Forest officially as there were some negotiations to be done about the fee and my wages, which dragged on over into the following week. I think in the end the fee was dropped by £5,000 so they could give me more money, and a deal was eventually struck with Birmingham, so I agreed to sign on the following Tuesday. I put pen to paper and signed a two-year contract with an option for another year. I had to take a drop in wages; I was on £125 a week at Blues and Brian only offered me £115 a week but I still couldn't say no.

I signed the contract and Brian said to me there and then:

'It took us bloody ages to get this contract signed. Now you've signed I want to get you in a Forest shirt as quick as possible, so can you play in the reserves this afternoon?' I thought he was having a laugh, wanting me to play hours after I'd signed the papers, but he explained, 'We've got a reserve team game and you're going to play. We're playing Wolves this afternoon.' I hadn't come to Nottingham prepared to play football so I told Brian that I hadn't got any boots or change of clothes. 'That's OK I'll get you some boots – I want you to play. I just want to get you in the shirt before Saturday's game.' What Brian had in his mind was not to pile too much pressure on me on Saturday when I was due to make my first-team debut. He wanted to ease me in by playing me in the reserves. I agreed to play that afternoon and, funnily enough, a lot of the Wolves lads playing were my old teammates like Phil Parkes and Geoff Palmer.

I was a bit rusty, as I hadn't played for about three weeks for one reason or another. I was given the number 9 shirt and played up front with Tony Woodcock, who was only young and was finding it hard to break through into the first team. Little did I know when I was on the pitch that all the first-team players were in the stand watching me play. They wanted to see what the new signing was all about. Brian was sitting in the dugout alongside Peter Taylor, watching me.

I played a god-awful game. I had visions of Brian sitting next to Peter saying to him, 'Are you sure he can play?' The players in the stand must have wondered what Brian had signed based on that performance. We won the game, and Tony scored the winner, but from my position it was a total disaster; the boots Brian gave me were crap and I hadn't played for a while. It was the worst game I'd played for ages, but Brian didn't say anything to me after the game, other than to report for training the next day. After that game, Tony went out on loan to Lincoln as Brian was planning to sell him during that summer.

It was normal for both Brian and Peter to get to know and understand their new players, and I remember Peter asking me a load of questions when I first joined, trying to find out if I had any vices. I think he asked me if I gambled – I didn't. Then he asked me if I went with different women – again my answer was no. He then asked me if I drank and I replied, 'Yeah, I like a drink but not to excess.'

Peter wasn't getting very far with me. 'Well there must be something you do?'

To which I replied, 'Yeah, I play football.'

I honestly didn't have any vices.

My full debut was against Carlisle on the following Saturday at the City Ground. I had three days of training and I stayed overnight in a local hotel on the Friday. I wasn't in good shape leading up to the game; I had blisters on my heels where those crap boots I'd worn on the Tuesday had been rubbing. I'll never forget the kit we had for that season – it was the worst kit ever manufactured. Nobody had ever heard of the kit supplier, U-Win, and the shirts looked as though they had shrunk in the wash; I had to keep pulling mine down, as it didn't fit properly. I think Forest only used them for one season, thank god! Regardless of the crap kit and blisters, I played up front alongside Barry Butlin and I put in a tremendous performance – in total contrast to the reserve game a few days earlier. Brian must have thought he was watching a totally different player. It was a walkover for us, and I scored and had assists in four other goals and worked my socks off for 90 minutes. We won the game 5–1 in front of a crowd of only 12,000. This time, I imagined Brian saying to Peter, 'Flipping heck, you're right. This boy can play,' but knowing Brian he probably didn't.

A few days after I had signed for Forest, the ever-astute Brian Clough, again acting on Peter Taylor's better judgment, snapped up 'veteran' defender Larry Lloyd for a bargain £60,000 from Coventry City. Larry had won major honours with Liverpool a few years before and was an experienced, tough central defender, just the player we needed at Forest. He was a big character too, and built like a brick shithouse. He had a bit of a swagger and arrogance about him, and when he signed I remember he lit a big fat cigar, looked around at the surroundings and said, 'Nice little club you've got here.'

Larry made his full debut in the away trip to Hull and went straight into a team who were already doing well, hovering around third or fourth place with my old club, Wolves, under Sammy Chung, heading up the league. We were accused of being a 'counter-attacking team' by some people, but that was a bit unfair because while our tactics were to attack teams full-on, we could also defend well. We had the nucleus of a decent side with the likes of Frank Clark, John McGovern, Ian Bowyer and John Robertson already established at the club. It was very rare that any of the reserves would get a look in as we had a fairly settled side, although Brian liked to 'mix it up' sometimes so that John McGovern and Larry would play together, or he would bring in Sammy Chapman to play with Larry and put McGovern into midfield. We also had Terry Curran on the right wing and he was fast, but from my standpoint, John 'Robbo' Robertson was one of the best wingers ever. He and Tony Morley (who I played with at Villa) were both unbelievable. Brian once compared Robbo to Sir Stanley Matthews, which just showed how good he was. If you marked him tight, he'd play one touch and play around you; if you dropped off he'd pick the ball up and run at you. He wasn't the quickest, but boy he could dribble past players, and you could rely on Robbo to deliver a pinpoint cross into the box exactly where you wanted it. There were also players in the squad who could do jobs and organise, like Martin O'Neill.

Early in 1977, an unknown striker called Gary Birtles was signed for £2,000 from Long Eaton United. Gary was a part-time carpet fitter who couldn't get a place up front and was dropped into a left-midfield role. Tony Woodcock had been out on loan to Doncaster and had played six games with them before the permanent deal to sign him broke down. Brian had no choice but to bring him back and Peter persuaded him to pair me with Tony in the Anglo-Scottish Cup semi-final game against Ayr United in early December 1976. The media frequently scoffed the competition but we valued the opportunity and took the game seriously – and it worked to our advantage. The gamble to pair me with Woody paid off and we both scored in a 2–1 victory.

We got to the final of the Anglo-Scottish Cup and played Leyton Orient on a heavy pitch. During the first half, a cross came in and as I was just about to connect to the ball with a volley their centre-back came in with a high tackle and hit me right on my instep. I initially thought I'd broken my ankle as I went down on the muddy surface. Jimmy Gordon, Brian's other trusted sidekick, was eventually allowed to leave the bench and ran on to the pitch to see how bad the injury was. Brian rarely allowed Jimmy to leave the bench: he would usually say something like, 'Sit down Jimmy and let him hobble around a bit. He's OK. He's not really injured.' Anyway, I eventually got up with the help of Jimmy and played on until I couldn't possibly carry on any longer. We won the game and the tie 5–1 on aggregate to win the cup.

I only had a few days respite in order to be fit for the crucial game on the following Saturday against Bolton, with whom we were competing for a promotion place. We had been neck-and-neck all season for that all-important third spot. Brian had no sympathy for players who were injured, so it was the same old routine again for me – ice, hot water, ice, hot water, have a walk around and get on with it. On the Friday before the game, Brian came in to the dressing room and said, 'Right, Jimmy, I'll take the players down to the park. You do the fitness test with him,' (as he pointed to me). Jimmy took me into the stadium and told me to have a little run on the pitch and that felt OK at first. He then told me to turn left and I immediately felt a pain shoot right up my leg. He then told me to turn right and that was OK. We continued this routine for about half an hour and he said he was going to try me with a ball. I kicked the ball a few times with the injured foot and there was no real pain but when I kicked the ball another way I felt the pain shoot up my leg again.

Suddenly, I heard a voice from the stand shout, 'He's fit!' You can guess who it was.

I looked at Brian and turned to Jimmy and said, 'It's OK I'll play.' I had no choice really – Brian had spoken.

You couldn't argue with Brian Clough, although sometimes I tried to.

Come match-day, I had my ankle strapped up to protect it a little bit from their two bulky centre-backs, Paul Jones and Sam Allardyce. We got a free kick near the end of the first half, Robbo delivered it right into my path and I drilled the ball into the back of the net to make it 1-0. I had no recurrence of my ankle injury until I got on the end of a cross from the right and just as I tried to connect to it, 'big Sam' did exactly the same as the Orient lad, and hit me on the instep. I ended up spinning round before crashing to the ground with the ball going out of play. As soon as that happened, the referee blew up for half-time, leaving me on the ground in a heap. My immediate thought was that I'd definitely broken my ankle. Everyone walked off the pitch leaving me to fend for myself and when I looked up I saw Jimmy Gordon sprinting across the pitch in the opposite direction and heading my way. When he eventually got to me he asked if I was OK to which I replied, 'I think I've definitely broken my bloody ankle now!' Jimmy was a small Scottish fella, about 5ft 6in tall and in his sixties, and he was trying to pull me up and somehow he got me on his back in a fireman's lift position and started to run across the pitch with me towards the dressing room. It must have been quite a sight for the fans watching in the stand. When we got into the dressing room, Jimmy threw me on to the treatment table and I was in excruciating pain. Brian then walked in.

'Right, don't think you're coming off, do you?'

I really felt as though I couldn't play any further part in the game but for some reason I just agreed with Brian: there was no point in arguing with him.

I said through gritted teeth, 'No, I'm not coming off boss. Don't worry, I'll stay on.' He had a tendency to wind people up like that but you just had to agree with him. Any other manager would have made the substitution, but not Brian. The club doctor then came to my assistance and I told him not to touch my ankle. 'If I take my boot off I won't get it on again because it's going to blow up. Just strap it up and I'll have to go out as it is.'

I went back on for the second half and limped through another 45 minutes in pain. We drew the game 1–1.

After that game, I went into Brian's office and had a discussion with him about why he continued to play me, even though I had a double injury.

'I don't understand, you ended your career through injury yet you don't have a physio and you want players to go out and play and give 100 per cent when they're not fully fit.'

He thought about my statement and looked at me and said, 'You know what young man? You play every game you can, because when I finished my career it was the saddest day of my life, having to watch people training and playing and I couldn't. Play every game, young man. Play every game.'

Those words stuck in my mind for a long time – and still do to this day. He was right, of course – as he always was – but at the time I was furious.

Brian would normally ignore the state of the pitch; we played on some horrendous pitches in the 1970s and he would tell the referee that the pitch was fine and playable, even if it was waterlogged, frozen or covered in snow. Brian would always ask the referee what he wanted; some autographed balls or pictures, whatever he wanted as long as the game wasn't called off. Jimmy Gordon wasn't really a 'physio' as such – Brian didn't feel the role of physio was required because players didn't get injured enough. Recommended 'treatments' were to put your foot in ice, put your foot in hot water and put your foot back in ice, or if you had a knee injury, do nothing but lie still and wait for it to heal.

I remember Brian usually sat in his office and telephoned down to the physio room in the hope someone would pick up so that he could give them an errand ... One day, Brian phoned through to the apprentices' room,

'Right, young man I want you to get tea for four people.'

The voice at the other end wasn't so polite. 'Fuck off!'

Brian was stunned, 'Young man. Do you know who you're talking to?'

The apprentice was equally responsive. 'Yes, do you know who you're talking to?'

Brian then said no, and the apprentice finished off by saying, '... well fuck off again, then,' and immediately put the phone down on the gaffer.

I don't think Brian ever found out who that cheeky apprentice was but if he did the apprentice wouldn't have lasted long at Forest, that's for sure. The apprentice was certainly brave (or stupid) but it was funny at the time.

I used to get changed right next to the physio room and the telephone was forever ringing. Because I was usually the closest one to the phone, every time it rang the players would shout, 'Can you get the phone, Withey?' and I would stop what I was doing and pick the phone up in a huff. I'd then relay the message to the recipient. One day I got so pissed off with the phone ringing, I picked it up and shouted, 'Maternity ward.' No one answered at the other end so I shouted out again, 'Maternity ward, can I help you?'

A voice finally responded and said, 'Young man, if you don't get off that phone you'll be in the fucking maternity ward.' I'll give you two guesses who it was.

I'll always remember the training ground at Forest, or more to the point, the lack of one; Nottingham Forest didn't have their own training ground so they had to use some land next to the River Trent, about a mile down the road from the City Ground, basically a park with two football pitches in the middle. We got changed at the City Ground and walked or ran the mile to the park. It was a joke! Even a club like Birmingham had their own training ground and changing rooms. The training was just as bad. Brian hardly ever took the training; that was left to Jimmy Gordon, who was a coach and the 'sponge man' (physio). Brian would stroll around the park with Peter Taylor and his dog, chatting. If anything needed to be said or anything was untoward, they would come over and have their say. It was laid back to say the least, but that was Brian Clough all over.

Training varied from day to day; five-a-sides, practice matches and shuttle-runs were the norm and it was a myth that Brian was a master tactician on the training ground. He did have a reputation of signing players who had knowledge of the game and who could 'sort things out' on a football field. In order to play for Brian Clough's side, you had to know what you were doing, end of. I'd developed a play with Woody at corners where I'd spin round to the far post, but Brian wanted us to do something a bit different. One day at training he noticed what we were doing and said to us, 'Right, Woodcock, Withe. When Robertson's on the ball on the left-hand side I want both of you to run to the near post.'

I disagreed with him and replied, 'Yes boss but I can take him in and spin round to the far post?'

Brian stuck to his guns and told us to do it his way: 'No! I don't want you to do that. I want you both to get to the near post.'

On the match-day following that session we did as we were told but a few weeks later I confronted Brian about it again.

'Boss, I think I can do better if I come out and spin, not just make the same runs.'

To that he said, 'No! I've got a daft Irishman called O'Neill. Every time you go to the near post, everyone follows you and O'Neill is there and he scores 15 goals a season.' He was right of course. Everyone would follow us, but up there popped Martin O'Neill in space and most of the time he'd score. He effectively played as a wide-right midfielder. It was true – Cloughie was a genius!

Every Friday before a match day, we'd have a team meeting and go to a cafe for coffee. It was the players' chance to speak up and talk about our football and the way we played, but we usually ended up listening instead to Martin O'Neill telling us about whichever murder case he was studying for his law degree. It was rather strange, and we'd usually take the piss out of him for it. Back then you'd never have thought of Martin as management material – he was more interested in law than football. The same could have been said of Robbo but they both proved us wrong there.

Even though Brian hardly ever took training, the one time I remember when he did, he took us down to the park and the first thing he said to us was, 'Right you lot, get yer bottoms off. Them bottoms – get 'em off. Right, get them socks rolled down.'

So there we were in the middle of the park, standing in our shorts and our socks rolled right down to our ankles.

'Right, I'm going to do the warm up with yer. Run through them nettles.'

We looked at each other, thinking he'd lost the plot. He was asking us to run through knee-high stinging nettles – but of course we did it, and you can imagine the language we used running through those stingers'.

When we came out the other end we were all covered in red blotches. Brian had no sympathy and carried on with his training routine.

'See that kiddie's playground? Go along them monkey bars then go round that swing. After that go round that roundabout.'

Here we were, top professional footballers running round a kiddie's playground and calling it 'training'. It summed him up really – it was in his nature to do things differently, but it seemed to work.

Brian had a certain aura like no one else. In a way he was a bit of a 'Jekyll and Hyde' character; one minute he'd do anything for you, next minute he'd try and wind you up or just piss you right off. The one thing a lot of people didn't realise was that he was a great family man, and unbelievable with kids. My son, Jason, was about seven at the time and used to go to every game. Afterwards you'd always find him in Brian's office. I'd go and knock on his door and there would be Jason sitting on one knee, with Brian's son, Nigel (who must have been the same age as Jason), sitting on his other.

Brian loved Jason and he'd tell me off when I went to collect him: 'I'll send them out when I've finished with them. Now get out.' When I went back to collect Jason, he'd insist on giving him a kiss on the cheek and a hug. He was the same with his own kids – he loved kids no matter whose they were. When it came to family, Brian was as affectionate as anyone else. He tried to take his kids everywhere – Nigel must have gone to every game with his dad. That was the side of him that not many people knew or saw.

He was also a great deflector, particularly when it came to criticism of himself. For instance, we played against Chelsea at Stamford Bridge towards the end of the season. We hadn't won in London for a very long time so the media were all over it. They had a new stand (the old East Stand), the first triple-decker stand built in England at a staggering cost of £3m – it looked huge compared to the other stands and was the beginning of an ambitious redevelopment at Stamford Bridge. However, the changing rooms were pretty small and simple, nothing flash, and after the game (which we lost 2–1) I was reflecting on the game, sitting on the edge of the bench with my head bowed. That was my normal routine after a defeat, as I hated losing. I'd reflect on what had happened in the game for several minutes then, once I'd left the dressing room, I could start thinking about the next game.

On that occasion, I must have been one of the last in the dressing room, along with Brian, who was chatting to someone but was interrupted by a knock at the door. It was a Chelsea official, who looked about 80 and was dressed in his club blazer. He asked for Brian.

'Yes young man?' Brian replied.

'Mr Clough the press are all waiting for you upstairs.'

Brian looked at the official, then looked around the dressing room and put his hand on his chin.

'Right, get 'em in 'ere.'

The official then said, 'No, no, Mr Clough. There's a press room upstairs.'

Brian, being Brian declined to go upstairs to the press room. 'No! I'm not doing it. Get 'em in 'ere. I want 'em in 'ere.'

I looked up from my reflective position and wondered what was going on. The poor old boy went back upstairs to instruct the media to gather in the away changing room. Brian shut the door and said to me, 'Young man, this is how to control the media – watch and learn.'

Everyone who was left in the changing room was intrigued by what was about to unfold. A few minutes later, the room was filled with media men. Some of them looked at me to see if I knew what he was going to say to them but I just shrugged my shoulders, as I was none the wiser. The place fell silent and Brian offered to answer any questions from the media. It was as if everyone was too frightened to ask a question; no doubt about it, they were all frightened to death of him.

Suddenly, someone asked, 'Well, Brian, you've come to London again and you've lost again. That's six times now?'

Brian thought about his reply and said, 'Yeah, I know. Emm, well! Emm, yeah.' He then started looking around and up and down the changing room and everyone in the room followed his eyes. Brian then broke the silence again and said, 'How much did it cost to build this stand?'

The media men looked at each other and they all must have thought he was losing the plot until someone piped up, 'About £3m Brian.'

Brian continued, 'Three million pounds, and they can't even put a bloody tile on the floor. The scruffy fuckers ...'

It was classic Clough rhetoric. Brian did a great job of deflecting the defeat by talking about the pitfalls of the new stand. That's the way he worked. The next day, the headlines were full of the Clough outburst and relegated the result to the foot of the page:

CLOUGH SLAUGHTERS THE MEARS STAND

Forest lose 2–1 at Chelsea

In the season we got promoted back to the first division, my first season with Forest (1976/77), we played something like 70-odd league and cup games, so Brian's theory that giving us time off between games would keep us fresh must have worked. It was something of a tradition at Forest that all staff associated with the club went to Cala Millor on Mallorca for a ten-day break. It was kind of self-funded as we contributed to what was called the Cala Millor fund. We were expected to play in a number of charity and testimonial matches throughout the season to raise funds for our end of season trip to Spain. It was Brian who introduced it and if some team wanted to play us in one of these matches Brian would insist they pay around £1,000, which they didn't know would eventually end up in our 'holiday savings'. At the end of the season, the kitty was counted, the flights and accommodation paid for and what was left was spending money for the players and directors. It was a way for the players to contribute to the holiday, even though it didn't cost us anything in real terms. If you played in the testimonial matches and didn't want to go (or couldn't go for any reason) you wouldn't get anything from a refund – someone else would simply take your place.

The break was meant to be a relaxing time for the players to unwind after a hard season, but families were not allowed to go. We had finished our season before Bolton and they still had to play Wolves at home. If Wolves beat them we'd be promoted. It was out of our control where we finished in the league, but obviously we were hoping for Wolves to beat Bolton so we could secure third place (in the day before play-off finals). I didn't go to Cala Millor with the rest of the club as I stayed behind to watch the Birmingham City game with my mate, Dennis Collett, so I was planning to fly out of Birmingham Airport with Larry Lloyd and a few of the directors on the Sunday. During the game, some of the fans were feeding me information about the Wolves score and I kept saying to them I only wanted to know the score at the end of the game – I wanted to blank it out of my mind. After the game, I still didn't know the score of the Wolves game and, funnily enough, my old boss, Willie Bell spotted me in the stand and told me the news I'd been waiting for.

'Congratulations, you've got promotion then. Wolves beat Bolton 3–1!'

Still, I only believed it when I saw it come up on the TV screen a few minutes later. Apparently, even on the plane, the pilot announced to the lads that they had gained promotion but Brian didn't believe it until he landed and phoned his wife, Barbara, who confirmed the news that we had been promoted by one point. It wasn't a bad first season for me at Forest – Anglo-Scottish Cup winner and promoted to Division One.

Howard Kendall had been right – Brian Clough was there to win things, and I didn't regret leaving Birmingham City for a winning team one little bit!

Larry and I flew out to join the rest of the lads on the Sunday afternoon. The club would always book the same two hotels, with the directors and management staying in the Bahia del Sol Hotel and the players in the Said. When Larry and I arrived we were dropped off just down the road from our hotel and we walked straight to the Manchester Bar, where all the lads were, and joined them for a few drinks. It was a celebration of a great but hard and long season, so who could blame us?

There were supposed to have been no rules and regulations on the trip to Cala Millor and it was meant to be a relaxing break, but Brian did have a few unwritten rules of his own. One of them was a dislike for his players having beards. I had a beard at the time and I'd arrived not having shaved for a few days.

Brian noticed I was unshaven and said to me one day, 'Young man, do you ever shave your beard off?'

I responded by saying, 'Sometimes, when it's hot usually.'

Then he said to me, 'Right, it's hot here. Shave your beard off and shave it off by tomorrow.'

As soon as he said that I thought to myself, 'Well I ain't shaving it off now!' Naturally, I did the opposite to what he asked and refused to shave off my beard. Needless to say, Brian wasn't impressed.

Something else that Brian didn't like was seeing us train while we were supposed to be relaxing. I didn't do too much during the daytime but at about 5pm I'd go up to my room and put my running kit on (against Brian's orders). I was a fitness fanatic and always had been, so lounging around all day and night wasn't my thing. I would then run along the beach, usually alone.

On one occasion I'd only just got on to the beach when I spotted Brian with his family. 'Young man,' he shouted, 'Come here. What are you doing?' I told him I was going for a run and he replied, 'I brought you here to relax; to let you wind down; to enjoy yourself and to do anything you want to.' He obviously didn't want me to run, but I responded by repeating what he'd just said, that he'd brought us here to do what we enjoyed.

'Yeah, but I enjoy running. I love running and I'm going for a run.'

Brian was gobsmacked and didn't have an answer to that so he just walked off. Training is one of those things about being a footballer that most players hate. I'd say that about 80 per cent of the players I've played with hated training. I was in the minority who loved it. I loved that I had time to think when I was running; my mind was free to wander as I took in the scenery. Unlike other players who would moan about running and would be out of breath in five minutes, I was relaxed about it. I was in my element.

The unique thing about Nottingham Forest was that the club wasn't a limited company. It was actually owned by a committee consisting of a chairman, a vice-chairman and a group of directors – and they had been voted in by the members. The committee wasn't made up of people who were high-flying executives or had a lot of money, but mainly local businessmen, like Fred Reacher, a local publican. Brian didn't like the players mixing with the directors, which is why we were in an adjacent hotel but separated from them. Whereas at Derby County, Brian was answerable to a board, at Forest he was not. I don't think he cared too much for directors anyway, and was once quoted as saying something like, 'treat directors like mushrooms – keep them in the dark.' It was a classic Clough quote!

Fred Reacher wasn't having any of that, however, as he used to like mixing with the players when he could. He'd sneak into our hotel behind Brian's back to have a drink and a chat with the players. Fred was a down-to-earth publican who didn't mind who he mixed with. He wasn't the only director like that – there were a few who wanted to mix with the players, but generally Brian didn't allow them to. To a certain degree it could be said Brian was a control freak but he balanced the books at Forest and only wanted the best for the club, so no one could complain.

One thing was certain about Brian and that was that he knew what he wanted and didn't suffer fools lightly. In the movie, *The Damned United*, it suggested Brian 'begged' Peter to go with him to Leeds in 1974 when he was managing Brighton, but that just wouldn't have happened. No way! With Brian it was black and white – Peter either stayed or he left, and he chose to stay at Brighton, so I think the film got that one wrong.

When we returned from Cala Millor, we went straight into pre-season training. I remember we went down to Plymouth to play in a testimonial match. The morning before the game, I spotted some of the directors and the club secretary, Ken Smales with their golf clubs and asked them where they were going. Although I had started to play golf back in my Wolves days, I hadn't actually joined a club. Ken told me they were off to play one of the championship courses in the Plymouth area, so I asked if I could join them. I think Ken thought I was going to join in on the play but I just tagged along. When we got back in the afternoon, Brian called me over.

'And where have you been?' he asked, 'How did you get on – did you play?' He was serious with his questions. There was no way any other manager would allow a player to play golf hours before a match, even a friendly.

Brian asked me again, 'Did you play?'

When I said, 'No, no, we've got a game tonight,' he must have thought I was mad.

'You went to a golf course and you didn't play? Why didn't you play? You won't get another chance to play a championship course again!' Like I say, you never knew what he was thinking.

Brian didn't give a monkey's whether we played golf or not, even a few hours before a match. We could have played 18 holes of golf and turned out in the evening to play 90 minutes of football and he wouldn't have given two hoots. He didn't mind you having a few drinks with your pre-match meal, either. It didn't matter what you did before or after the 90 minutes, as long as you gave your all on the football field. I learned a lesson from that, and following that tour I started to play nine holes of golf before training on the odd occasion. I'd obviously got Brian wrong on that front. However, when it came to having sex with your wife or girlfriend the night before a game, that was a different matter because he thought it would sap your energy too much. I'd always prove Brian wrong on that one, though.

In stark contrast to Brian, someone like Bill Shankly wouldn't let any of his players anywhere near a golf club, let alone a pint of Guinness – or a woman, for that matter. In fact, if he found anyone was on a golf course he'd probably go to the club and drag them back home; he apparently used to ring the local golf courses and tell them not to allow his players on the course at all, so I'm told.

I eventually joined a local club, the Stanton-on-the-Wolds Golf Club. The owner at the time asked some of the Forest players, including me, if we wanted to join the club, and Larry Lloyd, Peter Shilton and myself said we were keen to arrange an interview. It was the time of the energy strikes in the late 1970s and the whole area was suffering blackouts. We all went to the club to have a few beers before the interview and, indeed, the lights went out, but thankfully the beer pumps remained on. We'd been there for a couple of hours before I asked our sponsor when we were going to have the interview. Then the club captain came over and asked us if we'd bought a round of drinks and because we had he replied, 'Well, you're in then.' It was that simple and the shortest interview I've ever had. I had become a member of my first golf club.

Brian never wasted any time getting to work during the close season. The squad was trimmed of several fringe players, with the veteran defender Sammy Chapman crossing the Trent to join Notts County, midfielder Sean Haslegrave joining Preston and back-up forward Barry Butlin leaving for Peterborough. Brian somehow always managed to buy good players who would fit into his 'system' – or more to the point Peter Taylor found them and Brian persuaded them to join the club. Even though we had only just been promoted, we were everyone's favourites to go straight back down, probably because we only scraped in by the skin of our teeth, but Brian made a couple of key signings in Peter Shilton from Stoke, and Archie Gemmill, a player he had managed at Derby, for £25,000.

Brian wanted to sign a few more players but the one player he wanted to sign most of all was Kenny Burns, my old pal from Birmingham. One day, Brian and Peter called me into the office and Brian asked me about Burnsy.

'I'm going to ask you a question about a player. If I mentioned the name Kenny Burns, what would you say? What do you think of him as a player?'

I replied, 'Are you mad? He's a bloody nutter! He's a bit of a thug really.' I went on to say about him getting into all sorts of bother. I don't think Brian was interested in his personal life or his temper, though, as he continued:

'I'm not talking about that, I'm asking what's he like as a player?'

I replied, 'He's got talent. He can play. He can kick right foot, left foot. He's a good player but mentally he's a nutter. He doesn't want to play centre-forward – he wants to be a centre-half.'

In off the shin? Scoring that goal in the European Cup Final

Scoring a diving header for Newcastle at St James' Park

Celebrating after scoring

Me with Frank Clark and Nottingham boxer, Dave Needham

The picture was taken before my last (11th) England cap

Having my famous beard shaved for charity by the legend, Jimmy Greaves in 1984

Having a chat with Snooker great, Steve Davis before
the World Snooker Championship

Winning the Midland Sportswriters Player of the Year
in 1981 at the Central TV studios

Aboard a Mediterranean cruise ship with Ray Clemance and his family in 1983

Thailand head coach

Group picture at the airport after winning the 2002 Tiger Cup with Thailand

My father, Gerard Withe with my sons, Stephen and Gareth taken in 1986

Jason and I practicing heading at his school in 1981

At Villa Park with Kathy, holding the League Championship in 1995

In an attacking position with my strike partner, Cyrille Regis during the game in Iceland in June 1982

Another family picture taken at our home in Knowle, Solihull

Taken during our stay in South Africa while I was playing for Arcadia Shepherds in 1973

Me with Nigel Spink, Garry Thompson, Steve Hunt, Andy Gray and Pans People at The Night Out in Birmingham

Stephen and I in our new kitchen in 1983

Me with Gary Shaw celebrating winning the League in 1981 at Highbury

Tony Woodcock and I at Forest in 1978

Scoring against Spurs at Wembley during the Charity Shield in 1982

The aftermath of a training session at Villa's Bodymoor Heath training ground with Dennis Mortimer and Paul Rideout

In my Newcastle kit during 1978

The Birmingham City team in 1975/76

Showing off some of the trophies I'd won with Forest and Villa

In my Sheffield United kit during 1989

Putting pressure on the Sheffield United 'keeper, Jim Brown for Forest in October 1976, with Larry Lloyd looking on

In my Portland Timbers kit during a game in 1975

Scoring for Forest against Blackburn in November 1976
(Picture Courtesy of *Nottingham Post*)

Playing in goal for Villa against Coventry City In March 1984

The 14 players in the Villa squad who won the League in 1980/81

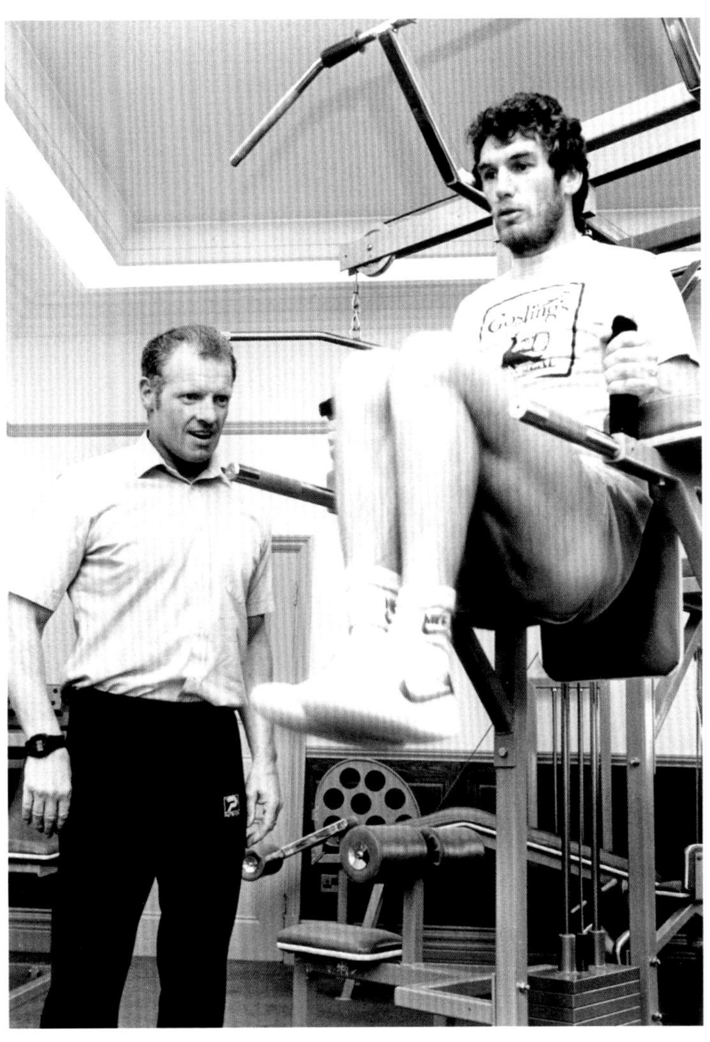

In training at Moor Hall Hotel gym with Tony Ford in 1984

With Gary Mabbutt during a 5-a-side tournament
while I was Wimbledon manager in 1992

The Villa team before the 1982 European Cup Final

After the Hungary game in 1983 where I had fractured my cheek and broken my thumb

Scoring for Forest at the City Ground against Manchester United in 1978

Thailand - Tiger Cup winners 2002

Being presented with an award from the Olympic Committee for winning the Tiger Cup with Thailand in 2002

The Thailand head coach after winning the 2002 Tiger Cup

With 'the gaffer' Ron Saunders with my Midland Player of the Year Award in 1981

Waiting with my staff for the final whistle of the 2002 Tiger Cup Final

'We've Won' – ready to celebrate winning the 2002 Tiger Cup

My other passion – golf. John Letters sponsored me while I was at Newcastle

The 1982 England World Cup squad

Finally being presented with the 1981 Golden Boot in 1992 –
only 11 years too late

On the top deck with the European Cup in 1982

The face of a winner. Playing through the pain barrier for Forest

Gareth - Jason - Stephen on holiday Cala Millor Mallorca Spain

Stephen - Gareth - Jason - Kathy on holiday Cala Millor Mallorca Spain

My debut for England v Brazil in September 1981

Brian looked at me and said, 'I don't want him as a centre-forward, I want him as a centre-half.' I told Brian he'd have to manage him closely. Brian was convinced. 'Right, I'll manage him, that's my job. If I can't, nobody can.'

The next thing I heard he'd signed Kenny for £150,000 and made him a central defender. Burnsy was, in effect, three players in one, as he had previously operated with success both in attack and defence at Birmingham City and he could do a good job in midfield as well, if necessary. Brian knew where he wanted the rugged Scot to fit into his Forest side; however, Larry Lloyd had suddenly found himself an ideal partner in the centre of defence. If you look back now, Brian knew he wanted to pair Larry Lloyd with Kenny Burns where no other manager would have even thought of that pairing; they were both slow and neither of them played from the edge of the box, but he wanted to play them up to the halfway line. You'd think if you had two centre-halves playing that far forward you'd be vulnerable to the ball being played over the top with pace, but Brian knew what he was doing with the two of them, that's for sure. Burnsy wasn't the best looking player ever to grace the City Ground and I remember Brian's classic line after he signed Kenny:

'The ugliest player I ever signed was Kenny Burns.'

Kathy was expecting our second child in the August of 1977, but I was due to go on the pre-season tour of Austria and Germany. I explained the situation to the gaffer and asked if I could stay behind until Kathy gave birth and then I'd join the tour afterwards. The answer Brian gave me wasn't what I expected and shocked me rather. He refused me permission to stay behind, so I had to go with the rest of the squad while Kathy stayed back in Nottingham, ready to give birth.

While we were in Germany, I seem to recall Burnsy getting into bother on several occasions. Kenny couldn't handle his beer and would be pissed after a few pints. Not only that, he'd brought his girlfriend with him on tour. Not only did she hold the reins on him about gallivanting around, he had Cloughie on his back too. One night, Brian had arranged for the players and wives (and girlfriends) to go out to a bierkeller with live entertainment. Barbara Clough was there too. After a few steins of German beer, Brian came over to us and warned us to behave ourselves and look after each other, but during the evening we somehow lost Kenny – he'd disappeared outside and was nowhere to be found. When it was time to go, we all marched outside in the rain and Brian noticed someone lying in the gutter. It was Burnsy. Brian looked at Barbara and then looked down at Kenny.

'Right, get the drunken bum on the coach.' Brian pointed to Larry Lloyd and me so we had to pick him up out of the gutter and put him back on to the coach.

The following day, Brian called a meeting and said a few words about the previous night while pointing at Burnsy.

'We've realised a few things. I don't mind you having a few drinks but it's obvious, young man, that you can't take your drink, so you won't be drinking any more.' He wasn't angry, but it was Brian's way of finding out what people were made of and what their personality was like. He wanted to see how his players reacted to certain things and situations, and in that particular case he had found out that Burnsy couldn't handle his drink. At Birmingham Burnsy was considered a bit of a 'Jack the lad', and I think Brian wanted to humble him a little bit – it was the way Brian got the best out of his players. That wasn't to be the last instance either.

One of the matches we played during the pre-season tour was against Austria Vienna. During the game, 'Shilts' (Peter Shilton) cleared a ball out of the box and it flew over my head. I turned, thinking their centre-back was going to head it clear, but as I turned I started to run, the ball bounced and the centre-back missed it completely. I was suddenly on top of him and we both jumped up for the ball; I was already in motion but he was in a standing position. I then headed the ball down thinking I was going to pass it to Woody, who was running past me. Unfortunately, the centre-back made contact with my head instead of the ball and smashed me in the nose. In the meantime, Woody picked the ball up and scored. Blood was pouring out of my face and I was unaware we'd scored. It felt like I'd broken my nose, and the referee had no choice but to stop the game from restarting. Brian allowed Jimmy Gordon to come on to attend to me, and when he got to me, he wiped my nose with a wet sponge and said in his broad Scottish accent, 'Nay, yer alright, yer alright.' What he was saying was that I wasn't coming off.

I yelled at him, 'But Jimmy, I've broken my nose! Give us some cotton wool, will yer?'

Jimmy gave me some cotton wool and I stuck it up my nose just to stop the bleeding as best I could. After about five minutes we carried on with the game. There were only minutes left to go and we were hanging on to the lead. A minute or so later, Robbo played a ball into my path and the same centre-back came up against me again and he punched me in the ribs as I tried to hold him off. Instinctively, my hand flew back and hit his chest. He clattered to the ground and started rolling around like a baby, although I'd hardly touched him. The guy was play-acting and rolling around as if he'd been shot, just typical of modern-day European footballers. The next thing I saw was the referee waving the red card in the air and pointing at me. I told the referee the player was acting and I hardly touched him but he wouldn't have any of it. I walked off the pitch in disgust and went straight down the tunnel into the changing room.

With only five minutes to go in the game, Brian walked into the changing room and came over to me.

'You know, you get the bloody goal for us, we're winning the bloody game and you let that ...'

I cut him off. 'He was punching me in the ribs and I'm not going to let that happen without reacting.'

Brian looked at me and then said, 'Well done for staying on the pitch. We'll get you a doctor for your nose.' He then disappeared to find a doctor.

Five minutes later, Brian introduced the doctor and low and behold in walked the bleeding referee! Yes, believe it or not the referee was a flaming doctor. He walked over to me, didn't say a word but grabbed my nose, twisted it and said, 'Yes, it's broken,' and walked away again.

We returned to the hotel after the game with my nose broken, still pouring with blood. Peter Taylor nonchalantly approached me and said, 'You've got another son,' and then walked away.

I called after him, 'What? What do you mean, I've got another son?'

Peter stopped and told me a bit more, 'Kathy's given birth and it's a boy.'

Peter then went off and told Brian, who came over to me to tell me they were going to get me on the first flight back home.

'You've broken your nose and can't play in any more games so we're going to get you a flight home.'

When I arrived home, I read the headlines in the papers and it was as though I'd been sent home because I'd got a broken nose or was sent off, not because I'd become a father again. Brian must have concealed the real reason for my early exit and told the press a load of bull. I went straight to the hospital to see Kathy and our new son (who we named Stephen) wearing a pair of sunglasses.

The first thing Kathy said was, 'Why you got the sunglasses on?' I told her that I'd broken my nose to which she replied, with the usual female sympathy, 'It doesn't look that broken to me. It looks alright.'

I think we had a family picture taken shortly after and when that picture was later developed, my nose looked broken alright; it was all over the place.

It took about two weeks before I got to see a specialist about my nose. He told me what he was planning on doing, which was to (properly) break my nose by hitting it with a hammer then try to put it back into place and straighten it up. That operation ended up being the worst experience of my life. It was awful. I remember going into the theatre and seeing the anaesthetist and the specialist talking to one another, and I heard one of them saying, 'He won't be out too long so you don't have to give him a lot. I'll just be straightening the nose today.'

The anaesthetist then got the needle ready to put the fluid into me and he said, 'Right then, Mr Withe, start counting to ten.'

Normally you don't get to ten as you're out for the count, but I carried on counting, '10, 11, 12, 13, 14 ...' and I was still counting in my head after 20.

I heard the anaesthetist say, 'OK, he's out now. You can start.' The specialist then tried to push some tubes down my throat and as I was still conscious, I was gagging as if to be sick. Even though I felt the tubes in my mouth, I couldn't move my arms or legs; I couldn't talk; I could see and I could hear but my body had effectively shut down through the anaesthetic. I wanted to move my arms but my brain said otherwise. By the time they got the tubes halfway down my throat, I had, fortunately, passed out.

The operation ended up being a success and I didn't know anything about it after that point until I woke up. I told the anaesthetist what had happened but he refused to believe it so I told him what he said before the operation and he still didn't believe me. If that had happened nowadays someone would have sued the hospital.

During the pre-season, former Notts County manager, Ronnie Fenton, was brought in to be reserve-team coach. One day, Ronnie was walking round the park (the training ground) with Peter Taylor, who was walking his dog as he usually did while Brian was walking with Jimmy Gordon. Brian wanted to know what Ronnie was doing with the reserve players so he asked Jimmy, who started to wander off to find out, but Brian stopped him.

'No, no don't bother. I'll sort it.'

So Brian shouted in the direction of Ronnie and Peter, 'Ronnie, Ronnie what are you doing?'

Ronnie ran across to Brian and explained, 'We've got a reserve-team game tonight and I'm just practising free kicks and corners.' Football was a simple game to Brian and he was horrified at hearing that.

'Nah, we don't do that here. We do five-a-sides. If it's a corner go to the near post. If it's a free kick, get it down and play. End of story!' He then walked off leaving Ronnie Fenton gobsmacked.

Ronnie said to Peter, 'I've been doing this for years and now he tells me I've been doing it all wrong!' That's the way it was at Forest; we never practised free kicks; we never practised corners; we never practised set-plays. It was just the basics. If you didn't fit into the style of play you'd be out of the team and Brian would sell you as soon as he could.

We had won promotion, and my partnership with Woody became the most feared outside of the first division. It goes without saying that Tony and I would not have scored the same number of goals without help from the other lads: everyone in that team was capable of scoring. Defenders hated strikers running at them at speed more than almost anything, and that's what Woody did best. The only problem was that he did things so quickly, I couldn't always keep up with him. The combination of power and pace was too much for over-pressed defences, but we realised the real challenge was still to come in the top division. In the second division, defenders tended to dive in early and give you the chance to get away from them, but we were under no illusion the same would be true in the top league. Players tended to stick with you and wait for you to make mistakes, so our game plan had to change. All the same, I set myself a target of 20 goals before my second season at Forest had started.

We opened the new campaign away at Everton, who were everyone's bet for the championship. Everton were without their midfield leader, Martin Dobson as well as the Scottish international, Bruce Rioch, but even more crucially, the 'Toffeemen' were missing their centre-forward, Bob Latchford. We beat them 3–1. The victory must have given the entire squad a dose of self-belief – on top of that which Brian had managed to instil in us already.

Next up were Bristol City at the City Ground. It was a tight game but the best chance we had was started by Robbo, who delivered a superb cross from the right wing. I met it on the edge of the box and the ball rocketed into the top corner. It was probably one of the best goals I've ever scored with my head. In fact, even Brian Clough called it 'special'; in fact, Brian was quoted as saying the last headed goal like that he had seen was scored by the great Tommy Lawton. We won the game 1–0 and all of a sudden we were top of the league with two wins out of two. Norman Hunter was playing for Bristol City that day and he told me if he had been marking me I wouldn't have scored. Lucky, then, that he was asked to mark someone else.

We then played our fierce local rivals, Derby County, at the City Ground, and I scored a brace in a 3–0 victory. It was an absorbing contest that reached its peak at the end of the first half when I hammered home our first goal with a firm left-foot volley that crept inside the post. In the 67th minute Robbo curled in a dangerous cross and I chested the ball towards goal to make it 2–0.

Going into the game at Highbury we had a poor record against London clubs. It was only the fourth game of the season and we were already losing 1–0 when Arsenal were awarded a free kick just outside the box. One of their defenders, Richie Powling was standing in front of our wall with Kenny Burns standing behind him. Powling was trying to push the wall back, but all of a sudden, I saw Burnsy lose his rag and tell him to 'fuck off', before head-butting him. Burnsy poleaxed Powling and he tumbled down like a sack of potatoes. Fortunately, the referee didn't see the incident, so Burnsy didn't get sent off. Nothing came from the free kick and we ended up losing 3–0.

Brian must have seen the incident and ordered a meeting after the game. He walked into the dressing room looking really annoyed.

'Right, that performance was a disgrace. And you, Burns, you're a bloody thug! You come from bloody Birmingham City and they didn't want you there. I'm your last hope, son. If you do that again you won't play in the first team ever again! You'll play in the reserves and train with the youth team. You're a bloody disgrace! We're not bloody thugs here. We're footballers. We've got talent ...'

Brian carried on laying into Burnsy for a few minutes, then started to talk about the game in general. He then turned to Peter Taylor and said, 'Peter, have you got anything to say?' No sooner had Brian finished his sentence, Peter opened his mouth, fuming.

'Have I got anything to say? I'll tell you what I've got to say. If I were you I'd look at yourselves in the mirror and ask yourselves, what's your contribution to this team? I can tell you what my contribution is.' Peter was his own man and wasn't afraid to speak out. He saw himself as an equal to Brian, not just an 'assistant' manager. He then went round the players, pointing at each and every one of us. 'You. I signed you. Him, I signed him.' He then pointed to Colin Barrett and realised he had not been involved in signing him and just said, 'Well, not so much you.' I don't think Peter was at the club when Colin signed.

I think Brian's rant did get through to Burnsy that day, because I don't think he did anything like that again.

The momentum had started early in the season, but the media were saying we hadn't played a team with any conviction. By early October we had won six out of eight games and we had Ipswich to come to the City Ground. Their captain, Mick Mills had put an article in the national newspapers and had gone on national radio saying something like, 'They might be top of the league but they haven't come up against a decent side and now they're coming up against a proper side in Ipswich Town.' That from someone whose team was mid-table at the time, although they were managed by the great Bobby Robson. On the day of the match, Mick pinned the newspaper article up on our dressing room door. Brian wasn't impressed when he saw it.

'Have you seen what this bloody Mills is saying about you lot? You can't bloody play. You haven't come up against a good side yet.'

We didn't need any more ammunition than that: we went out on to the pitch with all guns blazing and beat them convincingly, 4–0. I scored all four goals. We were rampant that night, and destroyed the pedigree defensive pairing of Kevin Beattie and Allan Hunter, as well as the combative attributes of Brian Talbot and Mick Mills in midfield. Robbo and I were on fire: he laid on all four goals for me to score. If he was marked one-for-one he'd usually skin his full-back, and teams tended to put two or three defenders on him, which created more space for me. I'd scored four goals but I was only doing what the boss told me. Brian told me to get into the box, take all the knocks and stick the chances in the back of the net, and that night he wasn't disappointed. It seemed to come easy, but to be fair everything was easy when you were working with Clough and Taylor.

After the game, I asked Brian what I thought was a simple question.

'So, boss can I have the match ball?'

He gave me a withering look and said, 'Young man. When you learn to play with it, I'll buy you a football.' Brian always played you down. Nevertheless, he took the match ball into their dressing room and went round every Ipswich player individually and got them to sign it. He then brought it back into our dressing room and I got it signed by our lads, and I got to keep the match ball. That was Brian all over. He always tried to deflect from what you'd done on the pitch.

A few weeks later, we played Manchester City at the City Ground and I scored a late winner but got fined £50 for getting booked for dissent. I had protested to the referee as he cautioned Larry Lloyd for fouling Brian Kidd. It was a full-blooded game, although it wasn't a dirty game. I wasn't too upset as my goal kept us at the top of the table, however, Brian wasn't happy with me (again) after that game and even threatened to put me in the reserves if I didn't improve my behaviour on the pitch.

I also remember playing in a game at the City Ground against Liverpool. Joey Jones was their right full-back and he was given the task of marking Robbo. The ball went out of play in the last third of the Liverpool half and I went to retrieve it. Joey tried to grab the ball from me, but I wasn't going to give it to him, so he punched me in the stomach on the blind side of the referee and linesman. I'd always worked on my abs so the punch didn't even make me flinch and I said to him, 'You'll hurt your hand doing that, Joey.'

After he realised it didn't hurt me he replied, 'You're right there, Withey.'

It was around that time that there was press talk of me being linked with several clubs including one in South America and a German club, St Pauli. The Germans apparently wanted me as their priority transfer target and had put in a £300,000 bid. I'd scored four goals in the first three games of the season and the local newspaper had reported that I had been watched by scouts from the Hamburg club after their local rivals, SV Hamburg, had signed Kevin Keegan for £500,000. I was still under contract with Forest and we were going for the championship, so nothing was done about their interest and Brian never mentioned anything to me about it (not that he would have, anyway). I knew we were more interested in buying players than in selling our best players. Apparently, Peter Taylor had suggested Forest could have made a lot of money on me, but pointed out I was 'more useful than the cash.'

I was top scorer with 11 goals by the end of November. I hadn't scored for six weeks when Brian issued a warning to me: 'Get back among the goals or else ...' Brian was a striker himself in his day (and a good one at that) and because of that he was demanding of me and that was hard, but I thrived on it. I guess I'd have been exactly the same in his position. However, he really laid into me via the media, saying I was at the crossroads of my career and holding everything up. He accused me of dropping back too deep, saying, 'If he drops back any further he'll be getting in Peter Shilton's way.' He threatened to leave me out of a League Cup tie with Aston Villa, but he played me and I scored in a 4–2 victory at the City Ground.

Brian had a habit of buttering up referees before each match and if I ever had a go at one he'd go ballistic.

'You know, young man. I've signed autographs and I've done this and that for these referees and YOU, you're having a go at him because he's made a decision you don't like. Everything I've done has gone out of the window.' Throughout my career, bad refereeing decisions inevitably used to wind me up, so I vented my anger at times, and that led to me missing more games through suspension than I did through injury. He hated players getting booked for arguing with the referee and he used to fine me (or anyone else) who did it.

There were always issues for Brian to deal with off the pitch and during the autumn of 1977 the England manager's job was up for grabs after the 'defection' of Don Revie to the Middle East. Our magnificent early-season form meant the general clamour for Brian's appointment to the national team was intense. He made no bones about his interest in the post and made little attempt to reassure our concerned supporters (and players) at the time. Not only did he take time to criticise our supporters for preferring to shout foul-mouthed abuse towards the opposition rather than get behind their own team in the game, he also questioned their right to try to sway him away from the England job when so many season tickets at Forest remained unsold in our first season back in the top tier of English football. It was a strange time.

Wembley beckoned in the League Cup. I scored two and created another in a 3–1 victory in the first leg against Leeds at Elland Road. We won the home leg 4–2 and I scored the opener. The season then took a surreal turn. As if Forest being top of the league, in the final of the League Cup and the last eight of the FA Cup was not enough, we also entered the pop charts. Teaming up with the pop group, Paper Lace, the club broke into the charts with the misunderstood classic *We've Got The Whole World In Our Hands*. For six weeks that anthem graced the charts, peaking at a respectable #24!

We were due to play West Bromwich Albion at The Hawthorns in the FA Cup, and we hadn't seen the gaffer for three days. It was not unusual for Brian to take us away prior to an away game, and on his return he decided to take us to the Burton Hotel. The hotel wasn't what you would call local to The Hawthorns, but it wasn't that far away either, situated between Nottingham and Birmingham. It was an unusual location to say the least, but Brian never did do anything the way anyone else would. It was also quite common for him to disappear for days on end, and whenever he did, we'd miss his presence around the place.

I'd scored 18 goals by the time we played QPR in the 5th round of the FA Cup but I committed a tackle in a 'late and dangerous manner.' A week before the League Cup Final, I got suspended for three games for reaching 20 penalty points, just at a time when I was on fire, scoring goals for fun. The club called for a personal hearing with the FA to plead for leniency and to try to rescind the suspension, so we had to go to Manchester. Brian agreed to take me to the hearing so I drove over to his house in Derby for 9am. While I was waiting for Brian, I noticed there was a bar of gold on the mantelpiece above the fire. I had to look twice. Brian told me a sheikh had given it to him; however, I think he put it in the skip in the end because it just wasn't his style. Anyway, Brian had arranged for one of the directors of Derby County to drive us in his Mercedes from Brian's house to Manchester. Brian and I ended up being half an hour late for the hearing but, surprisingly, the outcome of the 16-minute hearing was that the FA reduced the ban from two games to one. It meant I'd only miss the home game with Leicester and not the cup final. I'd only had nine bookings in my entire career before that season, which really wasn't bad for a striker in that era. Brian was anxious to make sure I'd play at Wembley as we already had Archie Gemmill, Peter Shilton and Dave Needham ineligible for the game.

After the hearing, Brian took us out to lunch and we were met by a few media guys. Brian, being Brian, offered drinks all round. At first I didn't want any alcohol, but eventually he insisted we all drink pints of beer with our meal. However, in typical Cloughie style, as soon as he bought a couple of rounds he said, 'Right, that's it, no more drink. We're off now.' We drove back to Brian's house in Derby, then I had to drive back home to Nottingham.

The usual ritual prior to match day was for Brian to give us sleeping tablets so we'd have a good night's sleep before any big game, but I didn't like taking them and I'd ask him if I could have a pint of Guinness or something with my meal, then have another pint to take to bed with me instead. He was generally OK with that, however, on one occasion we were all booked into single rooms so I went up to bed with my pint of Guinness and sat watching the TV for an hour. All of a sudden there was a bang on the door. I thought it was a few of the lads taking the piss so I ignored it. The banging continued, got louder and began to annoy me so I eventually got up and opened the door only to see Brian standing in the doorway.

'Right, what yer doing?'

I replied, 'Watching TV, boss.'

Brian said, 'Right, get downstairs in 15 minutes.'

You didn't argue with Brian, so I did as I was told. I went into a function room, and all the lads were sitting there dressed in their nightclothes or dressing gowns. No one knew what the hell was going on until Brian appeared with Peter Taylor. 'Right,' he said, 'I haven't seen yer for a few days so I thought we'd have a drink together.'

Brian looked straight at Robbo and he nearly shat himself, thinking he'd done something wrong. 'Right, Robbo. What yer having to drink?' As Robbo was the first one, he asked for an orange juice to which the gaffer replied, 'No! You're not drinking that shit tonight.' He then turned round and pointed in my direction. 'You'll have a pint of Guinness, won't yer?' I duly obliged. It went on like that until everyone had a drink, except for wee Archie Gemmill, whom we called 'the little nark' because he moaned about everything.

He piped up, 'I'm not having a drink. I don't want a bloody drink.' Brian insisted he should have one and eventually Archie gave in and said, 'If I have to have a drink, I want champagne.'

Brian agreed without hesitation and turned to the barman. 'Right, OK. Six bottles of champagne, barman, please.'

When the champagne arrived my glass was topped up, so I was drinking Guinness with champagne (Black Velvet), of which I must have drunk four pints by the end of the session.

So, the night before a big FA Cup quarter-final we just sat there for hours, drinking and talking about football with the boss. It was bizarre. However, in usual Cloughie style and as quick as it had been organised, we were suddenly ushered back to bed.

'Right, we've got a game to play tomorrow. Get to bed you lot!'

The next day, we all got up right as rain, had breakfast and drove to The Hawthorns only to get beat by the Baggies, 2–0. If I recall, 'Shilts' dropped a clanger for the first goal, which was unusual for him. Some of the players wondered if the reason we lost was down to us having a few drinks and staying up to get pissed the night before, but that wasn't the first time that kind of thing had happened, and we had won other games following a similar night's drinking.

Our preparation for the League Cup Final replay against Liverpool at Old Trafford was even more bizarre – Brian took us all to Scarborough for three days. On the first day we were there, he took us on a long walk along the beach and we stopped off at a pub. He wouldn't let us sit in the main bars, so we had to hide away in the corner out of sight of the public and, bizarrely, we couldn't buy pints so we had to have two halves. After a few half-pints of Guinness, Brian ushered us all out and he asked who wanted cockles and mussels, so we took another stroll along the front, tucking into seafood. We didn't do a lot of training in the three days we spent in Scarborough, apart from some cardio work on the beach.

To this day, I don't know what he was thinking and I wish I had asked him why he took us out on binges just before big games like that. I'm sure he must have given it some thought and not just decided on the spur of the moment. He really wanted us to win all three trophies but it wouldn't have surprised me if he'd said to Peter Taylor that he particularly didn't want to lose the championship and the League Cup. I'm pretty certain he wanted to win that double at least, and that's why he allowed the lads to let their hair down the night before the West Bromwich Albion FA Cup game. I think the fact that he had lost the treble when he was managing Leeds United played on his mind.

A similar thing happened when we played local rivals, Derby County, at the Baseball Ground early in the new year. It was a goal less draw and he came into the dressing room after the game and said, 'Right, you lot, I want you all at the airport tomorrow – East Midlands Airport and report there at 12pm – we're going to Spain.' As always when Brian said something out of the blue, we all looked at each other as if to say, 'Is he bloody serious?' So, we left the ground and went home to our partners to tell them we were going to Spain the next day – which was a Sunday. Again, it must have been planned because he sent flowers to all our partners knowing they'd all be pissed off. I think Kathy binned hers.

Anyway, he took us all to Benidorm for five days in the sun, which we didn't complain too much about. One morning, after my run along the beach with Colin Barrett tagging along, we noticed the swimming pool was covered over with a tarpaulin as it was out of season – it was January and it wasn't very warm, even for Spain. We were both sweating from the run and were greeted by the lads, who were shouting down from the balcony of the hotel, 'You lot – what you running for?' I gave them the 'bird' in response. Colin then had a bright idea.

'You get that end and we'll uncover the pool to make one lane and we'll have a swim.'

We pulled the tarpaulin back and started swimming in the cold water and the lads started shouting abuse again. Colin, for some strange reason decided he wanted to show off so he dived onto the tarpaulin.

I shouted to him, 'You stupid prat, you'll drown!' and the lads began to laugh their heads off. All of a sudden, the tarpaulin began to sink into the water with Colin in the middle of it and in the deep end of the pool.

Colin tried to keep afloat and shouted desperately, 'Withey, Withey I'm sinking. I can't get out.' I began to think he was going to drown so I swam towards him, grabbed his arm and locked on to him, with the lads still laughing in the background. I shouted up to them:

'He's drowning you stupid prats!'

I was treading water with Colin locked on to me as I was trying to get him out. Just as we got to the edge of the pool and before he was about to go under completely, I got him out and up on to the tiled floor. He must have been about a minute from drowning, his breathing was rapid and he began to splutter water. It was a good job I was there because I think he would have tried the same trick if he'd been on his own, only the consequences would have been fatal. It put a dampener on the mini-holiday.

Essentially, Brian had to be in control of EVERYTHING. He wanted to pull the strings with everything and everyone – the club, the players and everything that was happening around him. He knew the club inside out and wanted to run it his way. You could say Brian was a 'unique' manager. Control freak? For sure! A lot of people thought Brian did things off the cuff but I never thought that. I always thought if he did something he'd done it for a reason. He'd often do things to stimulate a reaction, whether it was from me or another player in the team. He did it a few times with me and my reaction was always, 'I'll show you ...' Brian Clough did things that no other manager would ever do – and I do mean NO other manager. He was very much one of a kind, and had his own way of managing.

As a football manager, there was no one better but as a person, as Larry Lloyd said to me once, 'I'd never cross the road to talk to him.' Larry found him a nightmare to talk to but to be honest I never had a problem with him. I always did my job to the best of my ability and if that was not good enough for him it wasn't good enough for me. To be fair, that's all that Brian ever expected of his players, to do their best on the football field. If there were any issues around the team you'd either be in the camp who didn't say anything or you'd be in the opposite camp and confront him – and I confronted him on several occasions. There were a few times when I'd actually ended up having an argument with Brian five minutes before the kick-off to a game – and survived. There aren't many managers who'd pick you for the next game after having an argument with them, but all Brian was concerned about was that you gave 100 per cent on the pitch. Very often he'd admit to doing or saying the wrong thing to you, but you'd never find that out if you didn't challenge him. Brian once said he wouldn't touch Kenny Burns with a bargepole but then signed him, and he was player of the year that same season. Kenny obviously proved Brian wrong, and fair play to him for that.

There's no doubt Brian was a footballing genius, pure and simple. Pre-match and half-time team talks were elementary and there were no complicated tactics involved whatsoever. Sometimes Peter gave the team-talks to the players, but he didn't seem to have the same effect as Brian did. Peter just didn't have the same repertoire as Brian, and while I'm not being disrespectful of Peter, we knew who 'the boss' was.

Brian had a great relationship with his players, and once described his team-talks as, 'We talk about it for twenty minutes and then we decide I was right.' Another one of Brian's classic team-talks was as simple as, 'Right, Lloyd, you're a centre-back, head the bloody ball. Burns, don't keep giving them the ball. Withe, you're a striker, score us a goal.' It wasn't all the complicated positioning we see in the modern game – it was simple stuff; football's a simple game and what Brian was telling us was all relevant. Everything he did was planned, although he did very occasionally slip up, like when he slapped those fans that invaded the pitch on that famous occasion at the City Ground in 1989. That was out of order, and out of character for Brian.

Brian did things which would never happen in the modern day Premier League, such as giving players two, three or even four days off at a time. If we won a game on a Saturday he'd come into the changing room after the game and say something like, 'Right, I'll see you Thursday,' and we'd look at each other in amazement. Nowadays, players are lucky to get Sundays off.

Overall, I'd say Brian was a pretty fair manager. He'd call you 'a bloody disgrace' when you'd had a nightmare of a game or praise you if you'd played well, and that's all you wanted as a player. At least you knew where you stood with him (most of the time, anyway). Most players took his criticism in one of two ways – they'd either let it get to them or take it on the chin. If he had a go at me, I would go out on to the pitch all guns blazing and try to prove him wrong, but then that's always been my attitude to life. Just after the League Cup Final in March 1978, Brian put something in the papers, I took it all in my stride and as a bit of a joke until Jason came home from school one day, crying his eyes out. I asked him what the matter was and he said all the kids at school were criticising me and quoting Brian Clough, who apparently said I was a 'crap player'. As soon as he said that I turned to Kathy:

'Right that's it. I ain't having that. Whatever he says about me, I don't give a damn, but when it affects my son, I'm not having that.' Kathy told me to go to see him, which wasn't as easy as it sounded because you'd have to book an appointment to see Brian.

The next day I reported for training and told Jimmy Gordon I wanted to see Brian. Jimmy asked me what I wanted to see him about and I turned round and said bluntly, 'It's none of your business Jimmy, just go and tell him I want to see him after training.' Jimmy duly went to tell Brian and returned to say he would see me after training.

Just before I went to see him, I went through in my mind what he'd said in the papers and I was still upset. As I was getting changed after training, Jimmy came over to me and said, 'He's ready to see you now.' I knocked on the door to his office (you had to knock otherwise he went ballistic).

'Come in. Right, sit down. Right, what do you want to see me about?'

I started to explain about the article in the paper, but he didn't take much notice of what I had said because the phone rang.

'Hang on. Hello. Yes, right. Umm, right. OK. Hang on. Hang on. Hang on.' Then he turned towards me and asked me out of the blue if I wanted a drink. I looked at him in surprise and said yes. Brian then continued his telephone conversation, 'OK, get us a bottle of champagne and a bottle of brandy. Who, the chairman? Right, OK.' He then put the phone down. 'So, why have you come in to see me?'

I was starting to feel myself getting wound up as I could see he was playing games and deflecting the point of my meeting with him.

'It's about this article in the papers!'

Then there was a knock at the door, 'Hang on. Hang on.' It was the chairman. 'You don't mind the chairman joining us do you? Come in mister chairman. I don't know what he's come to see me about, but I guess I will find out soon.' The chairman sat down and Brian asked me what I wanted for the third time and, again, I repeated myself.

'It's about these bleeding articles about me in the papers. It's not affecting me but ...'

There was another knock on the door and in walked Peter Taylor and he also sat down and joined us. As if it had all been pre-planned, the Clough/Taylor double-act started to get going. Peter asked Brian what I wanted, to which Brian said he didn't yet know, but possibly something about a press article. There was a pause and then Brian continued, 'Ah, I remember something about an article. Barbara said it was a bit unkind. I suppose really I might have been a bit unkind, but what's your point young man?'

The second he said that the phone rang again. 'Yeah, alright bring it in.' He put the phone down and we start chatting again. I was getting even more wound up and I could see myself getting angry with Brian.

'It's affecting my son.'

We were interrupted yet again when the door opened and the champagne appeared. We drank the champagne and the conversation went on in much the same way for over two and a half hours. In the end I don't think he answered my concerns. As I've said before, he was an expert in deflecting the blame away from himself.

I eventually got out of his office at 2pm and when I got home I couldn't get the key in the door thanks to the champagne. As Kathy opened the front door she knew straight away I was pissed and she shouted something at me like, 'I hope you've bloody seen him? Where have you been all this time? I've been waiting for you.' I said something incomprehensible, walked straight past Kathy and trudged up the stairs and straight into bed. No more than five minutes later, the phone rang and Kathy answered it. It was Brian:

'Did he get home alright, Kathy?' Kathy had no hesitation responding.

'And you can sod off for a start!' she stormed, and slammed the phone down.

Following the birth of Stephen the previous summer, we had decided that Nottingham was the place where we wanted to stay; we liked the house and the area we lived in and we'd got the house a lot cheaper than it should have been which was a bonus. (The valuation officer from the estate agent made a mistake on the value of the house that worked to our advantage, and we ended up with quite a nice house and a massive garden with a pond in the middle.) We were happy there, and I wanted to sign a new contract at Forest. However, not everything was rosy at the club. We were playing Ipswich at Portman Road in April 1978 and we had almost secured the league championship but it was a poor game and we were drawing 0–0 at half-time. Brian took me off shortly after the restart, as I hadn't been playing that well. I don't know how true the story is but apparently Peter Taylor was talking about me to Brian and allegedly said, 'He's had his day here – get him off.' So, he subbed me and, surprisingly, he put Frank Clark on, a full-back who was coming towards the end of his career. Frank was 34 and had played nearly 600 games – but he had never scored a goal. Obviously, Frank was confused at being brought on to replace a striker.

'Where do you want me play, boss?'

Brian said the obvious. 'Play centre-forward. Get up front and score a goal.'

Frank looked bewildered; he'd played all his life as a full-back and all of a sudden he was expected to win us the game. And would you believe it – Frank only bloody scored didn't he! He scored his only ever goal in his life after replacing me. Talk about celebration – I think he must have run from Ipswich back to Nottingham after scoring that goal. Unbelievable!

Going into the away game at Coventry we had two games in hand over our nearest rivals, Everton, and were leading the table by six points. We drew that game and didn't win in the league again that season – we didn't need to because we'd secured the championship by then, at Highfield Road with four games to go. We joined a small and exclusive company of clubs to have won the Division One championship the season after promotion from Division Two. We were unbeaten in our last 26 league matches, a run stretching back to November 1977, and lost just three league games all season. I must say here that if it wasn't for Peter Shilton in goal, we probably wouldn't have won the league as he must have saved us 15 points – he was magnificent that season. We only used 17 players all season, which was an incredible achievement in itself.

Straight after securing the championship, we all flew off to Vigo in northern Spain to celebrate and to play in an exhibition match. We were followed everywhere by the media, and some were even on board our flight. On the afternoon of the game, Brian decided we were all going on a boat trip so we all went off and the boat stopped off at a small fishing village. Just like our preparation for the League Cup Final replay, Brian had an idea we were all going to eat seafood, so he took us all to a bay side shack where they sold oysters. So here we were, a team of professional footballers and some of the media guys, eating oysters by the sea in Spain. Of course Brian paid for the three-dozen oysters (well, the club paid anyway). Not only that, he bought a few carafes of wine to wash them down with. We must have sat there for about an hour and a half until he decided it was time for us to go to get some sleep, as we had a game that evening. I can't imagine anything like that happening nowadays.

I'd just played the best football of my career, I was joint top-scorer and we had won a double with that great Forest side, but my two-year contract was up. I was also rumoured to be in line for an England call-up because the England manager, Don Revie had been to watch me several times. I was scoring goals for fun back then, but I think Revie refused to pick anyone from Forest on principle after what had happened in 1974, when Brian famously took over the Leeds management from Revie. Moreover, I couldn't see Brian recommending me to Revie, somehow. Under any other England manager I felt I'd have been capped much earlier, but I didn't complain. Having said that, there were hints in the media that I would be called up and I'm sure I read an article written by Revie around that time saying that I was the best English centre-forward around.

If I'd known what Brian was like before I'd signed the contract I would probably only have signed for two years, but he was insistent that I sign for the two years, plus one-year option. When we got promoted we hardly made any extra money through bonuses because finances were tight. We had just made history and won the first division championship and the League Cup and again we had no bonus scheme in place – we made absolutely nothing out of it, which was sad, really! At the end of the 1977/78 tax year my P60 said I'd earned exactly £9,990. At the time, I had no gripes about my wages, even though there were players at the club, like Shilts, who was given a huge increase to come to Forest. Shilts must have been on about £500 a week, while players like myself and Woody were on no more than £115. I even think Robbo was only on a miserly £90!

Winning the championship inevitably spurred everyone into renegotiating their contracts – including me. What Brian would do when players renegotiated their contracts was to call you into his office and ask you what you thought you were worth. He would tell everyone that there were two people in the team who should be paid the most money and they were the goalkeeper (who saves the goals at one end) and the striker (who scores them at the other end). When I went in to speak to Brian, I went in armed with the figure in my head that I thought I was worth. I had no desire to leave the club; both Kathy and I liked the city and I enjoyed being at Forest, so I saw no real problem in renegotiating my contract and getting the money I had in my mind. That was before the meeting with Brian. Not really knowing what everyone else was earning at the time, I had an argument with him about my wage demands. I'd been the leading goal scorer for the two years I was at the club so Brian, being his astute self, asked me what I thought I was worth, to which I replied, 'The same as Shilts'. He had a bit of a chuckle to himself and he asked me the same question again.

'Come on then. What do YOU think you're really worth?'

I gave him a more 'realistic' figure (but in hindsight I was underselling myself), suggesting £180 a week, which would mean a £70-a-week increase. I didn't think I would get anywhere near what Shilts was on and was only trying my luck with that one if I'm honest; nor did I think I'd get even double the salary. Brian ummed and ahhed, had a think for a few minutes and then came back with a figure of £170. To that I said adamantly, 'Well, no! The figure is £180.' I wasn't about to budge, but neither was he.

So he said, 'Well, right, I'll have a think about it.'

I walked out of his office none the wiser – and none the richer. It wasn't long before I found out what the other lads had been offered; Woody, Robbo and Viv Anderson had all been offered £200 a week; there were four or five players who had been offered the same wage he wanted to pay me. I was shocked and disappointed to say the least – I wasn't happy!

When I got home that afternoon, I told Kathy what had happened and said I'd shot myself in the foot a bit. I thought I could have gone back in again and asked him for the same as the other lads. A week went by with no further mention of my contract and I decided to go back in to see him.

He said to me, 'Right, have you had a think about what we were talking about last week?'

I played his game and deflected his question and put the ball back in his court.

'Yeah I had a think about it, have you had a think about it?'

He played his usual game and said, 'What's for me to think about?'

It was my turn to play hardball then. 'I told you, £180 a week.'

Brian held firm. 'Nah, I'm not giving it yer.'

I was furious because at the back of my mind (and he probably wasn't aware of this) I knew what he'd offered the other lads. He repeated what he was offering me.

'That's what I'm offering yer, £170.'

To that, I said outright, 'Well, I wanna leave.'

I think I shocked him a bit and he called my bluff.

'What? You want to leave the club? If you want to leave then put it in writing.'

I then stormed out of his office and banged the door behind me.

By then I had switched off and was thinking it just wasn't going to happen for me at Forest and I would end up moving on. It looked like Brian had forced the issue by getting me to put my transfer request in writing to show it wasn't him getting me out of the club, but it also made it look like I wanted to leave the club and he didn't want to sign me. That same day I spoke to the PFA and they advised me to put my transfer request in writing but address it to the chairman, not to Brian. Another week went by and he called me in again and said, not knowing I'd written directly to the chairman, 'Oh, you didn't put in a transfer request then? Are you going to sign?'

I told him I'd written to the chairman.

'I've put a transfer request in.'

Brian shrugged his shoulders and said, 'Well I haven't seen it – and I run this football club.'

As soon as I explained the transfer request was addressed to the chairman, Brian's face turned red and he picked the phone up and spoke to Fred's secretary.

'Is there a letter in there for the chairman?' She said there was and Brian told her to bring it in and he slammed the phone down. When the secretary brought my (unopened) letter to Brian he immediately opened it, read it and said, 'Right, you're out of here! Get out!' (Or words to that effect). He put the letter down on his desk and I walked out of his office.

Just before the start of the new season, I was called into a meeting with the rest of the lads, as I was still officially a Forest player. He told us that now we had won the championship, we were going for the European Cup and explained what the bonus scheme was. As we had received nothing from winning the first division championship, everyone listened intently when he explained we'd potentially receive something like £1,000 for each win in the European Cup. Effectively, he was trying to make amends for not having anything in place for the previous season. If the lads got to the final they would have made a tidy packet plus there was a huge bonus of £5,000 for actually winning the thing.

After the meeting, Larry called me over and said, 'Sign your contract – you'll be mad not to.'

I said, 'No, no I won't.'

He said, 'Don't be bloody stupid. Bloody hell, have you seen the bonuses?'

I was thinking more about which club I wanted to go to than bonuses, and told Larry, 'I don't give a monkey's. I'm not signing.'

As soon as I had made my intentions clear and he had told me to leave the club, Brian played hardball with me again and wouldn't let me go to any other first division club. I found out that West Bromwich Albion's boss, 'big Ron' Atkinson was after me, and a couple of other top clubs were keen to sign me as they'd heard I was on the transfer market; I think Terry Venables had made an enquiry but Brian wouldn't let me speak to him. I was included in the opening game of the new season against Spurs at home because he didn't have anyone else to play up front. We went to the hotel in Burton-upon-Trent for our pre-match meal as we normally did for a home game. It was a scorching hot day and by midday he told us to get some liquids down so he ordered me a pint of Guinness, which was typical. That wouldn't be allowed in modern football as it would be water or power drinks.

I missed a good chance during the game and Brian took me off during the second half. Apparently he said to Peter Taylor, 'Take him off. He's dried up. We'll sell him.' It turned out to be my last game for Forest.

Brian's plan was to bring in a young lad called Steve Elliott who was scoring goals for fun in the reserves but I don't think he stepped up to the plate. In the end, the only club he would let me go to was Newcastle, basically because they were in Division Two at the time and, therefore, I would pose no threat to his team.

After that Spurs game, Brian told me to go to speak to Bill McGarry, the Newcastle manager, who was sitting in the stands watching me play. Brian had already agreed a fee with Bill for £250,000, nearly six times the amount he paid for me. I went in to see Bill and we talked about wages; I had a figure in my mind but deep down I didn't want to join Newcastle, only because they were in Division Two. I knew about their supporters and the legendary number 9s of the past, but I still didn't really fancy it. Bill made me an offer and I initially turned it down. In my head I wanted to see out my one-year option and play for Forest on the money I was already on. I didn't want to leave Forest – why would I? We were in the European Cup for the first time in the club's history. I didn't want to go just anywhere and I didn't want to leave the first club that really wanted me. This was the time before the freedom of contract rule allowed players to leave for free; however, I felt I was being forced out by Brian and was willing to do anything to see out the extra year on my contract just to piss him off.

After my meeting with Bill, I saw Brian in passing and he asked me if I had sorted my deal with Newcastle and I told him I wasn't interested in it. He went bright red with anger and said, 'What do you mean you're not going?' I told him I wasn't signing and I wanted to play for Forest. He told me to stay where I was and he'd be back in five minutes after he'd seen Bill. When he came back, Brian told me to go in and speak to Bill again.

I'd known Bill for several years, as he'd been my manager at Wolves, and I knew what he was like. He said to me, 'I don't like what's happening here, but Brian's made it clear he doesn't want you. He's told us the fee is £240,000 so you can get more wages. That's the best I can offer you now.' When he told me how much per week he was prepared to pay me I agreed to sign. However, it wasn't plain sailing as he wanted me to sign a four-year contract but I only wanted a year, so we compromised on a two-year deal – and only if we got into the first division.

'I'm telling you now, Bill, if you don't get us up into the first division in the first two years, I'm leaving.' Bill talked the club up and promised he would do everything to get the club promoted.

In hindsight, I think that game at Ipswich on the 25 April 1978 was the beginning of the end of my Forest career, that Brian knew then he wanted me out and that's why he played hardball during my contract negotiations. I really think the reason behind me leaving Forest was what Peter Taylor had said to Brian that day: 'We've had the best of him now. We need to find an alternative striker.' Brian was hedging his bets a bit, not wanting me to go to another first division club; if I went to a rival club and started scoring goals there, his decision would backfire on him. I was 26 years old and not even at my peak, so I'm not sure why he felt that they'd had my best, and I'm sure the Forest fans were confused as to why I was allowed to leave. After all, I'd been top-scorer for the two seasons I'd played for the club and there was no one else to replace me.

The next season started badly for Forest and they only won once in the first eight games after I was sold, but they went on to be runners-up to Liverpool in the championship race. It was only by chance that Brian decided to put Gary Birtles up front, that his plan kicked in and worked, after the form of Steve Elliott wasn't good enough.

More importantly, Forest won the European Cup, so the lads got their win bonuses – and of course repeated it again in the following season. For a manager of a provincial team, to do what he did at Nottingham Forest was truly unbelievable. I really think Brian should have been knighted for what he achieved over such a short period of time.

Fans have often said to me I must have been kicking myself for leaving. Well no! I won things at Forest and I enjoyed it. I might have stayed and not played in the European Cup run, who knows? I don't like looking back and I have no regrets on leaving Forest. If I had looked back on every decision I'd made I would have gone mad by now: as always, I did what I thought was best at the time. Of course, I would have preferred to have played for Forest in the European Cup – but I would not have been happy playing on the terms offered by Brian Clough.

I've always said I have no regrets whatsoever!

8

Name That Toon

"I'm telling you now, Bill, if you don't get us up into the first division in the first two years I'm leaving."

****

I was about to join a club which had just dropped into Division Two at the end of the 1977/78 season and it was as though I had gone back to square one with my career. Richard Dinnis was replaced as manager by Bill McGarry at the start of the 1978/79 season, and I was Bill's first signing. It was Bill's intention to sign a lot more players to improve the squad in the hopes of gaining promotion at the first attempt. That was the promise, anyway.

I was well aware of the importance of the nostalgic number 9 shirt, previously worn by the likes of Hughie Gallagher, Jackie Milburn and Malcolm MacDonald, so I knew the fans would expect me to deliver goals. In fact, it was one of the main reasons why I joined the Magpies – that and their passionate fans. They say if you hang 11 Newcastle United shirts on a washing line, 20,000 fans will turn up to watch them. The fans were just football crazy up there, so the expectation was sky high when I arrived at St James's Park. However, I had cut down my chances of winning an England cap by joining Newcastle. Forest were always in the limelight, so naturally the players got more chances to show what they could do.

Most new players to the club stayed in the New Kent Hotel in Jesmond, which was about two miles out of the city and at that time owned by a Newcastle supporter called Alan Stalker. However, I ended up initially staying in the Holiday Inn, in a place called Wideopen, six miles from the city centre, which didn't go down too well with some people – including Alan Stalker. When I checked in at the Holiday Inn for the first time, the receptionist asked me if I was Peter Withe from Newcastle United and said that the inn-keeper was expecting me.

'He's in the restaurant and his name is Peter Taylor.'

My response was instant: 'You winding me up?' I told the girl that I just left a Peter Taylor in Nottingham – could it really be the same one? Surely it can't be him asking me to come back. Anyway, it became a bit of a standing joke with the lads, who all thought I was a bit of a 'big-time Charlie', staying in a different hotel to everyone else – but Bill McGarry had told me to stay there.

There was one time when the Holiday Inn was full and I had to stay in the New Kent. Their receptionist was, in fact, Alan's daughter, and she made a joke about me not wanting to stay in her father's hotel.

'Dad will be pleased you're staying in his hotel for a change.'

I hadn't met Alan so, in the evening, as that was the only time Alan worked, John Blackley introduced me to him just before we went out for a few drinks. It was a bit awkward actually, because he genuinely thought I didn't want to stay in his hotel. The usual after-game routine was that we'd all go out to a night club called Tuxedo Junction, and Alan would come along with us. As it was my first time at the club, I instinctively walked to the front of the queue, thinking we'd be let in as VIPs. I looked round and the rest of lads were standing at the back of the queue so I shouted out to them.

'What are you all standing there for?'

One of the lads replied, 'We're queuing up to get in!'

The doorman looked confused. I walked up to the doorman and said, 'Are you the owner?'

The doorman responded, 'No, no, Mr Quadrini's the owner.' I asked to see Mr Quadrini and told the doorman who I was. After a few minutes, I was allowed into the club and went to see Mr Quadrini, who was sitting in the restaurant. I sat down and introduced myself and explained what I wanted.

'You know we've got 12 players standing outside queuing up to get into the club? My point is that these 12 players will enhance your club because of who they are. You should want Newcastle United footballers to be in your club, and you absolutely don't want them queuing up – you should be making them all VIPs. They won't just have the odd pint of lager – they're serious drinkers these lads.' I sat with him for about an hour and he eventually gave me a VIP pass and some more for the lads. I went back outside to get the lads and gave them their passes.

Alan and I went to the bar and he bought all the lads a drink. As soon as they picked up their drinks, they all disappeared and left me and Alan alone at the bar, which allowed Alan to break the ice.

'All the players that come to this football club stay with me at my hotel, but you don't.'

I responded by saying it wasn't my choice not to stay at his hotel.

'Basically, you're peeved that I went to stay in the Holiday Inn rather than staying in your hotel? Do you think it's a personal thing between me and you?'

At that point all the players returned to the bar, and Alan said, 'Oh, alright. Can you get another round of drinks?' as he looked towards the barman.

I said to him, 'What are you doing?'

He told me he was buying all the players another drink to which I said, 'Well, you ain't buying me a drink.' I wanted to buy him a drink rather than him buying all the drinks all the time. I told the other players to sod off and made it clear that I was going to pay my way if we were to become friends and have a drink together. 'Where I come from, you buy a drink then I buy a drink. Not you buy a drink, you buy a drink and you buy another drink. And all those prats over there, they should buy you a drink as well.' I think that broke the ice and we later became great friends, and we always stayed at his hotel after that initial hiccup.

One night, Alan and his hotel night watchman, who was celebrating his golden wedding anniversary and had worked for Alan for many years, were chatting in the hotel bar and Alan invited him to have the party at the hotel. The night watchman shrugged his shoulders and declined the offer as he said he couldn't possibly afford to splash out that kind of money and it was a bit too upmarket for him anyway. Alan insisted he came and had a meal for four and he offered to pay for everything. He also offered to send his Rolls Royce to pick them up. When Alan told me about the Rolls Royce, I said to him, 'Where's the Rolls? I'll go and pick them up.' Alan didn't like that idea but I tried to convince him and said I would dress up in a chauffeur's uniform and hat. He eventually gave me the address, and it turned out to be on a rough council estate. There were kids playing football in the road and they all stopped and turned to look at this flash Rolls Royce driving up their street. I pulled up at the house, knocked on the door, and lowered my hat as he answered the door.

I lifted my head up and said, 'Your cab awaits you, sir.'

The guy nearly fell over and said in his broad Geordie accent, 'Bloody hell, man. Is that Peter Withe?'

All four of them got into the car and I drove them to the hotel. When we saw Alan at the hotel, the night watchman said, 'That's made my day. I can't believe it's my anniversary and you sent Peter Withe to drive me in your Rolls Royce to pick me up.'

Alan responded, 'I didn't send him – he volunteered to come and get you.'

He was all but speechless and said, 'Bloody hell. I can't believe it – bloody Peter Withe!'

After a few weeks living in hotels when we first moved up to the North East, we finally rented a house in the Ashington area, 15 miles north-east of the city, near the coast. We had sold our property in Nottingham, but rented a furnished house for a few months while we were waiting for our move to be completed and our new house was being renovated. Ashington is only famous for two reasons: the Charlton brothers were born there, and probably the most famous Geordie footballer of them all, Jackie Milburn was born there too. Ashington is a bleak place when it's cold, which is most of the time because of the wind that comes off the North Sea. One freezing cold night, we had a knock at the door and Kathy opened it to find six men wanting to speak to me. I went to see who they were and what they wanted and as it happened they were all Newcastle fans from the local working men's club who had somehow found out where I was living. The guys told me they wanted to take me out to visit some of the local social clubs in Ashington, which I agreed to, and we sorted out a suitable date and time. A few days later, they came to collect me, and one of the guys said, 'Let's see how many clubs we can visit today.' I asked how many clubs there were in Ashington. It wasn't a big town but there were 22 working men's clubs. I couldn't believe it. When I asked how many pubs there were in Ashington, the same guy said, 'There's only two.' As you can imagine, it was a very working-class town.

We visited the first club, and when I tried to walk in, the doorman stopped me and asked me where my CIU card was. I said matter-of-factly, 'I haven't got a card.'

He obviously didn't recognise me and in his broad northern accent he said, 'Well yer can't cum in here unless yer affiliated.'

The six guys who took me there all said who I was to the doorman. 'It's Peter Withe, the footballer,' but the doorman wasn't having any of it.

'I don't care, he's not coming in here without a card.'

One of the lads told him I was getting a card from the secretary but they had to make me an honorary member until I had a full membership card. By the end of the evening, we had visited 10 of the 22 CIU clubs in Ashington but, unfortunately, we had to have a beer in each one. Two or three weeks later, the guys came back for me and we managed to get to a few of the other clubs. I went two or three more times after that as well, by which time I'd probably visited all the clubs in the town.

Bill McGarry had always been a hard taskmaster when it came to his training regime, but the first thing I noticed at Newcastle was that he'd completely changed his routine since our days together at Wolves. He was a great advocate of physical exercise and still held his Tuesday or Wednesday sessions in the gym; although he'd sometimes vary it by doing a physical session on the training ground. The gym sessions included weight training, agility and circuits; however, if we had a mid week game, we'd skip the physical session.

I think it was after my first season at Newcastle that I decided I wouldn't do any exercise during the summer break. After every season I'd played since I was young, I'd always kept myself in shape by doing some sort of exercise routine, whether it be long-distance running or gym work. But after that first season at Newcastle, I decided not to do anything for six weeks. It turned out to be a big mistake and I regretted it when we returned to pre-season training, as I found it so much more difficult to get going again. Pre-season in those days was a long, hard slog, unlike what it is now, where players are monitored for their fitness and stay fit all year round.

Jackie Milburn, the iconic Newcastle striker of the 1940s and 1950s was asked by Bill to come to coach the strikers for a short time. Jackie had retired from the game about 18 years previously, but he was the club's all-time highest scorer and was (and remains) a true club legend, and a really nice guy as well. However, his first training session will live long in my memory. He'd been watching me train and pulled me to one side.

'Yer know I've been watching yers, and yer get too close to the defenders. I want yer to get up to 'em like five yards away, knock the ball past 'em and ding it into the net.'

That was his trademark, but I laughed and replied, 'Jackie, I can't do that I'm not as fast as you were. You ran the 100 yards in 10.4 seconds. You were like lightning.' He was, in his day, the fastest player around, and I think he thought everyone else was as quick as he used to be.

We played West Ham one Saturday afternoon, and I was sitting in the stands at St James' Park with Kathy and the kids as I was either suspended (most likely) or injured. If I remember rightly, the club used to put the players who weren't playing in a certain section of the main stand at St James' Park, and I seem to recall a petrol bomb was thrown by one of the home fans. I thought it was a firework at first, until it exploded. It either hit someone or it connected with someone and their clothes caught fire. I'd never seen anything like that at a football match before – it was pretty frightening and to this day I don't know what initiated the missile being thrown. I suppose it was in the middle of the era of football hooliganism of the 1970s. It wasn't as if the ground was full, in fact quite the opposite, so it was quite a strange incident.

It was always cold in Newcastle, and another game I remember was a mid-week game against Wrexham at home. We must have had every type of weather you could think of during that game – rain, hail, sleet, and snow. It was freezing – and I mean *freezing*. I made a conscious decision early in my career that I would never wear long-sleeved football shirts, and that day was no different. Every player that day wore long sleeves, except for me. Footballers didn't wear gloves back then, either – god forbid if they did as they would have got quite some stick from their teammates. The wind was blowing from the Gallowgate End, and I remember the Wrexham goalkeeper, Dai Davies, took a goal kick. The wind was that strong, the ball went backwards and straight out of play for a corner. I'd never seen anything like it before – and the balls were fairly hard in those days, not like the balloons they play with today. The conditions were terrible and Dai Davies was complaining to the referee all through the match. He wanted to abandon the game, but the referee said he had to play at least 50 minutes because the club would have to give the money back to the fans if he played any less. When we'd played exactly 50 minutes the referee called time, just as it started to snow again, and we all ran off the pitch as fast as we could. It was impossible to play football – you couldn't pass the ball or do anything with it. We all got back into the changing room and we were all soaked and shaking trying to keep warm, and I remember little Terry Hibbitt, who only weighed 8 stone wet through, wasn't in the dressing room. We all thought he was having a fag somewhere as he smoked. I went back out on to the pitch and there he was, lying face down in the snow. He'd collapsed because of the cold. I picked him up in a fireman's lift and took him back into the dressing room to warm up. We had these pull-out heaters in the dressing room, and I remember putting Hibby inside one of the heaters to get him warmed up.

While I was at Newcastle I must have scored dozens of goals with my head, and a lot of them were diving headers, such as the one I scored at St James' against Blackburn when John Connolly crossed the ball from the left, and I dived in at the far post to score. I remember another diving header which went into the net like a bullet when we beat Fulham 3–1 at Craven Cottage. People very often ask me what was the best goal I ever scored and I'd have to say I scored it when I played for Newcastle. We were playing Oldham, which was funny because that was the club I was meant to have made my first league appearance against all those years ago. We were leading 2–1 and I went back to defend a corner in the 89th minute and headed it away towards Mick Martin, who then headed it forwards and started to run with the ball towards goal. I was running down the left-hand side screaming for the ball to be played to me and I was 30 yards out, on the left side of the box. Mick saw me and crossed the ball and I caught it with my left foot on the volley to land in the top corner of the net. It was a screamer! We won the game 3–1 in front of my whole family, who had travelled all the way from Liverpool to watch me play. After the game I asked them what they thought of my goal.

'What goal, Peter? Oh, did you score? We left five minutes from the end.'

I wasn't amused. My entire family had missed probably the best goal I have ever scored!

Another funny memory is just after the club opened a new stand at St James' Park, and I think we were playing Charlton. I was running for the ball at full speed towards the new stand (opposite the main stand) and managed to catch up with the ball and back-heel it to keep it in play, but the momentum took me forwards. The club had just erected a two-foot fence around the ground and it was about ten feet from the pitch and about six feet from the front row, and as I was heading towards the fence at full speed I was thinking to myself, 'Oh shit!! Fence!! Jump!!' So I jumped the fence and then thought, 'Seats!!', somehow turned myself mid-jump and ended up sitting down in the front row of the stand with a Newcastle fan either side of me, each holding a pint of beer. I looked at the lad on the left, took his drink off him, and had a swig.

'Ah, Newcastle Brown Ale. Sorry boys, I've got a game to get back to, I'll see you later, lads.' These two lads looked at each other in amazement as I jumped over the fence and rejoined the game.

My first season ended with me as top-scorer with 16 goals in 43 appearances. Bill had spoken to the media during the start of my second season saying, 'I wouldn't sell him for a million pounds. He's priceless because I couldn't replace him. In his present form, Peter is a better player than Bob Latchford, who is in the England team. Where would you get a replacement for someone like Withe today for less than £1m?' I was fairly settled in the North East but I knew things could change pretty fast in football. During the season we were hit by too many injuries and used over 30 players. The club was crying out for success but the crowds were really low. If we had played in Division One we would have had 46,000 in the ground every week but Division Two was a poor standard, and the fans were fed up with mediocrity.

Towards the end of the season, my younger brother, Chris, signed forms for Newcastle. He was 16 years old and a winger, but was proving himself a valuable left-back, and could also play in various other positions. He was young but grasped his opportunity with both hands.

I had become a keen golfer during my spell at Forest and as we had just moved from Ashington into our renovated house in Melton Park, I had the choice of two top-quality golf courses, located literally on either side of the main road where our house was situated. The City of Newcastle course was on one side and the Bridle Path course (Gosforth Park) was on the other. I got to know two of the pros at Gosforth driving range and it was there I started to play what I'd call 'proper' golf. My official handicap when I joined Gosforth was nine, but most of the time I was playing to about two. I played with the two pros on a regular basis and I nearly always beat them, even though they were playing off scratch.

I also played golf with Bill McGarry. Most football managers didn't like you playing golf during the week, but I was playing *with* my manager – that just wouldn't happen these days, that's for sure. During a round one day, I remember Bill saying that he wanted me as captain but he had a 'thing' about centre-forwards being captain of the team, so he chose someone else. I was OK with that – I just wanted to play football and wasn't bothered about being skipper.

I hadn't really mixed with Bill during my short spell at Wolves, but when I was at Newcastle I seemed to be closer to him; I was older and a bit wiser I guess, and he seemed to have adapted his training to suit the developing game. Golf was our common ground: Bill was a keen and proficient golfer who played off a handicap of five and he'd very often ask me to play a round after training or at the weekend. I'd just bought a new set of clubs from a mate of mine – they were Ping branded clubs and a pretty decent set at that. I had to contact their Gainsborough factory one day because I thought the clubs were the wrong size and they invited me to go there to get measured up. Apparently, Ping manufactured the first golf clubs that could be adjusted to your size. I was imagining that they would just swap my clubs for a new set that better 'fit' me; however, when I got to the factory they went through all sorts of tests and told me what I needed – basically, clubs that were an inch longer. I also needed a 'green spot', which meant the clubs appeared more upright. Once they had sorted out what I required, one of their guys put my new clubs into a vice and started to hit them with a hammer in order to set them correctly, which I thought was bizarre but was apparently a standard procedure. In the end, they went through my set and changed the loft on all my clubs to make them suitable for me to use.

The first time I got to play with them after they had been adjusted was with Bill at the City of Newcastle Golf Club. We were both associate members at the club because we belonged to Newcastle United, where all the staff automatically became members. Bill had a better handicap than me and used to say, 'We are playing as men,' even though we only played each other for a few quid. We both had a real competitive streak, but he still refused to give me any advantage. The weather didn't really bother us, but on one particular day the course was waterlogged and made it difficult to hit the ball. We came to a par 3 that had a winding stream near to the tee which had expanded with all the rain. The rain was so bad we had actually discussed packing it in, so we decided we were going to complete the hole then retire to the clubhouse. Bill teed off first and he hit a shot to the par 3. I then hit this excellent shot to the green but, as my hands were soaking wet, the club flew out of my hand, over the stream and landed in someone's garden, situated only a few yards from the edge of the course. Bill burst out laughing but I stood there in bewilderment, and he asked me what I was going to do. I told him I was going to jump the stream, which was probably 12 feet wide. Bill said I was stupid.

'Bill, I'm going to jump the stream! I'm not going to leave my flipping club in that garden.'

I took a running jump, got to the other side but found myself up to my knees in mud because the grass was so soft. I tried to pull myself out but my shoes wouldn't move! Eventually I got out, soaking wet and covered in mud. I then made my way up to the garden fence, climbed over it in an attempt to retrieve my club but some woman caught me and ran after me with a broom, shouting at me to get out! Before I could explain what had happened she had chased me over her fence and back on to the course. I stopped to think how I was going to get back over the stream, which was an even harder task as it would mean jumping upwards over the stream and there was no room to take a run. Bill, who was on the other side of the stream stood there shouting at me.

'How you going to get back to this side then?'

I then threw my club over to the other side of the stream and made a running jump at it. I managed to get over the stream somehow, only to be greeted by Bill, laughing his head off. I was literally covered from head to toe in mud and I was soaked. We eventually finished the hole and retired to the dry clubhouse and ordered a cognac each.

When Bill was manager at Wolves, he'd organise golf days for the players on a fairly regular basis, and he did the same at Newcastle, but less regularly. I had become a member of the Variety Club of Great Britain and was linked to the children's charity Sparks and several other organisations, and got invited to many golf tournaments all over the country; how Kathy put up with me I just do not know. Kathy accompanied me some of the time, but it was difficult to juggle the tournaments with looking after the kids. I was always getting requests to play in golfing events, but they would usually be on a Sunday, which was awkward as it was a family day.

One of the funniest events I played in was the Ray Clemence testimonial event at Skegness Golf Club. We had to drive from Newcastle to Skegness, which was a hell of a journey as there was no M18 motorway at the time, so it was a cross-country route. We arrived at the club a bit late and as we pulled into the car park I found out that everyone was waiting for me. So I collected my clubs, sorted myself out and made a mad dash to the first tee. I was the first player to tee-off and, as soon as I arrived, the announcer introduced me to the crowd and also made people aware that there was a yard of ale competition in a tent halfway down the fairway. The competition was hosted by Hooters, who were a tacky American hospitality group, so there were a load of girls wearing not much other than hot pants and skimpy orange tops, trying to attract the attention of the crowd. I stepped up to the first tee and struck the ball firmly but hooked it, and the ball hit one of the Hooters girls right on the backside and then landed just inside the tent. I turned to the crowd gathered around the tee and said, 'Somehow, I don't think I'm going to get that ball out of there,' and the crowd burst out laughing. Luckily, that was the worst shot I hit all day, and the rest of the event went well; I even won the 'nearest to the pin' prize.

The first year I was at St James' the club were sponsored by Martell but the following year they were sponsored by Hennessey and the man-of-the-match for each home game was awarded a bottle of cognac. We had no short supply of cognac in our house while I was at Newcastle, that's for sure! As part of the sponsorship deal, we had to play a game in France against the second division side UA Cognac. All the players met at the airport and we asked one another if anyone had a boarding pass, but no one did. There was then an announcement over the tannoy asking for the Newcastle United players to make their way to gate 9. You can imagine our surprise when we found out the sponsors had laid on two private jets for us to fly in, one with 'Martell' on the side and the other with 'Hennessey' on its body. I hung behind for a few minutes and one of the lads asked me what I was waiting for.

I replied, 'I'm waiting to see which jet the boss is going to get on.' Bill boarded the Martell plane so I decided to board the Hennessey one. We were greeted on board by hosts and they offered us drinks – cognac of course. I started chatting to the hosts serving the drinks and asked one of them how long he'd been in the job.

He replied, 'No, no, I'm Claude Hennessey – I own the company.' I thought he was joking and asked him why he came on board to serve a bunch of footballers. 'Yes, yes, I wanted to make sure everything was perfect.' Throughout that short flight to France, Claude talked about the business and educated me on cognac.

The game was a typical friendly, but I scored another screamer. The goal was exactly the same goal as I'd scored the week before in a league match at Oldham, but when I weaved away to celebrate I saw the linesman had his flag up and had disallowed it for offside. Ten minutes later, I struck another sweet volley and, yet again, the French linesman put his flag up, but the referee, who was British, told the linesman to put his flag down and awarded the goal. In the space of three weeks I'd scored three of the best goals I'd ever scored but only two were allowed.

Newcastle was quite a sociable football club, and we'd very often go to visit different clubs around the city. On one occasion some of the players were invited to go to an ex-servicemen's club, and we were asked to join in on their games nights which were mainly darts and dominoes, but one night it turned out to be a set of 'tests' which had to be completed and usually involved eating or drinking. One of the challenges involved eating half a dozen cream crackers, which seemed ludicrous, but we took up the challenge regardless. Everyone had a chance to participate and when the lads asked me which challenge I wanted to do, I said I'd do whatever was left. When it came to be my turn, I was left with eating six hard-boiled eggs. I could eat like a horse back then so downing six boiled eggs posed no problem for me. The other guys had done it before against other clubs so they knew exactly what they were doing. The lad I was up against even had his own technique: he was taking the yolk out of the eggs and eating the whites before swallowing the yolks whole at the end. Everyone thought he was doing the right thing and I didn't know what I was doing because, apparently, the yolks make you choke. But by the time he was downing his fifth egg-white I'd already eaten all of my six eggs whole. He still had the six yolks to eat so I'd beaten him.

The next test was to drink a pint of beer, which I thought sounded more like it, but just as the referee started the clock he said, 'On your marks, get set ... Oh, we forgot to tell yer, you have to drink it through a straw and with your hands behind your back ... Go!' When the straws were put into the glasses, the game started and I downed my pint. I saw my competitor was still drinking his so I picked up my straw and put it into his glass and finished off his pint too.

The lads said they'd been playing their joker in the previous two games, which was why we won the challenges. It was great fun and we ended up doing it quite often as a group, going round to different social clubs in the area and mixing with the locals. Back in those days, we just did things off our own backs, unlike nowadays when the community officers organise events for players. You just wouldn't ask modern-day footballers to do anything like that – visiting hospitals is about the limit for a lot of players.

One of the downfalls of being a professional footballer is almost certainly that your career requires you to regularly uproot your family. That was not only difficult for Kathy and me, but also difficult for the kids. Gareth was born in Ashington Town when we were in the rented furnished house, shortly before we moved to Melton Park. We already had Jason and Stephen, so for a family of five to move from the Midlands to the North East was a major upheaval. Jason was eight at the time and he had a friend who lived two doors away whose father was a well-known comedian in the North East called Spike Rawlings. Little did I know back then, but Spike was an ex-professional footballer and had played for my old club, Barrow, in the mid-1960s. He got his first taste of showbiz in 1969, after the half-time entertainment failed to show up and Spike stepped in and performed in front of the crowd. In 1976 he shot to fame when he won the TV show *Opportunity Knocks* that led to his own TV show.

One day after school, Spike's son came running to our door in a panic and told us some kids were trying to kill Jason. Apparently, some kids had got hold of Jason and tied a rope round his neck; they weren't intentionally trying to kill Jason as his friend suggested, but were trying to pull him over a tree and in doing so were choking him. It was one of those games that kids play that very often goes horribly wrong. I managed to get to him just in time and took him home, but because of the seriousness of the incident I had to call the police. After a police investigation it was found that Jason was suffering at school – he was being bullied because I was a famous footballer. I didn't understand why he should suffer just because I was famous – were the kids seeking attention or were they jealous of Jason having a famous dad? I just couldn't come to terms with the reasoning behind their behaviour, but I guess it was one of those difficult incidents you sometimes have with your kids as they grow up.

I'm pretty sure most people think bullying and the like doesn't happen to famous people but I can confirm that's a big misconception: we've had our fair share of hassle over the years. We were just like any other family bringing up our kids, with all the trials and tribulations everyone has to face. I can recall an occasion when we'd all gone out for the day except for Jason, who had been naughty; I think he'd tipped Kathy's expensive Chanel perfume all over the bathroom floor, so we reprimanded him. We'd had a nice family day out (minus Jason, who was being looked after by the babysitter) but when we arrived home all hell broke loose. The babysitter was in a right state and explained to us that Jason had dialled 999 and told the fire service his brother's room was on fire. The fire brigade had acted on the call and had sent a fire engine out to our house while we were out. Of course there was no fire and the fire brigade had a wasted journey; it was a serious offence, so they left a note for me to ring them as soon as possible. When I went to see the fire officer he told me how serious it was to waste their time. He couldn't have been any more explicit and suggested I brought Jason in to see him. The next day I took Jason in to see the fire officer and he got a talking to from him, as well as from me. Suffice to say Jason didn't do anything like that again.

Looking back at my time at Newcastle and the support we had from the fans in those days, it's clear that the club was just desperate to get back into Division One – just as desperate as I was, really. I didn't want to leave the club at the end of the first season there, and it was in all the papers that I was going to be the highest paid player in Division Two and Newcastle were going to move heaven and earth to keep me at the club.

Alan Stalker said to me that day, 'Look, Peter, they're going to offer you a fortune to keep you here so why don't we open a wine bar in the city – Kathy and her friend Mary can run it. You can put your memorabilia up in the bar and it will make us £500 a week easily. You'll have your wages from the club and you'll have a healthy income from the bar. I'll fund the renovation and I'll get it up and running and get sponsors from breweries.'

It was a good idea but I wasn't sure and told him not to make any plans until I had a firm offer from the club.

We had finished that second season 9th in the league, one place below the previous season, and I guess that the two seasons I'd been at St James' Park hadn't worked out as I would have hoped. My contract was up, and it was standard practice when your contract was coming to an end that the club would send a registered letter to your house so you received it exactly two weeks after the contract ended. It was a strict timeline; it couldn't be any later or any earlier. If it was received any later or the letter wasn't sent at all, you were entitled to a free transfer. It was a bit of a strange rule; however, on the deadline of the two weeks, which was a Saturday, I received the registered letter. I thought (and hoped) the letter wouldn't come and I could get a free transfer but I signed for the letter and opened the envelope and read the contract offer. I was already on £240 a week and I read the detail of the offer and focused on the amount – £250 a week. I was meant to be the highest-paid player in the division and the highest-paid player in the history of Newcastle United, but all they offered me was a miserly £10 extra a week. All through the contract negotiations, Bill McGarry hadn't told me what they were prepared to offer me and all he said was, 'I've left it to them [the club] to sort it out.'

Anyway, I folded the letter up and put it in my pocket. Kathy and I often went to the New Kent Hotel for a meal and a few drinks, so I took it to the hotel where I was due to meet Alan, who only worked in the evening.

I said to Alan, 'You remember what we were talking about earlier on?' and I placed the letter on the reception desk in front of him and said, 'That came for me this morning.'

We left him to go into the restaurant for our meal and Alan started to read it and focused on the amount. His broad Geordie accent carried through to the restaurant.

'Them bastards! They've sold us down the river again. I can't bloody believe it.'

He was livid.

That was the last straw – I wanted to leave Newcastle.

I went straight in to see Bill McGarry on the Monday morning.

'Is that the final offer?' I think he knew that was all they were prepared to pay all along and then I said something like, 'I don't care what they offer me I'm going anyway ...' The club had called my bluff.

Bill didn't want me to leave the club because he thought they had a chance of promotion in the third season but it was too late. I told Bill that we had had the same conversation when I signed for him, that I had given it the two years I promised, but I needed to get back into Division One. For me, it was all about winning trophies, and at that time I could not see myself winning things at St James' Park.

It was fair to say Alan was our best friend while we were in Newcastle, so it was sad that we had a big falling out just before my contract was due to end. Alan ended up having a go at Kathy, although I wasn't there to witness it. Alan had apparently said to Kathy something like, 'The clothes on your back and the things you buy – us supporters pay for all that.' Kathy was furious, and as soon as we met up that evening she told me she wanted to leave Newcastle there and then. I thought what Alan had said was out of order and I told him so. I think he'd had a few drinks too many, but at the end of the day he had said those words, whether he meant them or not. It -eft a bad taste. We ended up walking out of his hotel that evening for the last time.

A number of offers from first division clubs had come in for me – both Aston Villa and Leeds United showed interest and I was now free to talk to other clubs. I had made up my mind that my future was away from St James' Park, so I drove to Leeds to speak to their manager, Jimmy Adamson, which turned out to be an experience in itself. I wanted to get something sorted out quickly, before I went on holiday, so I knew in which direction I was heading for the new season, but I also wanted to be sure I was making the right decision. When I got to Elland Road I met with Jimmy and he said the chairman would be joining us, and it was at that moment that alarm bells started to ring. Their chairman at the time was Manny Cousins, famous for the Cousins furniture chain stores. A few minutes later, Manny burst into the board room, introduced himself and told me who he was as I had no idea at the time. I jokingly asked him if he was going to give me free furniture, but he soon brought me down to earth and lowered my expectations.

'Anything you want, I'll give you 10 per cent discount,' he replied, and I immediately burst out laughing.

Manny was Jewish and ignored my laughter and carried on.

'We pay good wages here but we don't pay mega money.' I said I didn't want to know about how much they wanted to pay me as I was more interested in the team and how they would play me.

He then turned round and said, 'How much money do you want?'

I told him again that I didn't want to discuss money. 'It's not about money. It's not about your budget and what you spend on players.'

We carried on chatting about other things, and after another ten minutes he asked me again how much money I wanted. By now I was getting annoyed.

'Look, I've told you, it's not about the money.'

This pattern repeated five or six times, and I was getting browned off with his persistence in getting me to agree a wage, so I said to him in a serious manner:

'I want £50,000 signing on fee, and £25,000 a year.'

Manny went red and immediately spluttered, 'Err, well you won't get that here! We can't afford to pay that. You know, it would cost a lot of money just to buy you.'

I responded, 'Why do you keep asking me about the money, then?' I was calling his bluff and just quoted a stupid figure to get a reaction from him and to shut him up. Manny had said his piece by then and walked out of the room and left me with Jimmy, shaking his head.

As soon as Manny had closed the door, Jimmy said to me, 'That's what you have to work with sometimes, you know.'

Jimmy must have known that I wasn't going to sign for him, but he was a gentleman about it and asked me to let him know what I decided. I said to him that I would tell him either way and I also told him I had been targeted by other clubs. Apart from Villa, I later heard that West Bromwich Albion were interested in me and their manager at the time was 'big Ron' Atkinson. However, he didn't pursue his early interest in me because he had apparently taken advice from Wolves manager, Sammy Chung, who had warned 'big Ron' that I 'wasn't brave enough in the box.' Ron had made a decision based on someone else's opinion but he admitted to me years later that he had made a mistake in not signing me for Albion. I'd like to think Ron used his own judgement after that episode.

Another top manager, Terry Venables (then manager of Crystal Palace), was also keen to sign me but nothing materialised of that. Apparently, he'd promised their fans he'd make a big signing and I was his top target. But I was also attracting interest from America. Tulsa were talking in terms of phenomenal money, but there would have been problems because of their apparent refusal to pay a transfer fee. Had I gone there I could have been banned for life from football anywhere outside the United States.

A couple of days after speaking with Jimmy at Leeds, I got a phone call from Bill McGarry who said that Everton were in for me and wanted to pay £300,000 for my services. As an Evertonian myself, I was obviously very interested to talk to them; who wouldn't be interested in the opportunity to play for their boyhood club? As soon as I heard they were interested I rang Kathy and said, 'How do you fancy going to live in Liverpool again?' I don't think she was overly keen or very impressed but she didn't stop me going to speak to them. I rang my father before I left Newcastle to tell him I was driving to Goodison to meet with Gordon Lee, and he asked me if he could come with me. Of course I couldn't take him, so I said I'd see him before the meeting then go back home afterwards for a cup of tea.

When I arrived at Goodison Park, Gordon introduced himself and led me into the boardroom. It was ironic that Gordon had been Newcastle manager before Bill McGarry and had only left to take over at Everton in 1977. Just as at Leeds, Gordon said he had to wait for the chairman, Mr Carter to join us. Those alarms bells rang out again. I was a bit surprised at having to wait for Mr Carter after the debacle I'd just encountered at Elland Road with Manny, so I said flippantly, 'Who is Mr Carter? Does he pick the team? Does he know the tactics? Does he know where you see me playing?'

To all of these questions Gordon answered, 'No.'

I then said, 'So why do I want to see Mr Carter?'

Gordon looked shocked and surprised and then asked me, 'Oh, so you want to know them sort of things, then?' I was taken aback by that and carried on explaining what I wanted to find out.

'Err, yeah. I want to know what position I'm going to play; who's going to play with me; what system you're going to play.'

Gordon started to get a bit more interested in me then, and began to tell me about his plans for the Everton team. He told me he was selling Bob Latchford and about six other first-team players. I was thinking, 'If he's selling seven players, who's he buying?' Gordon then told me which players he was going to get in to replace these lads.

'Well, I'm going to get you for a start, then I've already got Peter Eastoe.' I knew Peter from Wolves and it seemed strange he was going to pair me with Peter because he hadn't got much pace even though he was a good finisher. He carried on, 'I'm going to look for another striker and a midfielder.'

The chairman, Mr Carter, then entered the room and introduced himself. The first thing he said was, 'We're getting rid of all the big hitters.' It dawned on me that the seven players he was trying to get rid of were all on good money and the club were going to downsize. The next thing he said to me was, 'How much do you think you'll cost?' I told him that Villa had put a bid in for me for £500,000. 'Nah, we're not putting anything like that in. We'll go to a tribunal – you're out of contract.' The next thing he said was the usual question all chairmen ask, 'So, how much money do you want?' I asked Mr Carter what his budget for players was but he ummed and ahhed a lot, and then he said to me, 'Well, we can maybe give you £400 a week. How does that sound?'

I told him I would think about it, as I had other teams interested in me. I was already on £240 at Newcastle (rising to £250) so that would be nearly double my money. He was expecting me to make up my mind there and then, but I told him I had other clubs to talk to (which I did). Again he kept trying to persuade me to make an instant decision. He knew I was an Evertonian so he was playing on that a bit, trying to get me to make a snap decision but I wasn't having any of it. In effect, what Gordon had done during our meeting was to convince me Everton were going nowhere, but I left Goodison without making any decision and went to see Dad before driving back to Newcastle to tell Kathy. She asked me what I thought and I said, 'Well, I'm not making any decision yet; I've got to talk to Villa first.'

My main motivation was not so much the money as to win things. I thought back to the dream I'd had six or seven years previously – the dream that one day I would play for Aston Villa. It was probably an innocuous dream, and some people might wonder why Aston Villa, but I still felt there was something in it. It occurred to me that maybe I would be joining Villa after all because their manager, Ron Saunders, was very keen to speak to me. But I was still 'owned' by Newcastle as they held my registration, even though I was out of contract. Prior to the Bosman ruling in 1995, owning clubs were able to prevent players from joining another club even if their contracts had expired, and at that time in 1980, the transfer tribunal had just been introduced to resolve disputes over fees between clubs when transferring players at the end of their contracts.

I was effectively in a state of limbo and I wanted to sort it out quickly. However, things weren't clear-cut. Relations between Villa chairman, Harry Kartz, and manager Ron Saunders had deteriorated. Dave Geddis had been brought in from Ipswich in the previous October but had failed to make an impact at Villa, so they wanted me in to score the goals. Apparently, Saunders had agreed a £750,000 transfer of Mick Ferguson from Coventry, but the board withheld the cash so that deal collapsed, and there was a risk to my transfer to Villa because of the rift between Saunders and Kartz.

I finally decided to see what Ron Saunders had to say and arranged to meet him at the Metropole Hotel at the NEC near Birmingham. Ron had checked into the hotel, so I went up to his 'interview' room. I didn't know it at the time but he'd apparently been interviewing other players all that day, so he hadn't booked it specially to meet up with me.

When I actually met with him he told me, 'I've got a very good team here. I've got a goalkeeper called Jimmy Rimmer; two centre-halves in Allan Evans and Ken McNaught; I've got a good midfielder in Gordon Cowans, one of the best in the country, and I want you to play up front with

Brian Little. You'll be a lethal partnership. Brian has played with centre-forwards of your stature before and he needs someone like you to take the weight off him to score the goals.' In my mind I thought he'd already got a great team and if I signed I'd only be adding to that.

Then Ron sold me the club in a couple of sentences: 'You'd be the final piece in the jigsaw. If you sign for this club we'll win the league.'

At that point I knew Ron meant business. He definitely knew who and what he wanted. Apparently, he had wanted to sign me in the previous season but for some reason the deal fell through. Ron was a winner. He was also a former striker himself so he knew what he wanted from me. There was no pressure for me to sign, unlike at Leeds and Everton, and more importantly, there was no sign of the chairman. The big difference between my meeting with Ron and the other managers was that he was open and honest about what he paid his players and what he wanted to pay me.

'All my top players earn £500 a week. I'm not one of these managers who will pay one player this much and another player that much. That way, the younger players have a goal to achieve – and that is to earn £500 a week. I've agreed a £500,000 fee with Newcastle so you'll get your 5 per cent of the fee.' It was refreshing to hear a manager know exactly what he wanted me to do and where I fitted in, and to say so adamantly that the club were going to win the league was music to my ears.

In those days, bonuses in football were almost as important as the weekly wages clubs paid the players. There was a hunger in the players, not only to play week in, week out but also to earn their bonus when the club won games. Ron told me about a new bonus scheme he was planning to introduce.

'It will be the best bonus scheme in the league. We'll be paying for success and not for failure. If we're in the top four you'll get a bonus of £500 a win, doubling your wage, and we have a sliding scale according to what position in the league the club are in.' Ron explained that there wasn't any appearance money on offer for the senior players because they were expected to be in the team, but for the younger players, there was – it was their incentive to get in the first team and stay there. It sounded like a fair scheme to me.

When the meeting had finished Ron asked me to go away and think about it. I promised I'd let him know either way very soon. I went away from that meeting with Ron in a positive frame of mind, and as soon as I got home I contacted Gordon Lee at Everton and told him what Ron had said. Gordon asked me what sort of money Ron had offered so I told him straight and he said he'd get back to me. Two days later, Gordon called me and offered me nearly £600 a week, £100 more than Villa had offered. I told him I'd decide within three or four days and would let him know.

A couple of days later, Kathy and I took the three kids to visit our friends, Dennis and Sheila Collett who lived near Stratford-upon-Avon, something we did on a regular basis. I'd already discounted going to Leeds, even though I hadn't turned them down, and it seemed to be a choice between Everton and Villa. That night, we sat down together and discussed all the pros and cons of moving to Merseyside versus moving to Birmingham. We discussed things like where we would live, and talked about the possibility of moving to the Wirral rather than Liverpool, an area where a lot of Everton and Liverpool players lived; we talked about schools for the kids and many other things like family ties and if we would have hassle from them if we returned there. There were pros and cons of moving back home but the number one thing for me was still whether I would win anything with Everton. The answer to that was no – there wasn't a cat in hell's chance. They had finished the 1979/80 season in 19th place in Division One, four points above the relegation zone, whereas Villa had finished in 7th place and were on the up. Added to that, when Gordon Lee had told me he was going to sell most of his first team it had rung alarm bells, and he was essentially building a new team from scratch. Ron Saunders, on the other hand, already had a good team in place and wanted me to complete the jigsaw.

I had virtually made up my mind to sign for Villa, but the local media had put up a story that I had been offered a three- or four-year contract totalling six figures to become 'the richest footballer in Newcastle's history', as a tempter to stay at the club. Bill had apparently said in the papers that if I did stay, I'd be there for life with the substantial offer. The crux of the matter was that I wanted to play in the first division again, so any offer Newcastle made me was simply not enough. The story was a load of rubbish. It was clearly all talk from the board who were anxious to appease the fans after a disastrous season. I don't think they ever thought I'd accept it anyway.

I'd decided in my head as soon as I met with Ron at the Metropole, but my heart was still thinking about my boyhood club, Everton. I told Dennis I was almost certain to be signing for Villa and had planned to go and see Ron again after that weekend. Dennis and Sheila had a huge house in Stratford-upon-Avon and it had a built-in sauna, which was somewhat unheard of in the 1980s. Before we went out for dinner, Kathy and I made use of the sauna and sat there for some time, relaxing and thinking about my future – our future – but our peace and quiet was interrupted by Dennis, who knocked on the sauna door to tell me Ron Saunders was on the phone and wanted to speak to me. He asked me what my plans were and I told him that I was planning to see him on the Monday. Ron asked me if there was a problem or a sticking block, so I told him I'd also spoken to Everton and Leeds. I also told him Gordon had offered me more money and they wanted to go to a tribunal to agree a fee. Ron was adamant he didn't want to go to a tribunal and was going to pay the full £500,000 fee. I told Ron the difference was another £100 a week and he then said, 'If I do something about the fee will you come and join us? I'll speak to Bill McGarry and come back to you in a couple of hours – I'll ring you back on this number.'

Ron kept his word and rang me back within a couple of hours.

'Right, the difference in the money we basically took off the fee. Because I'm paying £500,000 for you, they [Newcastle] don't want to go to the tribunal with Everton and so they have agreed to give you the difference.'

It basically meant Newcastle would pay me what was effectively an ex-gratia payment of £15,000 out of the transfer fee which equated to the difference between the wages Everton offered (£600 a week) and what Villa were prepared to pay (£500 a week) over the three-year contract.

It was a great offer, but honestly I would have turned Everton down anyway, as hard as it was for my inner child to face.

I hadn't signed for Villa yet, but I remember listening to the local radio station, BRMB that evening interviewing a few of the Villa players including Kenny Swain. They were asking their opinions on me signing for Villa and I was wondering where they had got the information from, as nothing had been made official. There was even a phone-in show about it saying I'd already signed. Later that day, Bill McGarry rang me to confirm the deal had been agreed with Villa and that he didn't want to go to the tribunal. I immediately rang Ron Saunders to tell him I'd meet him on the Monday to sign and assured him I wouldn't be joining any other club in the meantime. Ron wanted me signed up as quickly as possible just in case a late bidder came in for me.

The pros didn't stack up for me to join Everton – they weighed in favour of Villa by a mile in most respects. When I told my father I wasn't joining Everton he was gutted, but when I said I wanted to join a club because of what my head said rather than my heart I think he understood. I was 28 years old and it was a big decision to make. I didn't want my past ties to influence my decision – otherwise I would have signed for Everton for sure. It must be every boy's dream to play for his boyhood club – it had been my dream ever since I stood on the terraces selling programmes with uncle Harold all those years before. I got so close to fulfilling that dream, but the timing was all wrong. It brought back memories of when I was 13 or 14 years old and told my mates that one day I would play for Everton, to be dismissed with 'Yeah, right – in your dreams.' That was the heart talking, not the brain.

After two years in the second division at Newcastle, and having won things with Forest, I had to be sure that my next move would be the best for my hopes of winning a few more medals. I was still ambitious and thought I did enough to fulfil the Newcastle fans' hopes of me. My only regret was that we didn't deliver the success their superb fans deserved.

The time had come for me to emulate the success I had at Forest by returning to the top tier of English football. Besides, at the time, the first division represented the cream of the football profession and everyone wanted to play there.

It was nice to think I had the chance to play at Goodison but at the end of the day, the timing was just wrong. Everton were in a period of transition whereas Villa had the players they needed to succeed and wanted to add me to that squad. Everton just didn't have any chance of winning anything, and I had no regrets in passing them over in favour of Aston Villa.

9

Pinball Pete

"I've got a winning team here. You'll be the final piece of the jigsaw. If you sign for this club, we'll win the league."
Ron Saunders, former Aston Villa manager

****

On the Monday following that eventful weekend in Stratford-upon-Avon we made the short journey from Dennis and Sheila's to Villa Park to meet Ron Saunders. I'd given my word to both Gordon Lee at Everton and Jimmy Adamson at Leeds that I'd ring them as soon as I'd made up my mind which club I wanted to sign for. No sooner had I said hello to Ron, than I told him I wanted to ring Gordon and Jimmy to tell them I had signed for Villa. Ron wouldn't have it and said he wanted me to sign first. I knew what he was thinking at the time, and with hindsight, I'd have thought the same. He was thinking if I rang the other clubs they would offer me more money and I would change my mind. I reassured him that wasn't a possibility, but all he wanted was for me to sign.

He presented me with the contract and said I could sit in his office to phone the other clubs, but after I had signed the paperwork. After I had signed the four pieces of paper, Steve Stride, the club secretary at the time, took the contract away with him and left me to make the calls to Gordon and Jimmy. To be fair, Jimmy pretty much knew I wasn't going to sign for Leeds, but he thanked me for the phone call and wished me well. Inevitably, when I called Gordon Lee, he tried a last-ditch attempt at getting me to sign for Everton, but I told him I'd already made my mind up. He asked me if I'd signed the contract and I told him a bit of a white lie, and said not yet. Gordon wanted to go to speak to his chairman there and then, but I told him not to bother. It wouldn't have mattered if he'd come back and said he was going to give me £700 or even £7,000 a week; how could I have gone back to Ron and said Everton offered me more money and I was going to sign for them? There was no way I would have done that – some people may have, but I was brought up to be a man of my word and if I shook hands on something, I would hold to it.

Kathy and I went out for lunch to celebrate, and while we were eating, a party of kids wearing American football shirts walked in. I stared over towards them and who should walk in but my old Birmingham City manager, Willie Bell. He spotted me with Kathy and asked me what I was doing there, so I told him I was signing for Villa and he congratulated me and said I was making a good decision. Willie told me he'd left English football in 1979 to become an ordained minister and was now coaching a university soccer team called Liberty University. He wished me all the best and hoped everything worked out for me. It was a far cry from when we'd last met, all those years before.

We had started to think about where we wanted to live even before we left Ron's office; in fact we'd talked about it all weekend at Dennis and Sheila's. We liked Knowle, near Solihull, and it didn't take long to find a suitable property there. It just so happened that Ron lived there too – although our new house wasn't quite as big as his. It was just a question of selling the house in the North East and relocating to the West Midlands again. As it happened, it didn't take long to sell the house in Melton Park and we made a sizeable profit on it, which was a bonus. I also went on record saying that that house would be our last for a while, and I made a promise to Kathy that we wouldn't have to move again any time soon. She had followed me around the world and I owed it to her to settle down for a longer period of time. There's a saying that goes something like, 'behind every successful man there's a great wife.' Well, if it hadn't been for Kathy I wouldn't have found myself at Villa, nor would I find myself where I am today. We've been through thick and thin together and she's always encouraged me to do the right thing when my career wasn't going so well.

We needed a bit of stability for our boys as well. Jason was only nine years old and he'd already attended six different schools. One of the first things we did when we moved back to the West Midlands was to put Stephen and Gareth into a Montessori school in the area. I'll never forget it because they hated every minute there. The head teacher was a stern taskmaster and she noticed something wasn't quite right with Stephen and Gareth because they refused to move if they were told to do something. It became an issue and one the teachers suggested they might be dyslexic, so we went to get them both tested. We contacted someone who specialised in dyslexia and actually took all three of the kids to be tested, just to be on the safe side. As it happened, all three of them turned out to be dyslexic. When I read the report highlighting our kids' dyslexia, it could have been written about me as a kid. I was asked if I was dyslexic when I was a child and I responded by saying there was no such thing in those days, but I probably was. Nobody had ever heard of dyslexia when I was young and the fact that I hated school was beside the point; my worst fear was being asked to stand up in front of the class to read aloud because I simply couldn't read that well. When I left school I taught myself how to read, but to this day I still don't enjoy reading, and only read what I have to.

The house we bought in Knowle had a huge garden with fruit trees and plenty of space for the kids to play in. If the kids played at the bottom of the 150-yard garden you could just about keep an eye out for them, it was that long. One day, Stephen came running in shouting and screaming, 'Gareth's dying, Gareth's dying ...' When I looked outside I saw Gareth about halfway down the garden and all I saw was the blood on his face. I ran down the garden and picked him up but I couldn't make out where the blood was coming from. When I got him into the house I wiped the blood from his face and I noticed a hole in his head. When he'd calmed down he said he had run into a nail that was sticking out of a piece of trellis fence. We rushed him to the hospital, still bleeding, and when we saw the doctor he said he'd have to stitch up the wound immediately. The doctor then asked me to hold Gareth down while he stitched up the wound, as he was too young for a local anaesthetic. It wouldn't happen these days but back in the 1980s the doctors weren't happy for kids to have anaesthetics. Poor Gareth didn't know what was going on and almost screamed the hospital down through the pain of being stitched up. Having had stitches without a local myself, I knew what he was going through. It's a little bit easier when you're an adult, but young Gareth was understandably terrified.

£500,000 was a club record signing for Villa at that time. After all the upheaval of signing for a new club and relocating (again), we managed to get away for a couple of weeks before reporting for pre-season training at the start of July 1980. Unlike the previous pre-season I kept up a routine, as I knew that Ron's training would be tough going. I'd heard he was an old-school, hard taskmaster; that probably stemmed from his army days. I soon started to settle in and got to know the lads a bit. Dave Geddis came up to me after training one day and said he didn't realise how fit I was.

'You just run for fun, don't you?' Dave was a fit lad himself but he had a funny stride when he ran; however, where he had the pace, I had the stamina. I think I had shocked the backroom staff and the players because I was such a fitness fanatic.

The training at Villa was very tough. Quite often we would drive to a quarry near to the training ground at Bodymoor Heath and run up and down hills for the whole morning; it was either that or we'd be running round the circumference of Bodymoor several times. There was a very competitive edge at the club and that came across in the training – even running up and down the hills of the quarry would end up being competitive. I was the new player at the club and some of the apprentices thought they could beat me; but if they beat me once they didn't beat me the second time because they didn't have the mental stamina for it. I'd had a certain mental toughness all my life and that drove me on. I hated losing – always have done, still do and always will. Fridays would always mean five-a-sides and at the start of the season, Ron and his assistant, Roy MacLaren, would join in; however, I think they made a decision halfway through the season that the backroom staff wouldn't join us any longer, probably because we were playing at such a high tempo that someone might have got hurt.

Talking of apprentices, I thought some of them flitted around the place too much and had an 'easy come, easy go' attitude to the game that used to upset me. I wish I'd had the same training facilities at the age of 16 that they enjoyed but I also knew that working on the docks, getting up at 6am and not arriving home until seven at night didn't do me any harm. Some of them needed a year or two in industry, I thought; however, I loved working with the lads. One day, we met a dozen children in wheelchairs at Bodymoor after training, and I loved meeting them. It did me good to see those kids and I hoped it did the apprentices some good as well. It was easy to come into training and feel down in the dumps (everyone does it at some stage) and take everything for granted, but seeing those lads in wheelchairs I quickly realised I had nothing to moan about. At Newcastle we spent a lot of time visiting children in hospital, many of whom had only six or seven months to live. That taught me a lot about life's values.

I used to drop the boys off at school in the morning on the way to training at Bodymoor Heath. I usually got to the training ground before most of the other first-team players. I'd ask three of four of the youth-team lads to train with me while I was waiting for the other senior players to arrive. As time went on some of the other lads like Nigel Spink and Gordon Cowans became aware of this routine, so they would make the effort to come in earlier to join my pre-training session. All through my career I'd done more than was required so that I could be the best, whether it was practising my shooting or heading in general or something more specific. If I missed a chance due to poor technique I'd want to go out and work on that. Of course, what helped me also helped the team. If I practised shooting, the goalkeeper would be practising shot stopping; if I practised heading, the wingers would be practising their crosses and the goalkeeper his catching.

There was a culture of vitamin taking at Villa that I had never encountered at any other club I'd been at. I couldn't believe it – there were tablets for anything and everything. I remember Ron asked me one day how my sleeping pattern was.

'Well, I sleep like a baby,' I told him.

He told me about all the tablets he could offer; if I had anxiety he'd have a tablet for it, if I couldn't sleep he'd have another tablet for that; but I told him that a pint or two of Guinness usually did the trick. Ron was a forward-thinking manager who was always on the lookout for new and different methods to improve his team's chances, and this was one of them. He tried to make sure that all of his players took their vitamins after training: 'Don't forget to take your tablets, lads,' he'd say. However, it was up to the individual if he wanted to take them – most did but I chose not to. I have always hated tablets and I would always refuse anything basically because I couldn't swallow them. I didn't believe you could solve something by taking a tablet – I mean, I've never even taken headache tablets. I remember one particular day I returned home from training and I was absolutely shattered. Kathy gave me a cup of tea but I didn't realise until I woke up she'd put a sleeping tablet in it. I had a bloody great sleep that night though.

Apart from the tablets, Ron even had a faith healer called Olga Stringfellow come in (the same one used by top players at the time including Bryan Robson and Glenn Hoddle). She came to Bodymoor a few times but I only met her twice. She would come to talk to some of the lads, but it wasn't for me. Although no one knew at the time, I recently found out that Ron had started studying meditation at the age of 23. Some people ask me now how the likes of Ron and Brian Clough would get on in the modern game, and I really think that both of them would have been just fine: they were both adaptable and could cope with change.

I didn't know much about Ron Saunders before joining Villa, only what I'd heard from other players and a bit about him on TV. He'd already enjoyed some success at Villa in winning the League Cup in 1977 and his Villa side had had a few top-ten finishes in the league. However, he saw the 1980/81 season as the time to really push for the championship. I was the only player in the squad who had won the league and I think that was why Ron brought me into the fold. It was Ron's vision even before I joined the club to pair me with Brian Little, who had spent his entire playing career at Villa Park. Brian was a natural goal scorer and thrived when he played with a so-called 'big man' up front. He had played alongside some top strikers like Andy Lochhead, Andy Gray, John Deehan and Keith Leonard, but his playing career effectively came to a halt in April 1980 during an away game at Old Trafford when he suffered a knee injury. He never recovered and, sadly, at the age of 26, Brian retired from the game. It was a great loss to the club. He must have been devastated and, for me, it was a shame I didn't get a chance to play with him. However, later that year, Ron gave Brian his first break into coaching and a job as Villa's youth-team coach.

When one door closes another one opens and the emergence of a Villa youth-team player called Gary Shaw meant I would partner the blond-haired Brummie up front instead of Brian. Gary had played in three-quarters of Villa's games during the previous campaign, mainly on the left, but he was going to be Brian's replacement. Although Gary was ten years younger than me, our partnership worked from the start. In those days the strike partnership was inevitably a 'little and large' duo, unlike in today's football where there's usually one striker with a quick player behind the front-man. Our partnership was similar to the one I had with Trevor Francis at Birmingham and Tony Woodcock at Forest, in that we both scored goals but would also make goals for each other. It was also similar to the link-up I had had with Alan Shoulder at Newcastle. Although Gary wasn't the fastest, he had that natural instinct inside the box which made him look quick.

Our opening match of the season was away at Leeds. It could have been me playing against Villa had I signed for Jimmy, but I knew I had made the right decision as we beat them 2–1, with goals from Tony Morley and Gary Shaw. After winning the first home game 1–0 against Norwich I scored my first goals for Villa in an away draw at Manchester City. It wasn't until midway through October that I scored my first goal at home, and we were playing Spurs when I scored our third, at the famous Holte End. I will always remember that goal because it was probably one of the easiest I've ever scored. Their goalkeeper parried a shot away and straight into my path, and I hammered it into the net from about three yards – I couldn't miss really.

The first time we played Everton at Villa Park we were doing quite well in the league, but we lost the game 2–0. It wasn't what I came to Villa for – to lose to my boyhood team and the team I'd turned down. They had a defender called Mick Lyons who was a fit lad and pretty decent, and he taunted me after the game and was giving it all the chat.

'We stuck it up yer today. You should have come and joined us.'

In the changing room afterwards, Ron came in and said, 'That was the kick up the backside you needed. You all think it's going to be easy when you're flying but that's what happens when you don't put 100 per cent effort in.' Ron was right. We didn't play well on the day and carried too many players. We needed toughening up and he was the man to do it.

Ron was an ex-boxer and he used the toughness he'd learnt in the boxing ring to toughen his players up. He'd often walk past you in the corridor and punch you in the stomach unexpectedly, or get close up to you and grab hold of you round the head. Some of the lads wondered why he did that, but we later found out that he was, in fact, smelling your breath, making sure you hadn't been drinking the night before – at the same time as roughing you up, especially the younger lads.

Whatever Ron did after that Everton game seemed to have done the trick because we went on an incredible run which saw us win nine out of the next 12 league games and climb the table from 10th place to top of the league.

There was only once that I remember Ron and me disagreeing, and it was after a home game with Wolves. We'd won 2–1 and I played up front with Dave Geddis as Gary Shaw was injured. Dave was brought in from Ipswich as a replacement for Andy Gray but Dave was no Andy Gray – he wasn't even a centre-forward really, if I'm honest. We were two different animals. So for the first time ever, Ron called me into his office and told me he was going to leave me out of the next game and he was going to play Shawy alongside Geddis up front. He said I hadn't been effective enough in the last game.

'What do you mean "effective?"' I asked.

He replied, 'You seem a bit lost.'

I tried to explain that someone else (Dave Geddis) was trying to play my role when he should have been playing Gary Shaw's role. I went on to say when Dave played previously, he played in my role as an out-and-out striker, but in that game, he was effectively stepping on my toes.

It appeared Ron wanted me to play Gary Shaw's role. Gary wasn't the same type of player as me and I felt I couldn't play his part. I said to Ron that Dave should have made the runs into the far post, not me. I had to play outside of my usual position during that game and wasn't able to use my strengths.

Ron took it all in and agreed with my assumptions. He must have called Dave in after I'd left and explained what I'd said. Later that day, I spoke to Dave myself and explained what he should be doing in Shawy's role; that he had the pace to get into the near post areas and that he could then play differently to how I played. Basically, I was saying he could feed off me.

Needless to say, Ron didn't drop me for the next game, away at Crystal Palace.

No player likes being suspended but I missed three games during the December, including the local derby against Birmingham City. Dave Geddis happened to step into my number 9 shirt and scored a brace as we won 3–0 at Villa Park. He became the local hero for the weekend. We got through those three games with only one win and two defeats and I often think I could have helped the side out if I hadn't got myself suspended, but that's football I guess. I got suspended again in March for another two games, after reaching 30 penalty points. At the time I was blaming myself for losing those games and it was at a time the team needed the steadying influence of its experienced players. I'd scored five goals in the previous four games, playing as well as I'd ever done, so the suspension came as a blow. I was hoping Dave Geddis would play well and wasn't frightened of losing my place in the side. Individuals were not important in that Villa side as it was a team effort; and I never believed I had a guaranteed place.

I was on 14 league goals and wanted to beat my Nottingham Forest record of 16 goals in a season. I returned to face Leicester at Filbert Street and we won that game 4–2, and I scored a brace, equalling my personal record. We showed great character in the second half, coming back to win the game. We were top of the league and it looked like we would take some shifting. I was well on my way to scoring 20 league goals. Not only that, but the media were starting to call for me to be picked for England, with the 1982 World Cup not far away.

In the next game against West Bromwich Albion at Villa Park, a near-capacity crowd of 48,000 saw us beat our local rivals 1–0. I scored the winner, seeing off Albion's faint title chances. Dave Geddis played up front with me, in place of Gary Shaw, but in the 89th minute, Brendon Batson made a fatal blunder of making a back-pass. I read the situation perfectly and picked the ball up before Tony Godden. I lobbed it past their goalkeeper and was grateful when the ball rolled into the net, even though it seemed to take an eternity to get there.

Ipswich were always our main rivals that season but in the games we played against them we made a lot of mistakes, especially at Villa Park in the April, with five games to go. If I remember rightly, Des Bremner gave the ball away when we were all pushing forward and that led to Eric Gates scoring a great goal. We had three or four good chances after that; we had a penalty turned down when Gary Shaw was brought down in the box and we ended up losing the game. The fans and the media thought we had blown our chances. However, Ron was famously interviewed after the game by the BBC commentator, Tony Gubba, who intimated that the championship chase was over for Villa. Ron cleverly turned the interview round on Tony and said, 'If you think this is finished, do you want a bet against us?'

The Friday before our last home game of the season, against Middlesbrough, we trained as usual and all the players had lunch together. I noticed some of the lads seemed a bit tentative so I asked them what the matter was and they informed me that Middlesbrough were one of Villa's 'bogey' teams. I told them in all the games I'd played against Middlesbrough I'd never lost against them and, more importantly, always scored. That piece of information seemed to perk the players up a bit and most of them appeared to become positive about the game ahead. At the time it seemed like a good idea and it worked, even though it was a little white lie.

I remember talking to Tony McAndrew about that game when he was working at Villa with me in the 1990s and he told me the manager of Middlesbrough in 1981, John Neal had a team meeting with the players before the game with us and told the players the man to stop was Peter Withe. They had a centre-forward called Billy Ashcroft, a fellow-Scouser from Garston, the village next to the one I grew up in. Ashcroft told his manager that he'd play centre-back to try to mark me out of the game. When the game got under way, I hit the post early on and had a couple of other chances saved by their goalkeeper, Jim Platt. I think the BBC *Match of the Day* commentator, John Motson, said that Middlesbrough couldn't get out of their own half during that period – I had a point to prove after telling everyone my white lie, so I ran and ran trying to score. Tony McAndrew told me he'd said to Billy just before half-time:

'Are you going to get anywhere near Withe to mark him out of the game?'

Billy replied, 'He won't stop running!'

Luckily for me, I kept up my run of scoring against Middlesbrough and we beat the Teessiders 3–0.

After that game we felt there was no way Middlesbrough were going to beat Ipswich, so it was up to us to go to Highbury and get a result; we only needed a point to win the championship. It was all but over, but we still had a job to do. Our destiny was in our own hands at Highbury on 2 May 1981. The fans at Villa Park that Saturday afternoon were in a jubilant mood and celebrating as if we had won it already; however, Ipswich had a game in hand so we all thought the celebrations were a bit premature.

On the way down to Highbury, the atmosphere on the team coach was strange, if not a little subdued. We were looking forward to it like any other game and the plan was to go out and do what we had done all season, to play our normal offensive game. However, Arsenal had something to play for – a third-place spot – so it wasn't going to be a typical end-of-season match.

As it was, our game plan back fired on us. Willie Young scored the first goal for the Gunners and just as we were trying to claw our way back into the game, Kenny Swain made a mistake to let Brian McDermott in on goal, and the ball bobbled into the net. It was 2–0 to Arsenal before we knew it, but we could hear the buzz in the crowd at the Clock End where the 20,000 Villa fans were standing. Jimmy Rimmer, who was at that end in the second half, was trying to gather information from the Villa fans who were telling him that Ipswich were losing and he was trying to relay it to the players on the pitch. The information about the Ipswich score spread amongst the fans and all we could see and hear were Villa fans singing and dancing as if we were winning the game! As a player on the pitch we couldn't get our heads around what was happening, as we were losing 2–0 and trying to get on with the match. Eventually some of us got wind of what was happening at Ayresome Park and when the referee blew the final whistle, we were trying to get off the pitch as quickly as possible to confirm the score. Instead, we were mobbed by 20,000 Villa fans who were invading the pitch. We didn't play well at all; in fact I'd go as far as to say it was one of our worst performances of the season – but it didn't matter after all.

When we finally reached the dressing room, Ron was still waiting for official confirmation of the result from Ayresome Park even though 20,000 fans already knew it. A reporter finally confirmed to Ron that we were the champions and at that point the celebrations started in the dressing room. It was all pretty surreal. We really wanted to go back out on to the pitch once we found out the news, but the security guys told us it would be too dangerous to even go into the stands, as there were too many fans outside. The champagne arrived in the dressing room and we were all singing and dancing. Paul and Henry Fewtrell, who were friends of some of the players, managed to gatecrash their way into the dressing room and told the security guys they were reporters. They had a video camera with them so they took footage of the celebrations. Being footballers in the 1980s it wasn't a case of shaking the bottles of champagne everywhere because bubbly was far too expensive to waste, so we decided just to drink it. I remember some of the press lads and Terry Weir (Villa's official photographer) were all in the dressing room taking pictures of the celebrations. After an hour or more, we had to get on to the coach back to Birmingham but even then we had a job to get on board as there were hundreds of Villa fans still outside, waiting for their heroes to emerge.

All in all it was a fantastic but bizarre day, losing a game but, more importantly, winning the championship, Villa's first in 71 years. It didn't matter in the end we were champions of England! We were worthy of the crown and we did it with only 14 players. It was an incredible achievement that has never been beaten since (nor ever will, I believe!). Even more remarkable, there were seven lads who played in all 42 games. The other three lads in the squad, Colin Gibson, Eamonn Deacy and Dave Geddis were just as important as the starting 11. The great thing about that team was that there were lads who could step in if we had injuries. Gary Shaw and I scored 41 goals in 38 games and Tony Morley chipped in with 12. We all struck up a good understanding from early in the season, and our goal record showed just that. It was a similar situation at Forest when we won the championship in the 1977/78 season – there were players who could cover almost every position. I think in that season I played at centre-half at least once.

At Forest, we clinched the title with a few games to go, but in the 1980/81 season it was much closer and went down to the wire. Ipswich were everyone's favourites to win the league and the two other trophies but ended up winning just the UEFA Cup. They had been in the top two or three of the table for most of the season and it must have been heart-breaking for their players and manager, the late Bobby Robson, that they missed out on the league title – even more so because they beat us three times that season (including once in the FA Cup).

I spoke to Bobby about that before he passed away and he said Ipswich 'had the better team.'

I countered that by saying to him, 'That isn't actually true. Yes, you might have beaten us three times but it's not measured over two or three games, it's measured over 42 games and over 42 games you didn't win the championship – we did. You might have had good players or better players even but you weren't the better team because if you were, you would have won the championship. Not only that, it wasn't just a point or two points that we won the championship by, it was four points.'

He couldn't argue with that really.

I don't have any memories of the coach journey back to the Midlands after the game or the celebrations afterwards. With the championship won some of the lads went out on the town, but I went with Jimmy Rimmer, Ken McNaught and Kenny Swain and our wives to our usual Saturday-evening haunt, The Nags Head in Hockley Heath, for drinks, sandwiches and a big silver plate of chips. We knew how to treat our ladies after such a monumental achievement.

Even though we had just won the biggest prize in English football, none of us watched *Match of the Day* when we got home, basically because we had played a shocking 90 minutes of football at Highbury!

On the Sunday we had the official celebration and the open-top bus tour of Birmingham. We started the tour at Villa Park and most of us were still in recovery from the night before. It was a horrible, grim and grey day and not the kind of day you wanted to get aboard the top deck of an open-top bus. It was the beginning of May but it was freezing and we all sat on the lower deck, under cover at first. But as we got nearer to the crowded city centre streets we decided to go up top. We were amazed at the number of fans that had turned out along the three-mile journey from Villa Park to the Council House; people were lining the streets, on top of buildings, in treetops and someone even managed to climb up a lamp post. The streets were packed with people waiting to see the new champions of England.

When we arrived at the Council House, we met up with our wives and girlfriends. Terry Weir was there to greet us and he took some amazing pictures of us inside the Council House. I recall there was a spectacular group picture of all the players, the wives and girlfriends and all the kids. Dennis Mortimer went to collect the trophy and we were all then presented with our medals by the Football League vice president, 'jolly' Jack Wiseman, who was also vice-chairman of Birmingham City. I'll always remember his catchphrase was 'Swinging.' One funny thing that stuck in my mind from that day was that Jack said to Ron he had one spare medal left. Ron offered to take the spare medal to give to Roy MacLaren, Ron's assistant coach. At the time, I was talking to Eamonn Deacy, our left-back who had only made 11 full appearances, six starts and five from the subs bench, during the season.

I said to him, 'Where's your medal, Eamonn?'

He said he didn't receive a medal.

'What do you mean you never got a medal?'

He said in his Irish accent, 'I didn't tink I'd played enough games to get one so I didn't go up to get me medal.'

I told him he should have gone to pick up his medal as he had contributed to the side winning the league. I wasn't having any of it so I immediately went up to Ron and told him Eamonn didn't pick up his medal. Ron then went over to Roy MacLaren and explained the situation and Roy gave the medal back to Ron.

A few minutes later, Ron spotted Eamonn and asked, 'Eamonn, where's yer medal son?'

Eamon said the same to Ron as he'd said to me, 'I didn't get a medal, boss. I don't tink I deserved one.'

Ron asked him how many games he played and when he said he'd played 11 – six full appearances and five as sub, Ron said, 'Well you deserve a medal. You played enough games and you were part of the championship-winning team,' and duly gave Eamonn his medal.

When Eamonn received his medal from Ron, he burst into tears. Eamonn was always a very unassuming guy and very quiet and humble and we all agreed with Ron that he deserved his medal.

Eamonn was one of those guys who would be the centre of most other players' jokes because of the way he was. Basically, most of the players would take the piss out of him, always in a pleasant way though, and he'd always just brush it all off, to be fair to him. He wouldn't say boo to a goose off the pitch but on the field of play he'd kick anyone in his way. I remember the Christmas party during the championship-winning season was held at The Belfry and I went over to Eamonn and said, 'Eamonn, it's Christmas. Are you having a pint?'

Eamonn, who was a devout Catholic and never touched alcohol, said sharply, 'You know I don't drink. I never have a drink.'

I egged him on a bit and tried to persuade him to participate: 'Come on Eamonn, you must have a drink. It's Christmas.' Again, he said he didn't drink but I wasn't having it. 'OK then but you like fruit juice though don't you?' He agreed to the juice so I went to the bar and ordered him a jug of sangria. I gave Eamonn this huge jug stuffed with fruit and sangria (and a few extra shots thrown in for good measure) and I said to him, 'Here you are Eamonn, here's yer fruit juice. Don't let anyone else drink it will yer? It's just for you.'

While he was drinking his 'fruit juice' I wound him up about his love life. His girlfriend lived in Ireland and her name was Mary. I said to him, 'How's Mary? Have you done the deed yet, Eamonn?'

He immediately flew off the handle and said, 'I don't do tings like that, and I don't!! I can't do that until I'm married. I'm a Catholic. My religion doesn't allow it.' I told him I was a Catholic as well but it didn't stop me!

Eamonn was very much into his religion. Everywhere, and I mean everywhere, we went as a team, he'd want to know where the nearest church was so he could go to pray. He was a great lad and it was so sad he passed away in February 2012 at the tender age of 53 – God rest his soul.

After the medal presentation we had a few drinks and chatted to the dignitaries, then went out on to the balcony of the Council House to greet the fans and to lift the trophy. The scenes from the balcony were unbelievable. Ron said a few words to the adoring fans and some of the other lads said some things until I grabbed hold of the microphone and started to control the proceedings, as I felt it had got a bit out of hand. I started to talk to all the fans and mentioned there were five Scousers in the side, but that received a cold reception until I said we were all adopted Brummies and then the crowd went wild. The celebrations went on for a fair few hours and eventually we all went our separate ways back home.

The celebration continued that week with the Midlands Sportswriters Player of the Year Awards dinner, held at the old ATV studios in Birmingham. It was a prestigious event hosted by Gary Newbon with a comedian on the bill called Ian 'Sludge' Lees, who was hilarious. I won the Player of the Year award, as expected I suppose and Gary Shaw won Young Player of the Year. More fittingly, Brian Little received a lifetime achievement award. The weird thing about the evening was that Brian Clough presented me with the award; it couldn't have been any sweeter. When I was called up on stage to receive the award, Gary Newbon looked at Brian and put the microphone in front of him and said, 'Just before you present this award Brian, can you answer this question? Were you right to sell Peter Withe?'

Brian replied quite matter-of-factly, 'Yes I was right to sell Peter Withe but I dropped a clanger in not buying him back.'

That left Gary Newbon speechless. I suppose that comment by Cloughie, in itself, was a compliment from someone who didn't do compliments.

That wasn't the only award I won that season as I also won half a dozen or more Aston Villa supporters clubs awards from individual branches. I also won the Aston Villa Player of the Year award. That one could have gone to any of the 14 players who were in the first team that season – everyone did a great job, and quite honestly, I didn't expect to win at all.

However, my season was made complete when Ron Saunders called me into his office and told me I'd been selected to play for my country in a friendly against Brazil. It was my first call-up. I'd also been selected for a couple of Home Championship games too. At the age of 29, I thought my chances of winning my first cap for England had gone, but having said that, I was playing the best football of my career. (More about my England career later in the book.)

It had been three weeks since we'd clinched the championship at Highbury when my season finally ended playing for England against Scotland at Wembley, an experience I'll never forget. As I wasn't going to be involved in the World Cup qualifiers the following week, I flew to Los Angeles to join the Villa lads for the last four days of their post-season holiday. Kathy and I arrived in LA and we met up with the team at a hotel in the middle of the city. I don't know why they picked that particular hotel because the location was awful. The hotel itself was in the middle of being modernised and the swimming pool was out of action during our stay, so we had to share the pool at another hotel down the road. We spent four days with the team and visited several theme parks before they all flew back to Birmingham, but Kathy and I stayed on to spend another ten days in California and spend some time with Jason, who also came with us. We decided to hire a car and visit a friend of mine called Chris Dangerfield, who lived near Redondo Beach. I think we drove around for most of the ten days we were there as Kathy and I always liked to visit new and different places. We didn't like to park ourselves in one place for too long – we're still very much like that now, really.

When I look back now, it was incredible that we only used 14 players throughout that season (42 games in those days). A similar thing had happened at Forest when we won the championship using 17 players – that would be unheard of in today's Premier League. People played in different positions to accommodate back then; we had Des Bremner playing at centre-back when either Ken McNaught or Allan Evans got injured (and he also stepped in as a midfielder and as a full-back); Gary Williams was a right-back but played at left-back for most of the season; he also played at centre-back too. In a way, Bobby Robson was probably right when he said Ipswich had better players because their team was full of internationals whereas we only had one player who had played for his country at that time, Jimmy Rimmer (who had played one game for England back in 1976). Having said that, I still thought at the start of that season that we, as a group of players, were good enough to win the league as Ron had predicted. I'd signed a four-year contract with Villa in the summer and in my first season we'd won the championship. I enjoyed every minute of that first season. It was a pity I didn't sign for them earlier in my career, but I was a late starter in football so I had a lot of catching up to do. Ron told me before I signed I would be leading the line, a target man and a character in the team and he proved to be right.

The similarities between the Forest team I'd played in and the Villa team were clear to anyone looking for them. There was a great blend between youth and experience in both teams; we had the same adventurous attitude and looked to win every match, whether it was at home or away. When you look through the spine of that Villa side there were leaders – myself, Jimmy Rimmer, Ken McNaught and of course Dennis Mortimer, who was the captain – but it's fair to say there wasn't a 'figurehead' in the side, someone who would go round threatening people if they weren't doing their jobs or giving someone a kick up the backside when they needed it. In some respects that was my job at times, as I was the one telling my teammates to get stuck in, shouting out the orders and encouraging the lads.

Thinking about some of the characters we had in that championship side and the players who influenced the rest of the team, I suppose I was amongst the more aggressive players on the football pitch. Then there was Ken McNaught, who was a lovely, placid guy off the pitch but once the whistle blew he'd kick you up in the air if it meant he got the ball; him and Allan Evans were horrible centre-halves to play against, particularly as a pair. I did play against Ken a couple of times; he was a thinker and an organiser but he would get his head or foot in when it counted and would sacrifice himself for the cause. Allan was also a hard-man – strong and aggressive – and together, they would have done anything to stop attacks short. Ken wasn't the fastest in the world but 'Evo' was pretty quick and read the game well. Gordon 'Sid' Cowans was a quiet and shy character, in his early twenties then but already a great player and on the verge of playing for England.

Des Bremner could run all day. Although I'd say I was probably the fittest player in the club, he would come a close second. Des was fit in terms of being match fit; his strength was his stamina to run around the pitch for 90 minutes. Then there were the younger players; Gary Williams, Kenny Swain and Gary Shaw. When you look at the side, we just seemed to gel together as a team, on and off the pitch, and to a large extent that was all down to Ron. I've played in teams where some players hated one another but they knew for the team to function they had to play together.

We all got on at Villa and we had a competitive edge about our team. Everyone had the ability to score a goal so the reliance wasn't on the strikers. It all came down to what we did on the pitch on a Saturday at 3pm – Ron made sure of that. He was 100 per cent for his players and Aston Villa FC. The training was full-on and at no time did we ever get bored of it. There's nothing worse than being out on the training field, cold and bored, but at Villa the sessions were short and sharp – and hard work – and there was no time to be bored. During training and five-a-sides on a Friday prior to a game, we'd kick each other up in the air and we wouldn't ever refrain from putting a tackle in. It was Ron who built that mentality into the team and he was quite right in my mind to do so. Ron would let Roy do the warm-ups and then he would come out and tell us what we were going to work on for 45 minutes, and then we'd finish up.

Off the pitch, because most of the lads lived on the northern side of Birmingham, we didn't usually go out much as a group. However, a few of us who lived on the south side – me, Ken McNaught and Kenny Swain – would go out to a local pub in the Knowle area for a few drinks and a meal after games. The only times we went out as a team were official club functions, but I don't think that was a bad thing because all that mattered was what happened once we were on the football pitch together. Believe it or not, we did have some club rules about when we were allowed to drink; alcohol was forbidden on the Thursday and Friday before a Saturday afternoon match. That's probably why Ron would get you in a headlock in order to smell your breath. Thursdays were always golf days and I'd go with some of the lads to either Ladbroke Park Golf Club near Solihull or, if we decided to play in the north of Birmingham, Barracks Golf Club (now called Whittington Heath) near Tamworth. The media perceived Ron as being some sort of 'sergeant major' type but he always turned a blind eye when it came to the lads playing golf during the week. He must have known it went on, but didn't ever say anything – to the senior lads at least.

There were five or six of us who were members of Barracks Golf Club, so after we'd played a round of golf we'd go into the clubhouse to have a few beers and always order chip butties. We'd finish the day by going for a meal and a couple more beers – but we'd never go overboard as we were conscious of the club rules.

Gordon Cowans, who always played at the Barracks Golf Club, said to me one day, after we'd played a round of golf there, 'You know when we go in your car, you drive like a madman. You're driving and you're racing people on the road but when you've had a drink, you drive like a bloody snail.'

I replied, 'What does that tell yer, Gordon? I drive like a maniac when I'm sober but when I've had a few drinks I don't want to have an accident or get stopped by the police for speeding. Doesn't that tell you anything?'

Gordon was the opposite though and he almost paid for it one night.

At the time, Gordon wasn't married and had a sporty three-litre Ford Capri fleet car, whereas I had a family-friendly Ford Cortina. Gordon told me a story about when we'd been for a drink after golf and he'd driven back to meet Jackie (who was his girlfriend at the time and is now his wife). He was going so fast he hit a lamp post full on, not far from Jackie's parents' home. He must have hesitated, left the car, and then ran from the scene of the crash. When he got to Jackie's parents' house, he was shaking like a leaf and he had to explain what had happened. Jackie's father sat him down and tried to calm him and gave him a brandy. Shortly afterwards, the police arrived and asked to speak to Gordon, who came to the door with a brandy in his hand and smelt of booze. The police didn't stay long. It was obvious Jackie's father knew that if the police came for Gordon they would breathalyse him and he'd get arrested for drink-driving. But because he'd got to Jackie's parents' and had a drink in his hand when they arrived they couldn't breathalyse him, and there was no proof of him driving under the influence. He got away with that one and was lucky, to say the least.

I've always taken my sport seriously, not just on the football field but also on the golf course. All throughout my professional football career everyone wanted me to play in their golf tournaments, up and down the country, and sometimes abroad. All I had to do was turn up, play golf and enjoy the evening that inevitably followed. When I was with Newcastle, I met a guy by the name of Peter Taylor, not Brian Clough's right-hand man, but a hotelier who worked for the Holiday Inn in Newcastle. One day, out of the blue (after I'd moved to Villa), Peter rang me and told me he'd moved to the Holiday Inn in Aberdeen. After some small-talk, he invited me to a big golf game involving all the major oil companies. Apparently, it was an annual event and it was a big pro-am tournament. Peter wanted me to be part of the event and told me there were a number of pros flying to Aberdeen from Birmingham Airport. I agreed to attend but only after I'd played for Villa on the Saturday (at Villa Park).

When Kathy and I arrived to checkin for out flight I looked around and recognised a few faces including legendary golfer, Sam Torrance. I caught Sam's eye and he came over to me and said, 'Have you played today? How did you get on?'

I told him we'd won the game and that I was playing in a golf tournament in Aberdeen. Sam had just come from the State Express Classic golf tournament at The Belfry and he said he was playing in the tournament as well and it soon became apparent we were flying on the same plane and heading for the same tournament. Sam asked us to join the rest of the group, which included fellow golfers, Brian Barnes, who must have been 6ft 6in tall, and Sandy Lyle and his partner, Christine Sharp. We eventually walked out on to the tarmac (there were no gates in those days). We took one look at the plane waiting for us and Kathy stopped me, pointed at the propelled plane sitting on the tarmac and said, 'I ain't going on that bloody thing!!!'

Brian Barnes, who also hated flying, whatever the size of the aircraft, started to shit himself and pointed to the aircraft, 'We're not flying on that are we?'

With a lot of persuasion, we all got on the plane and Kathy and I took the seats at the rear. Eventually, the pilot got on and shut the door behind him. Brian noticed the empty seat next to the pilot and asked him, 'Where's the co-pilot?'

The pilot started laughing and said there wasn't one for the flight. Brian became anxious and asked the pilot, 'But what would happen if you have a heart attack then?' The pilot assured us all that wouldn't happen and everything would be fine. Brian eventually calmed down and we took to the sky.

Once in the air, Sam asked the pilot if there were any drinks on board. The pilot said there was a drinks box at the rear of the plane so I pulled it out and acted as barman. There were all kinds of beers, miniatures and soft drinks in the box so I served everyone with a drink to help calm everyone's nerves.

We didn't realise at the time but the flight was going to be over two hours and by halfway I needed the toilet so I stood up and walked towards the back of the plane, where I thought the toilet door was.

The pilot shouted out, 'What you doing?' I told him I was going to the toilet. 'We haven't got a toilet on this plane,' he replied.

I sat down again and thought to myself that I desperately needed a pee. I'd had a few pints at Villa Park after the game and had a pint at the airport and before boarding the plane. I was that desperate; in the end I opened a can of beer, drank the contents then peed into the can. By the time we landed all the contents of the drinks box had been drunk.

We arrived in Aberdeen in one piece but there wasn't a lot of time to freshen-up at our hotel before dinner. We came downstairs to find out which table we had been allocated, and one of the organisers said Kathy had to sit down while all the golf professionals and celebrities were announced and paraded into the ballroom. Once Kathy was shown to our table she was asked what she'd like to drink; Kathy asked for a Bacardi for herself and a whisky for me. A few minutes later the drinks arrived but they weren't glasses – they had given us a bottle (yes, a bottle) of Bacardi and a bottle of whisky. There was no expense spared at that do, that's for sure – it seemed everyone had their own bottle of whatever they wanted. As the night progressed, I slowly got though the bottle of whisky and started to feel the worse for wear. We didn't know anyone on our table but I did notice that no one else was drinking, and asked one guy about it.

'We've got a big day tomorrow so we need to try to keep sober to win the tournament.'

As we got up to go back to the room after the dinner, I noticed there were loads of bottles left on the tables (which had been paid for) so we grabbed about six bottles of wine between us and took them upstairs. But by that time we were both out for the count and didn't drink any of them.

In the morning, Kathy woke me up and said she'd had a strange phone call in the middle of the night from Sam Torrance. Kathy was tired and she'd had a few drinks that night but she was adamant she'd spoken to Sam at around 3am. Sam had apparently said he wanted to buy some drinks but couldn't as he wasn't staying in our hotel, so he asked for our room number so we could pay for them. Half asleep, Kathy couldn't comprehend where she was and thought he was downstairs (thinking she was at home and Sam was in our lounge). Kathy apparently gave Sam our room number and went back to sleep. I thought it was a bit strange but took her word for it.

Not having that much sleep after having a skinful the night before isn't the best preparation for a round of golf, especially if you've got to play with pros. However, I made it to the course, the Royal Aberdeen, and decided to play a few practice shots before I was due to tee off, and bumped into Sam. I asked him what time he turned in but he said he'd come straight from the party. After a quick chat with him I was introduced over the PA system and I went to tee off. The last thing I felt like doing was playing golf, but I put my ball down on the tee.

I looked over at Sam and said, 'Sam, I can see three balls.'

Sam replied, 'Pick one and hit it.' So I did, and hit a perfect drive straight down the middle. I was on Sam's team and by the end of the round he'd shot a course record round of 63 and I'd shot a two-over-par 74 (off a handicap of eight) and played out of my skin. In the end we lost the tournament by one shot. The tournament had a decent prize of around £5,000 to the winning pro; however, Sam won a trophy for shooting his record round. He handed it over to me.

'You can have that. Without you I wouldn't have shot a 63. Every time we got to hole you took your driver at it and hit your driver down the middle.

I'm the professional and I'm thinking, this is a tree-lined fairway. There are five holes on the course where I'd never use my driver but you did.' I was a big hitter back then but Sam was an even bigger hitter and could hit the ball 50 yards past my best shot.

It turned out to be a great weekend. Brian Barnes was that petrified of flying back on the same propelled plane that he didn't turn up at the airport for the return to Birmingham and caught a scheduled flight to London, along with Sandy Lyle and his partner.

After that weekend, Sam introduced me to John Letters, a Scottish company who made golf clubs and bags. Their logo was a golden goose and, apparently, all the professionals had them in those days. It wasn't too long before he got me one with my name on, and I was very grateful to Sam for doing that for me.

I played in another pro-celebrity tournament shortly after that, in Cheltenham for the Golf Fanatics Society. Kathy came around the course with me – although as it turned out I wished she hadn't. I was playing really well until I hit a shot on to the green but a long way from the hole, so I asked Kathy to stand by the flag. I attempted a 50-yard putt and saw the ball get closer and closer to the hole so I shouted to Kathy, 'Take the flag out,' but Kathy couldn't get the flag out fast enough as it was stuck. The ball approached the hole, hit the flag and landed about two feet away. That putt lost me the tournament and comedian Eddie Large took to the stage after the event and thanked Kathy for allowing him to win the tournament by not getting the flag out.

During the summer break I went to play golf in Tenerife. I met a friend of mine called Paul Gaskell at a hotel near to Manchester Airport. Paul organised pro-celebrity golf tournaments. He'd organised one in Tenerife and invited Norman Wisdom to the event as an ambassador. While we were having a meal at the airport hotel, Norman asked us if we'd like a drink. Paul was taken aback a bit and whispered to me, 'He must like you two as he's never bought a drink in his life – he just doesn't buy anyone a drink!' It was the first time I'd met Norman but he was as mad as a hatter. When we arrived in Tenerife, he was hyperactive. He must have been in his mid-70s but he was jumping around and doing press-ups and jumping on and off the stage – he was full of life, even at his age. Amazing! We asked him how he kept himself so fit and full of beans. 'There are two things that go when you get to my age,' he replied. He paused then, and we all gathered round closer to him, anticipating some words of wisdom from Norman. He continued, 'The first thing to go is your brain.' He paused again for a moment, then said, 'And I can't remember the second.'

Well, we all just keeled over in fits of laughter. It was hilarious at the time.

The teams had been sorted out, and being the lowest handicap golfer in my group I was marking the card. We had a football referee in our group called George Courtney, and when we played the first hole, one of the players shot to the left and George shot to the right. In the meantime, Kathy was walking with us to locate the balls so I told her to go to help George find his and I went to look for the other player's ball. I looked over to Kathy and she seemed a bit miffed about the whole thing and I asked what the matter was.

She replied, 'His ball's under a tree and he kicked it, not once but a few times.' I said she must have been mistaken but she insisted she was right so I started to watch what was going on more intently.

When the round ended the guy said he'd shot a five but knowing what had happened, I replied, 'What about the fresh air shot? You have to count that.'

As I had the card he didn't get a score.

****

I found Ron Saunders very much in the mould of Brian Clough, but where Brian went out of his way to praise individuals if they played well (and slated them if they didn't) Ron found it very difficult to recognise players on an individual basis, although he did praise us in his own way. Like Brian, Saunders was all for the team. He had found a team who had bonded as a unit and were always going to win things because everyone trusted each other and knew we were aiming in the same direction. I took that into my own coaching career in later life because it was a philosophy that was proven to work and I believed in it. Ron was also unique as a manager, just like Cloughie, albeit in a completely different form. Ron had his tablets and vitamins, but he also kept a bottle of Rémy Martin cognac on a table in the dressing room, and some of the lads used to have a swig of it before they went out on to the pitch. The cognac served two purposes, to calm the nerves and to clear the air passages. It would also give you that warm feeling as it went down. I would never participate before a game – I'd always leave it until afterwards. I didn't see anything wrong with it though – it was one way of coping with pre-match nerves and footballers had been doing it for years before our time. It was mainly the senior lads who would have a swig or two – or in Jimmy Rimmer's case three or four. After the game, I'd have a swig of Rémy and the lads would always (not surprisingly) empty the bottle.

Unlike the pre-match routines that modern-day footballers go through, when I was playing we were left to our own devices; there were no group warm-ups as such and I was the type of person who wanted to be left alone anyway. Ron had a routine where he would go round and talk to each player individually and make sure everyone knew what their jobs were on the pitch. I didn't need Ron geeing me up (or anyone else for that matter). I knew my role in the team and just wanted to concentrate on the next 90 minutes. He'd always start by talking to Jimmy Rimmer then move on to the next player, and so on, quietly talking to every single one of us. I bloody hated it – and I would do anything to escape his pre-match chat. As he approached me I'd go and hide in the toilet or disappear somewhere – I didn't want Ron coming up to me and getting into my 'zone.' I think after a while he realised how much I hated it because he'd come up to me say something like, 'Where have you been?' I'd tell him I was in the toilet or in the corridor and he'd go on to say, 'You know what you've got to do today?' and I'd just nod and agree with him and tell him that I just wanted to focus on the game. He would just say OK, and move on to the next person.

I didn't deliberately ignore everyone (including Ron) in the dressing room but I was always in a semi-trance state, preparing for the game and thinking every time, 'This is THE game.' I remember a time when I was playing for England and Gordon (Cowans) was playing and we were in the tunnel together, about to walk onto the Wembley turf.

He looked into my eyes and said: 'You're getting into the zone aren't you?'

I replied, 'What?'

He repeated what he'd just said; 'You're getting in that trance again aren't you?'

Gordon distracted me for a moment from my semi-trance state and I replied nonchalantly, 'Yep, looking forward to the game, Gordon ...' and I immediately returned to my zone. I suppose it was just my way of coping with nerves before a game. If a player says he's not nervous before a match he's not up for it in my book; I got nervous before every game I ever played, but once I crossed that white line I was ready for it, and the nerves disappeared. I would say, however, that players learn to manage their nerves as they get older and more experienced. I know for a fact that I never, ever had a sleepless night prior to a game – any game – whether it was a friendly or a cup final.

As a player, I was emotionally involved in every game I played in, and I would go so far as to say that I changed when I crossed the white line and stepped out on to a football field – I bet every footballer feels the same. It was as though nothing else mattered in life once I stepped on to the pitch and the game started. I had no 'friends' on the field of play – no matter who they were on the opposing team. That mentality applied to any sport I played in – even now, I'm the same when I play golf with the lads, play cards or even tiddlywinks with my family. I am a very competitive person and I hate losing, no matter to whom. As a footballer, crossing the white line was about giving myself another opportunity to win a game. That mentality was with me from childhood. Even as a young kid playing in the park, people couldn't believe how competitive I was – even in a meaningless match. Very often I'd chase after the ball as if I was playing in a cup final whereas most of the other lads would have given up on it. I was always the one who would win the ball back for the team, and I did it time after time, during every match. I'd never really thought about it before, but looking back, my father was a very competitive player, and even though I was really young I must have picked up on that. I was a lot like him as a player, in that he'd very often get involved in arguments and was a physical kind of player. I suppose the edge that gave to my game was the difference between me and my elder brother, Gerard, who was a better player but didn't have the same competitive spirit. If someone said to me, 'You can't do that – that's impossible,' I would always say, 'Is it? Watch me,' and I'd go and do it.

The one thing that linked all the clubs I played for after we returned from South Africa was golf. There's something intrinsic that links football and golf, and most club managers back then encouraged it, probably because they were keen golfers themselves. Ron was a very keen golfer and the area we lived in, as mentioned previously, had several clubs within a radius of a few miles. As soon as I joined Villa and moved to Knowle, Ron asked me if I was going to join Copt Heath Golf Club, a very exclusive club which didn't let just anyone become a member. I knew Copt Heath from my time at Birmingham City as I was lucky enough to play there as a guest a few times, but now it was my local club and I started to befriend a few members during the course of the year. Some of the members I played with were just normal, everyday guys; one guy was a fishmonger from Solihull and he said there would be no problem in me becoming a member so I took his advice and filled in the forms and applied.

My application was vetted and I was asked to go to an interview at Copt Heath. It was held in a huge, brand new boardroom in the clubhouse. The chairman, who was an elegant gentleman in his 70s, asked me to sit at one end of this huge table, which must have had the capacity to seat 30 people, while he, his secretary and about a further eight board members sat at the other end. You can picture the scene. Copt Heath always had a reputation of being posh, a bit 'stuffy' and full of business people – and it was exactly that and more. I thought it was a bit formal and a bit old-fashioned to be interviewed to become a member of a golf club, and to be interviewed by ten people seemed a bit excessive, but that was the procedure back then. Once the formal interview got underway, the questions started to flow.

'Mr Withe, why would you want to join Copt Heath Golf Club?'

I thought about that question for a few seconds but I didn't tell the truth, and replied, 'It is just around the corner from my home' and then gave them a bit of flannel about it being a top-class golf club, etc. The committee members turned their noses up at that answer but when they asked me what my handicap was I told them, 'I play off seven,' and they seemed quite impressed by that at least. They continued with all sorts of irrelevant questions and the routine rigmarole, until they asked me the most important question of all:

'What do you do for a living?'

I told them, 'I play football.'

The boardroom suddenly fell silent and there was a pause while they all looked at each other. The chairman replied, 'Oh right, umm ... do you play rugger?'

'I played rugby when I was at school but not any more,' I replied. 'I'm a footballer now, a professional footballer.'

They carried on quizzing me for a few minutes more until one of them asked me, 'Well, what exactly is this football?'

I told them what football was and said again that I play football professionally. I began to wonder what planet they were on – I thought everyone knew what football was. Then they asked me if I played cricket and I told them that I did in summer, but emphasised that I didn't play cricket professionally. I don't think they got the fact that I was a professional footballer; they didn't know what football was or what a professional footballer did. The interview lasted an hour – an hour too long – and it was strange and hard work to say the least. I was told I would hear the outcome shortly.

A week or so after the interview, I still hadn't heard anything from the golf club and I kept asking my friends who were members there if they could find out what was going on. One day, I was with one of my friends in the club-pro shop, talking to the club professional, and asked him if he'd heard anything about my application. His face dropped like a lead balloon and he suddenly went pale.

I then asked him, 'Do you know something?'

He replied sheepishly, 'Oh, haven't they sent you a letter?' He obviously knew something because a few days later I received a letter saying my application had been turned down but no reason was given. In other words, I was 'blackballed'. In golfing terminology, blackballing is a traditional form of secret ballot. A white ball or a 'ballot' constitutes a vote in support and a blackball signifies opposition. In short, one or two objections are sufficient to defeat a proposition of the vote. Basically, they wouldn't let me join.

I later found out that they wouldn't let me join because I was a footballer. Fortunately, golf clubs have moved on since those days.

When I told Ron what had happened, he wasn't really surprised and he reacted as if he knew I wouldn't get in. His thinking was if I got in, he'd apply, so naturally he decided not to apply after hearing about my experience. After being turned down by Copt Heath I then turned my attention to the nearby Ladbroke Park Golf Club, which was only a couple of miles away in Tanworth-in-Arden – and didn't have the same old-fashioned, stuck-up interview process as I'd just encountered at Copt Heath. However, they still interviewed newcomers and I remember before mine being introduced to a guy who looked vaguely familiar. It turned out to be Mike Hailwood, the famous British Grand Prix motorcycle road-racing champion, regarded by many as one of the greatest of all time. He'd retired in 1979 and had opened a Honda dealership in Birmingham. He told me he was also being interviewed to join Ladbroke Park, and as we chatted for a few minutes we agreed to have a game together if we managed to get in as members. A week later I heard on the radio he'd been killed in a road traffic accident. I was stunned. I couldn't believe that he'd raced in 50 Grand Prix events and several 24-hour Le Mans, yet he was killed going over a hump back bridge in his car. Mike had apparently set off in his Rover with his children to collect some fish and chips and as they returned along the A435 Alcester Road through Portway, Warwickshire near their home in Tanworth-in-Arden, a truck made an illegal turn through the barriers on to the central reservation, and his car collided with it. His daughter was killed instantly. Mike and his son were taken to hospital, where Mike died two days later from severe internal injuries at the age of 40. His son survived with minor injuries. The truck driver was fined just £100.

Some months after I'd been blackballed by Copt Heath, my eldest son, Jason, who had been playing golf for a couple of years (since the age of seven or eight actually), asked his friend, George, if he wanted to become a member of Copt Heath golf club. George didn't actually play golf, but his father, who was a bank manager (not surprisingly), did play. Jason was playing off 9 or 10 by that time, which was pretty good for a nine-year-old, and he was also a junior member at Ladbroke Park, so when I heard Copt Heath were looking for new junior members, I asked Jason to see if he could get in. There was method in my madness, as I thought if my nine-year-old son could get in, then why shouldn't I be allowed to become a member? I told Jason not to mention my occupation unless they specifically asked because they would blackball him as well. A few days later, both Jason and George went for an interview at Copt Heath. I asked Jason when he returned home if they had asked him about my occupation and he said they didn't mention it. A few days later, Jason received the same sort of letter from Copt Heath as I did – he'd been blackballed as well – yet George got in. Nothing against George but he'd never played golf in his life, but was allowed to become a member of a golf club, probably on the strength of his father's occupation. I was livid but I had no real choice but to let it lie. The board must have found out that Jason was related to me but I had no proof of that, of course.

There is a touch of irony attached to the story of me being blackballed by Copt Heath. A few years later, George asked Jason if he wanted to go out to the cinema to watch a movie, but Jason said he hadn't any money because he hadn't done his paper round that week. George said he'd pay as he'd won some money on the one-armed bandits. Jason asked him how he could play the one-armed bandits at his age but he didn't answer the question. That happened a few times more and both Kathy and I became a bit suspicious of where his money had come from. We later found out that George was thieving from the members of Copt Heath Golf Club. The club must have known what was happening and had put up CCTV cameras all around the clubhouse and caught George on film, picking the pockets of the members. The committee subsequently banned George from the club. When we heard what had happened we both had a snigger about the fact that they'd let in the wrong one! Even now, every time we drive past Copt Heath Golf Club we make a one-fingered gesture at it.

I found out years later that all the old-timers on the Copt Heath committee had died or been replaced, and the club had re-invented itself as a more 'friendly and forward-thinking' club that welcomed new members, regardless of class or occupation. Even footballers are allowed in now, I hear, but you won't catch me playing there, that's for sure.

****

After an incredible first season at Villa, it was straight back into training in early July, then a six-week period of preparing for the new season. We opened the campaign with the traditional Charity Shield at Wembley against FA Cup winners, Tottenham Hotspur. We drew the game 2–2, so we shared the trophy for six months each. I scored both our goals; the first was from a Tony Morley corner, then Ray Clemence dropped the ball into my path and I hit it into the roof of the net to make it 1–0. It was Ray's debut for Spurs and one he'd rather forget. After Spurs went 2–1 up in the second half, Tony sent over a cross and Ray and I collided; I managed to make contact with my head and the ball went into the empty net.

As champions, our first game at home was against Notts County, but we lost it 1–0 in front of a disappointingly low crowd of 30,000. Winning the championship obviously meant the return of European football, but this time it was the club's first time in the European Cup, which back then was a straight two-legged knockout competition. In the first round we were drawn at home to FC Valur from Reykjavík. Gary Shaw was injured so was replaced by Terry Donovan, but we still won the game easily 5–0 and I scored a brace. In the away leg, we won 2–0 with Gary Shaw returning and scoring both goals. In the next game we were drawn away at Dynamo Berlin in a game where Tony Morley gave his famous finger to Ron after he'd scored his second goal. We won that game 2–1 but the story behind the finger was that it looked like Ron was going to leave Tony out of the team for that match and he'd bet Tony he'd never score two goals because he was 'too flash.' That wound Tony up, and when he found out he was actually playing against Berlin, he obviously wanted to show Ron he was right in picking him – and wanted to prove Ron wrong that he couldn't score twice. Before the incident, I think we were defending a corner and had cleared the ball and Tony picked it up and ran the length of the pitch, beat three players and scored his second goal. He instinctively ran towards the bench and gave the finger sign to Ron as if to say, 'This is why I should be in the team!'

Incidentally, I think that goal won European goal of the season in 1982.

We found out early on in the European campaign that we had to change our style of football a little; you had to keep possession, otherwise the European teams would capitalise. We were a very good counter-attacking side in the league and that seemed to suit us in the European games as well, so we didn't have to change that much. We could defend in numbers but then, with the likes of Tony and Gary, we had the quality and the pace to counter-attack, especially away from home – as Tony's second goal against Berlin demonstrated. The pace and skill he showed to score that goal was amazing – even on the bobbly pitch.

There was a break from European games after the Berlin victory but by the start of February we were struggling in the league and were in the lower half of the table – not where we were expected to be as reigning champions. On 8 February 1982, we all reported as normal to the Bodymoor Heath training ground and went out for our usual warm-up with Roy MacLaren. After the warm-up, he gathered the squad together and gave instructions on what training we were going to do. I remember seeing Ron in the distance walking across the pitch, and the next thing I saw was him sitting on his haunches, coughing and spluttering. Jim Williams (the physio) spotted Ron and came running out of the changing rooms to attend to him – I assumed someone must have said something to him that Ron wasn't feeling very well. Jim then took Ron back inside and the next thing we saw was Ron driving himself out of the gates of the training ground.

However, after training that day, I went to watch Jason play in a five-a-side tournament in Solihull and as we arrived back home at around 9pm, I noticed a load of cars in the cul-de-sac where we lived. It wasn't a small cul-de-sac but you wouldn't go down it unless you lived there so I assumed something serious had happened or one of the neighbours was having a party (and we hadn't been invited). I drove the car on to the drive and when I got out of the car, I was greeted by a load of lights shining in my face and the ITV reporter, Tony Francis, stuck a microphone under my nose.

'What are your thoughts of the events of the day?'

I honestly didn't know what had happened so I replied, 'What events? What do you mean?'

Tony must have thought I was hiding the truth and went on, 'Well, Ron Saunders.'

My immediate thought, after last seeing Ron on his haunches on the training ground that morning was, 'Bloody hell has he died?'

Then Tony continued, saying, 'He's resigned. Ron Saunders has resigned.'

To which I said, 'Well, thank god for that!'

Tony looked at me as if I'd gone mad or I was pleased Ron had resigned. Suddenly Tony had a story and I could see the headlines in the morning papers:

Peter Withe Happy at Ron Exit

Obviously we had both got the wrong end of the stick so I just added, 'No comment. I haven't got any comment, sorry.'

Ron lived round the corner from me so I managed to get back into my car and drove round to see him. When I got to Ron's house, Roy MacLaren was there with Jim Williams. I asked the gaffer what was going on and the first thing he said was, 'They [the board] won't let me manage the club.'

Ron was left to run the club from top to bottom and did everything that Brian Clough did at Forest. Everything went through him – even petrol claims got signed by Ron. Strangely, he was probably the only football manager to have his own private secretary, a lovely lady called Jane, and you couldn't get to Ron without going through her. She was the go-between, if you like, because she managed his schedule. Reading between the lines, I believe Ron had a disagreement with the (then) chairman Ron Bendall about the budget for players. Ron had always wanted to spend the rest of his managerial career at Villa but he had become increasingly disappointed with results on the pitch and had disagreements with Ron Bendall over how the club was run. He was apparently frustrated that there was no money in the kitty to improve the squad – he was also told he'd have to sell before he could buy new players. Ron wanted to sell Dave Geddis for £500,000 and use the money to bring in a few other players but Bendall refused to give Ron any of the transfer fee for Dave and wanted to plough the money back into the club.

I recall Ron said to me one day that he was looking at buying Trevor Francis and he asked me what I thought of him as a player. That would have been the signing of the century for Villa. Ron wanted more competition for places and looked at signing another striker to compete with Gary Shaw and myself. Ron wasn't sure about Gary Shaw's scoring ability – whether he was capable of scoring enough goals every season – so he obviously wanted to look at getting in another proven striker, but wanted to include Dave Geddes in the transfer to offset the fee. Gary had a great season, scoring 18 goals when we won the championship, but Ron didn't think he scored enough goals in the six-yard box – most of his goals were 'worldies.' Ron, being a striker himself in his day, knew all about scoring in the six-yard box and that's what he wanted from his strikers.

It was a myth that Ron resigned for health reasons. The club were basically in debt to the tune of £1.6m and had an £800,000 overdraft to deal with, so Ron's team-building had to be put on hold – and against his wishes. Not only that, the chairman had apparently thrown away Ron's three-year rolling contract. He saw that as a vote of no confidence in him and it left Ron on a sticky wicket.

It had obviously come as a major shock and disappointment to everyone at the club that Ron had resigned but we all knew the club wouldn't fall apart and we had to carry on regardless.

The next day we all felt a bit flat on hearing the news about Ron, so Roy MacLaren gathered the troops before training to say that Ron Bendall's son, Donald would be visiting the training ground to talk to all the players. Donald Bendall couldn't have been any older than me at the time, so that news didn't go down too well with the lads, but when he arrived after the training session he announced that Tony Barton was going to be temporarily replacing Ron as manager and Roy MacLaren was going to be his assistant. Young Donald Bendall then started to have a pop at Ron and once he started bad-mouthing the gaffer I stood up and interrupted him.

'Have you finished 'cos I ain't listening to this!' and I duly walked out, to be followed by Dennis Mortimer, Ken McNaught and Jimmy Rimmer. We all wondered how he had the gall to stand in front of the players who had won the championship and slag off their manager. It was a disgrace! Donald didn't bother saying anything else and left the training ground.

Tony Barton was very much a behind-the-scenes man before he was parachuted into the hot-seat vacated by Ron. In fact, Tony had watched me while I was playing for Newcastle and was the man who showed me around the club when I first signed for Villa. He hadn't even sat with the coaches in the dugout during matches; he was called the assistant manager to Ron, but in effect he was a scout. Yet he had been made manager of a team just about to play a big quarter-final tie in the European Cup.

The good thing about Tony taking over was that he didn't change anything, as he knew the club and the players. If another manager had come in from outside he would have undoubtedly changed everything from the training routine to some of the players in the squad, so in that respect, it was a smooth transition for us. However, Tony wasn't a strong character like Ron was; no disrespect to Tony, who was a very nice man, but he didn't have that strength of character you'd expect a top football manager to have. It was strange having Tony as the gaffer because, although everyone knew who Tony was, we'd hardly ever see him around the place. Having said that, the players weren't too shocked to see him as Ron's replacement in some respects, as the assistant manager stepping into the manager's shoes seemed to make sense.

The first leg of the European Cup quarter-final tie was in a place called Simferopol, 300 miles south of Kiev. The pitch at the Kiev stadium was unplayable due to the freezing Russian winter, so the match was moved to another stadium on the Black Sea. If we thought the conditions in Berlin were bad for our previous tie then the trip to Russia was the ultimate footballing nightmare. We were promised 'luxury' hotel accommodation when we arrived in the city, but were put up in a hotel called The Hotel Moscow, which wasn't exactly The Ritz.

From the moment we arrived we couldn't wait to leave. The club had decided to take no chances with the dubious Russian hygiene and had taken their own food for the trip. The hotel was no more than a youth hostel – and a bad one at that. The beds were not unlike what you'd expect to see in an army barracks. When I first tried to open the door to the toilet in my room, it banged against something and I couldn't figure out what it was. When I got into the toilet I realised the seat was right behind the door and I swear there was a plate on the back stating it had been made in 1901.

When you ran the water it came out all shades of green and yellow, and I ended up removing a couple of tiles from the floor because they were loose and cracked. My feet were sweaty and sticky and as I lifted them up the tiles just came away with them. It was disgusting.

I think we did well to escape with a goalless draw.

However, in the second leg, it was a completely different game and one of the greatest European nights ever seen at Villa Park. The pitch wasn't the best I'd have to say – wet and muddy – but we won the game 2–0, with goals from Shawy and Ken McNaught.

Even though our league form hadn't improved much, we were now in the semi-final of the European Cup, and drawn against Belgian champions, Anderlecht. Tony and Roy had been installed as permanent manager and assistant manager for their efforts in taking over from Ron, for moving us up the league table with only two defeats and for making progress in the European Cup. The first leg of the semi-final at Villa Park was a tough game, but Tony Morley scored the goal to take to the away leg. In the second leg, I scored a perfectly good goal, but it was ruled out and to this day I don't understand why. We held out for a goalless draw. However, the game was over shadowed by a moment of madness from an off-duty British soldier. With football hooliganism at its height in 1982, we witnessed a sad scene at the Émile Versé Stadium (now the Constant Vanden Stock Stadium). Just as the home side launched a first-half attack – which ended with a shot over the bar – the mayhem started. A Villa fan in a claret polo shirt appeared in the goalmouth, lying down in the box before being dragged away by half-a-dozen policemen. I remember intervening at one stage, trying to persuade him to leave the pitch. The fan was an off-duty soldier who claimed he was trying to run away from fighting on the terraces. The game was held up for several minutes but luckily it continued shortly after the incident and we went on to win the game 1–0, and a place in the European Cup Final.

Anderlecht later called for the match to be restaged and for us to be banned but that was dismissed by UEFA. It would have been harsh to have to play the game again, even more so to be banned. However, the club did receive a punishment – our next home European match (which would be the following season) was to be played behind closed doors. Villa were also fined 50,000 Swiss Francs, which was in effect a gentle rap on the knuckles in terms of financial loss in the light of what was laying ahead for the club – the final of the European Cup and the biggest game in the history of Aston Villa FC.

10

VE Day

The European Cup Final
Rotterdam 26 May 1982

"Shaw, Williams, prepared to adventure down the left.
There's a good ball played in for Tony Morley.
Oh, it must be! It is! Peter Withe!!"
Brian Moore – former ITV commentator

****

If you believed the media hype before the game, Bayern Munich were already 1982 European champions; it was a total mismatch, given that they had a side full of internationals and we only had two, myself and our goalkeeper, Jimmy Rimmer. Bayern were a side that had the likes of Rummenigge, Breitner, Dremmler, Augenthaler and Hoeness – all world-class players and German internationals – and we were a team of relatively unknown but solid players who were punching above their weight with the 'big boys' of European football. On the flip side, we had nothing to lose. It was the biggest match in the history of Aston Villa Football Club. We were going to enjoy every minute of it, and if we had a chance, we were there to spoil the party.

The build-up to the final was the same as for any other match – you wouldn't have thought it was the European Cup Final. Having said that, we were always relaxed before big games and I've said previously that I used to like to have a couple of pints before I went to sleep, rather than taking sleeping tablets like some of the lads did. As it happened, Jimmy Rimmer,

Ken McNaught, Dennis Mortimer, Kenny Swain and myself found a bar and had a few tots and talked about the upcoming game, so I slept really well the night before the big game.

Come match day, we were almost carefree, walking round the pitch an hour before the kick-off, taking in the atmosphere of the Feyenoord Stadium. We were taking pictures of one another and waving at our loved ones in the crowd. It was very special and one of those memories I'll never forget. As we approached kick-off time, we sensed the nervousness in the German camp, but on a personal level, I was well into my zone as we entered the tunnel. I didn't want to speak to anyone before the game (as usual). Unlike today's group warm-ups on the pitch, back then it was always your choice how you'd warm up and psyche yourself up before games. I remember I clasped my hands as if I was praying in the tunnel; in fact I was rubbing my hands, relishing the game ahead and thinking to myself, 'Let's get this won.' I was fully concentrating on how I was going to perform during the 90 minutes.

Gordon Cowans looked into my eyes before we went into the tunnel and said:

'You're getting ready for this aren't you? You've got that "Withe glare" in your eyes.'

I was really looking forward to it – why wouldn't I be? It was the biggest football match of my entire career and I was relishing the chance to take on one of the best teams in Europe – we all were.

The atmosphere in the stadium was fantastic; our supporters had travelled in the thousands to be amongst the 45,000 crowd, which wasn't even capacity for the stadium; but we could hear their deafening noise all the same. In the tunnel before we entered the stadium, you could see the tension in the faces of the Bayern players – all the pressure was on them – but our lads were all laughing and cracking jokes. It was a major achievement for us just to be there and we were going to make the most of it. It looked like the Bayern players weren't giving us the respect that we deserved. Tony Barton (our manager) helped us stay relaxed; he was as laid back as they come and treated it as just another match, which it was really. We were full of confidence that our name would be on the cup at the end of the evening.

About ten minutes after kick-off, Jimmy Rimmer unexpectedly put his hand up and waved to the bench. He was injured and couldn't carry on. He had cricked his neck in training and was given two pain-killing injections before the game, so he must have been in some discomfort, but he made himself fit for the start – it was the European Cup Final and he would have done anything to be fit. Unfortunately, Jimmy went off. Our substitute goalkeeper, Nigel Spink didn't know anything about it at the time – he was sitting on the bench, not really expecting to get a look-in. He'd only made one appearance in the Villa first team and all of a sudden he was taking centre stage in the biggest football match in the world. It was like, 'Go on Spinksy, you're on now mate. You'll be alright. Just don't let one in!' He couldn't have had any nerves as he was literally thrown in at the deep end, ten minutes into the game. I watched Nigel run into his goal and rub his gloves and I thought 'He'll be OK.'

A few minutes later, he saw his first action when a ball was lobbed into the box and he jumped and caught it cleanly with both hands. He made three or four really good saves after that, although he was taken by surprise at one point when an overhead scissor kick from Rummenigge flashed inches past the post.

I also had an early chance to score – a header which went over the bar. The second chance I had was from a ball played into the edge of the box; I turned on to my right foot and I tried to bend the ball into the top corner but I over hit it.

We were doing OK for the first hour. I was in the middle of the pitch battling for the ball and I knocked it out to Gary Williams, who then played in Gary Shaw. Shawy turned inside from the left, Tony Morley made a run and Shawy looked up and played him in. All of a sudden, Tony was in a wide position facing Dremmler, jinking in and out, he managed to get to the touchline. There was one occasion during the game that I was being marked by Klaus Augenthaler so I did my usual, which was to drift off him into space as he followed the ball, but I just walked towards the path of the ball to see what he would do. Augenthaler followed me and started to drift to the near post, just the place I wanted him to be. I peeled off him, positioned in the middle of the goal. Tony drilled the ball across the box and in my head everything was happening in slow motion. I was thinking, 'We've practised this move a hundred times ... now finish it.' All I had to do was to make good contact with the ball with my right foot and it was in the back of the net. As the ball came towards me, it hit a divot in the penalty area. It bobbled on the pitch and hit the top of my foot and hit the post before it went into the back of the net. I wish I could say it was a 35-yard screamer that hit the net so hard it burst the netting, but everyone would know I was lying. It probably wasn't the most beautiful goal I ever scored but I can't remember one I've cherished more. A lot of people said (and still say to this day) that the ball came off my shin but that's a load of rubbish – it definitely came off the top of my foot. If it wasn't for the divot, I'd have had a clean strike at it and I would have drilled it into the net.

The scoreboard read: **FC Bayern 0, Aston Villa 1**

My momentum carried me forward and I ended up in the back of the net with the ball. I couldn't get out of the goal net for a few seconds, and I remember grabbing hold of the net looking at all the Villa fans cheering in front of me. By the time I managed to untangle myself, Shawy had already got to me, then Gordon came flying in, dived on top of me and shouted, 'Get down you big bugger,' and wrestled me to the ground.

Now, there's a nice little story which connects the picture of me getting tangled up in the net with the boots I wore on that night in Rotterdam. While I was playing in Portland in 1975, I met a little-known businessman called Phil Knight, who owned a sports footwear company in Beaverton, Oregon. The company was previously called Blue Ribbon Sports in the 1960s but it later changed its name to NIKE, Inc. When I met Phil, the company specialised in running shoes and only sold them in the US; however, knowing I was one of the big names playing soccer in Portland, Phil asked me if I wanted to wear a pair of soccer boots the company were about to launch. We agreed a deal for me and some of the other lads in the Portland side, and we became some of the first players to wear NIKE, Inc. soccer boots in the NASL.

Fast-forward to the 1981/82 English first division season and NIKE, Inc. were an established company in the US but wanted to establish themselves in the European market so they contacted me to see if I wanted to wear their boots for that season. Of course, I obliged and a deal was done which made me the first player to wear NIKE, Inc. soccer boots in the UK. If memory serves me right, Ian Rush was also asked.

So, when I was photographed scoring the winning goal in the 1982 European Cup Final, the camera focused on my boots and the now-famous NIKE, Inc. 'swoosh' logo.

After a few minutes of celebrating the goal, it was backs-to-the-wall stuff for the next 23 minutes, but I always felt we had enough left to grab another goal – I really didn't see it as a case of just hanging on to the lead. I was shouting to the lads to 'hit the ball into the channels' – I'd chase them all day long. The important thing for us was to keep possession of the ball and, during those 23 minutes, I could hear Brian Clough in my head saying, 'Win the ball. Keep the ball ...' Funnily enough, Brian was in the stadium co-commentating with Brian Moore for ITV, so I guess he was probably saying the same thing on TV. There was one sticky moment when Hoeness had a goal disallowed for offside (and it was clearly offside if you look at it again on TV). If he had done something different in that move he may have played himself onside to equalise and it would have been a totally different game – but it wasn't and we were still winning!

The longer the game went on, the more we were all thinking, 'When's it going to end?' Finally, the French referee blew the whistle. We had won the European Cup! We could barely contain our excitement at winning Europe's biggest prize, but the neutral observers were probably wondering how we had beaten the German champions, being as Bayern were quoted as 5/4 odds-on favourites before the game. It was no fluke and I just remember looking at their players; looking at Breitner; looking at Hoeness, looking at Rummenigge, all crouched on the floor with their heads in their hands, all totally devastated. It could easily have been us on our knees but we were the ones celebrating. The Germans probably couldn't believe they had lost to the ranked outsiders. I think they had thought, 'Aston Villa? We'll beat this lot, no problem. We've beaten better teams than them.' What they didn't realise was that the 'British bulldog spirit,' or whatever you want to call it, had overcome many a great British team in the past; Liverpool had won the cup three times and Forest twice in a row in the previous five years. At that time, English clubs were dominating European football and one of the reasons for that was the never-say-die spirit we had (and still have) in this country. Villa simply added to the run.

As for Villa, we had a team who would run through brick walls for one another. We had a great work ethic; we could defend and counter-attack at pace. I don't think Bayern saw that in us. They just took it for granted they were going to win.

The looks on their faces after the game said it all. I went round the Bayern team and shook hands with every one of them, thinking that if I was in their shoes I'd probably be in the same state. I made a mistake though, as I swapped my shirt with Klaus Augenthaler. We didn't have replacement shirts like they do now, and in hindsight I wouldn't have swapped my shirt with anyone. (I kept Augenthaler's red Bayern shirt – more about that later). When you've just scored the winning goal in a cup final, your mind's not really on the future and you do things without thinking. I asked Dennis Mortimer about it after the game, and he told me he had in mind that he wasn't going to swap shirts with anyone, because he didn't want to go up the steps to collect the cup wearing a Bayern shirt.

We couldn't wait to go up those steps to collect our prize – the biggest club prize in world football. Most of the lads were behind the goal celebrating with our fans, but one of the UEFA officials asked Des Bremner to gather the players together and after several minutes we remembered that we still had to collect the trophy and our medals. All the wives and girlfriends were sitting near to where the cup was to be presented so we waved at them as we walked up the steps. The one thing I remember about collecting my medal was seeing Brian Clough, who was with Brian Moore and sitting right behind the dignitaries, giving the thumbs up to Kathy. Brian had contributed (massively) to my development as a player and I think he was very proud to have seen me score the winning goal, although he probably wouldn't have admitted it to me. He knew how I was feeling at that moment, having managed Forest to two consecutive European Cups a few years previously, and knew I'd missed out on winning it with Forest.

After we had collected the cup and our medals, I was pulled away from the crowds by several members of the media, all wanting to interview me. There were a few pictures taken of the lads with the cup, without me on them because I was being interviewed. After the TV interview I started to walk back to celebrate with the lads, only to be tapped on the shoulder by a UEFA official with a foreign accent.

'Mr Withe. You have to go behind the stadium to caravan to be dope-tested ...' I couldn't believe it and responded in accordance.

'You're joking.'

The official wasn't joking: 'No, no. You and one other and two German players have to go to doping.'

It was a UEFA regulation that two players from each team had to undergo a post-match test to ensure no banned substances had been used prior to the game. The other Villa player to get a tap on the shoulder was Ken McNaught and he wasn't very impressed either. We were duly led away out of the stadium, literally minutes after receiving our medals, and told to enter a shabby old caravan, parked underneath the main stand. The two Germans were Dremmler and Augenthaler and they were asked to sit opposite us while we all waited for the official. We were given a specimen bottle, about the size of a half-pint glass and were asked to fill it up. We'd just played 90 minutes of football and they asked us to piss in a half-pint-sized bottle – were they bloody serious? All four of us failed to provide samples so all we could do was sit and wait. I looked out of the window and saw this guy walking past the caravan carrying a crate of beer so I ran out of the caravan and caught up with him.

'Hey, where you going with those beers?'

He said they were for the Villa dressing room so I grabbed the crate off him and said, 'Not now they're not. Give them here.' I took the crate inside the doping caravan and put the crate of beer in-between me and Ken and the two German lads,

'Come on we'll have a beer.' I opened two bottles of beer and offered Augenthaler a bottle but he refused and so did Dremmler. Ken accepted and we downed a bottle or two each. It was a choice of water or beer and we chose beer. It seemed like an eternity waiting to give our sample. I was the first one to pee in the bottle. The official then asked about the beer, so I explained we'd been drinking it. The official wasn't impressed as he said it would affect the test but there was nothing he could do about it because I'd already drunk a few bottles.

After being tested, I went back to the dressing room, leaving Ken with the two German lads. I was expecting the lads to be there in the dressing room celebrating, but I walked into an empty room, with the exception of Jim Paul, the kit man. Looking round, all I saw were my own clothes hanging up, Ken's gear and Jim clearing up the mess. I was still in my football kit and hadn't bathed yet, but all the other lads had done all that and had packed up and gone. I noticed there was an unopened bottle of champagne, so I grabbed it and took it into the bath, which was still full of hot water. I lay there in the bath on my own with a bottle of champagne having just scored the winning goal in the European Cup Final, and thought to myself that I was the luckiest person on earth. I remember Jim telling me that the coach would be leaving in a few minutes to take us back to the hotel in Amsterdam, where the winner's party was taking place; however, Jim said they were going to lay on a car for me and Ken to take us there as we wouldn't make the coach in time. After about 20 minutes, Ken came into the changing room following his doping test and he said the German lads were still there.

'I think they'll be there all night!' Ken got into the bath and had a swig of champagne.

'Can't believe this, can you?'

The reality of it hadn't hit us yet.

We got changed, gathered all of our gear together and managed to catch the team coach, which had been waiting to take us back to the hotel in Amsterdam, a journey of about 45 minutes from the Rotterdam stadium. On board the coach we had a problem – where on earth do we put the European Cup? We tried every place possible including empty seats and on the floor of the coach, but without success. I then had an idea. I took the huge, heavy cup and put it in the safest place on board – in the toilet. It wasn't in the toilet *bowl* but resting upright on the seat so it wouldn't fall over. The journey to Amsterdam passed quickly. We all seemed to get a second wind as we reached the outskirts of Rotterdam, and our joviality returned with a vengeance. When we reached the Apollo Hotel in Amsterdam we almost left the Cup on the coach until Tony Barton suddenly asked, 'Where's the trophy?' In our celebratory state we had all forgotten where it was, so Ken and I got back on and searched the coach to retrieve the Cup. There was a panic because no one could find it, and we were reminded of a certain World Cup trophy that went missing in 1966 until I remembered where we'd put it for safe keeping: 'We've found it. It's in the crap house.'

We finally met up with the wives and checked into the Apollo Hotel in the centre of Amsterdam with just about enough time to freshen up and have a quick change of clothing before dinner. We went down to the banqueting suite to be greeted by table upon table of amazing food; every type of food you can think of was lined up on these banqueting tables. The champagne was flowing in abundance. In my ultimate wisdom I said to Ken, 'We should have a sip of champagne from the cup.' Ken was up for it and we went in search of a few bottles of champagne. After three bottles it had barely made a puddle in the bottom, so we carried on pouring this expensive champagne into the European Cup 26 bottles later it was almost full to the top. We couldn't believe it. It took 26 bottles to fill the cup!

Then I thought, 'Hang on a minute, we've got to pick this bleeding thing up.' I tried to lift the cup but it weighed a tonne. It was so heavy, it took two of us to just lift it off the ground but then we had to think of a way to move it around the room. We managed to transport the cup around the room and gave all the players, wives and girlfriends a chance to swig out of it, but because of the way the cup was shaped and how heavy it was, we ended up drowning most people in the process. When it came to Kathy's turn she was sitting on a ledge near an open window and when she came to take a gulp she slipped and lost her balance and drowned in champagne in the process. I had to grab her hand to stop her from falling backwards and out of the window. It was lucky she didn't end up in the canal, two floors down!

When it was time for bed, at some stupid hour of the morning, I must have taken four bottles of unopened champagne with me to our room – it would have been a shame for it to have gone to waste. Fortunately, I don't suffer from hangovers so the following morning I got up as right as rain for breakfast, and it was then that the reality of us winning the European Cup hit home. It was an amazing feeling as what we had achieved only several hours before began to sink in.

It was only an hour's flight back to East Midlands Airport and we knew we would be greeted by the media as we arrived back home. I can recall Gordon crawling around the floor because he thought he'd misplaced his medal, but Tony Morley eventually owned up to having taken it, to the relief of Gordon. We agreed a routine for me and Dennis to walk out of the aircraft and walk down the steps, holding the cup together, followed by the manager and the rest of the lads, so that the press could take their pictures.

The following day, Birmingham City Council hosted another civic reception for us at the Council House. The city centre was filled with Villa fans as they viewed the celebrations from every possible vantage point, desperate to greet their footballing heroes.

It was real – Aston Villa were officially the best team in Europe.

Celebrating after scoring the winner in the European Cup Final against Bayern Munich in May 1982

Arriving back with the Villa lads after winning the European Cup in 1982

11

Have Boots Will Travel

"This is the biggest wrench of my career, moving from Villa."

****

Where does a team go after winning the league *and* becoming European Champions in the space of two seasons? There are only two ways to go; you can win another trophy, like Nottingham Forest did straight after their 1979 European Cup triumph, or you can head the other way.

Without Ron Saunders at the helm, Aston Villa were destined to head in a downward spiral.

Although we were European champions, our 1982/83 league campaign started disastrously with three straight defeats. Although these were followed by four back-to-back victories – I even scored a brace against my former club, Nottingham Forest who were still managed by Brian Clough – the club were still in a financial mess. There were allegations that thousands of pounds had gone missing in connection with work that had been carried out on the North Stand at Villa Park in 1977, with around £700,000 not accounted for. We had been successful on the pitch for a few years, and with that we had tremendous support, so there must have been a lot of revenue coming into the club. People were wondering why we were not doing the same as Liverpool and spending money on new players to boost the squad.

On the pitch we were defending the European Cup, and our opening game was at Villa Park against Turkish champions, Beşiktaş J.K. That game will always be famous for one thing only – it was played in a totally empty stadium. Policemen, photographers, journalists and club directors were amongst the few to be allowed to witness the game. The match was played behind closed doors as punishment following crowd disturbances involving Villa fans at the previous season's European Cup semi-final against Anderlecht in Brussels. We won the game 3–1 anyway and I scored our first goal.

The return leg was memorable for another reason. We stayed at the Hilton Hotel that overlooked the stadium and I roomed on my own, which was unusual. I will always remember being woken up on the morning before the game by a noise. It was 8am and when I opened the curtains I saw a stadium full of people. My first thought was that I'd got the kick-off time wrong so got dressed quickly and ran downstairs to find Tony (Barton). I asked Tony what time the kick-off was and he confirmed it was 8pm. He obviously knew what had happened – the club had told fans they would only get into the ground on a first-come, first-served basis so they opened the gates to the ground at 8am. The stadium was absolutely rammed and there were people queuing up outside. I'd never seen anything like it – twelve hours before kick-off and the stadium was rammed.

If that wasn't enough to contend with, on arrival at the stadium our coach was shaken and banged on by hooligans. We somehow managed to get into the stadium safely. When we came out to warm up on the pitch we were 'welcomed' by all sorts of abuse, and anything and everything was thrown at us. The crowd went berserk, screaming and shouting, 'Welcome to Hell' at us. I thought a bit of reverse psychology might be the answer – it often works wonders in those situations. I noticed that the disabled fans didn't have a specific area dedicated to them. I asked our kit-man, Jim Paul, how many sweatbands, badges and other such items of memorabilia we'd brought over. I told the players to get some of the stuff together, and my idea was to walk along the side of the pitch before kick-off and give out a bunch of sweatbands and other items to all the disabled fans in their wheelchairs. While we were doing that, the crowd were still slaughtering us until they realised what we were doing, and then there was total silence, followed by applause. My idea worked a treat. The game itself was a bit of an anticlimax as it ended 0–0, and all in front of 45,000 passionate Turkish fans (who had waited all day to watch the game). It was incredible!

CHAPTER 11: HAVE BOOTS WILL TRAVEL

After our 0–0 draw against Coventry City at Highfield Road on Saturday, 6 November 1982, former Villa player, director and local sports-shop owner Harry Parkes came into the dressing room and claimed he had purchased the club from the Bendalls. He said that nothing would change and Tony would remain as manager. However, what Harry didn't realise, and what no one else realised at the time, was that during that weekend, Doug Ellis had flown to the Isle of Man to secure the shares from Ron Bendall. By the Monday, 'deadly' Doug Ellis had purchased 42 per cent of the shares and had returned to the club as chairman. Harry Parkes's bid had been scuppered.

The club that Doug took over was in dire straits – it was in debt and he had to cut costs everywhere. The feeling locally was that if Doug hadn't stepped in, the club would have gone under. Whatever people say about Doug Ellis as the chairman of Aston Villa, he was a financial man and he knew how to trim a company if needed.

Things needed to change – and they did.

Before Doug became chairman, we had a clause in our contracts that allowed us to have a club car up to the value of £6,000; my car was a Ford Cortina Ghia but Doug changed that because he'd arranged a new sponsorship deal with British Leyland for a fleet of Maestro cars for the players to drive around in. If I remember rightly, the club wanted to take the £6,000 deal out of our contracts and to replace it with one of the fleet Austin Maestros. They were one of the cheapest British cars ever built, and three of us refused to do it, and even refused to be involved in the photography session with the media to promote the sponsorship deal. Of course, Doug didn't like that.

On the playing side, one of the first things Doug had to organise was a trip to Tokyo, Japan for the World Club Cup against the Uruguayan side and South American champions, C.A. Peñarol. It was probably the last thing Doug wanted – to pay out for a trip to Asia for the team, the backroom staff and directors – but it had to be done. I think Doug paid for economy flights for the players and tried to get us upgraded to business class for free – it obviously didn't work, as we had to settle for the cheap seats.

Checking into the hotel in Tokyo, the first thing I heard was a voice in the distance shouting, 'Withey, Withey, over here.' It was the former

Whitesnake guitarist, Bernie Marsden. I asked him what he was doing in Tokyo, and he replied, 'I'm big in Japan, you know.' He had split from Whitesnake and had gone solo and he'd actually become very well known in Asia.

When Bernie was in Newcastle with Whitesnake a few years previously, the group's agent had invited me backstage to meet the lads. Bernie was a big football fan and I asked him, if I got him my Newcastle number 9 shirt, would he go up on stage and wear it? Fair play to him, he did just that. Whitesnake were considered 'the loudest band in the world' at the time, but when Bernie got up on stage wearing my football shirt during that concert at Newcastle Town Hall, the crowd went absolutely wild. The noise was deafening – and that was without the music. That shirt is hugely iconic in Newcastle so it went down well with the crowd. Kathy came along to that concert, even though she was pregnant with Gareth, so he was introduced to heavy rock at a very early age! After the concert, we met up with Bernie and spent some time together over dinner and a few drinks, and we've been friends ever since.

I'll never forget Tokyo – it was an amazing place, truly stunning. I recall borrowing some golf clubs and several of us went to a driving range, but it was no ordinary driving range – it was on the 7th floor of a building and the range was in the shape of a triangle, covered with nets.

Tony Barton went into the World Club Cup game in a positive frame of mind.

'We are here to win it. We will treat the game as seriously as we did when we won the European Cup,' he said. We had virtually the same side as we did in Rotterdam, with the exception of a youth-team player called Mark Jones who replaced Kenny Swain. The game itself wasn't one of our best, but we adapted to the poor pitch and I thought we gave a decent account of ourselves. We had a lot of possession during the game, but they caught us on the break. This led to a shot that bobbled and hit a divot, leaving Jimmy Rimmer to parry it away, only for one of their players to follow up and score. The only other thing that stands out in my memory of that game is their hideous yellow and black striped kit – which probably wouldn't be considered so hideous nowadays. The prize for man-of-the-match was a brand-new Toyota car, so we were playing to win the game and impress the panel; but in the end we failed to impress anyone and lost 2–0. It was a long way to go not to give our best performance and that was the most disappointing thing about it. At the end of the game, when it came to handing out the medals, there were more medals than players – it was a total farce! I think in the end, Doug took the spare medals and even gave one to anyone who had made the trip to Tokyo. I couldn't believe it! The event had been devalued big-time in my opinion by all these medals being handed out like confetti.

A few weeks into the new year of 1983, we had another new cup to challenge for. The European Super Cup was a two-leg affair between the European Cup winners and the UEFA Cup winners – and we were up against the might of Barcelona. It was the first time I'd played in the Nou Camp (officially known as Camp Nou), a fantastic stadium, huge and intimidating. The one thing I'll always remember about the Nou Camp was that it had its own chapel actually in the stadium.

Barcelona had a certain Diego Maradona playing for them at that time, but we heard before the game that he had been ruled out because he had contracted Hepatitis B. Even without Maradona, they had a great side with the likes of Migueli, Bernd Schuster and Quini. During the build-up to the game, the headlines in the Spanish press made two key players out to be superheroes of sorts:

'Tarzan' Migueli v 'Hulk' Withe

The first leg failed to capture the imagination of the Catalan fans. Only 45,000 saw the game at the Nou Camp and it was like playing in an empty stadium (well, it was half empty – or half full!). Again, we had the same side that played Peñarol and we held them up to half-time, when Schuster started to exert his influence on the game. Marcos Alonso scored in the 52nd minute, the only goal of a fairly tame match.

The second leg at Villa Park was a completely different affair. We were without our skipper, Dennis Mortimer, through injury, so Ken McNaught led the team out that night. It had been a superstition of mine that I always went out on to the pitch last but Tony Barton stopped me before we went out.

'You always go out last. Is it that you always want to go out last?' I told him I actually would prefer to go out first and walked away but he asked, 'When you said you'd rather go out first, what did that mean?'

I replied, 'Well, what do you think it means? Who goes out first?'

He was a bit surprised to learn that I actually may have wanted to be captain and said, 'Oh. I never thought about that. That's why I never asked you to be captain of the team.' I said to Tony he should have asked me the question but I guess if you don't ask you don't get. Funnily enough, I did get to captain the team a few times after that, in Dennis's absence.

The second leg at Villa Park was a bad-tempered affair, and one of their defenders, Alberto, was sent off for deliberate handball. All the same, by half-time we couldn't get a grip on the game and went in at 0–0. Late on in the second half, I think it was about ten minutes from full time, we had a free kick. Gordon usually took our set-pieces and we had a plan where I would start to walk away from my marker with the intention of losing him when Gordon pinged the ball into the box. However, on that occasion, Migueli grabbed me by the elbow as I tried to spin away from him. My immediate thought was to shrug him off me and to get away from him but he fell over in the box and the ball fell to Gary Shaw, who slotted the ball home for the aggregate equaliser. While we were all celebrating, Migueli was lying in a heap and his face was covered in blood. Their goalkeeper went absolutely berserk and pointed his finger at me so I shrugged my shoulders as if to say, 'What are you on about?' Maybe I did catch him, and in today's football, I would have been sent off if the referee had spotted my elbow. It wasn't intentional, though – it was a reaction to try to get him off me and, fortunately, the officials didn't see anything so the goal stood.

We were on level terms and smelling blood, pardon the pun. I knew Migueli would want revenge so I told the players to give me the ball knowing full well he would try to kick me up in the air – and indeed he did, but he didn't hurt me and I just shrugged it off and got on with it. The game went into extra time and, on 99 minutes, Mark Walters, who had come on for Tony Morley, was tripped in the box and Gordon scored from the rebound after his spot kick was saved; however, when Gordon went to collect the ball from the net their goalkeeper kicked him up in the air and would have been sent off if the referee had seen it. At that point, the game turned nasty and the tackles really started to fly in. Barcelona were livid. Our third goal was scored by Ken McNaught from a diving header but they continued their gruesome tackling and Marcos was sent off, as was Allan Evans for a second booking; they should have had at least four sent off including their goalkeeper, who took that swipe at Gordon. The whole of the Barcelona team just lost it that night and the match could have easily been abandoned if the referee had sent off the number of players he should have (including me). The headlines in the Spanish press the next day read:

Hulk sucia

In English it translates to 'dirty Hulk' – and it was directed at me, which was a joke really. I suspect Migueli was complaining to the Spanish media that I had used unnecessary force and it resulted in him having a split lip and a broken nose. I remember Dave Geddis saying to me after the game, 'Are you proud of that?' I answered that I wasn't proud of it, but it happened. I didn't go out and intentionally belt him in the nose because when I was a player, I took a bit and gave a bit more but I never intentionally tried to injure anyone. Having said that, if anyone got in my way, I would run through a brick wall to get a goal or help my teammates, and if that brick wall happened to be the opposition, then so be it. Some people say that the way that I played was dirty, but I dispute that. I wasn't a dirty player at all – I was just hard. If I was chasing a ball with a defender in front of me, I went to chase the ball not the defender and if he was in the way, well, I would have done anything to get the ball. I had no fear. I would dive in to get the ball and have the chance to score, even if there was a defender's foot in my face. There was never any intention to hurt anyone on my part – I simply wanted to let players know they were in a game. I'm sure during that era all centre-forwards were the same. You don't see that any more in football – the game has changed and you can't touch another player without being cautioned.

I can only recall one or two instances where I warned players for doing something they shouldn't have done and both games were testimonials. One time I was playing at St Andrews and I was in the same side as the great George Best. There was a young full-back playing for Blues and he went after George from the start, I guess wanting to make a name for himself. On several occasions, George was running down the wing and the lad flew in, feet first, at George and the great man was kicked up in the air. I went over to George and asked if he was OK and he shook his head so I said to the lad, 'Are you stupid or something?' The young full-back shouted something back at me in a fit of temper and I told him to calm down. Several minutes later the same thing happened again but I said to the youngster, 'Hey you! You see all these people in this stadium? Do you think they have come to see you? These people have come to see him [pointing at George], George Best. They haven't come to see you kicking him so let him have the fucking ball.' The young lad carried on swearing at me and refused to calm down – he was still angry as hell. I turned to George and said, 'George, I'll fix it.' I waited and waited for the right moment and, when we had a corner, I went shoulder-to-shoulder to this full-back, and when we went to challenge for the ball, I smacked him in the mouth. When the chump landed on the ground, I looked over him and said, 'It hurts doesn't it lad. Stop kicking George or you'll get another one!' I think by then he got the message because he never went anywhere near George (or me) for the rest of the match.

A similar thing happened when I played for the Aston Villa Old Stars and a 67-year-old Johnny Dixon was targeted by a young lad who kicked him up in the air. I gave him the same treatment I'd given the full-back. It was funny that Johnny was an old-school footballer. He always wanted to play football, even at the age of 67, and before the game he'd instructed the manager not to take him off.

Johnny was brilliant during that game; he played balls up to me and shouted, 'Hold it, hold it Peter' while I was being kicked left, right and centre by the centre-half.

I managed to hold the ball up and then shouted back to Johnny, 'When you getting here?'

Obviously, he wasn't as fast as he used to be in the 1950s but he was a true football legend all the same, and it was an honour to play with him on that day.

I had established a great partnership with Gary Shaw over the course of 18 months at Villa. I was feeding off him and he was feeding off me, and I looked out for him too. In those days, players would very often threaten or kick you or try to intimidate you to put you off your game, especially against the young and inexperienced players like Gary. If anyone threatened Gary I'd go and sort them out. I would usually say something like, 'you're not dealing with him, you're dealing with me now ...' The one thing I learned early on in my career was that if you got kicked, and you were hurting, you never stayed down, and never gave them the opportunity to think they'd got one over you. If I ever got kicked or someone did something to me I always got straight up, even if I was limping, and I'd always give them the 'Withe glare'. Someone told me that my eyes glared and pierced through people. I used to stare at them as if to say, 'You think you've got one over me – well think again.' When I was younger my mother used to say I had staring eyes, so I guess I've always done it.

Some players physically feared other players, and Ray Clemence once said to Kathy, 'As soon as I saw your husband's name on the teamsheet it put the fear of god in me and I wouldn't come out for crosses.'

Steve Foster was another player who feared playing against me. I spoke to him about it once and he said, 'You wouldn't take any shit from anyone and I hated playing against you.'

The 'Withe glare' stemmed from playing against Dave Watson when I was about 21 years old. Dave was playing for Manchester City at the time and I split his eye open by accident and it was bleeding fairly heavily. When I mentioned it to him on the pitch he turned round and gave me a piercing look that went straight through me. The next time I came into contact with him he tackled me and I ended up on my arse in 'row Z'. I never forgot that look though and I kind of adopted it as my own. Ironically, I ended up playing with Dave for England a few years later in my career.

Liverpool was one of those games where you'd expect to be involved in hard tackles and off-the-ball incidents, as they had players like Graeme Souness with a reputation for being 'hard-men' at that time. When we played Liverpool at Villa Park during the 1983/84 season, half the pitch was frozen and would have been considered unplayable nowadays. I made a tackle on Kenny Dalglish – well, I went straight through him actually, although I'd gone for the ball, and he went tumbling over. Souness wasn't happy about my tackle and came over to make his point, and we had a bit of a tête-à-tête, shall we say. I said something like, '... yeah, you want to try and sort me out? Anytime you want.'

Then Kenny got up and came over to me and gave me some verbal. I told him in to 'keep it shut' or 'I'll come and sort you out as well ...' or words to that effect. I must have given them both the 'Withe glare.' Ironically, they got a free kick and scored from it, so I learned my lesson that day. We lost the game 4–2.

Although the likes of Souness were considered tough guys during that era, as much as they took they also gave back – maybe even more so. Having said that, there was never any malice in the tackles those guys made. It was just a case of looking after themselves and backing up their teammates. Going back a bit further, the likes of Tommy Smith, Norman Hunter and Billy Bremner were in the same mould, I'd say. I will never forget playing for Wolves as a youngster, standing in the tunnel with our winger, Dave Wagstaffe who wasn't the toughest player in the world, when Tommy Smith handed Dave a piece of paper. Dave, being kind of naïve said, 'Ahr, thanks Tommy. That's really nice of you. Thanks.' He then opened up the piece of paper and read it. Tommy's note simply said: 'Do you like hospital food?' Dave didn't know what to say, so he asked Kenny Hibbitt, our captain, if he could play on the opposite side of the pitch! Dave played right-wing that day instead of on the left.

There were also certain players who you'd get to know would act like babies if you ever threatened them or went in hard on them. I never verbally abused anyone for no reason. I say never – what I mean is that I'd never go up to someone unless they'd done something to me in the first place. I remember a long time ago when I was playing for Portland and came up against, arguably, one of the most cultured centre-halves around, Mike England, who was playing for Seattle Sounders. He whacked me in the face and I stood up to him and went eye-to-eye, giving him some verbal. In hindsight, as a youngster I should have shown him some respect, as he'd been a great player with Spurs and a Welsh international. I felt a bit guilty afterwards to be honest, but that's the way it was in the 70s.

As a centre-forward I'd always have a battle with goalkeepers as well. Ray Clemence always said I was a nightmare in the box. Very often I would tell the wide players like Tony Morley and Des Bremner to test the goalkeeper and see what he was about. I'd tell them to cross the ball into the box to give me a 50/50 challenge. Very often I'd clash with the goalkeeper and some of them wouldn't challenge me again, but the good ones, the tougher ones, would come back and challenge me for the next one as well. Even as a goal-keeper, you were allowed to smash the centre-forward and challenge hard. These days, the centre-forward can't get anywhere near the goalkeeper.

There was only one player I remember that I actually chased after on the pitch because he wound me up so much. He was a footballer called Paul 'Max' Miller, who played in defence with Graham Roberts for Tottenham in the early 1980s. I was playing for Villa and Spurs were on the attack, and I was watching the play but he was more interested in where I was looking. We were standing on the halfway line and he started making some small-talk, but I wasn't listening to him. Max made sure neither the linesmen nor the referee were looking, then all of a sudden, he smashed me in the face with his elbow. I rolled back but didn't go down. The one thing I learned from being a striker was never to let the centre-half think you're hurt, so I just stood my ground and gave him the 'Withe glare.' He took one look at me and started running and I started chasing him across the pitch while the play was going on down the other end of the field. There was blood pouring down my face and I said to myself, 'I'll get him!' but I suddenly stopped myself and realised, if I got caught, I'd be the one getting sent off, not him. The referee noticed what was going on and stopped the game but I told him there wasn't a problem. I remember Miller pointing to Graham Roberts then pointing to me as if to say, 'You mark him 'cos I ain't marking him any more.' He was frightened to death of me after that glare. That was the first and only time something like that happened to me throughout my entire career, and to this day, I think it was very snide of him to do it. It would have been picked up on camera these days and he'd have been suspended for sure.

I don't think I ever got sent off for being too physical, though. If I ever did something physical to another player it was never intentional. I was usually arguing with the referee or disputing his decisions more than anything else. If I jumped in the air for a ball, I'd use my arms for leverage and to keep myself in the air longer, and sometimes I (unintentionally) hit the defender with my arm. Those sorts of challenges are fouls in today's game, but in the 1980s they were a fair part of the game. I was never fearful of getting stuck-in where it hurt; I'd very often come off the field of play with cuts and bruises and the odd broken nose, and I'd very often get a kick in the face because I dived into a challenge. In fact, when we played Arsenal late in my Villa career, Viv Anderson finished my singing career before it even began when he kicked me in the throat and nearly broke my windpipe (unintentially of course). I later went to see a surgeon called Mr Shamoo about it, but not before I'd played another game. I couldn't get an appointment to see him for a few days and he asked me if I'd played since the injury and I said, 'Yeah, I played last Saturday.' He told me not to play for the next three weeks:

'Because of where the windpipe is, if you get another blow it will snap and you'll be dead. We won't be able to do anything for you then – finished! Unless there's a doctor in the stadium and he pushes a tube into you straight away, but even then, I don't think you'd survive.'

After explaining the consequences of playing again, he put a camera down my throat and examined me and confirmed the damage. I said to him off the cuff, 'What about playing the piano?' He said I'd be OK with that, to which I replied, 'Well, I couldn't play it before ...' It was funny because as a consequence of the operation, my voice literally changed. Before damaging my windpipe, I could actually sing a bit; I wasn't a great singer but I could hold my own, but afterwards, my singing voice sounded like a rough growl.

All-in-all, going to Villa had proven to be a great move for me personally. In the three seasons I had been there we had won three trophies, and even in the season after the European Super Cup win, we managed to get as far as the quarter-finals of the European Cup. We came up against a very strong Juventus side that included six members of the Italian World Cup-winning team, plus the outstanding Michel Platini and the Polish striker, Boniek, so it was a good effort even to lose to such an immense side. I also scored in Turin in front of a crowd of 70,000. We finished in a commendable sixth place in the league that season, which meant we would automatically qualify for the UEFA Cup the following season – European qualification for the third season in a row. However, it was around that time there was talk that the squad was going to be broken up.

With the European Cup win in the past, Tony decided he would stamp his authority on the team, and so the European Cup-winning side started to be dismantled. With the departures of Tony Morley, Dave Geddis, Ken

McNaught, Jimmy Rimmer, Andy Blair and Pat Heard, we saw new players arrive in Mervyn Day, Steve Foster and Alan Curbishley. Gordon also missed the season due to a serious injury. Prior to this, it was obvious that the winning side of 1982 was going to be broken up as the likes of Gary Shaw, Dennis Mortimer and Allan Evans were being left out of the side on a regular basis. Whether those departures were Tony's decision was not known – they all went far too quickly and easily for my liking.

****

It was around this time that we made a big life decision regarding our family. Kathy and I always wanted to have a girl, but having had three boys we agreed that we wouldn't have any more kids. Kathy then decided to have her Fallopian tubes tied and the surgeon who performed the operation told us it had been a success, which was obiously good news. However, a day or so later, and after I had been training in the morning Kathy said she'd been feeling unwell so she went to see her local GP but due to her symptoms she was referred back to the surgeon who had performed the original operation. We went back to the clinic and after giving Kathy a check-up we were then informed she'd had an ectopic pregnancy (a pregnancy outside of the womb). The surgeon who had performed the original operation on Kathy had clearly informed us that there was no chance of her becoming pregnant again - yet, she clearly had, but sadly it wasn't the outcome we'd hoped for. We soon realised it was serious and could have been life-threatening so she was rushed into the local hospital to have a procedure. It was an emergency operation: it wasn't a case of moving the egg into the womb because that simply wasn't possible. I guess the symptoms were similar to having a miscarriage, either way it wasn't a nice thing to go through. Luckily, that operation was a success (if you can call it that). Kathy always believed that it would have been a girl, and for many weeks and months had a very tough time coming to terms with our loss. To this day, Kathy still has that same feeling that she lost her little girl. It was a very sad time for the whole family.

****

There was one notable match during the 1983/84 season in the local derby at Highfield Road against Coventry City. Spinksy had to go off injured with concussion and in those days there was only one sub, so as we didn't have a spare goalkeeper, I went in goal with the score at 2–1 to Coventry. I'd already scored our goal and now it was my job to keep the goals out. We drew the game 3–3 in the end – needless to say my defence let me down! I actually pulled off two miraculous saves to keep us in that game. After I'd put the gloves and goalkeeper shirt on, the Coventry forward, Terry Gibson, attacked us down the left, so I covered the near post in case he shot. Instead, he crossed the ball to the far post and I shuffled across my goal. As I got to the far post, Dave Bennett hit a volley sweet as a nut so I dived full length and made a great save; the only problem was I made the save with my private parts. While the lads praised me for my efforts I stood there in agony – my balls hurt like crazy! I recovered sufficiently to make another great save at full length but that time I parried the ball out with my hand – not my balls, but Terry Gibson followed up to score. It was the only time I kept goal as Spinksy didn't play again that season and was replaced by Mervyn Day.

In the summer of 1984, Tony Barton's short but eventful reign came to an end. The real reason why Tony was dismissed may never be known, but it came as a bit of a surprise to me and the rest of the lads, even though we knew recent results weren't that great. The story going round was that Tony had refused requests from Doug Ellis to cut the first-team playing staff and youth-team numbers in order to reduce the club's overdraft. Tony didn't have the same discipline or strength of character that Ron Saunders had but he was a lovely guy, an absolute gentleman and you have to give him credit for helping us win the European Cup.

I knew by then that my time at Villa was coming to an end, but even before a new manager had been appointed, I had a phone call from Doug Ellis saying he had agreed to sell me to Southampton – without me even asking for a transfer. I wasn't happy but I spoke with their manager, Lawrie McMenemy two or three times, and we actually agreed terms. Doug accepted a transfer fee of around £200,000. Shortly afterwards, the Shrewsbury Town manager, Graham Turner was appointed and became Villa's youngest-ever manager at the age of 36 – only a few years older than myself, in fact.

When we returned to pre-season training, the first thing that Graham did was to call me into the office for a chat. I thought he'd spoken to the chairman about the Southampton deal, but when I asked him he had no idea Doug had even made the deal.

I said to Graham, 'He's agreed to sell me. I've spoken to Lawrie McMenemy and I'm going to Southampton.'

It made sense to me that Lawrie would want me as he preferred older players and at 33 I fitted into that category. However, it was obvious that Graham had no idea what had gone on before he had arrived at the club, and he wasn't very happy about it. He promised to go away and sort it out. He had been watching me train on my own before the main training session and I think he was impressed with my attitude.

A few days later, with my situation still in limbo, Graham called me into the office again and said, 'The deal's off. You're not going anywhere. I've checked and you're still under contract with Villa. I'm not letting you go. I want you to stay because I see what you do and I see what a reaction it creates in the other players. You're an inspiration to everyone here and you're an inspiration to me. I've never seen anyone do what you do on the training ground.'

Although I was happy I was able to stay at Villa, it was disappointing to a certain degree not to get my chance at Southampton, who in the previous season had finished second to Liverpool in the first division.

We went to a pre-season training session at the Alexander Stadium in Birmingham. We did a number of different things there, but the main reason we went was to do the Cooper Test, a 12-minute run around the track at your fastest speed. Most players would manage about seven laps of a 400-metre track running flat out, but the better runners would manage eight laps, I'd guess. All of the players asked Graham what he expected us to do, and he told us to do what we liked, but if any player could run nine laps they'd have the afternoon off. So, Graham had thrown down the gauntlet, and I was the type of person who would pick up the glove. I'd need to run a 1 minute, 20 second lap to do it, and I set out at a good pace, lapping players who couldn't keep up, and they all encouraged me along the way. As I came round the final bend I started to up my pace and thought I'd do it easily, but out of the blue Graham blew his whistle to stop the test! I couldn't believe it: he'd blown his whistle 10-15 seconds too early and I hadn't reached the finishing line.

The funny thing about the on-off transfer to Southampton was that I'd previously been in contact with Howard Kendall, my old Birmingham City captain and now Everton manager, about a possible transfer to my boyhood club. Bearing in mind I had already turned them down to go to Villa in 1980, I had another chance to fulfil my father's dream for me, to play for Everton. However, it wasn't my decision not to go to Goodison Park; Doug Ellis had slapped a stupid transfer figure on my head, around £400,000 I think, which was out of the question for Howard. They signed ex-Villa striker, Andy Gray, instead for £250,000. What a wise move he made because later that year, Everton won the FA Cup, and the following season they won the league championship and European Cup Winners' Cup. Andy scored in the final of the Cup Winners' Cup and he also reached another FA Cup final a year later, but he ended up on the losing side as Everton were defeated by Manchester United in 1985.

I was disappointed on missing out on the move to Everton (again) and, even though Andy was a few years younger than me, I couldn't help thinking, what if ... ?

Bobby Gould, the then Coventry City manager, also made an enquiry about me and we met to discuss a deal, but that was a non-starter because Bobby was trying to do the deal himself but the club wouldn't back him with the money. They made a £200,000 offer for me, but Villa made it clear I wasn't for sale.

Towards the end of the 1984/85 season, my contract at Villa was running down and Doug offered me a one-year extension, but I wanted a two-year deal because I thought I was still fit and could carry on playing at the highest level. I had played a year under Graham at Villa and my last game was at Anfield on 11 May 1985 where we lost 2–1 to finish mid-table. I had scored 92 goals in 232 games in all competitions – roughly one goal for every three games.

How ironic it was, then, that Andy Gray, who had gone to Everton two years earlier when I had the chance to go there, came in to replace me in July 1985 for his second spell at the club after winning three trophies with the Toffees. Football is full of coincidences, it seems.

It was the biggest wrench of my career, moving from Villa after those five fantastic years. Following my departure after Doug Ellis refused to give me a two-year contract, I had a few offers from other clubs, but nothing concrete materialised.

I then started to think about what I wanted to do after I retired from football. I took my first coaching badge in 1982 while I was still playing for Villa, just after we'd won the European Cup. In those days, it was an eight-week course, one day a week and the only day of the week I could do was a Sunday. On the course there were only three professionals – myself, Dennis Mortimer and Dave Geddis, together with several members of the public from all walks of life. We had to drive to a random field near Wolverhampton every Sunday for those eight weeks, and there wasn't one Sunday amongst them that it didn't rain.

On the final Sunday we had an assessment. We had to pick a topic or a footballing scenario coaching a small team. One of the non-professional lads had the scenario 'midfield play', so he had ten minutes to get his point across to the likes of Dennis and Dave.

After five minutes, he hadn't said anything so my friend Dorien shouted to him, 'Five minutes have gone ...' The lad suddenly sprung to life and went straight up to Dennis.

'Dennis, this is what's happening. You're in midfield and you're in trouble so you need help, don't you?'

Dennis looked a bit bemused but played along with it: 'Yeah, yeah alright.'

The coach continued, 'What I want you to do is to shout, "HELP, HELP," – OK?'

So Dennis went off and for the next five minutes ran around the pitch shouting, 'Help, help ...'

Those who watched that session just burst out laughing.

After the last session, it was raining (again) and we were all buzzing because we'd completed the course, so I asked my son, Jason, to go to get a bottle of whisky out of the car. I'd won a huge bottle of whisky which had been rolling around in my car for a while, so I thought it would be nice to share it with the lads. I found some plastic cups and everyone had a tot to celebrate.

Fast-forward to the summer of 1985 and I decided to take my A Licence at the FA School of Excellence at Lilleshall. It was a two-week course and, again, it was a mixture of professional players and non-professionals – unlike today where professionals and non-professionals take separate courses. During one session, the topic was 'goalkeepers' and the coach was a guy called Mike Kelly, who I knew from my Birmingham City days. I was following a few of the lads on to the pitch and noticed one lad had a bag with him, and I asked someone else why he was taking it on to the pitch. He replied, 'Goalkeeper – he's a goalkeeper.' His name was John Bilson. Mike addressed the group and said we were likely to get a topic on goalkeeping and asked the group if there were any goalkeepers present, so John put his hand up straight away, along with another lad called Malcolm Crosby, an ex-Sunderland goalkeeper. It turned out to be John's fifth attempt to pass his full badge after he'd failed the previous four. I was thinking of putting my hand up actually, as I'd played in goal on occasion and considered myself as being pretty handy, but decided not to when John put his hand up – I fancied my chances scoring goals against him, knowing his previous record. Mike then asked the group for some strikers, and I didn't need any encouragement to volunteer for that, along with three others. I said to Mike privately, 'I want to play against John,' and he agreed, so he asked John and Malcolm to go for a warm-up while most of the group watched them from a distance.

While we were watching, we noticed John wasn't very good and didn't seem to move when the ball came towards him. When the time came for me to test John with some crossing and finishing, I was expecting to score every time, but out of the three shots and two headers against him, he bloody saved every one. The rest of the lads ribbed me about it, 'Withey, it's obvious you can't score goals against good goalkeepers like John.'

One of the shots was a volley: I hit it sweet as a nut and he dived the opposite way, but still managed to get a knee to it so it went over the bar. Another shot hit him on the head and went over the bar. In fact, every shot hit him anywhere but the hand. Looking back it was so funny because John really wasn't very good in goal, yet I couldn't score against him. John actually believed he was a good goalkeeper. At the end of the course we all had a bit of a collection and presented him with a goalkeeper's shirt with 'Dino Zoff' on the back, 'Being as you're such a great goalkeeper, look what we've got for you, John.' Not only was John absolutely ecstatic he'd received the shirt, he was also happy because he'd passed the course (at last).

John somehow ended up being Academy Director of Football at Leeds United in later life.

There was a farmer from Cornwall on the course too – yes, a farmer – and his name was also John. He had the scenario titled 'crossing and finishing', working with the strikers. What you had to do in that scenario was to get someone to cross the ball so the striker could get on to the end of it and score. John asked two players who couldn't even cross the ball properly to play as wingers – but he put professional strikers in the middle to score the goals. The head of coaching, Alan Wade, used to have the job of walking round the pitches watching the play, and he stopped to watch what was happening on our pitch. He must have been bemused because he watched crosses coming in from all angles but none of them reached their destination (the strikers) as they flew over the bar or out of play.

Alan stepped in and asked John, 'What's your name?' Alan continued, 'Tell the wingers what you want, John.'

So, John explained to the wingers that he wanted them to 'get down the by line and cross that ball in the middle for that striker over there.'

Alan asked more questions, then, 'Tell 'em how to strike the ball, John.'

So John carried on explaining, 'I want you to hit the ball with the inside of your foot ...'

Alan was pushing John to explain in even more detail, and after a few minutes, the coach who was taking the session stopped the play and called everyone in.

'John, it didn't really go that well, did it?'

John replied, 'Well, I thought it went alright, I did, until that cunt (pointing to Alan) poked his nose in!'

To that, Alan burst out laughing.

On those courses back in the 1980s you'd always get people who weren't professional footballers, and there used to be some crackers I can tell you.

If I remember rightly, if you were a professional player, the PFA would fund a percentage of the fee, maybe 55 per cent, so the first course – it was called the preliminary in those days – only cost me £50. The A Licence (full licence) was residential at around £650 but the PFA funded some of that as well. The non-professionals obviously had to pay the full amount. When I did my Pro-Licence in 2001 it cost me just under £5,000 and I had to come back from Thailand to do it over several weeks.

When I came back to do my full licence at Warwick University, along with a bunch of lads from Coventry City FC, we had Derek Fazackerley doing our coaching. The scenario was that Sunderland were going down, in the last game of the season, playing Manchester United at home. So, the would-be coaches had to come up with a game plan to deal with the scenario, but there had to be an 'if' element – something like, what if we go all-out attack and concede a goal? Then we had to think about things like: do we play four strikers or play with one up front and pack the midfield, for example. Derek was wired-up to a microphone so everyone could hear everything he was saying, and at one point he shouted out a chorus of swear words because he didn't like something he saw on the pitch.

So I said to him, 'Derek, Derek, you'll have to watch your language because there are parents listening and watching you.'

On another day during my full licence residential, one of the lads was trying to coach 'attacking play' and as strikers we had to pick two centre-backs who were professionals. It didn't go to plan because the centre-backs were so good, nothing got past them. Brian, the coach for the session, tried playing with two strikers, three strikers, four strikers, then he tried four strikers and two midfielders, but the centre-backs still couldn't be broken down – they were that defensively strong. The head coach watched the session unfold and said, 'Brian, something's gone wrong here.'

Brian (the coach) gathered everyone in and replied, 'Yeah, I've worked out what's going wrong here. Come in everyone,' and while he was talking he pointed to the two centre-backs, 'You and you, fuck off.'

That solved the problem. Of course, Brian failed the course because the idea was to coach the strikers to get past the defenders and he failed to do that.

Some of the things that go on during those courses are hilarious and the people who go on them make the whole experience worthwhile.

****

I knew I was still fit and could give a club three years or more, but I spent that summer without a club until I spoke to Ian Porterfield, the (then) Sheffield United manager, who I knew anyway. Ian said he'd been chasing me for a while and wanted to sign me on a three-year contract. I signed for United just before the start of the 1985/86 season. Big Ken McNaught, who had left Villa in the summer of 1983 following the change of ownership, had spent a season with West Bromwich Albion and then went on loan to Manchester City and the funny thing was we both signed for Sheffield United at the same time that summer of 1985. Not only that, Ian Porterfield made two other significant signings in Phil Thompson and Ray Lewington, who were both 'veterans' as well. We were all in our early 30s so we quickly became known as the 'Dads Army.' It was around that time that my eldest son, Jason, signed for West Bromwich Albion, managed by Ron Atkinson.

Sheffield United were in Division Two at the time and had only just escaped the drop in their previous season under Ian so we were under no illusions about what we were going into. Kathy and I decided we weren't going to move to Sheffield; nor did Ken, so we travelled back and forth to Sheffield together, sharing the driving. The agreement I had with Ian was that I didn't have to travel there every day, so we only went two or three days a week to train.

United supporters were unhappy with Ian because the fans' favourite, Keith Edwards, had been dropped to the bench in favour of his 'aged' colleagues. We started the season very brightly, and after a 3–0 win away to early season promotion favourites Portsmouth, we were fancied for another promotion chase. However, injury and bad results saw the club's fortunes falter, and the crowd's anger turned on the manager, who, after a 5–2 defeat to Norwich, was sacked after a car-park demonstration. It was funny, because Keith Edwards was an out-and-out goalscorer and to this day holds a number of records for scoring – he scored 114 goals in 191 appearances for United. He only played a few games in the top flight so scored most of his goals in the lower leagues. However, we did play several games together, and I remember in one game, he was told to stay up the field when we defended set-pieces. Keith had a bit of pace about him, and normally the opposition would have to leave two defenders back to mark him. At one point in the game we were defending a corner and I got a header in to clear the ball away which landed in Keith's path on the halfway line. One of the opposition centre-backs tried to nick the ball, but Keith rolled him and set off towards goal with me in hot pursuit. As Keith headed towards the box on the right-hand side, I had caught up and was alongside him, but as the goalkeeper closed him down I thought he'd just roll the ball across the box to me and I'd have an empty net to score. He elected to shoot, and missed the goal at the near post. I asked him why he didn't pass to me as I'd made a 70-yard run to get into a good position, but he reckoned he didn't see me, to which I replied in no uncertain terms, 'The best players see the shot and see a teammate.' I wasn't too happy as you can imagine, but he wasn't the only player ever to do that.

At the end of the season, Ken had tried to manage a recurrent swelling in his knee which he'd acquired after an operation back in 1981, and had unfortunately developed deep vein thrombosis. A blood clot had remained in his calf, limiting his movement. He was forced to retire as a Sheffield United player when he was told a broken leg could result in the loss of the limb. That meant I would have to travel to Sheffield on my own during the second season at United. Not only that, Ian left the club and the chairman promoted the youth-team coach, Billy McEwan as manager. Billy was only two months older than me, and I think he felt a bit uncomfortable dealing with guys of his own age. The change of manager was a problem for me, because my agreement with Ian that I would only travel up to Sheffield for training a few days a week was questioned by McEwan. He wanted me to come in every day, but I told him that I had agreed not to travel every day with Ian. McEwan then said it wasn't written into my contract so I'd have to do as he wanted. I did it for the remainder of the season, even though the daily commute was a real pain. Billy signed a few players, and one of them was Peter Beagrie, a wide player who could play on either wing, or if needed, made a decent striker. He was famous because when he scored he would do a somersault, which was something players just didn't do back then.

I remember we played a game at Bramall Lane, not sure who it was against but Peter seemed to be pleased with his performance, so I asked him how he thought he'd done. He told me he thought he'd done great, and the crowd liked what he did. I then asked him how many crosses he got into the box (not many) but he didn't know and asked me why I asked. I told him my thoughts and offered to do a bit of training with him on the Monday, and he agreed. Monday came, and we trained at Bramall Lane, so we went on to the pitch and I asked him if he could go into the middle while I crossed some balls over for him to score. He seemed pleased with that, so I went out on to the left wing and made a run with the ball, but I faked the cross and dragged the ball back to my right foot, and he shouted at me, saying he'd made a run to get on the end of the cross. I repeated that trick five or six times, and he started to get annoyed.

So I asked him, 'What's your problem?'

He replied, 'I'm making the runs to get on the other end of a cross that doesn't come to me.'

I told him, 'Now you know what it feels like. I do shuttle-runs every game, not knowing when a cross is going to come in from you. If you have time, go and watch a couple of wingers I have played with who are the best in the business, John Robertson and Tony Morley. They measure their game on how many crosses they supply to the forwards and the bonus for them is when they score goals themselves.'

I think I got my message across loud and clear because he got a move to Stoke and then to Everton later in his career.

We finished 9th in Division Two and at the end of the season I spoke to my old playing partner, Garry Pendrey. Garry was the manager at Birmingham City then, and he offered me a way out of the daily commute to Sheffield. I'd joined United on a free transfer and I think Billy just wanted me out of the club as he agreed to release me at the start of the 1987/88 season; however, there were a few issues with my contract and we couldn't sort them out in time, so Garry asked me to join Blues on loan, with a view to giving me a two-year contract once I'd sorted my contract dispute with Sheffield. It was a way out of Sheffield United, and as we were still living in the Midlands at the time, playing for Blues again was appealing, especially at the age of 36.

I made my (second) debut for Blues in the home game against Shrewsbury Town in mid-September, but I broke my arm in that game. Garry had asked me if I would have a pin put in my arm so I could return quicker, which meant rather than being out for over eight weeks, I only missed four games before I returned to the side again, although the arm wouldn't have fully mended. I played seven more games for Birmingham before the start of December and one of those games was against Sheffield United during which I scored my only two goals for Blues in that spell. Of course, you're not allowed to play against the team who loans you now, but in those days it wasn't a problem. The United fans obviously weren't happy that I played in that game, and they made it known.

Shortly after my final game, at home to Leicester, Garry reneged on his word and told me he wouldn't be signing me after all. That episode impacted our friendship, as I felt he'd made a promise to me then broken it. However, I'm too long in the tooth to continue with the animosity it caused back then, and to this day I still see Garry when I attend Blues games. I think at the time he was put under some pressure by Ken Wheldon, the then owner of Blues, but it's all water under the bridge now anyway.

The next season I was still officially a Sheffield United player so I had to go back to them and face the supporters who had given me a load of abuse for scoring a brace for Blues against their team. Billy McEwan asked me to play in the home game against Reading but when my name was announced before the game, the Blades supporters booed, even though I was wearing the red and white striped shirt this time. However, I have always had the resilience to get on with things and I soon won the fans over as I went on to score a brace in a 4–1 victory. When I scored my first goal it was in front of the home fans, and I didn't celebrate but faced the fans with a huge smile on my face as if to say, 'OK, you booed me before the game, now you're cheering my goal ...' Irony seemed to play a part a lot in my football career and there was no shortage of it during that spell.

During that season I had to have a knee operation at the Priory Hospital in Birmingham. While I was recovering from the surgery at home, I remember being in terrible pain one night and I didn't want to wake Kathy or the kids so I went downstairs and sat in the lounge. I decided to have a tot of cognac and was looking at my left leg as it seemed to be a bit swollen. As I pressed my finger on to my shin it didn't come out, which didn't seem right; however, I took myself back to bed. I told Kathy about it when we woke up and she advised me to call the surgeon, Dr Pearson. The doctor asked me to come to the hospital as soon as I could, so I arrived about 20 minutes later and was admitted straight away. I had to go through a number of tests and then had a venogram, an X-ray which involves injecting dye into the vein to check how the blood is flowing through the veins. After all that, I was placed in a room waiting for medical staff to come to see me. I was dressed only in a gown and was freezing cold and shaking, but the male nurse told me not to be nervous.

'I'm not nervous I'm just bloody freezing,' I told him, so he went off to get me a blanket. Finally, a doctor came in and said he'd have to insert a catheter into my main artery in my leg, just around the groin area. He gave me an injection and told me he'd be back in 10-15 minutes, after the anaesthetic had taken effect. On his return he told me he was going to insert the catheter and when he started to dig the needle into my leg I jumped. The doctor asked me why I jumped so I said I felt the needle but he told me he'd put a lot of anaesthetic in me so I shouldn't have felt anything. As he couldn't have given me any more I told him to carry on. I remember it being painful for a while and then, all of a sudden I felt as though I'd peed myself, and I felt a bit embarrassed about it. The doctor told me to keep still as he'd got the catheter into the correct place but as I looked down to the floor I saw a pool of blood and realised it was from my artery – I hadn't pissed myself after all. The doctors and nurses spent a long time taking X-rays as they kept getting it wrong, so they kept pumping fluid into my leg while the X-ray machine was moving up and down ... It was a complete nightmare.

The tests finally came back and the diagnosis was that I had DVT – deep vein thrombosis or, in layman's terms, I'd had a blood clot. That in itself was very dangerous, because if the clot moved it would be fatal, so I had to remain in hospital overnight. I felt like a pin cushion, because they were giving me all sorts of drugs – warfarin, heparin – and constantly taking blood samples to see if they had the right blood coagulation. If I had the wrong blood coagulation and subsequently got a cut or got injured I could have bled to death.

At that stage, I was so bored of waiting around in the hospital, I decided (against doctor's orders) to go for a stroll, so I left my room and went on to the ward. I met a couple of lads who had just had open-heart surgery and they showed me their scars, which were the length of their chests. While I was having a chat to them the nurse came up to us and told the lads to go for a walk outside for about 15-20 minutes, but ordered me back to my bed as it was dangerous for me to be walking around.

Eventually, the doctors completed the tests, got the blood coagulation right and I was allowed to go home after a week in hospital; however, I had to go back every week to get my blood checked and to check my medication. I was able to train on my own but couldn't get involved in game situations for a while.

Results weren't going too well and Billy McEwan was sacked in January 1988 and replaced by Dave Bassett. I met up with Dave and liked what he had to say and he was looking forward to seeing me play in his team; however, I had to tell him that even though I looked fit enough, due to my DVT I couldn't play for any length of time, although I ended up playing a part in the last three games of the season. I played against Huddersfield who had already been relegated, and who we had to beat to secure our place in the play-off. In those days, the team who finished third from bottom played the third-placed team from the league below, and that team happened to be Bristol City. In the 43rd minute of the first leg tie, their centre-back elbowed me in the side of my head and I received a depressed fracture to my cheek. I had to go to a Bristol hospital to have an operation and ended up staying there for a few days. The operation went well but my football season ended, and because we lost the play-off over two legs, we were relegated to the third tier of English football during that 1987/88 season. All credit to Dave though; he got the club back up to Division Two in his first full season.

The main thing that I learned from three seasons at Bramall Lane was that I would never, ever let a player do what I did, and that was to travel every day for 90 minutes to train for two hours and then do the same journey to get back home. It didn't do my body any good as it was the only time in my entire football career that I had a strained calf muscle, and that was due to all the driving I did. By the time I got out of the driver's seat when I returned home after training it used to hurt like mad and I couldn't move.

I was without a club again at the end of my Sheffield United career and I was at an age where I had to consider packing it in. I'd heard about a managerial vacancy at Huddersfield Town and thought I would enquire about the job. As it happened, I received a phone call from Eoin Hand, the former Ireland manager and the (then) assistant manager of the Yorkshire club. I had actually played against Eoin while we were both in South Africa all those years ago, and we had a chat about Huddersfield and he said he had been lined-up for the manager's job. I told him I'd put an application in, which he knew about, but out of the blue he asked me if I'd consider being his assistant manager, if he did get the job. Not only that, I agreed to play as well as being the assistant manager, prolonging my footballing career in the meantime. I was still fit so it seemed to make sense.

Eoin got the job as expected, and he appointed me as his assistant manager/player/coach. The club had just been relegated from Division Two and had finished rock bottom in the previous season, so it was our job to recover the club's fortunes.

After living in Solihull for eight years, Kathy and I decided we would uproot the family and move north to Huddersfield because of the job. Jason, however, had been signed by West Bromwich Albion so he stayed in Birmingham with a friend. We managed to find a lovely place in a village called Farnley Tyas, three miles south of the town and situated up on a hill. I used to take the training and, of course, I ran the boys ragged. One session during pre-season, I decided to take the players up to Farnley Tyas and we ran there from the training ground. The hill goes on for miles and our house was almost at the top of the hill, so we stopped for a few minutes and walked past my house; of course the players didn't know where I lived and I asked them if they wanted a drink. They all looked at each other and then they looked at me as if I had gone raving mad.

'Where are you going to get a drink around here?' It was in the middle of nowhere and the nearest shop was a good distance away. Then I spotted

Kathy outside the house and said to the lads, pointing at Kathy, 'I bet I can chat that bird up over there and get a drink from her.'

The lads looked at each other again, and one of them said, 'You've got no chance.'

I approached Kathy and explained the plan and in a soft voice, I said, 'Can you just get us a few drinks, please, love ...' and we chatted away for a bit and then, out of the blue I gave her a big kiss on the lips.

The lads were transfixed and couldn't believe what they'd witnessed, and when I came back, one of the lads said, 'How did you do that?'

I replied, 'Well, I've just got this charm, you know ...' Kathy then came out with the tray of drinks and I thanked her. The boys couldn't believe it.

After our break for drinks, we continued along the road and arrived at a football field and did some training there then returned to the training ground. The training I provided at Huddersfield wasn't dissimilar to what I went through at some of my previous clubs and involved a lot of running, but the difference was, I ran with the lads and I was always at the front – that's how fit I was.

I will say though, that my coaching was not just about running: I tried to make the training interesting and different on a day-to-day basis.

During October 1990 I heard the sad news of the death of Peter Taylor, Brian Clough's right-hand man. Peter's friendship and partnership with Clough had been strained on various occasions in the past and it was said the two never spoke after Taylor pinched Robbo from Forest when he was manager at Derby County in 1983. I know Brian was deeply upset on hearing the news, and although it had been reported that he wouldn't attend the funeral, he did. I travelled alone from Huddersfield to attend the funeral at St Peter's Church in Widmerpool, Nottinghamshire. I stood at the back of the church with Frank Clark as all the seats had been taken. Shortly before the beginning of the funeral, a procession of footballers and ex-footballers walked through the church to take their seats. The funny thing about seeing all the lads walk through the church was that I didn't recognise my old roommate, Larry Lloyd, and Frank had to confirm who he was. He had put on so much weight, I didn't recognise him. After the formalities of the funeral and the burial, we all went out to a local pub to have some drinks and I spoke to Larry for the first time in ages.

'Flipping heck, Larry, you've put on a bit of timber!'

Larry replied, 'Yeah, I've been doing a bit of weights.'

I said, 'What, you been eating them?'

12

England

"Do you know what son? I said to you just come down to help us out and you've put in the most magnificent performance from a player I've seen for a long, long time. I wish I had 11 players of the same spirit as you played with. You were absolutely magnificent."

Sir Bobby Robson, former England Manager 1982–1990

****

On the Monday after the city-centre parade to celebrate Villa's 1980/81 league championship, Ron Saunders called me into his office and asked me if I'd like to play in another game, so I agreed. I thought he was asking me to play in another testimonial game, but he then said, 'How do you fancy playing up front with Kevin Keegan?' I didn't understand what he'd said at first so he repeated it, 'Yeah, playing up front with Kevin Keegan. I've had someone on the phone who wants you to play in this game.' There was a brief pause, '... and how do you fancy getting your first cap for England?' I was also pleased for our captain, Dennis Mortimer as he was called up to the squad as well. Then Ron explained the game was against Brazil at Wembley on the following Wednesday, so I had about eight days to prepare myself.

At that time, I had started to reflect on my past. Even when managers were telling me I'd never make it, I'd just accept their opinion – then try to prove them wrong! I always said to people I was like a good wine – I got better as I got older. However, I've always believed in my own ability, and I'm also a great believer in fate; meeting Derek Dougan in South Africa all those years ago was a matter of meeting the right person in the right place at the right time. If he hadn't encouraged me I probably wouldn't have come back to England to play for Wolves, and that's where my long journey in football truly started.

Throughout my career it had been my ambition to play for my country, but I'd always felt that the opportunity had passed me by. However, I'm not the sort of person who gives up easily and my motto has always been, 'try, try and try again.' Despite my age at the time (I was 29) I still wanted to play for my country. Even had I been 39 years old, my determination to fulfil that ambition would have been just as great. I'd reached the age when England caps seemed nothing but a pipe dream, but I kept on dreaming anyway because that's the kind of person I am. My dream came true.

It capped off an extraordinary season; winning the championship, scoring 21 league goals, being voted player of the year and being capped for the first time at the age of 29 – not a bad season. As it happened, Kevin Keegan got injured and I made my debut for England *and* took the number 9 shirt. There was a World Cup coming up in Spain (1982) and I wanted to be part of it. Life couldn't have been any better and I felt like I was walking on cloud nine.

One of my favourite boyhood teams was Brazil and it was like a dream come true that I had been selected to play against them at Wembley. I think my soft spot for Brazil stemmed from seeing them at Goodison Park during the 1966 World Cup. Pelé was an idol of mine (as he probably was for millions of lads of my generation). To me, he was the perfect footballer.

At that time, England was blessed with great strikers – the likes of Trevor Francis, Mick Channon, Kevin Keegan, Paul Mariner and even Bob Latchford were in front of me in the pecking order. At the bottom of the list were Cyrille Regis and myself. Cyrille was very quick and created a lot of trouble for defenders because he got on the ball so quickly, whereas my qualities were in laying the ball off and getting into the box quickly. All in all, Ron Greenwood was spoilt for choice, which was great for him because it meant everyone was trying that bit harder to impress.

So, on the 12 May 1981, only ten days after winning the championship with Villa, I stepped out in front of 75,000 fans at Wembley to make my debut for England. I remember the day so well. While I was getting changed I looked around the dressing room, with the likes of Kenny Sansom, Ray Wilkins, Bryan Robson and Ray Clemence beside me, and I was thinking, 'Why has everyone got two shirts?' I asked one of the lads, because at club level, we only had one shirt. I think it was Ray Wilkins who told me that at half-time you'd change your shirt and then swap with an opponent, and then you'd have the original shirt to take home.

Surprisingly, I was no more nervous than I'd ever been before a game. To make your international debut at Wembley is a major achievement for any player, so I was determined to take it all in my stride. It was also Alvin Martin's debut and both of us were thrown in at the deep end playing Brazil, but Alvin, who was only 22, felt like he was in deeper water than me, as he had to cope with their attacking players. There was a capacity crowd of 100,000 to witness that great Brazil side, which included Zico, Junior and Eder.

For some reason we played in red shirts that day, even though we were at Wembley. Not that it mattered – we could have played in pink shirts, it wouldn't have made any difference. The game kicked off and I felt like an 18-year-old again – well I was playing like one, giving the ball away far too often during the opening stages of the game. I told myself to relax and enjoy my first cap; normally I thrive playing in front of big crowd and after a while I began to relax and started to play my usual game. We conceded an early goal in the 12th minute when Zico scored, but we gave a good account of ourselves and, low and behold, in the latter stages of the game, we were looking for an equaliser. Kenny Sansom ventured forward and crossed the ball to me and I headed it down as I was off balance, then hit it on the half-volley, beat the goalkeeper but hit the left-hand post and rolled out for a goal kick. I couldn't believe I nearly scored on my debut. In another move, I soared above the defence and headed the ball down firmly and saw it spin out, off the goalkeeper's knees for a corner. In the end, we lost narrowly 1–0. It could have been a dream debut but it wasn't to be.

I also took Ray's advice and exchanged shirts after the game with Luiz Carlos Ferreira, the Brazil number 4 who was marking me all through the game – so I had both shirts, and went home happy.

The difference in standard between league and international football was remarkable, but I thought we matched the Brazilians on the day. They tackled hard but I didn't mind that as I could handle the physical side of the game. I actually found it easier to play at international level because I was playing with the best bunch of lads in the country who helped each other out, both physically and by talking to each other on the pitch. It was just great to be in the side.

My day had come – and not before time.

****

That was my first taste of international football and I enjoyed the whole experience, even though we lost the game. The manager at the time was Ron Greenwood, who I found to be a very good manager. Greenwood was famous for the selection of the first black player to play for England, Viv Anderson. He reportedly stated, 'Yellow, purple or black – if they're good enough, I'll pick them.' It was a bold statement at the time and I respected him for that. Ron was very knowledgeable about the game; he was a very good tactician and always coached the players himself. He just told me to play the same game as I did for Villa, which suited me down to the ground. He had a few excellent coaches in his backroom staff including Don Howe and Bobby Robson, who not only helped with coaching but also did some scouting too. There was also World Cup winner Geoff Hurst, who came in to help out occasionally. Working with a legend like Geoff was special. Ron had worked with Geoff at West Ham where he had been drafted into the coaching team to work with the strikers.

Don Howe was a very good coach and Ron's right-hand man. He was brilliant in fact; he was always only too pleased to help a player improve and would put on extra training sessions if you asked him to. Don had time for anyone who wanted to learn and practise. He loved football and had an infectious personality. Everyone warmed to him and most of us wanted to emulate his character. His knowledge of the game was immense and he strived to do better and always wanted you to improve as a player.

Joining the England squad opened my eyes to different training methods and drills. We had a really fit squad and some truly skilful players. I never thought I'd be working on fitness when I went to join the England squad but we actually did some serious fitness training. Bryan Robson and Terry McDermott were both fitness fanatics like myself and were super fit. Terry McDermott was as thin as a rake and would pick at his food – but would also like a pint or two, like a lot of the lads did. Funnily enough, there was at least one player who didn't drink in the squad and that was Trevor Brooking, or 'Hadleigh' as we called him (after the TV series at the time). Trevor was always smartly dressed, impeccable in fact. He was a teetotaller and he claimed he never swore. In fact, he hated swearing and he'd very often go berserk if he heard any of us swear on the training field. Ironically, he was caught using the f-word on camera when he was caretaker manager of West Ham in 2003.

I soon realised that those rivalries on a Saturday afternoon turned into good friendships once you put that white or red shirt on. We all had the same goal, and that was to play and win for England. There were certain (internal) rivalries though, mainly between the strikers and goalkeepers who were fighting for one or two places in the team. There was a great rivalry between Peter Shilton, Ray Clemence and Joe Corrigan at the time – three great goalkeepers. The goalkeeper position is unique in that keepers are always competing with one another for that one position between the sticks; but Peter, Ray and Joe all worked with one another. It was left to the manager to pick the best goalkeeper on the day. Ron had previously made a statement that he was going to play Peter and Ray alternatively, but I don't think it worked out like that. It would have been interesting if he'd just made one of them his number one goalkeeper to see how many caps they would have ended up with. Looking back, at that time Peter and Ray were England's two best goalkeepers. Personally, I had only played with Shilts (at Forest). I knew Ray fairly well and he was a great goalkeeper but Peter was the best I'd worked with – he was just phenomenal. With regards to his training and everything he did on the pitch, he was head and shoulders above anyone else.

I remember after I'd played my first game for England and I received my salary cheque from Villa, I just sat staring at it, because the total was so much more than my usual salary. I immediately went to see the Villa club secretary, Steve Stride.

'What are these extras in my salary, Steve?'

Steve confirmed that the extra was my England appearance money. I seriously had no idea I would be paid to play for England. When I got home I told Kathy about it.

'Flipping heck, I can't believe I get paid to play for England – I'd have played for nothing!'

Kathy immediately replied, 'You bloody wouldn't! If you're given money, you take it!'

I think it amounted to about an extra £125, which was a fair amount back then, and it meant that Kathy could spend a bit more money on the kids. I believe the England players these days donate their purse to the England Footballers Foundation – fair play to them for that.

Talking about extras, playing for England also brought in gifts such as new Sony Walkmans, as Sony were one of England's main sponsors, and sunglasses from Ray-Ban. Footballers love freebies, and that was just the tip of the iceberg. Not only were you given stuff, you could also order products at huge discounts. I remember one time I ordered a TV, video and camera from Sony for next to nothing. All footballers get boots from their boot sponsors, but it was like Christmas every time you played for England. Talking about sponsorship, since I'd been at Newcastle I was sponsored by the car manufacturer Talbot (now Peugeot) and they gave me their latest model, the Tiago. It was the widest car I'd ever driven and on one trip I think I packed eight players in it! But by far the best freebie was when Ray Clemence's agent asked us to go on a Norwegian cruise for free (although we had to pay for the children) in return for making a few guest appearances while on board.

At your club, you'd be expected to do media interviews for nothing, but with England, there was a 'committee' who organised the interviews and then chose who would do them. We were all part of a pool of players who would actually get paid for being interviewed. On one occasion, I'd just driven from Birmingham to the West Park Hotel, the team base for home matches, to join up with the rest of the squad and was met by the press officer. He told Peter Barnes and me that we were expected in Birmingham to do a Q&A at the Night Out (night club). I was a bit annoyed to say the least as I'd only just arrived from the Midlands.

'You could have told me before I'd set out. I've just come from Birmingham!!'

The press officer then replied, 'It's OK Peter, you're both flying up there.'

I thought it was a waste of my time; however, Peter Barnes was absolutely crapping himself, as he hated flying. To make matters worse, it was pouring down with rain and the plane was a six-seater. As soon as Peter saw the plane he turned round and said he was going to hire a car and drive to Birmingham himself. However, fair play to him, he eventually plucked up enough courage to get on the plane. I think we both spent a few hours at the Night Out and then had to return back to London the same evening. Peter took the plane back because he couldn't get anyone else to take him back to London, but he promised never to go in one of those small planes again.

Playing for England was brilliant and it was an exciting time for me, but there were times when I was staying away in hotels that I had to find ways to fill the time and alleviate the boredom. Luckily, we were allowed to go outside of the camp, so we'd go out to the pub or, on one occasion, about eight of us went to the local cinema to watch the latest movie, *The Woman in Red* with Gene Wilder. Can you imagine the likes of me, Kevin Keegan, Ray Wilkins and other England footballers sitting in a cinema eating their popcorn watching a movie? When the opening scenes came on the screen we nearly dropped our popcorn all over ourselves; our eyes were fixed on that famous sexy scene involving Kelly LeBrock's red dress. What a start that was! It actually turned out to be one of the funniest movies I've ever seen.

I soon found out that playing for England helped you meet some big celebrities you'd never have expected to meet. Dave Watson was a big rock fan and during our downtime with England, he'd very often go to concerts at Wembley. On one occasion he told us he was going to see Status Quo at the Wembley Arena so six of us tagged along with Dave. Before the concert we found ourselves in a private room and we got to chat with the Quo lads. It was the same after the performance; we went backstage to meet up with the lads again.

Eight days after the Brazil match, we were due to play Wales at Wembley in the British Home Championship involving England, Wales, Scotland and Northern Ireland; however, this was the year when the competition wasn't completed and so failed to produce a winner. The English and Welsh FAs declined to play at Windsor Park because it was deemed too dangerous to travel in Northern Ireland following IRA leader Bobby Sands' hunger strike. His death had provoked a storm of protest and violence by republicans in Northern Ireland. Anyway, in what was seen as a pointless competition, I played in our two games against Wales (where we drew 0–0) and was substituted by, of all people, Tony Woodcock during the Scotland game at Wembley, which we lost 1-0. I was then called up into the squad for two World Cup qualifiers against Switzerland in Basel and Hungary in Budapest, but didn't play in either.

Every time we played at Wembley, we always stayed in West Lodge Park Hotel in Enfield, North London, which was situated opposite Hadley Wood, an exclusive golf club set in beautiful woodland. One day, before a Home International game, Kevin Keegan and I decided we'd have a game of golf at Hadley Wood and were lucky enough to acquire a couple of 'partisans'. Hadley Wood was such an exclusive club, members of the general public didn't get much of a chance to play on it, so they used to allow staff who worked on the greens to play the course at certain times. On that particular day we heard there were a couple of guys going round, and Kevin and I were allowed to join them.

When we reached the 14th tee, one of the guys, pointing at a huge mansion behind a 12-foot hedge, told us that Bernie Winters lived there. It was ironic because we'd bumped into Bernie in the hotel the previous evening but we didn't know he actually lived on the course. Bernie had told us that he lived not far from the hotel so we asked the lads where he lived and they said he lived right on the 14th fairway. To our surprise, there was a monument of a giant hand right outside his house with both fingers pointing upwards in a 'V' pose. Kevin and I were intrigued so we all went along to see the house. Apparently, the club had blackballed him from the course, so Bernie had this huge monument built in defiance to the golf club. Incidentally, the reason why he was banned from the course was because he was Jewish. Funnily enough, we played on another course in North London that was actually run by Jewish golfers because their community weren't allowed to become members of most of the other courses in the area.

I remember one evening before a midweek international at Wembley, Ron Greenwood told us we were going out into central London as a group; he told us we were going to see a show! Now, you can imagine the shock the players felt after being told they were going to the theatre to see a show. The show we were meant to be seeing was *Anyone for Denis*. It was a parody on the relationship between Denis and Margaret Thatcher, who was the Prime Minister at the time. I'd never been to the theatre before so didn't know what to expect. However, once we got there, all most of the lads were thinking of was knocking a few pints down. I actually thought the show was brilliant and hilarious, but the other lads didn't bother to watch it and stayed in the bar throughout the performance.

After a World Cup qualifier in Norway in September 1981 – where the Norwegian broadcaster, Bjørge Lillelien famously said live on air, 'Your boys took a hell of a beating ...' – Ron Greenwood decided he would resign from the England job. However, some of the senior lads like Kevin Keegan and Trevor Brooking tried to persuade him to stay on. Kevin and Trevor made the case that the players wanted to see the job through and qualify for the 1982 World Cup. Eventually their persistence prevailed and Ron did stay on.

I don't remember the date, but on one occasion, Ron called five Villa players including me up to the squad. The other four were Dennis Mortimer, Kenny Swain, Tony Morley and Gordon Cowans. I think we were called up on the Sunday (after playing in a league game on the Saturday) for the midweek international game. We all drove down to the West Lodge Park Hotel in North London together, to join the rest of the squad. On the Sunday evening I joined most of the lads in the local village for a few pints. The guy who owned that particular pub didn't rush us to leave at closing time (which was 11pm back then); he used to lock us in to carry on drinking after hours. Some of us, including my Villa teammates, decided to return to the hotel. When we arrived we were greeted by the coaching staff: Ron, Geoff Hurst, Don Howe and Bobby Robson, lined up like a firing squad. They confronted us about our drinking session and told us to get straight to bed. It just so happened that we had returned before some of the other lads so we felt a bit hard done by.

It was the first (and only) time anything like that happened while I was in the squad. Ron must have known players went out drinking but he had never done anything about it before. Maybe Ron thought he'd wait in the hotel lobby and catch us in the act but if he'd waited a bit longer he would have caught the rest of the lads as well. When we met the other lads at breakfast the following day, it was apparent that Ron and his staff hadn't still been waiting for them.

Having said that, the drinking never seemed to affect my training, as I'd always train twice as hard after a night out – and that would have been the case for most of the lads there. In fact, I was the one who would say to Don Howe, 'Don, we're not doing anything today, can I do some extra training.' Sometimes I'd challenge Kevin to a finishing competition – and I'd usually win. It was more than just another way of passing the time – it doubled up as a valuable training session.

At the end of the 1981/82 season I played in a testimonial match for Brian Little, who had retired during the previous season. Ironically, that was the only time I got to play alongside Brian for Villa. The game was at Villa Park and I was playing for an Aston Villa XI against an England XI. It was the last chance for players, including myself, Gordon and Tony, to show Ron that they were good enough to go to the World Cup in Spain. Brian scored a hat-trick, although he still claims he only scored two in that game. Most players on the pitch were fighting for places in that World Cup squad, so the game was pretty competitive as we fielded a strong side and beat the England XI. The FA had also arranged two further warm-up games prior to Ron picking his final 22 for the World Cup. Ron picked two squads consisting of 32 players, although he didn't call them 'A' and 'B' squads. I was in the second squad who travelled to Iceland and it was my last opportunity to show him that I was good enough to be picked for the World Cup. I played up front with Cyrille Regis but he pulled his hamstring in the first half and that ruined his chances of being picked for Spain. After the game it was a case of waiting for a phone call from Ron Greenwood to tell me if I'd be included or not.

It was normal practice that you'd first find out if you'd been picked for an England squad via your club manager (or club secretary), then you'd find out in the media. However, when it came to picking squads for the World

Cup or the Euros, you'd be called personally by the England manager. I was at home when Ron Greenwood eventually called me a day or so after returning from Iceland.

I picked up the phone and he said, 'It's Ron Greenwood. I've just spoken to one of your playing partners, Tony Morley, and have given him the bad news that he's not in the squad.' By the tone of his voice I thought he was going to give me bad news as well, but he carried on. 'Those are the worst telephone calls I have to make ... but I've got more pleasant news for you. You're in the squad.'

He told me I'd get a letter to explain when and where we were to report in. After getting off the phone with Ron, I gave Tony a call and he hadn't taken the news very well at all. He was absolutely gutted that Ron had picked Peter Barnes in preference to him. None of us who had a chance to get into the squad had made any holiday plans because we thought we had a chance of being selected, so Tony told me he was going to book a holiday to get away from it all. I was gutted for him.

For me, though, it was a chance to meet up with my old Forest teammates Tony Woodcock, Peter Shilton and Viv Anderson, players I hadn't seen for a few years. The only disappointment was that I didn't get the number 9 shirt, as the squad numbers were in alphabetical order of surnames, except for Peter Shilton (who kept number 1) and Kevin, who was captain and kept his famous number 7. I was allocated the number 20 shirt and Woody was given 21. If I had the choice I'd always choose number 9, but in this case my surname dictated the number. As it happened, Glenn Hoddle got the number 9 shirt.

For me, there wasn't any chance of a holiday because it was straight into training with England and then off to our base in Bilbao. We arrived at the hotel and it was in stark contrast to the five star hotel complexes that the modern-day England players are used to. It was a small, family run hotel, not fancy. However, that wasn't how *The Sun* newspaper portrayed it in a newspaper article that had the headline, 'Hotel from Hell' and a picture of a dead dog on the beach. As it turned out, the way the family looked after us was amazing. They went to so much trouble to make sure our stay there was to our liking and put in a room full of video games, board games, a snooker table, a table-tennis table and a darts board, so we wouldn't get bored. The food was superb and made from local produce. Being in the heart of the Basque region, security was intense – we even had two tanks following the team bus everywhere we went. Even when we went outside the hotel, we would have armed security men following us.

Before the opening game against France, we were all worried about the great French midfielder, Michel Platini. Ron called us all in for a meeting and made a statement about our opponents.

'Don't worry about Platini. I'm not going to ask you to man-mark him. He's not that good. We'll do our own thing. Don't worry about him.'

As soon as Ron had said that, I thought to myself, 'You can't say that about Platini.' We all knew he was their main threat. If anyone was going to do something, it was him. We thought Robbo was the ideal guy to man-mark him and stop Platini from playing but Ron had other ideas.

As it happened, Ron's ideas worked out brilliantly and we beat France 3–1. It turned out that the nearest man to Platini was, in fact, Robbo, although he didn't man-mark him, but he did stop him playing. To cap it all, Robbo scored the opening goal in a scenario we'd worked on in training many times. Stevie Coppell threw the ball in, Terry Butcher flicked it on and Robbo arrived in the box to score. You sometimes wondered whether Ron was being tactically dismissive of our opponents, in the same way as Bill Shankly used to tell his players not to worry about the opposition but to concentrate on their own game.

After the game, Ron told us all we could have a drink but we had to stay in the hotel. We could also invite our families (if they were there) to the hotel, but on that occasion Kathy and the boys remained back in Birmingham. The following day, Ron gave us the day off, which didn't suit me because if I wasn't playing or training I'd always want to do something, so I asked the coach, Don Howe, if I could train on the beach, which was literally over the road from the hotel. Don advised me that if I was going out on my own, I had to take the security guys, so there was me with a bunch of cones and a ball being escorted to the beach by three security men all armed with machine guns. These three lads were positioned at strategic places just watching me on the beach while I was training and running around them, doing my own routine for an hour and half. It was bizarre! As it was early in the morning it wasn't as if there were many people around but those people who were there couldn't get anywhere near me and probably wondered who the hell I was and what I was doing training on my own. Don came over to speak to me during my training and said, 'I've never seen anyone do that before.'

That wasn't the only time I trained on my own. In fact it became a bit of a habit and some of the other lads in the squad got wind of it and joined in. The likes of Kevin Keegan and Joe Corrigan would join us in shooting sessions on the beach on the odd occasion.

Kevin, as a player, was magnificent and as a captain he was very forthright in what he wanted to do and what he wanted from his team. He was a high-profile player but unfortunately he got injured during the qualifying round, along with his roommate, Trevor Brooking. Before the tournament started I thought we had a good chance of doing very well, maybe even winning, but those injuries reduced our chances considerably. To go through the qualifying round and not lose but get knocked out was a bit hard to take.

It was inevitable that Bobby Robson was going to take over from Ron because he'd been groomed in the background. It could be said that when Bobby did eventually take over in the summer of 1982, he had a liking for his own players and Paul Mariner was one of them. However, I'd like to think he was an unbiased manager and picked his players on merit or quality. Either way, my chances were few and far between once Ron left the England job.

I have to say I was disappointed at not starting a game in the World Cup finals but I never once gave up hope of getting a recall. That recall came in a European Championship qualifier against Hungary in April 1983. I had watched the lads on TV in the European Championship qualifier against Greece, and when I saw all those crosses going into the penalty area with no end result, I felt sure I would have got on the end of some of them. England had loads of free kicks that night but if I had been playing I'd have scored from one of them and unlocked the doors for us to win the game. At the time, Trevor Francis and Paul Mariner were playing well for England, so it was only right that Bobby kept faith with them.

The way I found out I'd been recalled to the squad was a bit bizarre. Kathy and I had returned from a weekend in Blackpool to be greeted by the constant ringing of the phone. It must have rung a dozen times and eventually I picked it up and it was a reporter friend of mine, Dave Horridge, who was the *Daily Mail* (Midlands) correspondent (even though he was a fellow Scouser). Dave asked me where I'd been.

'Bloody hell mate, Bobby Robson's trying to get hold of you. He's been trying all weekend.' Remember there were no mobile phones in those days so getting hold of people was a nightmare. Dave told me to ring Bobby straight away and gave me Bobby's number.

When I phoned him, he too asked me where I'd been. After I explained, he pleaded with me to come down to the West Lodge Park Hotel, as he hadn't got a fit striker left in the squad. Of course, I told him I'd leave immediately! By the time I spoke to Bobby it was about 7pm so I'd get to the hotel by 9pm on that Sunday. He said there was training in the morning so there wasn't much time to rest up.

Bobby met me at the hotel and asked me if I was fit to play. He went on to explain about the (1984) European Championship qualifier on the Wednesday against Hungary: he had no fit strikers so he was banking on me saying I was fit.

However, Bobby went on to say, 'I've got to be perfectly honest with you, this is just a one-off game. I just want you to fill in as I've got all these injuries to the strikers.' I was playing the best football I had ever played and I told him I was ready to play. At the age of 33, I was thrilled to be considered for England again – even if I hadn't played I would have been grateful to Bobby for the chance to make a contribution. I never really expected to get back into the England squad, yet as long as I was able to play it remained my ambition. I was conscious I hadn't scored in my previous six England appearances but I'd never considered myself as an out-and-out goalscorer – there was more to my game than just scoring goals. A lot of people thought my game was about hustle and bustle and barging goalkeepers into the back of the net. Those sorts of comments were a bit insulting, if I'm honest – I preferred to see myself as being competitive in the box.

We trained on the Monday and Tuesday and I did my usual extra finishing work, and Bobby announced the team on the Wednesday. My name was called out, and so was Gordon's (Cowans) and he announced I was partnering Trevor Francis and Luther Blissitt during the first half. I did a bit of dribbling in the right corner of the pitch and gained a free kick that Gordon hit left-footed into the box and Trevor Francis got in front of his marker and scored. In the second half, we were on the attack and the ball was played to Sammy Lee. I peeled off my marker into a far-post position and Sammy picked me out with a cross-field pass for me to chest down. I hit a perfect half-volley that went straight across the goalkeeper into the net. I'd scored my one and only goal in that game against Hungary and we won 2–0. During the game, I got a whack in the face but brushed it off and then fell awkwardly on my thumb in the second half. I didn't think anything of the injuries throughout the game and it was only when I got into the communal bath and tried to clear my nose that someone noticed my face had swollen up, and I was ordered to go to hospital to get it checked out. I explained to the doctor what had happened and also told him about my thumb. To cut a long story short, the X-ray showed up a depressed fracture of the cheekbone and I'd broken my thumb. Fortunately, the fracture wasn't bad enough for an operation and I was told it would heal naturally if the doctor strapped my thumb up. It was bad enough, though, that I missed Villa's final four games of the season. I could have played in the last game; however I was suspended anyway.

I think I proved to Bobby that I was an international-class player that night. He was quoted as saying; 'Peter will be good for England until his legs give out.'

When we got back to the hotel, after a few hours in hospital, Bobby knocked on the door and said, 'Do you know what son; I said to you just come down to help us out and you've put in the most magnificent performance from a player I've seen for a long, long time. I wish I had 11 players of the same spirit as you played with. You were absolutely magnificent. You got that free kick and scored that goal that inspired us for the rest of the game.' I thought he was going to cry as he was so sincere when he said those words. I must admit I felt like bursting into tears as well.

Bobby loved the game so much he sounded so passionate and carried on praising me: 'I'm going to tell you this, son. If we get to the Euros you're coming with us. I'm going to take you. You have shown the sort of passion that we need and it's infectious to the other players.' He must have spent half an hour in our room, talking me up. However, that was my only goal for England, and we failed to qualify for the 1984 Euros, finishing second to Denmark. In those days, only eight teams competed and only the group winners (and the hosts) qualified for the finals. At the age of 34, it would have been my last chance to play in a major championship but it wasn't to be.

A week or so after the Hungary game, I was facing a bit of a dilemma – whether to have a knee operation or wait and offer myself for selection for England's three-match tour of Australia in June 1983. I honestly didn't know what to do. I was back in the England reckoning, and I wanted to stay there. I'd psyched myself up to do well against Hungary and tried to convince a few people that there was more to my game than crash, bang, wallop. At the same time, I didn't want to let the Villa down as I had a responsibility to the club. An operation would have needed six weeks recovery time. England were due back from Australia in the middle of June, so an operation would have disrupted my pre-season training.

Bobby was an enthusiastic character and was a fair manager who cared about his players. One time I remember he gave us a Sunday off from training and told the lads who lived in the London area they could go home for the weekend, but the ones who lived further afield had to stay in the High Wycombe area, near the hotel. Ray Clemence's agent lived in the area and knew some of the players would be on their own, so offered to take us all out to a local pub for Sunday lunch. I think there was myself, Trevor Francis, Gary Mabbutt and Peter Shilton and we went out into the country to an old pub. After about three or four pints of some strong beer called 6X, we were all feeling a bit tipsy and hungry to say the least. We were finally led into a huge hall that must have held around 200 covers and shown our table, and soon ordered our meals and wine. All of a sudden, a woman appeared from nowhere and told us to hide all the drinks anywhere we could, so we all started to take the beers and wine off the table and hiding them behind plant pots and curtains – anywhere there was a space. We sat there in bewilderment and asked her what the hell was happening.

'It's the police. It's the police.' It was after 3pm and they hadn't got a licence to serve after 2.30pm, which was the legal drinking-up time back in the

1980s. A few minutes later, I'm not kidding you, I've never seen so many policemen storm a room.

Fortunately, there happened to be a solicitor sitting on an adjacent table and he obviously knew who we were, so he approached me (as I was at the head of the table) and said, 'The police are going to come round and start asking questions. You don't have to answer any of them. This isn't anything to do with anyone in this room – it's to do with the landlady of the pub. She's the one who broke the law. Legally, you don't have to say anything and my advice would be not to say anything.'

One of the coppers decided to approach Trevor, who was sitting at the opposite end of the table but he didn't see me shaking my head so he started talking. I then told Trevor he didn't have to say anything, so he just said, 'I've got nothing to say.'

A few minutes later, the chief of police approached Trevor and tried to get something out of him, but Trevor declined to make a statement. The police then suddenly disappeared and as soon as they'd left the building all the wine bottles and glasses reappeared on to the tables and we carried on eating our meals as if nothing had happened. It was a very strange Sunday lunchtime indeed.

We returned to the hotel and I phoned Kathy to tell her what had happened. However, when we reported for training the following morning, someone from the restaurant or a member of staff had obviously tipped off the media and a dozen or so newspaper reporters were there, waiting for us outside the training camp. None of us commented to the press but we weren't surprised that the story was all over the newspapers that morning. It even made the front page of *The Sun*! Inevitably, Bobby wasn't happy about it and called us all in for a meeting to ask us to explain what had happened.

'You know, I've read through this article about half a dozen times but there's no substance to it. They've blown this out of all proportion because I made the decision to give you a day off and you made the decision to go where you wanted. They're totally out of order,' he said.

If you read the article it was full of nothing really. It was a non-story. The press hounded us for the rest of the week trying to get someone to make a comment but we remained tight-lipped. The whole episode put a dampener on preparation for an important game, and it was a lesson for us all.

It is interesting to compare what the media were like back then to what they're like now. These days all top footballers are in the spotlight and can't do anything without it being in the papers, or more to the point, on social media, but that episode was a huge story back then. The story suggested we were smashed out of our faces, but the reality of it was we'd had a few drinks and were having a nice Sunday lunch, just chatting and joking amongst ourselves.

Eighteen months on from my previous appearance in an England shirt, Bobby called me into the squad for the World Cup qualifier against Finland at Wembley. It was the autumn of 1984 and Paul Mariner had taken an injury. It came as complete surprise, being such a long time since my last game, even though I had been a substitute in the game against Hungary in the October of 1984. I always felt I was good enough to make the squad, even at the age of 33. It proved that it doesn't matter what age you are if you're playing well and scoring goals – there's always hope. Unfortunately, I didn't make an appearance in that game, and I never got my chance to go to the European Championships because we didn't qualify for Euro '84.

I did get selected to play once more for England, in a World Cup qualifier in Turkey in November 1984. I remember playing at Highbury for Villa on the Saturday and being told I was in the squad in place of Paul Mariner, who'd got injured in that game against us. If I remember rightly, we had to walk from the changing room under the stadium to the tunnel that led on to the pitch. There wasn't much space in the tunnel and the Turkish players were quite close to us. I was at the back of the line and Terry Butcher was at the front and we looked at one another and shouted simultaneously, 'Let's get into 'em.' If you recall, Terry was a 6ft 4in giant and I was 6ft 2in, and I can tell you the Turkish lads jumped out of their skins when they saw us and probably shat themselves. We took that spirit on to the pitch.

Turkey kicked off, and straight from the whistle they played the ball back to their midfield. I closed their midfielder down very quickly, and as he hit the ball forward towards the striker, Terry won the ball and played it forwards towards me. I won the ball and headed it towards Tony Woodcock and he went on to score our first goal and set the tone for the rest of the game.

Although I didn't score, I had a hand in five or six of our goals as we cruised to an 8–0 victory. Unfortunately for me, I didn't get another chance to play under Bobby after that, even though it was probably one of my best games for England.

If I had to sum up my England career in a sentence, I would say it was better late than never. I was very proud to go out and play for my country, I played for two of the best managers in Ron Greenwood and Bobby Robson and won 11 caps. However, I honestly think if Brian Clough had been given the chance to manage England back in 1977 when he was interviewed by the FA, I would have had the opportunity to earn far more caps. In my opinion, Brian should have been given the chance to manage our country, no question – he was certainly good enough. Brian's philosophy was, whether you were 16 or 40, if you were good enough you'd play. I felt sorry for him in a way, because he really wanted to be England manager. He was very patriotic and wanted to lead the national team. I honestly think he would have won things for us, but it wasn't to be.

In the end, Brian made a statement aimed at the FA hierarchy that didn't go down too well:

'I'm sure the England selectors thought if they took me on and gave me the job, I'd want to run the show. They were shrewd, because that's exactly what I would have done.' The FA, god bless them, took the safest available option in handing Ron Greenwood the job – no disrespect to Ron. There can be no question that it should have been Clough's time to take on the England team, even though he had unfinished business at Forest. England's loss was very definitely Nottingham Forest's gain.

I was involved in a squad that included Paul Mariner, who was knocking the goals in for Ipswich, a club managed by Bobby Robson. Paul was a good striker but he and I were very different as players – I actually think he was the type of striker I could have played alongside. If you look at that Ipswich side at the time, they also had the likes of Whymark, Brazil and Gates playing up front in different positions so Paul wasn't really your classic big centre-forward.

To put that England shirt on was a dream come true. All the players felt that way, which made it all the more special. It wasn't about the money.

I was called up at the age of 29 and played 11 times over four years, and went to the 1982 World Cup finals. The biggest disappointment was not playing any part in those finals in Spain. I had every confidence I'd get a game, but it never happened for me.

13

Dr Who?

"I'm a grown man. I make my own decisions in life."
Paul McGrath, former Aston Villa defender

****

To play 38 games in my last two seasons when I was in my late 30s was some achievement in itself, and in doing so, I proved to 'deadly' Doug Ellis he was wrong to sell me in 1985, given I didn't want to leave Villa in the first place. After my introduction into football management and coaching, I had a call out of the blue from the Villa secretary, Steve Stride, early in 1991. Steve said they wanted me to be assistant manager to Dr Jozef Vengloš, who was the first manager born outside Britain or Ireland to take charge of a top division club in England. Dr Jozef was the ultimate guinea pig when he was introduced to a bemused press-pack by Doug Ellis in July 1990 with the words, 'Do you know who this is?' Few people (if anyone) recognised who Dr Jozef was and he soon became known as 'Dr Who?' despite leading the Czech Republic to the quarter-finals of the Italia '90 World Cup just weeks earlier. It wasn't long before everyone in the football world knew who Dr Jozef was.

I had been recommended by Steve Stride to be Jo's assistant manager but he later confirmed my appointment after reading up on the impact I had made at the club while I had been a player, and the deep feeling for the club I therefore carried. Some people have said he simply researched ex-Villa players and picked me out of a book about the club, but that story simply isn't true.

I had actually spoken to Jo some years before he came to Villa. His record and achievement spoke volumes but he knew it would take him a while to get used to the English league. He wanted his team to play good football and be as comfortable on the ball as the top European players were. I was excited at the prospect of working with Jo.

Villa had called and I couldn't turn them down, so I drove down to Birmingham and met Jozef at his house to talk football for a couple of hours. John Ward was the Villa assistant manager under the Graham Taylor regime at the time, but I had a feeling that they wanted a stronger character to be Dr Jozef's assistant, and I fitted the bill. I accepted the job and we arranged a deal with Huddersfield to release me from my contract.

Kathy and I first needed to find a new place to live back in the Midlands and, because it was mid-winter, we had to find one pretty quickly, before the snow blocked us in in Yorkshire. The housing market was flat at the time and we had to sell our house in Farnley Tyas as well; however, we found a place in the Dorridge area of Solihull – funnily enough on land owned by Doug Ellis would you believe. He had planned for five houses to be built in a small cul-de-sac but only one had been built as yet and he made a point of telling everyone that I was going to be living in one of his houses. Kathy had initially picked the house out a few years earlier when we were first looking to move from Knowle, but we hadn't gone ahead with it, so it was pretty strange that the same house had come on to the market again now – maybe you'd call that fate?

Dr Jozef had inherited quite a decent side at Villa; a side who had finished second to Manchester United in the previous season following the resignation of Graham Taylor, who had been appointed England manager for the 1990 World Cup in Italy. With the likes of David Platt, Paul McGrath, Gordon Cowans, Nigel Spink, Dwight Yorke and Tony Daley in the side, there were indications that Villa were going to push on, but the writing was on the wall, even before my arrival. No one has a magic wand to make a club successful but it was a dream to come back to Villa. I'd spent five happy years at Villa and I wasn't afraid of finding myself in charge of players who used to be my teammates, such as Gordon Cowans and Nigel Spink. They knew they would get the same treatment as everyone else – you can't have favourites in football. I'd played with pride and passion and those traits were the very least I expected to see from the team. The players were told that if they deserved praise they would get praise, but I knew I needed to be a bit tough with them as well, on occasions. I'd spent two and a half years with Huddersfield and I'd learned the importance of attention to detail and discipline – on and off the field. I know I was guilty of dissent sometimes in my playing career, but I paid heavy penalties for that, and I learned from those moments of madness.

It was a big risk to bring in Dr Jozef, but looking back, he was a pioneer for the likes of Wenger, Mourinho and all the other foreign managers who have been in English football since. Dr Jozef was far ahead of his time with his footballing philosophy, but he inherited a most uncontinental system and a squad of players he could change only marginally. He was expected to accomplish great things instantly, and he certainly tried his best. There would be no more launching the ball upfield – but the players we had in that side, the likes of Tony Cascarino, were built to play that way. In came new coaching methods and terms like 'transitional play' and out went lots of running and long balls. The players were expected to understand how to 'play' the ball.

We started well in our first game in charge, at home to the champions, Liverpool on Saturday, 12 January 1991. I received a standing ovation from the massive Villa crowd and we repaid their praise with a well-earned scoreless draw. However, subsequent results under Dr Jozef were mixed to say the least with more defeats than victories, and fans began to wonder what Doug Ellis had been thinking when he appointed Dr Jozef. Having said that, there were a few highs; a home victory against Inter Milan in the UEFA Cup was probably Dr Jozef's finest hour, and some fans were convinced that he was the man who'd eventually take Villa to the promised-land. But all that changed when we crashed and burned in the San Siro in November 1990 – before I'd re-joined the club.

It was a bit of a strange set-up because I was technically the coach under Dr Jozef, but he took the training sessions; I felt the roles were reversed in a way because it felt like I was the bloody manager and he was the coach! I was the one who was seen talking to the media after games and giving pre-match press conferences, while Jo was coaching the players. I didn't get out on the training field as much as I thought my role required me to because of the managerial tasks I had to do. There were a lot of things about the English game that Jozef couldn't get used to, and one in particular was how a player can perform at such a high level on a Saturday afternoon when he didn't train on a Monday, Tuesday, Wednesday or Thursday, and only did a bit on a Friday. Of course, I'm talking about Paul McGrath. Jozef used to scratch his head at how such a talented player could work like that. I didn't know Paul that well, but I knew he had a strong mental attitude that made him play at a high level once he took to the football field on a matchday. I was only finding out about his problems as I went along; to think how much alcohol he drank and how well he performed – in some ways it was incredible, really. Sometimes he went out there on the pitch and I'm sure he was drunk. The biggest ally Paul had at Villa was the physio, Jim Walker. He looked after Paul, virtually 24/7, even though Paul lived in Manchester.

Talking about Paul, my first meeting with him was when I was asked to play in Mick Martin's testimonial in Dublin in 1983. Having played with Mick at Newcastle, I agreed to play for the World XI vs. Republic of Ireland XI. Our team consisted of the likes of Ozzie Ardiles, Dino Zoff, Kevin Keegan and Trevor Francis, to name but a few. However, we didn't have a centre-back so Mick said we could have a young Irish lad as our centre-back – that lad was young Paul McGrath. After about ten minutes, I said to Bryan Robson, 'Who the hell is that centre-back playing for us?' Bryan told me he played for Manchester United. I asked Bryan why he wasn't in the United first team, but apparently he had been injured. From that game on, I realised Manchester United had a great talent on their books. After the game, I didn't get too much of a chance to talk to Paul because he quickly got changed and left straight away but the rest of the players stayed behind and had a few beers in the players' lounge.

However, I managed to catch him briefly before went home, and said to him, 'By the way, that was some game you played for us.' He didn't say much in response and seemed a bit shy, even though he'd had a few beers before he left. After reading his autobiography, you soon realise why he was drinking and it was unfortunate that he didn't have anyone to guide him or mentor him during his early career.

The only time I had a problem with Paul was when the club went over to Hong Kong for a tournament. We'd played a couple of games already and we decided to allow the players to do what they wanted for an evening. Some of the lads wanted to go for a drink but even I had to get permission from Dr Jozef for that. He wasn't very keen on them going out to have a few drinks but I tried to persuade him otherwise.

'Look, if you don't let them go out for a couple of drinks, they'll sneak out anyway. You need to control them so let them go out, as long as they're back by 12am.'

Dr Jozef didn't understand why footballers had to drink, but he left me to make the decision. I promised him I'd get the lads back in their rooms by 12am. I relayed the information back to the lads and I asked them not to let me down.

Meanwhile, Dr Jozef and I were at an official banquet representing the club and we were invited to go out afterwards to a famous party destination in Hong Kong called Joe Bananas. When our hosts mentioned Joe Bananas I thought, 'I bet the lads have gone there, too.' As soon as we entered the building, I spotted the lads at the bar and I turned to Dr Jozef and said, 'Jo, you don't need to be here. You need to go.' He had obviously spotted the players as well and he agreed he didn't want to be there. Dr Jozef wasn't a drinker but stopped for a quick drink then went back to the hotel. It was 11.20pm and I realised the lads had promised they'd be back at the hotel by midnight, so I approached them and said, 'Look lads, I don't want to stay any longer so make sure you're back at the hotel by 12.' I went back to talk to the officials and by 11.45 I saw the lads drift out of the bar so I walked out with them. While we were waiting outside for a taxi, Gordon Cowans decided he wanted to go back in so I asked him, 'Err, where you going Gordon?' He told me Paul was still in Joe Bananas.

I went back in and spotted Paul sitting in a booth with a couple of girls who had taken a shine to him. I walked over to him and said, 'Paul, we're going! It's a quarter to 12.'

He looked at me and said in his softly spoken voice, 'I'm a grown man. I don't need people telling me what to do. I do my own thing.'

I basically ignored what he'd said and repeated, 'Paul, we're going.' He wouldn't have any of it and carried on talking to the girls.

By this time, Gordon was standing next to me so I took my coat off and said, 'Sid, go and get us a drink.' Gordon asked me what I wanted and I asked him to get Paul and the girls a drink as well. While Gordon was at the bar, I sat down and looked at the two girls and said to them, 'I don't know who you are but if I put you in a taxi with him (pointing at Paul), will you go back to the hotel and have a drink with him there? As long as he's in the hotel, he's OK.' They looked at each other and agreed.

I then started talking to Paul and he repeated, 'I'm a grown man. I make my own decisions.'

I then asked him, 'So, you're different from everyone else, then?'

'What do you mean?' he said.

'Well, everyone else has gone but you're still here. You want to be different. You're the star are you?' I started to reason with him.

Gordon then came back with the drinks, put them on the table but before anyone could pick up their drink, Paul got up and said, 'Peter, come on. Let's go.'

We left the drinks on the table, untouched, and walked out of the bar. Gordon asked me, 'How the hell did you do that?'

In the taxi back to the hotel, Paul put his arm round me and said to me most sincerely, 'Thanks. Thanks for that.'

For the rest of that trip no one saw Paul, apart from Jim Walker as he stayed in his room the whole time.

There was another incident on that trip, but it didn't involve Paul. We were at the airport coming back from Hong Kong. There was a young player called Chris Price, our full-back, and he was drunk before we'd even got to Hong Kong airport. I noticed he was in a right state and I told him to behave. As soon as I spoke to him, Chris started having a go and began to swear at me. I wasn't going to stand for any of that and I was in the mood to knock him out. I felt myself getting het up, so I put my hands in my pockets, thinking as long as my hands were in my pockets I couldn't hit him. I walked towards the check-in desk, talking to him, telling him, 'You need to calm down. If you don't calm down, I'm going to have to take you into the toilet.' Fortunately, Gordon was Chris's mate so he came over to see what was going on, while Chris did something he really shouldn't have done and that was to point at me with his finger. By that stage, my hands were out of my pockets. Gordon saw I was wound up and pulled me away just in the nick of time. If I'd have hit him, that would have been the end of my coaching career.

About a day later, when we had arrived back in Birmingham, Chris came in to see me and apologised for his behaviour but I refused to accept his apology. 'You WILL apologise outside, in front of the manager and all the players.' I took Chris outside and said to the lads, 'Pricey's got something to say.' He then apologised in front of everyone and I thought fair play to him for doing that. I later found out he had similar issues to Paul McGrath around booze.

There were some players, the likes of Tommy Smith, Souness, Hansen, Bremner and Hunter, who were real hard-men of the game during the 1970s and early 1980s. Those guys could look after themselves and get on with the game. Then there were certain players who had a reputation for being a 'tough guy,' but really weren't – they could hand it out but couldn't take it back. Vinnie Jones fell into that category for me. He had a hard-man reputation which he gained from being part of the 'Crazy Gang' at Wimbledon. There was one game which I distinctly remember while I was assistant manager at Villa, and it involved Vinnie, who had just moved to Sheffield United at the start of 1990. The tunnel at Bramall Lane in those days was very narrow and the dressing rooms were fairly close together. When the two lots of players met to go out on to the pitch through the tunnel, I followed Vinnie who was standing just behind Gordon 'Sid' Cowans. Vinnie had a ball in his hand and was bouncing it off the walls and the ground. I looked at him and saw he'd got the ball in a position ready to throw at the back of Sid's head. The ball poleaxed Sid, but he managed to keep his balance somehow – the ball hit him at some speed and must have hurt. Being behind Sid I saw it happen and wasn't happy about it, so I tapped Vinnie on his shoulder and said, 'Pick the fucking ball up! Throw it at me and we'll see what happens.' I wasn't having him pick on Sid, who was only nine stone and 5ft 7in. Vinnie mumbled something in reply so I repeated myself. 'Go on, pick the ball up and throw it at me!'

Vinnie then pointed at me and shouted an obscenity at me and said, 'You've had your day you have!' He then ran off on to the pitch.

I think that proves my point? Hard-man? Nah!!

That season ended up a total disaster and Villa finished just two places above the Division One relegation zone. There were a lot of rumours flying around about Dr Jozef at the end of the season, particularly about him leaving the club, but when I asked him about it he wasn't sure what he wanted to do. I tried to persuade him to stay another year to transform the side but I don't think he had any intention of staying on to be honest. In the end, he pulled the plug and resigned by mutual consent with Doug Ellis after just one season in charge.

With a vacancy in the hot-seat, I was pushing to get my chance to be manager of Aston Villa FC. I had made it known to the powers that be that I wanted to be given the chance, but Doug ended up giving the job to 'big Ron' Atkinson and he brought in his own staff and Andy Gray to be his assistant; however, Ron insisted I remained at the club and asked me to take on the reserve team.

When we started pre-season training I was still a good runner, so Ron asked me to do the running sessions with the players. That was like giving chocolate to a child – I loved it. I will always remember that Nigel Callaghan came back for pre-season and he was a little overweight; sorry, he was a lot overweight. Nigel was only 5ft 7in tall but he probably came back the same weight as me. Ron obviously wasn't happy and told him that he wouldn't play for Aston Villa with that weight on him; in fact, Ron actually warned Nigel he wouldn't wear an Aston Villa shirt again being overweight. Ron then asked me to help Nigel get fit as quickly as possible so I came into Bodymoor Heath at 8:45am on the first day, got changed and met up with Nigel to run through his fitness regime. I told Nigel that he needed to do some running so I took him over to The Belfry and we started running 9 of the 18 holes on the course. Nigel wasn't used to distance running so he wasn't happy with what I was asking of him, but I explained the reasons for doing it and I think he started to understand after a while. We increased the distance every day and sometimes I'd take him out in the afternoon as well as the mornings. On top of the running, we'd do other training as well. Normally, pre-season lasted around four to six weeks, and after the sixth week Nigel came up to me and said it was the hardest pre-season he'd ever been through, but he thanked me for getting him fitter than he'd ever been before – and for shifting the excess weight.

Nigel eventually got his place back in the team after that strenuous pre-season.

Up against Pelé in America

Aston Villa team prior to kick off in the European final against Rottherdam

Team picture at Bodymoor Heath after winning the championship

Team picture at Villa Park after winning the European Cup

George Best played in the Villa team testimonial

Playing against Manchester City (Asa Hartford)

Beating Gary Shaw to the ball in the air

Stephen and his wife Petra, Skye, myself and Kathy

Me with Skye my Granddaughter at Villa Park

Myself, Kathy, and Granddaughter Skye

Myself and Kathy on our first holiday to Wales 1968

Kathy, Grandson Aaron, his wife Aubree, and myself at their wedding

Myself, Jennifer (Gareth's wife), Isla, Aaron, Cara, Kathy, and Gareth

Kathy, myself, and Granddaughter's Cara, and Isla

Myself and Kathy, Perth Australia

Jason and his wife Sharon, myself, and Kathy

Jason and his wife Sharon, myself and Kathy, enjoying a meal

Myself, Kathy, and my Mum and Dad

Tommy Smith, Liverpool vs Blues

Stephen and Gareth, with some of the medals I won

Gordon Cowans, Ken McNaught, and myself

My time at Thailand as head coach

Thailand vs South Korea having won the golden goal

Tiger Cup winners - Virach - Vijat

Arsenal's pre-season tour of Thailand. Arsene Wenger, and myself at the press conference

Gareth's wedding, and his wife Jenifer. Very rare, when we are all together like this

The Withe family at Gareth's wedding

Nakhon Pathom

Gareth wearing my first debut England Cap, against Brazil

Myself, Toni Iommi and Kathy

Myself and Gezzer Butler, at one of the Villa games

Robbie Williams plays in Bangkok and he asked to meet us before the gig

My other sport, playing in the Nailcote Hall Par 3 Championship, which I won

Myself and Gordon Banks

Myself, Bobby Charlton,Kathy, and Jason

Myself, and Ron Greenwood

Me and Jason, practicing heading

My injuries against Hungary, and Stephen broke his

Family holiday, Disney World Florida

Myself and Nigel Spink, Town Hall victory parade of European Cup

My Mum and Dad, with Jason, Gareth, Stephen

A collage of former clubs

Myself with Sam Torrance

Myself, Rossana (David's wife), Kathy and actor David Bradley, who are both keen Villa fans

Myself and Kathy with the championship trophy 1981

Klaus Augenthaler and myself exchanging our European cup shirts back at Allianz stadium

Ken McNaught, Kenny Swain, Dennis Mortimer, new owner of Aston Villa Dr Tony Xia, Tony Morley, and myself

Myself, Aaron, and Kathy at Providence Park Portland Timbers

Myself, Kathy, Sharon, Jason, and Nick Sharon's boy, who has been a part of the family for many years

Myself, Kathy, Cara and Isla

Enjoying a pint with Gareth and Aaron

Myself, Kathy, and the European Cup

14

Taming the Crazy Gang

"I want you to steady the ship and to toughen them up."

Sam Hammam, former Wimbledon FC owner

****

At the start of October 1991, while I was still at Villa, I received a phone call out of the blue from Sam Hammam, who was in charge of Wimbledon FC. I didn't know Sam that well and had only met him a couple of times before but he was adamant he wanted me to be his next manager. Sam told me that the club had lost a bit of discipline over the previous few years and the players were getting away with murder. Basically, he wanted someone to 'steady the ship and to toughen them up.' During its meteoric and record-breaking rise through the football league to the top flight and that famous 1988 FA Cup victory, Wimbledon fostered the 'Crazy Gang' image and Sam encouraged bizarre rewards and initiation ceremonies for new players.

Sam asked me to meet him in a service station on the M1, somewhere between Birmingham and London, and he didn't take long to offer me the job as Ray Harford's replacement at Wimbledon. Sam said he needed to meet his board of directors so they could ratify the appointment, and he asked me to drive down to one of the director's houses for a meeting with all the other board members present. I think it was his way of pacifying the other directors, making them feel part of the decision-making process.

Kathy and I drove down and met with the directors and they asked me all sorts of questions. The chairman was a very articulate old gentleman named Stanley Reid. He'd been on the board at Chelsea and Sam thought of him as a father-figure to the club. I stayed with him once, in his big, old house in Wimbledon, which he'd converted into six flats. He had two flats – one on the ground floor he stayed in during the summer and one on the first floor he stayed in during the winter. Incidentally, he later offered me a basement apartment to live in but when I subsequently told that story to the other directors they said he'd forgotten to tell me someone was murdered in that apartment.

I was eventually appointed manager of Wimbledon FC on 7 October 1991 on a three-year contract, which had been verbally agreed when we met at the M1 service station. I started work that same day. I met up with the lads on the training ground and was introduced as the new manager. I wanted time to look at the staff and make a decision on my assistant. Sam had arranged for the team to go abroad for a team-building exercise and some of the players didn't want to go. I informed them it was important they went and after some huffing and puffing most of the players made the trip.

On that trip I was doing a warm-up session one day and I joined in. It involved turning quickly and after about ten minutes I tried it and ran bang into one of the players, which caused me to have a nosebleed. The physio was very concerned and wanted me to stop, but I said it was fine and asked for some cotton wool to stick up my nose. When the bleeding stopped I continued with the session.

The trip abroad was called for because we had a gap in the fixtures – we'd played Norwich at home and won that one but didn't have a game for nearly two weeks. My first game as manager was to be against QPR. The training and team-building went reasonably well and we started work on preparing for the game. I'd had a chance to look at the staff and had made a decision to appoint Mick Buxton as my assistant. I'd known Mick since his days at Huddersfield and felt his experience would be invaluable to us.

I was still living in the West Midlands but a friend of mine had an apartment in London so I took up her long-standing offer to stay there during the week. The logistics of getting to and from the West Midlands from Wimbledon were a nightmare, but it was even more of a nightmare to drive to the training ground from the offices at Selhurst Park (Wimbledon started to ground-share with Crystal Palace at the start of the 1991/92 season). Some people thought I was mad for taking the job in the first place, and even madder for wanting to make the daily journey to and from the training ground. But I saw it as my chance to make the step up from the reserve team coach at Villa to a management role. After all, Wimbledon were a first division team so it was a decent job – it was a no-brainer really.

When an opportunity like that arises you've got to take it!

We had a good squad of players, even though some of the old 'Crazy Gang' members had moved on. We still had John Fashanu, Warren Barton, John Scales, Terry Phelan, Robbie Earle and Lawrie Sanchez. One of the first things Sam said after appointing me was that I had to sell some of the 'profitable' players, but he also made it clear that I would have to have replacements in line before I could sell. That wasn't a problem, as I knew some of the lads wanted out anyway. On my first day taking training, Terry Phelan came in to see me and said matter-of-factly, 'Well boss, when can I go?' He'd apparently been promised a transfer by Sam but he didn't waste any time telling me he didn't want to be part of my team. It was my first introduction to the club – a bit of a baptism of fire and it became my first battle in the world of football management.

I soon found out that the club had an unusual mentality about it. There were some big characters in the dressing room and I felt a little resentment from certain sectors of the camp, probably because there were quite a few London-based players and I was from the north. One thing I had to sort out almost immediately was John Fashanu's contract renewal. Fash had a flamboyant agent called Eric Hall, who had an outlandish fashion sense, the catchphrase 'monster', and was famous at the time for smoking huge cigars. We had a meeting arranged at Terry Venables's club in Kensington called Scribes, and I remember he was discussing things that should have been discussed privately, before meeting me.

One thing he wanted for Fash was a bonus for scoring goals to which I said, 'Eric, you can't give a bonus to someone for scoring goals. There will come a time during a game when someone else will be in a better position to score but he will take the chance himself and that could cost us the game.'

Eric defended Fash, 'Nah, Fash isn't like that.'

I continued, 'If you think about it, it's only human nature. If he's faced with a choice of either trying to score himself to get £200 or passing to another player in a better position and not get £200 he'll choose to score himself every time.'

Eric didn't respond to that.

The meeting lasted well over two hours and we still hadn't completed the deal, even though in principle he'd agreed to stay at the club. Fash asked me if I wanted a lift back to my apartment, which was less than a mile away, so I declined and decided to walk home. On my way back home I recapped the meeting in my head and about five minutes later, Fash pulled up beside me in his car.

'I've followed you for the last five minutes. You look … well, I thought you'd be jumping up and down now I've agreed to sign and stay at the club.'

I looked at Fash and said, 'Well, why?'

Fash was a bit taken aback by my response and repeated, 'Because I've agreed to sign and stay at the club and to score goals for you.'

I couldn't believe what he was saying to me, 'What did you expect? Did you want me to do somersaults and cartwheels down the street?' Fash must have thought I'd be excited that he'd agreed to extend his contract with us. 'I don't get excited about things like that. I get excited about winning games and winning trophies.'

Whatever he wanted me to say, Fash couldn't get his head round my philosophy but I guess we're all different.

Fash was Fash, and was one of the longest-serving players at the club and our leading striker – he'd scored 20 goals in the previous league season so he deserved to be listened to I suppose, but I wasn't going to get excited about him agreeing a new contract. Besides, he always turned up late for training and he was the only person I've ever known to have a new excuse every time he turned up late.

He'd come into training and say something like, 'Gaffer, you wouldn't believe it ... I've run over a cat. It wasn't dead so I had to make sure it got to a cattery.'

He'd just come up with the most ridiculous and bizarre excuses ever and we'd all just say, 'Fash, just pay the fine. I don't want to know. Don't give me any more excuses.'

The strange thing was I didn't know just how much Fash really wanted to play football – it seemed football interfered with his life, somehow. If I'd given him the choice of playing football or being a television personality, he'd probably have chosen the latter. I believe football was a means to an end for him. If I had asked him just to play on a Saturday and to take the rest of the week off, I think he'd have snapped my hand off.

Wimbledon had a certain system that was described by some as 'long ball' but it was obvious to me that there were players there that could actually *play*. I wasn't going to introduce a new style to these players, but I certainly wasn't going to tell them to 'lump it' up to Fash. Players like Robbie Earle and John Scales could play, so I was intent on using those guys and to mix it up a bit. However, the old school players like Fash, Phelan and Sanchez just wanted to play the tried and tested system. That wasn't a problem as such, but I felt we were capable of playing a better style of football.

We had a lot of fit and quick players in the squad with the likes of Phelan, Scales, Joseph and Barton – they were all fit lads. Of course, I was still fit enough to take the running sessions, and guess who'd always be up the front? Whatever task I set the lads, I would do the same task as well – I told the players I wouldn't ask them to do something I couldn't do myself, and I was fitter than some of the players, which was worrying as I was over 40. I guess I wanted to lead by example as I felt I could still run and still take the training.

I'd always finish training with a closing task: for example, if anyone hit the crossbar from the 18-yard line they could finish training. One day, I set a task to kick the ball from the centre circle into the goal without bouncing. We were there for about ten minutes without anyone hitting the net. In the end, Fash looked at me and said, 'Gaffer, you're winding us up. You can't do this. It's impossible.' To that, I took the ball and showed the lads how it could be done. I turned to Fash and asked him which foot he wanted me to do it with and he said, 'Right foot.' Fash wasn't having any of it, 'You're winding us up aren't you?' So, I pinged a ball with my right foot and it hit the back of the net without bouncing. Fash wasn't happy and muttered something to himself and then said, 'It was a fluke,' and asked me to do it again. So I hit another ball with my left foot and, again, it hit the back of the net without bouncing.

The lads stood there astounded. 'OK, I've shown you it can be done, now get on with it.'

Fash piped up again, 'Gaffer, you couldn't do three out of three.'

Of course, I hit the third shot into the goal.

I had to stop the session in the end because most of the lads couldn't hit the target; some did but most couldn't get anywhere near the net. I can't really remember but I don't think Fash got anywhere near the target somehow.

Occasionally, after training some of the lads would have a bet to see who the fastest runner was. So Fash, Phelan, Joseph and Scales would often race and have a bet on the winner but Fash was that fast, he won more than he lost. I often watched it when I had finished the training session so I offered to race Fash for £100. Fash dismissed my offer as if to say it was a non-contest and egged me on.

'Gaffer ... gaffer, come on. What distance?'

He soon realised how good I was at running, so I replied, 'Pick your distance. I'll race you for £100 – any distance you want.'

Fash chose a distance of 100 yards and I even said he could pick anyone to start the race, so he picked Phelan. 'On your marks, get set, GO!' he shouted.

I was running as fast as I could but Fash decided to take it easy and appeared not to take the race that seriously and still finished in front of me and celebrated his victory.

When I finished the race I went up to him and said, 'Have the £100 in the office after training.'

Fash looked at me and replied, 'What do you mean, gaffer?'

I explained the bet: 'I said I'd bet you £100 to race you. I didn't say I'd beat you.'

Fash looked surprised and was wound up about it so I continued, 'Well, you should have listened to what I said for the bet.'

The other players cracked up as Fash had been duped.

How a team plays is partly dictated by results, so when a team isn't winning the manager has to decide whether he sticks with the philosophy of playing decent football or reverts to 'route one'. I spoke to Mick Buxton on several occasions about it, and he agreed it was a case of getting the best out of the players we had in order to get results; however, sometimes in football you just don't get the breaks. Before the game at Arsenal on New Year's Day I asked our full-back, Terry Phelan, to do a job for me and he replied, 'What do you mean "do a job"?' I asked him to mark Ian Wright as he was their main threat. Terry didn't have a problem with the instructions and seemed fairly happy with his task. Well, Wrighty didn't get a kick all through the game and Terry followed him all over the park. During the game, we had three or four good chances to win, but we ended up with a 1–1 draw. In another game, we played Liverpool at home in November, only six or seven weeks into my managerial reign, and I gave a team talk prior to kick-off. Our defender, Roger Joseph spoke out while I was trying to gee the players up.

'Yeah, come on let's get into these Scouse bastards!' he shouted.

I don't think he realised I was a Scouser and he'd just offended me but I didn't say anything.

In the Friday session before that Liverpool game, I got the players to do set-plays. I had recently given a debut to Neil Ardley, who was a wide player, and I asked him to take the corners on one occasion. When he went over to take the corner, I noticed he had his head down and wasn't looking at what was happening around him, so I told Roger Joseph to go to the halfway line and stand there looking uninterested and then use his pace to make a run to the edge of the penalty box where Neil would then play him in for a shot or a cross. All went well in the training session but on matchday it all went to pot. We were attacking the end where all the Liverpool supporters were and we got a corner on the right-hand side. Roger did his part by not looking interested in the play, but Neil was looking at the ball, which wasn't part of the set-play, so I screamed at him from the dugout. Meanwhile, Roger made his run and was screaming at Neil, who then remembered what he was meant to do and tried to rectify his mistake. He took the corner so quickly he kicked the corner flag instead of the ball! You can imagine how the Liverpool fans behind that goal reacted – they absolutely slaughtered him.

By the time we played West Ham at Upton Park early in the new year, both teams were struggling at the wrong end of the table. I was on the touchline thinking we were doing OK. We scored the first goal and dominated the play until Fash missed a great chance to make it 2–0, which would have been a true reflection of the game. Warren Barton, our young full-back, then gave the ball away cheaply, lost possession and tried to chase after their winger, who ran into the box. Barton did well to catch up with him and to get back on goal-side and all he had to do was stop the cross, but he simply hacked the guy down inside the box to give away a stupid penalty. I stood on the touchline in shock thinking, 'Why would you do that?' The worst thing was Hans Segers saved the penalty, but in the process got booked for moving before the ball was struck and had to face another penalty. They scored from the retake and the game fizzled out into a draw. I was pretty annoyed after the game and I had an argument with the referee (which was unusual for me) about his decision to award a retake. In the changing room I said to the players that the Sunday papers would highlight the stupid penalty we gave away and wouldn't give us the credit we deserved. I told the players that the journos wouldn't write about the 80 minutes that we controlled the game and that to me was the most frustrating thing about it. It was the story of the season, in that we had taken the lead in a lot of games but couldn't hang on to it to see the job through, so ended up drawing or losing. In fact, over the Christmas period we drew five games back-to-back and they all ended 1–1. It just wasn't good enough.

As time went on, little niggling things started happening behind my back. Sam had installed me as his manager to toughen the lads up and to instil some discipline, but one day he told me not to do what he'd asked me to do, which was a bit confusing. Reading between the lines, I had a feeling he wasn't happy with the results and he wanted me to try another approach. To me, we weren't playing badly but the results weren't going our way and we were making elementary mistakes that cost us several games. It all seemed to come to a head after the defeat at Selhurst Park against Chelsea on 18 January. After the game, I drove back up to Birmingham, as I did following most home games. When I got home, I received a phone call from a friend who asked me if I was leaving Wimbledon. Obviously, I knew nothing about it so I didn't comment.

The following day, my son Stephen collected the Sunday papers and noticed there was a story on the back page that I was no longer the Wimbledon manager. I picked up the paper and read the article that said I'd been sacked. After only 15 games in charge, although we had only won one game (but had drawn eight) Sam had sacked me, behind my back.

I refrained from speaking to him or anyone else at the club, but later that same day, Sam rang me. He wanted to meet me at the same service station on the M1 where he had offered me the job. When I turned up to meet Sam, Vinnie Jones's father was with him, as they were both on their way to Scotland to do some shooting.

Sam said to me, 'You know why we're here?'

I told him bluntly, 'You know what the most disappointing thing is? You told the media before you told me.'

That flustered Sam and he tried to make out he didn't tell the media I'd been given the boot. He then started to question the results and said things hadn't worked out as he had wanted. He went on and on about nothing really. He mentioned that he couldn't afford to see Wimbledon go down and because we were at the foot of the league, I became a casualty. It became clear to me that I'd lost my job simply because of poor results. I had no problem with that to be fair – he was the owner so he made the choice of getting rid of me.

Having said that, I told him I was disappointed that he didn't have the guts to tell me to my face, or at least pick up the phone. I went on, 'In fact, you should have told me after the game as you must have known that's what you were going to do.'

After that, we went our separate ways; I drove back to Birmingham, officially jobless, but that was just the start of it.

A few days later, after just 105 days at the helm I was replaced by the club's reserve team coach, Joe Kinnear.

Looking back to when I was appointed as Wimbledon manager, I'd agreed a three-year deal on the Friday and on the Monday I'd started work, so I didn't get a chance to sign the paperwork – even though I did read through it. There was so much in the contract, and I refused to sign it until certain items were removed, but that never actually happened. In hindsight, I shouldn't have verbally agreed to it until I had read the paperwork. I guess it was like playing a game of cards with Sam – he had 50 and I had the two remaining cards. He had total control of me and wanted everything his way. Sam was a total control freak when it came to his managers but he'd done a fantastic job at Wimbledon while he was there. He ran that football club from top to bottom. I learned a lot from Sam and a lot about management from my time at Wimbledon – although some things I'd rather forget.

Even though I was no longer Wimbledon manager, Sam offered to pay me for six months or until a settlement had been agreed. His argument was that I had shaken hands on a three-year contract (verbally), which in law was a binding contract I suppose, even though I hadn't signed the paper version. When the LMA (League Managers Association) got involved they advised me not to accept any more payments and they put me in touch with a solicitor. The previously friendly banter with Sam then turned into a war of written words via our solicitors, and he stopped my payments.

The solicitor went on a crusade to try to disprove Sam's case and tried to get the full two-year contract paid, but in the end I was advised to take the offer of six months' salary. The case was a total mess and the solicitor working for me made a complete hash of it all. One minute he was telling me he was going to take Sam to the cleaners, the next he was advising me to take his offer. It was a complete shambles and it got totally out of hand. I eventually got some money, after about six months, but so did the solicitor, and I was left with very little compensation in the end. I should have received a 'benefit in kind' of six months' salary that would have severed my (verbal) contract with Wimbledon. If I had received that, I wouldn't have involved the solicitors, but unfortunately I took advice from the LMA.

Within weeks of agreeing the settlement, I was signing on for the first time since 1971.

15

Back at the Villa

"We'd always like to believe everything will be hunky-dory – but in reality, life just isn't like that."

****

I'd just been through the most harrowing and stressful time of my life, what with being sacked as manager of Wimbledon, the subsequent dismissal case and trying to keep my family together. I'd also had other family matters to deal with which were causing me some grief.

Things could only get better – well that's what I thought.

It's never easy bringing up kids. We all have highs and lows throughout life, and that's a never-ending story where kids are concerned. We'd always like to believe everything will be hunky-dory but, in reality, life just isn't like that. The kids had had a few run-ins with bullies back in Nottingham and in Newcastle, but it was still a shock to find Stephen had been bullied at school again in Solihull. Stephen was just five years old in 1982 when I scored that iconic winner against Bayern Munich that clinched the European Cup for Villa. With Kathy cheering me on in Rotterdam, Stephen was with the family of Norman Bodell, the coach I became friends with during my Wolves days, so he didn't really have any recollection of that night in Rotterdam. However, what followed it was years of bullying, and from one lad in particular, when Stephen was at junior school. It had started up again at senior school while I was at Wimbledon.

When I lost my job at Selhurst Park the kids at Stephen's school brought in copies of the national newspaper stories that suggested I had been sacked and they tormented Stephen because of it. The bullying, which had begun five years previously, was all due to the fact that Stephen was the son of a famous footballer. When his elder brother Jason found out about it he went to find the lad and gave him a piece of his mind. I went to see Stephen's head teacher at Arden School in Solihull on my own, as Kathy didn't want to come face-to-face with the lad accused of bullying – or his parents. I said to the head teacher that I'd told my children that if anyone bullied them they should defend themselves in some way. He told me that was wrong and that 'violence didn't make things right,' to which I replied, 'I don't give a monkey's about that! Someone is bullying my child in your school. Unfortunately, you haven't done anything about the bullying and it's escalated.'

It escalated because the lad's parents went to the local newspaper making out it was Jason who was the culprit for defending his brother, and it only made the headlines because it was my son who was involved in the story. If it had been anyone else's son, it wouldn't even have been printed. I actually couldn't believe the newspaper had bothered printing such a story because it was a nonentity really – a story with no substance. Shortly afterwards, we had a meeting with the lad and his parents but his mother sat there in front of the head teacher and denied her son was bullying Stephen and stood by her story (which had been printed in the newspaper). In response, I said she should have come to me rather than going to the media, as it made the situation ten times worse. The head teacher didn't like the story going into the newspaper as it showed his school in a bad light and he assured us that he'd 'get to the bottom of it.' I left it with him to deal with, and to be fair the head teacher and Stephen's form teacher interviewed all of his classmates individually in order to deal with it. When they had finished the investigation we were invited to another meeting at the school with the lad and his parents and the truth finally came out.

The mother didn't accept the conclusion of the investigation and had to be convinced her son had been in the wrong, after which she duly apologised to us both. Her son was then suspended from school for six weeks and the bullying stopped. Stephen recently met up with the lad who bullied him all those years ago and the lad admitted he didn't know why he bullied Stephen and said he regretted it. To that, Stephen's reply was, 'Yeah, you wouldn't have done it if I'd been stronger because I'd have knocked your head off.' It's funny how life brings up these twists and turns because even stranger,

Stephen's younger brother, Gareth, was best friends with the bully's own younger brother for a long time, but he tragically died at the age of 18.

Things got worse when Stephen was diagnosed with type 1 diabetes. By chance, he was diagnosed around the same time that he'd started to be bullied again and it came as a shock to us all. There was no family history of diabetes, so it was a total mystery. Stephen had gone away on a camping trip and his friend mentioned when they returned that he thought he drank a lot of water, more than normal – pint after pint after pint. I knew then there was something wrong. We took him to the hospital for a check-up and the doctor knew by the symptoms that Stephen was diabetic. They did a blood test and he was kept in hospital for a week until his blood sugar levels were stabilised.

We knew Stephen would face a difficult time, as type 1 diabetes involved injecting yourself with insulin, which was a big thing for a 13-year-old to deal with, but one he had to face up to. Not only did Stephen have to learn all about diabetes and the treatment, but both Kathy and I had to learn too. Stephen initially found it hard to inject himself so I had to do it for him. He didn't really come to terms with it; it resulted in Stephen becoming a bit of a rebel and if I'm honest, he went off the rails a little bit. Going off the rails when you're a diabetic is not recommended because your sugar levels and moods can fluctuate so quickly, and Stephen struggled, big time. However, we soon learned the signs and knew when he needed his insulin. We really felt for him, especially at such a difficult age.

Somehow we got through that terrible six-month spell and, fortunately, I managed to find another job in football that meant I no longer had to queue up at the dole office. I responded to an advert for the PFA's Community Scheme, went up to Manchester for an interview and got the job as the West Midlands Area Manager. It was a completely different experience, but I needed a new challenge at that time. The scheme was self-funding and the job involved visiting the community officers of various football clubs in the West Midlands. I had the biggest patch of the four area managers, as my area covered as far north as Stoke and as far south as Hereford. It was more of a coordinating role, advising the community officers on what they needed to do, running the soccer schools and visiting local schools. One of the biggest problems I faced was at Birmingham City, because the club wouldn't give away any tickets for home games to the local schools. They gave away some tickets for the minor games, but when it came to the bigger games, they were reluctant. Eventually, Blues sacked their community officer and asked me if I'd like to take over, but it would have meant even more travelling than the job I already had with the PFA. I had a think about it and agreed to do the role only if I had my son, Jason, as my assistant. Jason had done his badges but wasn't working at the time and Blues agreed to that.

I held the Blues post for a few months and in the end Jason took over my role because I was offered a job at Villa as Director of Youth Development (the equivalent of the modern-day academy). Ron Atkinson was the Villa manager at the time and I'd already worked under him when I left to become the Wimbledon manager. The position was vacated by Dave Richardson and I was interviewed for the role by Ron, who offered me the job there and then. Ron also allowed me to carry on with my radio and TV commentating, which I'd just started with the BBC and Sky, as long as it didn't interfere with my coaching role. I assured him it wouldn't.

Thanks to Ron, I was back in football at last – and back at the Villa!

I had always enjoyed the coaching side, so teaching youngsters from nine up to the age of 16 suited me down to the ground. Gary Shaw had just retired from football at the young age of 30 and was at a loose end, so I initially asked him to help me out with a bit of coaching. I gave him the under-14s team to coach and he reluctantly agreed, although he really wanted to coach the older lads. At any one time, we must have had around 100 kids on our books and I can honestly say I knew every single one of them (and their parents).

Part of my role was to coach the coaches. There were two coaches for each age group and they were all complaining that they hadn't been properly compensated by the club for the work they'd put in. Some of them were coaching two nights a week and even Sundays, and what Villa were paying hardly covered their expenses. In the end, I went to Doug Ellis and asked if he was willing to pay the coaches a bit more money for their time. Amazingly, Doug obliged and eventually I got them an increase to around £50 a session.

Coaching kids at that age, in my opinion, isn't always about results in games – it's about producing kids who can progress to bigger and better things; kids who can be turned into apprentices and move up to the reserves and eventually into the first team. That has always been my aim; to develop players to become better footballers. At the age of 14, the parents could decide where their kids would go, but until the age of 14, they had to stay local. I remember we lost quite a few talented kids to the likes of Manchester United, where most kids became small fish in a big pond. Doug didn't like losing youngsters to our rivals but at the same time he was reluctant to give the kids any money to sign professional contracts and that was one of the reasons why we lost some talented youngsters at Villa. One lad from the Walsall area who was on our books wanted £20,000 to sign for Villa, but in the end he signed for Wolves and Doug wasn't happy. In truth, he was a talent, but he wasn't worth that sort of money for sure. However, in the meantime I told Doug I'd signed an even better player for nothing. His name was Darius Vassell and he went on to be a regular in the Villa team and also picked up 22 caps for England. We also signed up the Moore brothers, Luke and Stefan and Boaz Myhill to name but a few – and they didn't cost any money.

I enjoyed going on to the training field and showing the coaches what I wanted from them and what I wanted from the lads. It was also my role to sign young lads who I thought could make a difference at Villa. You could always spot the talented lads who would make it and it was a case of looking after them to make sure they achieved their goals, but at the same time, looking after all the other lads in the same way. The biggest problem I found was actually the parents, and how they controlled their kids. Every parent thinks their Johnny is the best, and I found it hard to tell the parents that their son wouldn't make it at Villa. Joe Cole's father must have taken his son all over the country and visited every league club, including Villa, just to meet the likes of Ron Atkinson, Terry Venables or Alex Ferguson. Joe was always going to sign for West Ham, but he was a talented lad and he could have had his pick of any club in the country. It was probably fitting that he ended up at Villa towards the end of his career.

Doug Ellis ran the whole club on a shoestring budget, and the youth development was no different. Coaching wasn't my only remit in the role of Director of Youth Development. Among the twenty or so jobs I can think of were driving the minibus around and making sure the kits were clean for training and matchdays – all with no one to help me. On a typical Sunday morning I'd be there at 8am before anyone else, making sure everything was in place for the matches, and then I'd walk round to watch the games, and on the rare occasion I even had to reprimand a few parents too. One particular parent hit his kid in front of everyone on the pitch so I told him, in no uncertain terms, not to do it again. I made it clear that the training ground was my domain.

'You! You're not allowed to hit your child while you're on the Aston Villa training ground. If you are away from the training ground I have no jurisdiction over you, but do not hit your son because of football. You're NOT doing that to your child here in front of everyone else. I'm not having it.'

The parent ended up apologising to me afterwards. 'I'm sorry. I just get frustrated. I get frustrated with the kids.'

The number of times I had to calm the parents down during matches was unbelievable. I used to say to them, 'Don't have a go at your son – he's trying his best.' In the end I had to put up ropes so the parents couldn't get on to the pitch.

That was the era when the governing bodies wanted us to make the players aware that winning wasn't the most important thing in the world and taking part was paramount, but I thought at the time it was a ludicrous philosophy. I had a meeting with some coaches and the parents to explain it. We had to adapt to it but it became evident to me that certain things were happening, so I decided to arrange a meeting with the coaches one day to discuss it.

'You know when I said winning wasn't the most important thing? Forget it. It's out of the window. It's got to the stage now that the kids just don't give a monkey's. They're losing their appetite to win a football game. They have just taken it the wrong way. Every game now, we try to win. The attitude of the players is changing and I don't want that. I want a winning instinct. Some kids have got it and always will but some have lost it. So we need to change. We're going to go to every game and try to win.'

I explained it to the coaches and then I stated my philosophy to the parents and the kids. I wanted our teams to play football the proper way and to win every game. It was plain and simple. It didn't matter if kids made mistakes during games – that happens all the time and we were there to rectify their mistakes in training, but I wanted them to learn how to play football to win the match. I demonstrated to the coaches that they needed to teach the kids to adapt to different positions and told them they needed to initiate these methods into their programmes. Most of the coaches were ex-players, but some were ex-school teachers and the majority took it on board.

I have a thing about how my coaches should act during training and to see someone putting hands in their pockets was, for me, the worst of misdemeanours. Even if I saw Gary (Shaw) standing on the touchline with his hands in his pockets, I'd go give him a pair of gloves.

'If you put your hands in your pockets, what does that say to the players? They're going to put their hands in their pockets too. So don't put your hands in your pockets and don't allow the players to do the same. We're here to play football.'

Shawy would always give me that look and have a moan. Then one day, I asked my son, Jason, to assess Gary when he was coaching, but as it turned out, Jason ended up taking the session. He was a good coach and had gained his lower licence at the age of 16. When I went over to Shawy he told me Jason wanted to take the session and he was just standing there watching (with his hands in his pockets). Gary was also a bit of a charmer and you'd very often see him on the touchline chatting to the parents, especially the mums. That was Shawy all over. Gary knew how to coach but I don't think he could put it into practice and explain what he wanted the kids to do. His heart wasn't in it, to be honest.

In November 1994, Ron Atkinson was suddenly sacked as Villa manager following a 4–3 defeat to Wimbledon, only days after being given the dreaded 'vote of confidence' by Doug Ellis. The side that had come close to winning the football league championship just 18 months earlier was ageing and they just weren't performing, even though they had won the League Cup in the previous season. Brian Little was appointed Villa manager and I immediately had several meetings with Brian about my position. He asked me how the job was going and I explained what my role was and that it was hard work on my own, so Brian suggested Brian Jones should come in to help. I knew Jones, as he was the assistant to

Dave Richardson, who had been Youth Development Officer under Ron. Having Jones on board allowed me to carry on coaching the kids, but not have to worry about driving the minibuses and all the other peripheral jobs, freeing me up to do a bit of scouting.

During 1996, Brian's first-team coach, John Gregory, left to take charge of Wycombe Wanderers. I asked Brian if he wanted me to step in to coach the first team, but Brian had another role lined up for me. He brought in the chief scout, Malcolm Beard, to replace me because he wanted me to be the head of European scouting for Villa. At the time, it was a minor role but he assured me that European scouting was about to become a massive job for every football club. How right he was: all clubs now have them in place, so it was a great forward-thinking move by Brian.

The role took me to every corner of Europe and beyond. I think when you do a job like that which takes you all over the world watching players, you only find satisfaction when your recommendations turn into definite signings. As far as I can remember, we only signed one player while I was in the post and that was Stan Collymore from Liverpool, and funnily enough, I didn't recommend him to Brian anyway! Having said that, I did go to watch the brilliant France under-21s play in the middle of nowhere with the intention of watching an unknown lad in their midfield. In the event, he ended up playing in three different positions, including centre-back and striker. His name was Patrick Vieira. Of course I recommended him to the club, and we all know what happened to him ... On the same night I noticed another lad playing up front for France. His name was Thierry Henry. I recommended him as well, along with a third player – Robert Pirès. I followed their progress and watched them three or four times, but the club didn't sign them. I also recommended a Swedish under-21 international called Freddie Ljungberg and as it happened he said he wanted to come to Villa but had already signed for Arsenal. Brian asked me to look at Jaap Stam, who was playing for PSV Eindhoven in Holland at the time, and I watched him several times but I didn't fancy him, even though Brian thought he was a really good player. That is why football is different to any other profession – we all have our own opinions on players and you have to go with what you see. In the end those five players were snapped up by the likes of Arsenal and Manchester United but they could easily have signed for Villa.

Every time I went to watch a certain player, I'd spot someone completely different and recommend him to Brian, instead. When I was supposed to be watching Jaap Stam, I ended up more interested in the PSV striker, Michael Mols. I'd been to France, Holland, Germany, and all the Scandinavian countries – anywhere anyone said there was a player who I'd be interested in. In the end, though, nothing came of it – no signings for Villa. That meant to me that no one trusted my judgement, as the club wouldn't pay out for the players, or they wanted too much money. I had an old goalkeeping friend, Bryan King, who was based in Norway and I recruited him to be our scout in Scandinavia. He turned out to be a great scout for us in that neck of the woods because he spoke the language and knew everyone on the circuit. Incidentally, we had an opportunity to sign a young Zlatan Ibrahimovíc – but again, that didn't materialise.

In 1998, I was away in France watching players and I had asked Allan Evans to go to watch a game for me as well. That meant two of the staff who Brian could talk to were not there to offer support and advice over a meeting he had with Doug Ellis, and that led to his resignation. Brian was his own man, and if he felt he wasn't getting the full backing of the club he would react. Unfortunately on that occasion, he did.

When John Gregory took over the role vacated by Brian in 1998, I asked him what he wanted from me as a scout – what types of players he wanted. His answer was, 'better than what we got.' That didn't give me much help, to be honest. It was a broad request and I thought I had already recommended players 'better than what we got' with the likes of Vieira, Pirès, Henry and Ljungberg, but Villa didn't buy into them. I thought I was wasting my time in a way, even though the job was enjoyable. While I was scouting, I was mixing it with a bit of commentary for Radio 5 Live and Sky Sports, which I really enjoyed doing. One September evening, I was commentating for Sky on a Villa game in Europe. Villa were playing Strømsgodset IF from Norway in the UEFA Cup. Right after the match, I was due to fly to Germany to watch a player in another European game the next day. However, before the game started, I had a phone call from the FA to inform me I had been selected for an interview for the position of head coach of an Asian national side and I'd have to be in London the next day. I'd seen the advert on an FA circular and applied for the post, not even knowing what country they were recruiting for. Obviously this clashed with my scouting role and the game in Germany, so I was wondering how I could fit it all in. In the end I went to Villa secretary, Steve Stride, to ask if I could travel back to the UK on the club's plane, and I made an excuse that someone in the family wasn't well or something. Steve obliged and got me a ticket home.

The following day I drove down to London for the interview with the FA for the job with an unknown Asian national side.

I was told there were a couple of people lined up for interview and I was one of them. It was a bit of a bizarre situation because the English FA had arranged the interview for me to become the head coach of another country, and I didn't even know what country they were interviewing for until I got to the FA headquarters. I arrived and was told I would be meeting the General Secretary of the Football Association of Thailand, Worawi Makudi and the head of TV Channel 3 in Thailand, Brian Marcar. They both interviewed me and offered me the Thailand job there and then. They appeared very keen to secure my services and even asked how soon I could start; however, the English FA representative told us that they could NOT offer me the job and the process had to be formally discussed by the FA.

When I left the interview I was collared by Jason Hughes, who at the time was working on the England 2006 World Cup bid. Jason knew they would offer me the job even before I went in for it, but he said they weren't in any position to do that. I left the FA headquarters a little confused and bewildered and went straight home. There was a bit of a delay which lasted a few days and I went backwards and forwards to the FA a few times until I was later called into the FA headquarters for further meetings and they finally told me that they were willing to give me a three-month contract as head coach of the Thai national side. I was stunned and disappointed.

'What do you mean, three months? You expect me to give up my job at Villa and go to Thailand for three months?' They told me that there was a funding issue and after the first three months, further funding would be required. I told them in no uncertain terms that I wasn't going for just three months. They assured me that the extra funding would be in place but eventually we compromised on a six-month contract. I agreed on the deal and said to them that I'd prove that I could be successful and they'd have to give me a longer deal.

After being offered the job I went back to Aston Villa and spoke to Steve Stride, who was the director, secretary and everything else at the club and a true Villa supporter, but more importantly, a good friend to me. I explained the position to him and asked for his advice and without hesitation he told me to take the job – he didn't say why but I got the impression John Gregory wanted to change things round and bring in his own people, which I understood. It was just as well I'd been given the opportunity at that time.

16

A 'Farang' in Bangkok

"You are now the hero of Thailand. You will never, ever be forgotten in this country."
Chaiyong Khumpiam, former Thailand goalkeeper

****

Little did I know, but I was going into the middle of a major world football scandal involving the team I was about to manage. No wonder they didn't hang around finding a new coach.

Before I had been confirmed as head coach for Thailand, there was a huge scandal brewing during and after the Tiger Cup group stage match between Thailand and Indonesia. The game was marred by an unsportsmanlike attempt to fix the match before it had even kicked-off. At the time, both teams had already qualified for the semi-finals, but with knowledge that the winners would have to face hosts Vietnam in Hanoi, while the losing team would play the supposedly weaker Singapore; neither team fancied winning the game.

Apparently, the first half of that game saw very little action as both teams barely made any attempt to score. During the second half both teams scored, partly thanks to half-hearted defending, resulting in a 2–2 tie after 90 minutes; however, the real infamy didn't take place until extra time, when an Indonesian defender allegedly kicked the ball into his own goal with a Thai attacker running towards the ball. It was a totally farcical game. It wasn't match-fixing so much as neither side playing to win. FIFA imposed a fine on both teams of US$40,000 for 'violating the spirit of the game.' In the semi-finals, Thailand lost to Vietnam, and Indonesia also lost to Singapore, pitting the teams against each other once again for the third-place play-off, where Indonesia eventually won by a penalty shoot-out. In the final, the un-fancied Singapore produced one of the competition's biggest shock results by defeating Vietnam.

After that farce, the Football Association of Thailand contacted the English FA and asked them to recruit an established coach to improve the footballing side and to move the game in Thailand forward. I later found out that they were given the CVs of ten different coaches and the FA were pushing for Colin Murphy, who was the ex-coach of the Vietnam national football team and had led the team to a bronze medal at the 1997 Southeast Asian Games. However, there were two things that were against Colin – he was 'unknown' to most people, and he had walked out on the Vietnam team – and then disappeared. The Thai FA dismissed his appointment and, after a few more names had been thrown into the hat, I appeared at the top of the pile. Everyone in Thailand knew me as the player who scored the winning goal in the 1982 European Cup Final – and no disrespect to Colin but he was an unknown name even to me. In short, the FA of Thailand wanted someone that the Thai people knew to restore some pride to the national team.

For me, it was a chance to show the world what I could offer – I wasn't fazed by coaching a national side and moving to another foreign country. To me, living and working in Asia wasn't as daunting as people might first think. Remember, I went to South Africa at the age of 21 so moving to Asia would be a doddle, I thought. Don't forget, I also coached and played in the US, so Thailand was just another country on my list. It would be a new and exciting challenge, but what I probably didn't think about at the time was that it would probably spell the end of my chances of getting another top job in the UK. There's sometimes the perception that if you're not working in England, you're not learning the game and that's when you tend to be forgotten. That sort of thinking takes us back to the dark ages – as if being a national coach of another country isn't learning!

We eventually arrived in Thailand on 22 October 1998, a day before Kathy's birthday. We were met by the hysterical Thai media and were greeted by one of the Thai management team, a guy called Thawatchai – known locally as 'Big Hoi', who whisked us away from the airport to check into a hotel. The hotel wasn't the best hotel they could have chosen to impress the new head coach and his wife – it was close to the stadium and therefore in the middle of nowhere. After we arrived in Bangkok, we went for dinner and we were whisked into a huge room and, as I looked around it, I noticed there were lots of girls with numbers on their dresses. I could only imagine what was going on in that room, and I was sure it must have been something dodgy – and it was. We later found out it was the type of hotel you could visit just to 'meet up' with girls, shall we say. We quickly moved away from that room into the bar area, which wasn't much better to be honest. When I went to the toilet I noticed I was followed in by a guy, and he came up behind me while I was having a pee in the urinal and started to massage my back and neck, so I told him in no uncertain terms to 'fuck off'. He quickly stepped away, but as I went to wash my hands he started to massage my back again.

'Eh, I told you once lad, fuck off!!' When I came out of the toilet and told Kathy about it, she couldn't believe it and went ballistic. We later found out that it was common for this kind of thing to happen and it wasn't a sexual gesture – merely another way of pleasing the hotel customer.

It was certainly an interesting welcome to Bangkok, I thought!

After a day acclimatising and getting over the jetlag, I had a meeting with the Thai FA to agree my brief. My initial task in hand was to prepare the team for the Asian Games and my brief boiled down to how well we did in that competition. In other words, if we did well the FA would consider extending my contract after the initial six months; however, it turned out to be a rather strange meeting. They explained their stance to me but none of it made any sense. Effectively, they wanted me to be the coach of the national side but they weren't going to publicise the fact that I was actually the head coach because, as they put it, 'it would put pressure [on me] and we don't want to exert any more pressure on you.' Pressure didn't worry me, but they insisted that I would be 'the advisor' if anyone in the media asked what my title was. So, I reluctantly agreed to be 'the advisor' to everyone else but secretly I was the head coach. I went along with it, although I thought it was a bit strange.

The head coach's role in Thailand was the top job, but I also had a manager in Thawatchai and an assistant manager called Virach Chanpanich. What they didn't say to me when I was offered the job was that I wouldn't be doing one job, I'd be doing about ten (at least). I wouldn't just be first-team coach but I'd have to be the Olympic coach, under-23s coach, under-19s coach, fitness coach, goalkeeper coach and even the sports physiologist, among other things. We had four weeks to prepare the team for the Asian Games that were due to start in Bangkok on 30th November 1998. The FA asked me if it was long enough but I said I didn't know until I got out on to the training ground; I had to get a group of players I didn't know fit and strong enough to compete, so my task was massive to say the least. Added to that, I didn't speak their language. It was going to be the biggest test of my life!

Arriving from a totally different continent and not knowing anything about Thai football or the players I would be coaching was a bit of a culture shock to say the least. I was handed the names of 30 players that I'd be working with but they could have been anyone in the world – I hadn't a clue who they were, and my first challenge was to reduce the numbers down to a squad of 22. I had no idea what their abilities were or how much work I'd have to do before I could pick 22 players. I was also asked to change the players' way of thinking, though I knew I couldn't do it through my favoured technique of shouting and swearing. Unable to speak the language, I decided I had to rely on other skills, such as body language and physical demonstrations, in order to get the best from the players. I didn't have time to learn the language, but I picked bits up as I went along, which is the best way really. Communication between the players and me was at times hard work but at least several of the players spoke some English. My captain, Kiatisak 'Zico' Senamuang spoke better English than I spoke Thai, and we had five players who played their league football in Singapore (and everyone spoke English there). Even though they spoke Malay in Singapore their communication was through English, so they could understand what I was talking about on the training field. What they did was to translate my English and relay the instructions to the other players in Thai. Very often, my instructions to the players got lost in translation and on several occasions that led to some contradiction of what I'd said, so I used to say to the translators, 'Don't translate if you don't understand. Just tell me if you don't understand and I'll explain it again.' My assistant manager, Virach did most of the translating and would relay what I said in the same tone.

During one of my first sessions, I demonstrated to a player called Natthaphong Samana how I wanted him to deliver a ball into the penalty area and I must have demonstrated it at least four times. Even at my age, and after having a hip replacement, I could still kick a ball a fair distance but this lad just couldn't do it and I was getting a bit frustrated with him because it was a basic footballing skill. The next day we all gathered again for another session and I looked around the group and Natthaphong wasn't anywhere to be seen.

'Where's Natthaphong?' I asked the group.

After a few minutes of silence one of the coaches approached me and said, 'He won't come back. You shouted at him.'

I couldn't believe it. 'Shouted at him? What do you mean he won't come back? You need to get him here now – I need to speak to him.'

The coach went back into the changing rooms and he persuaded Natthaphong to come back out. He reluctantly came and sat down with the group and I said to him, 'If you think that was shouting you want to see me when I'm really angry. I wasn't shouting – I was trying to get the best out of you but you need to listen to what I'm saying and show me what you can do.'

Through an interpreter he listened, bowed his head, apologised and agreed to try harder. I explained to the group it wasn't anything personal and I'll have a go at anyone if they're not trying hard enough. Natthaphong was fine after that but from that episode I learned not to be so hard on them and tried to express myself in a different way. Losing your temper isn't something that's tolerated in Thailand because you tend to lose face and that's why they appear to laugh or smirk. I soon learned to change the tone of my voice when I explained something to the players.

That was the first time it occurred to me that the job was going to be harder than I imagined.

Out on the training ground I had to face the media every day, and they asked me questions about my role, but I gave them the preferred answer that I was 'the advisor.' I didn't really think they believed me at the time, but on one occasion the general secretary of the FA came to me and said the media were all asking questions like why would an 'advisor' take every single training session and none of the Thai coaches take any themselves? My cover began to wear a bit thin after a while, and the FA decided to make a big announcement to the media that I was not 'the advisor' but the head coach. As I said before, it was a strange situation they put me in.

There was one occasion during the build-up to the Asian Games when my manager, Thawatchai, came up to me and said the team had to attend a function so we couldn't take the training session that day. They asked me if I'd like to attend and I asked what the function was. He said it was a meeting with the King of Thailand, Bhumibol Adulyadej. He had reigned since June 1946, making him the world's longest-reigning monarch and the world's longest-serving head of state. The occasion was to mark the start of the Asian Games and all the athletes were having an audience with him to light the flame for the Games. It was the chance of a lifetime so I replied, 'Are you serious? It would be an honour and a privilege for me to attend.'

We had to be at the function three hours before the King was due to arrive in order to take our places. I was looking at the lines and saw that they were in alphabetical order so I began to wonder if we came under 'football' or 'soccer'. It turned out we were assigned to 'football'. My spot must have been less than 20 yards away from where the King was going to stand, and as I was by far the tallest person in the audience, I must have stood out like a sore thumb. When the King arrived and began his speech, I noticed a number of mobile phones going off around me, and more worryingly, people were actually answering them while the King was speaking. In Britain if that happened you'd probably get sent to the Tower, but it seemed like it was tolerated in Thailand. I was shocked. Not only was it a high-profile event, I thought it was sheer bad manners.

After the King had finished his speech I spoke to the person who actually organised the event and told him what I'd witnessed. I said to him, 'I'm not being funny but while I'm living and working in your country I consider myself as Thai and I'll adopt your rules, but next time please, please could you tell everyone to turn their bloody mobile phones off before someone gets up on stage. To me that's an insult to your King. It's a bloody disgrace!' He went numb and was shocked by what I'd told him. Normally, Thai people are very placid but if anyone mentions anything bad about the King, people don't take too kindly. As it happened, the next function I attended, he actually told everyone to switch off all mobile phones before someone started speaking so my little chat had some effect after all, even though they didn't take it too well.

Being the national football coach, I was invited to many functions and asked to attend lots of charity events, and one that sticks out in my memory was an event that was organised by British Airways for a group of terminally ill, disabled and orphaned children. Those kids had never set foot on a plane in their lives and BA laid on a jumbo jet to fly them on a short journey along the coast and back to Bangkok. I was asked to attend along with some well-known Thai movie stars; in fact, I'd say the movie stars wanted me there as much as the kids did! It was a memorable day for the kids and for me, as I got the chance to sit in the cockpit during the hour-long flight. The kids were in their element and couldn't get over the fact that I was on the plane with them. Those kids had nothing in their lives; their parents couldn't even afford the basics like wheelchairs, let alone a flight on a plane. It was very humbling for me to be there and brighten up their lives, even if only for a couple of hours.

On another occasion I was told (not asked) to take the players to meet the government finance minister in Songkhla which was three hours flying time away. The FA wanted me to travel by plane on my own while the players went on a coach. I refused to leave the lads to travel by bus on their own, so I refused the offer to fly and told them I'd travel on the coach. There was no reason for us to be there to be honest: they wanted us to travel all that way just to be present for a ministerial vote. When we got there I couldn't believe what I witnessed. We were asked to play a game against a local team that was attended by a few thousand people, and afterwards there was a big function for us to attend. The minister addressed the audience and asked the players to walk on to the stage one-by-one, and gave each player an envelope. In every envelope the players received was .... a picture of me with the national kit on. When I took to the stage I received an envelope as well ... with a picture of me wearing the national kit. To me that was strange – very strange. After the parading on stage, I told my assistant coach if they wanted to give the players anything they should give them money, not a photo of me. I later found out that the hosts had to give a gift to their guests and in that case it just happened to be a picture of me in the Thailand kit. It was embarrassing.

That wasn't the only time we visited Songkhla. On another visit I did a training session with some kids as a guest of the mayor. After the session, Kathy and I went to the office to meet the mayor and, again, we received a gift. In Kathy's case she received a piece of cotton, probably enough to make a shirt or blouse with – but I think Kathy didn't think there was enough material. Again, I thought it was strange but we accepted the gifts in good faith.

Thai football was at rock bottom before my arrival and I knew it would take something like a miracle to restore the faith of the fans and the media, but I was up for the challenge and my philosophy was, 'let's see how it goes.' The Asian Games were the second largest multi-sport event after the Olympics, and held every four years, and football is just one of the 44 sports played. We were in Group F along with Hong Kong and Oman. We beat Hong Kong 5–0 in the first game and then went on to beat Oman 2–0 in the second game and played really well. Apparently, the victory over Oman was a surprise to everyone in Thailand, because there was a belief that they couldn't beat Middle-Eastern teams, and especially in that game because they had a Brazilian coach at the time. We topped the group, and that meant we went on to the next stage and into another group. In Round two, we were in the group with Qatar, Lebanon and Kazakhstan. We drew the first game against Kazakhstan, beat Lebanon and lost the final game against Qatar which meant we finished second in the group behind Qatar with the prospect of facing a harder quarter-final tie, but we were at home so anything was possible.

Our quarter-final tie was played against a powerful South Korea side at the Rajamangala National Stadium, a brand new stadium which had been opened especially for the Games and had a capacity of 65,000, but come matchday, there must have been more like 85,000 in the stadium. You'd never seen a stadium like it. I've no idea how they managed to pack so many people in there – it was unbelievable and must have failed every health and safety rule in the book (if there were any). After 43 minutes our centre-forward was sent off with the score 0–0 but within ten minutes of the sending off we scored through Zico; however, with only four minutes to go our centre-back gave away a free kick on the edge of the box and was sent off for a second yellow card. We were down to nine men but still leading and my stress levels increased when the free kick was looped through the wall. Our goalkeeper seemed to catch it, and then dropped the ball and it ended up in the back of the net. I was warned about things like that before I took up the job but I'd never witnessed anything like it before; I knew bribery was rife in Asian football and I was warned about the players and told to keep tabs on them all. When the goal went in to equalise I was confident that if we could keep them out and I could get a chance to talk to the players, we could win the game – even with nine men. I asked my backroom team, who were sitting on the bench, 'Please tell me this is a golden goal tournament.' because I knew they had them in Asia. An official told me it was, so that gave me the opportunity to speak with the players and get them to follow my plan. I knew we were capable of scoring but wasn't so sure about defending for another half an hour with only two centre-backs on the pitch.

My team-talk at full time (through a translator) was intended to instil confidence into the players and I told them how we would win the game with nine men. Thawatchai, my translator said my team-talk raised the hairs on the back of his neck. Apparently, it was such an inspirational speech he just knew we were going to win the game. I told the players that I needed the centre-backs to push forward with the ball to try to create a scoring opportunity. Five minutes into extra time, we were awarded a free kick, probably around 35 yards out, on the left touchline. I was looking away from the play, organising our backline while our left-back, Dusit played the ball to our midfielder, Thawatchai Damrong-Ongtrakul, who took one touch of the ball and hit it. As the ball started to rise it looped straight into the back of the net. Fortunately, I have a vision that when I look at one thing I can see other things around me so I just caught the action in the corner of my eye for that split second. Ongtrakul went berserk and ran the full width of the pitch with both his hands in the air as if he'd scored the winning goal in a World Cup final – and to the staff, players and the supporters, that was probably how it felt. You'd never seen a stadium erupt into such scenes of celebration. My inspirational speech before extra time was executed to a tee. Chaiyong Khumpiam, our goal keeper came up to me and said in broken English, 'You are now the hero of Thailand. You will never, ever be forgotten in this country.' I said I wasn't worthy of that but he repeated the statement and insisted I was, so I just agreed with him and shook his hand.

Never in the history of Asian football had a team won such a high-profile game with only nine men – it just hadn't been done before. After the euphoria of winning the quarter-final in such a dramatic fashion, I don't think we were ready for the semi-final tie against Kuwait. I had just got back to the bench when they scored straight from the kick-off, and it rattled us. I think the players were still thinking about that great win against South Korea. Unfortunately, we were beaten 3–0 in that game and Kuwait were the better team on the day. That left us with a consolation game for third place against a physically bigger and stronger China side, coached by the ex-Fulham midfielder, Bobby Houghton. We were beaten by the better side and finished the tournament in fourth place, which was very respectable and an achievement in itself as we weren't expected to get through the first group stages.

Our achievement in getting Thailand to fourth place equalled that of the 1990 team and it was enough for the Football Association of Thailand to extend my contract by another six months. So unexpected was the fourth place finish that the Thai government gave the players a bonus (which I found out was the equivalent of £1000) as they just missed out on the medals (as the prize money was only paid to gold, silver and bronze medal-lists). We were also invited to a function hosted by the Thai Prime Minister and all the players had to meet him. I was asked to meet the PM as well and it didn't surprise me that he spoke very good English as he congratulated us. After our chat, the Prime Minister gave me an envelope, and all in front of the Thai media. I posed for several pictures with the envelope (which I later found out contained money) in my hand and as soon as I turned away to re-join the players, a woman appeared from nowhere and snatched the envelope out of my hand. I confronted her and asked her why she had taken the envelope. I went to find Thawatchai and I explained to him what had happened and he told me that because I was a 'farang' (a foreigner), I wasn't entitled to the money from the government (according to some). I told the woman (who apparently worked for the Thai government) never to do that again and said I'd never come to a function like that again.

'You give me an envelope just to take pictures for the publicity then you take it off me. I've not got a problem if you don't give me an envelope in the first place, but don't ever give me something then take it back off me again.'

My manager, Thawatchai wasn't happy, and had a go at the woman, and eventually recovered the money on my behalf. The principle wasn't taking the money off me as such, but being given the money, letting the media take pictures of me receiving it, *then* taking it off me. It was all very bizarre.

By the time the Games had finished it was almost Christmas, but as the Thai people don't celebrate Christmas we decided to come back to the UK for the festive period and to recover from a hectic few weeks and our introduction to Thailand.

When we returned to Thailand after our Christmas break, we decided to look for a more permanent place to live, seeing as we'd been living in a poor-quality hotel since our arrival. We were taken to view an apartment we had been recommended but which seemed a long way out of the city – in fact we were driving all the way out towards the airport. We arrived at the complex and the estate agent opened the door of the apartment. To our horror we were greeted by the sight of a couple lying in bed, and when Kathy walked in she wasn't very impressed at all. We all walked out and closed the door behind us. We viewed another apartment with my assistant manager, Virach, that was right in the centre of the city on Soi 16 (soi is the name for road or street) and it turned out to be just the place we wanted. It was a really nice apartment but the FA weren't very impressed with it for some reason, probably because it was a lot more expensive than the dodgy hotel they were paying for. The Thai FA must have been run on a shoestring budget because they only paid for my accommodation and transportation; the English FA paid my salary. In the end, we moved into that apartment, and Virach ended up paying the rent.

Following our success at the Asian Games my services were in demand. I was very often asked by government ministers to be photographed with them in order to help their campaign and to show off to their constituents. One time, I was even ushered off the training ground by the President of the Football Association of Thailand, who was standing for election at the time and had walked on to the training field to ask me to come to a school and coach some kids. He had already promised the school he would bring me there for a coaching session, without even asking me first. I told him, in no uncertain terms, that I wasn't going to do it as I was preparing the team for an important game. The next thing I knew the councillor's entourage had driven the car on to the playing field and as they approached me a door opened and a voice inside the car told me I should get in the car.

'No, no. I'm coaching. I told you I'm not going.'

The voice inside the car told me again, 'You don't understand. If you don't go, he'll lose face and if he loses face, it will not go down well. You've got to get in the car.'

It left me with no choice so I got in the car after I'd begrudgingly asked my assistants to take over the training.

When we got to the school there were thousands of people waiting to greet me, including around 500 kids. I thought I was there to coach some of the kids for half an hour, but to my surprise I was asked to coach all 500 kids with only two balls available and a few cones. In the end, there were a few other footballers and coaches there, so I organised it pretty well and a good day was had by all. It only occurred to me later on that I was being 'utilised' and they expected me to do a lot of promotional work for the hierarchy. It seemed that the public saw me in a different light to how people in the hierarchy saw me; the public just saw me as the coach for the Thai national football team but the hierarchy saw me as some promotional figurehead. I didn't really want to get involved with it all but I was asked to do lots of promotional events and it would have been seen as wrong to turn them down – I didn't have a choice really.

Thai people are generally sceptical of foreigners ('farang') but, moreover, they are reluctant to acknowledge foreigners who have achieved things in their country. So, whenever I was announced by a public figurehead leader to do a speech or something, I was addressed as a Peter Withe, staff coach' or 'part of the coaching staff' and never as 'Peter Withe, head coach.' It was something I couldn't get my head around, but at least the public (the fans) knew who I was, so in my mind the public figures could have called me anything – it was better than being called an 'advisor' anyway. In any other country I'd be an important figure but in Thailand it wasn't like that. I think they are still happy that their country is the only nation in Southeast Asia never to be colonised, and so they don't have any other country telling them what to do.

The longer I spent in Thailand the more I understood how the country worked. I also learned how to get the things I wanted – although it wasn't easy. If I asked for things directly, most of the time I wouldn't get what I wanted – because it was me (a foreigner) asking. I eventually had to change my tack and try another way of asking. We always trained in Bangkok but I had an idea that if we trained in different parts of the country, in Phuket and at other venues, we would become more popular with the masses, so I told my assistant coach of my idea and he didn't really make much of a fuss about it. However, two weeks later, a representative of the Thai FA approached me and said, 'We've got an idea. We think we should go round the country to train and play matches.'

As if I'd never heard of the idea before, I replied, 'What a good idea. That's brilliant.'

Rather than saying, 'That was my idea in the first place ...' I just told them it sounded like a great idea. It was easy. I decided from then on, that was the way I would have to get things done.

Among the nicest people we met while living in the city was the British Ambassador to Thailand, Sir James Hodge and his wife, Lady Frances. There was a close-knit ex-pat community in Thailand and with Kathy and me in town, we became part of that scene. Sir James and Lady Frances always invited us to every function they held at the British Embassy. Sir James made it clear to us that he was there to help us at any time and that was really comforting. In fact, just before we had moved into our new apartment, the British Embassy arranged a function especially for us, which was a really nice gesture. It was a party to welcome us as a couple to Bangkok and to make sure we felt at home. However, the delegation of ten Thai people from the FA who were invited felt a little uneasy when they set foot into the British Embassy as they had stepped out of their normal, comfortable environment, but they made the effort and I am sure they enjoyed being spoilt by Sir James and his team.

The good thing about those types of functions is that very often you'll meet people who can open doors for you. One such businessman I met was a chap called Mark Woodruff (nicknamed Woody), who owned a bar in the city called Chequers. Woody was a Villa supporter, so I guess that brought us together. We ended up going to his bar after the function and started to get to know even more ex-pats in the process, and after a few drinks there we headed back to the hotel we were staying at for that night which was called the Town in Town. I asked one of the barmaids to call a taxi and told her where we wanted to go. However, what should have been a 15 or 20 minute drive in a taxi turned into a scenic tour of Bangkok, so I got the taxi driver to stop the taxi and asked him if he knew where he was going, and he replied that he knew where Chinatown was. I then said to him 'No, not Chinatown, we want to go to Town in Town.' I didn't know whether the taxi driver wasn't a local or couldn't read road signs, but he was driving us miles away from the hotel and in the opposite direction, and we'd been in the taxi over half an hour. He didn't have a clue and continued to drive around aimlessly. In the end he kept stopping every time he saw another taxi to ask them where to go. I was keeled up in the back of this taxi dying for a pee, so when I saw a hotel ahead I cried out to him, 'Stop. Just stop here!' I jumped out of the cab and ran to the hotel and headed into the nearest toilet just in time. When I returned to the taxi I asked the driver to take us to the Town in Town and he pointed over the road – we were literally opposite the bloody hotel already. When he told me the fare I told him to 'sod off' and said I wasn't paying for him to get me lost.

Roger Fewtrell was another ex-pat who was well known in the community. I knew him from my days at Villa and I was aware he had a bar in Bangkok. I managed to get Roger's number from Mark Woodruff who also knew Roger, and arranged to meet him at a pub called the Bulls Head not far from where we were living. Roger was always known for being the life and soul of any party so he'd made a real effort to gather around a dozen of his people to meet us in the Bulls Head. Typically, the champagne was flowing and we all had a great time. Roger obviously knew a lot of people in Bangkok, so he suggested we go to a bar that he co-owned in Soi Cowboy. We had no idea about Nana Plaza or what the area stood for as we were new to the city but we soon learned that the bar was in the heart of a red-light area. When we arrived I looked around the place and thought to myself, 'This doesn't look like a "normal" bar to me.' All I saw were loads of scantily dressed women parading around the place. Some were topless and I'd be lying if I said I wasn't distracted by it, even with Kathy with me, and she wasn't impressed with the choice of venue. Needless to say Kathy didn't go there again after that night.

Living in Bangkok everyone seemed to know where I was at any one time – even with a population of six million people. It is the capital of

Thailand, but it seemed like a 'small' town. Anything I did or anywhere I went, it seemed that the entire population knew about it. When we had visitors from the UK come over to stay, they couldn't believe how famous I'd become in Thailand, and my sons, Jason, Stephen and Gareth even said I was more famous in Thailand than I was back home. It seemed that everywhere I went, even the most obscure places, everyone wanted to take a picture of me or get my autograph. It was flattering and humbling really, knowing that, as a foreigner, I had such an influence on the people of another country. Even now, I recently went back to Thailand, and people still recognised me. Once one person knew I was in town it was like a chain reaction and suddenly it seemed like the whole population came out to greet me, just like it was back then. It was really amazing to think that there are millions of people in Thailand who haven't got two pennies to rub together, but through just talking to them and spending some time with them I made them very happy.

One good thing I found out about the Thai people was that there was a strong family unity, and when their parents grow old, the children look after them and they all live together. On the downside though, there are certain things that go on in Thailand that are illegal but go on regardless: drug trafficking, prostitution, gambling and cross-dressing are a few activities that make Thailand a playground for tourists and illegal immigrants. All these things are rife in Thailand but they go on because they are the main income for tourism. The longer you spend in a place the better you get to know it and the longer we lived in Bangkok the more we got to know where not to go – and Patpong and Nana Plaza were the areas we avoided. That was until my old mate, Ray Clemence came over to visit us.

On arrival in Bangkok, Ray told me his old mate, Doug Livermore had told him he had to go to look at the bars, so he insisted we took him and his wife, Vee (who was friends with Kathy, being from Liverpool herself) there, and we reluctantly obliged. Every bar we went into that night with Ray and Vee, people came up to me and took my photo and word got around that the head coach of the Thailand football team was in the area. Although Ray insisted on wanting to go there, he couldn't believe his eyes – it was a real eye-opener for both of them. We went into one bar and saw women were doing all sorts of weird sexual things like firing darts, bursting balloons over our heads and smoking cigars (and not in their mouths). To the thousands of tourists it would have been a laugh but in Bangkok it's an industry. For me, I can't see anything entertaining in it.

After an hour of walking in and out of bars in Nana Plaza to get a flavour of Bangkok, we went to the quieter Soi Cowboy area. We walked into a bar and there was no one in there apart from some 'girls', hiding behind a pillar pointing at Ray and making sexual gestures at him. Ray asked me if I'd seen the girls. I knew what was going on but Ray hadn't clicked, so I told him:

'Ray. I'm just going to tell you one thing. Kathy and Vee are the only women in this bar.' Ray was confused, 'What do you mean?'

I repeated to Ray, 'They're the only women in the bar.'

After a few seconds he twigged. 'You're joking.'

I then pointed at the 'girls' and confirmed it to Ray, 'They're men.'

Kathy also showed Ray that they weren't women by ushering the two 'girls' over to our table, 'So, what have you had done then ladies ...?'

They then began to run through the 'treatments' they'd had. By that time Ray was nearly in stiches on the floor – he couldn't get his breath so I explained to Ray that most of the 'girls' we'd seen in the bars in Nana Plaza were actually fellas.

Funnily enough about half an hour later four (actual) fellas walked into the same bar and looked over to us and said, 'There's Peter Withe and Ray Clemence.' In those days there was no Facebook or Twitter so we were pretty safe that our pictures wouldn't be splashed all over the world a few minutes later – thank god!

It has to be said that we found Bangkok a contrast of cultures – it had some of the world's most insalubrious places but on the other hand, there were some beautiful hotels and restaurants in the city. One hotel we went to a few times was the Mandarin Oriental, one of the most unique hotels in the world. One Sunday, Kathy and I took Jason and his wife, Sharon, there for lunch. Jason and I were wearing shorts, not casuals but properly cut smart shorts, and as we approached the entrance to the restaurant we were stopped from entering because of our attire. I was annoyed because people were passing us wearing jeans! When I questioned the decision the duty manager told us guests of the hotel could wear anything they liked but if you weren't staying at the hotel there was a strict dress code. Meanwhile, Sharon wasn't having any of it so she went off to find the manager and explained that they were refusing entry to the head coach of the Thailand football team and his family. That caused a bit of frenzy, and the manager came over to apologise and said we could go into the restaurant after all. As soon as he'd said that I told him politely that we wouldn't be coming to his restaurant and we all walked out of the door. I thought it was a cheek, one minute refusing us entry and as soon as he found out who I was, allowing us in. A similar thing happened not long after that episode when we tried to enter the roof restaurant of the luxury Banyan Tree Hotel. That day we'd been shopping and had a few bags in our hands so we decided to go there for a drink. When we approached the entrance we were told we couldn't go in because we were wearing open shoes.

Having to rely on taxis to get across town wasn't ideal – the FA had promised me the use of a vehicle so I told them I wanted a car as soon as possible. The very next day they provided me with an old Volvo – plus a driver. The driver was made available whenever we wanted him to drive us around. One Saturday morning, Kathy and I wanted to go shopping at a department store called Robinsons so we gave strict instructions to the driver to park the car and wait for us to return. When we did return to meet the driver there was no sign of him. We stood there holding bags and bags of shopping, waiting for the driver to take us home. He didn't have a mobile phone to call him on but he eventually turned up half an hour later – minus the car.

'Where have you been?' I quizzed him.

The driver began to smirk and he looked a bit sheepish but I was getting wound up so told him to go to get the car. By the time he returned with the car another half an hour had passed so I quizzed him again, 'Where have you been?' Again, the driver smirked as if he was embarrassed about something. I'd lost it so I just pointed and gestured at him. 'Keys. Just give me the keys and go,' – or words to that effect.

The driver tried to explain but just asked in broken English, 'I'm finished?'

I replied, 'Yes, you're finished, now sod off!'

He kept saying, 'Sorry, sorry ...'

I didn't think about it at the time but I didn't have a Thai driving licence, but I just wanted to get back to the apartment. When I calmed down a bit I decided to drive him back to our apartment and then called my assistant to ask him to explain to the driver what his job was.

He didn't last long after that and we soon got another driver, who was only 5ft 3in tall and had a nervous twitch, but was a lovely guy who would do anything for us. One day, Jason was with me in the back of the car and we were stuck in traffic on our way to training. After about five minutes of being stationary he started to mutter to himself and then he started to shout out loud, which was unusual for Thai people. A few minutes later he jumped out of the car and headed directly for a truck right in front of us. The truck had ten lads in the back of it, but that didn't bother our driver who headed straight for the truck driver and, without hesitation, belted him across the face for no apparent reason. Jason and I were still in the back of the car, being stared at by ten pairs of eyes. Jason went mad, got out of the car, picked up our driver by the scruff of his neck and threw him back into the driving seat.

When he'd got his breath back I told him in no uncertain terms, 'Don't you ever do that to me again.' He knew he'd done wrong and put his hands over his face in shame. Funnily enough he didn't last long either, because one of the staff seconded him to drive for him.

After going through a couple more drivers I eventually asked one of Jason's friends, whose father used to work in the British Embassy to get me a driving licence so I could drive myself. He took me to the driving centre and the people behind the counter recognised me and wanted a picture and an autograph, which I obliged, and within an hour I had received my Thai driving licence, no questions asked.

Of course, part of the culture shock moving to another country (and another completely different continent) is the difference in the food, and Thai cuisine is known the world over for its strong aromatic components and spiciness. It's also known for its balance of sour, sweet, salty, and bitter tastes. It takes some time to get used to all those flavours – I loved it but Kathy didn't like any of it at first. She didn't like the spiciness of the food and most of the food didn't agree with her, mainly coriander, and as that herb is used in most Thai dishes it was a problem. My favourite dish was Tom Yum, a very spicy clear soup to which fish or meat was added – I couldn't get enough of it. So imagine the culture shock when I tried to introduce pasta to the player's diets – the Thai players hadn't even a clue what pasta was. They'd eat egg noodles no problem but pasta, bread or potatoes – no chance. All I wanted to teach them was to take in carbohydrates. I'd tell the players that to sustain energy levels for 90 minutes they had to have carbohydrates before games because the rice the Thai players ate wasn't what was considered a high-energy carbohydrate. I had so much trouble getting the players to eat pasta that I even did a deal with them; I told them they could eat what they liked every day, except for the day before a game when they had to eat pasta or other high-carb foods. A few of them, the better players who wanted to perform at a higher level, took it on board, but the majority refused. I was amazed when we travelled to away games with the national side, that we'd be taking up to 15 skips and 10 of them were full of food, whereas back home, for domestic away games, we'd often only take three or four skips full of kit and accessories. Food was a big part of the Thai way of life and very important in the diet of the players. Never did they eat food that hadn't been brought from home; we'd always take our own special rice, chilli paste, meat and vegetables, as if we didn't trust anyone else's food.

The players back then didn't earn very much money at all but I remember a very poignant moment when my captain, Zico, said to me they'd got some money left over from bonuses they'd earned for the Asian Games and had decided to donate it to a local orphanage. That to me was very special because I'd worked with a priest called Father Joe, who looked after an orphanage for all sorts of kids who had been left on the streets for whatever reason. I asked Zico how much money they had collected and I agreed that my assistant manager and I would put the same amount in. I felt very humble that my players had even considered doing it in the first place. So, we decided on a date to visit the orphanage, and when we arrived there everyone was very excited to see the head coach of the national football team and some of the players had come to visit them. We went there during lunchtime and as I was watching the kids eat their meals, I noticed there were probably a dozen kids on one table who had been kept away from everyone else. I asked one of the nurses why and she said they had HIV. I was horrified to see that these kids had been isolated because they had HIV. Having already spoken to a doctor at the British Embassy about HIV I'd been educated about the disease. I felt there was ignorance about HIV in the country and that was sad. I was in awe of the players because they went and sat with all of those kids, fed them food and cuddled them. I think most footballers from anywhere else in the world wouldn't have gone anywhere near those kids, which is quite sad really.

The success in the Asian Games had whetted the fans' appetites for more and a few high-profile 'showpiece' games had been arranged in the February for a four-nation tournament called The King's Cup. The event involved different international teams and was held annually in Thailand. We were up against South Korea, Hungary and Brazil. Although we lost 4–1 to Brazil, we finished a respectable third in the group. The funny thing was Brazil brought over two sides, the under-20s, and the full side, and they only played the full side against us because we hosted the event; their under-20s played the other two teams, so in that respect we did well.

The following season we played Brazil's first XI again and were beaten 7–0 but we played very well and could have been three up after 20 minutes whereas Brazil probably only had a dozen chances in the whole game and scored seven goals. After that game, their coach Vanderlei Luxemburgo came up to me and said, 'I see English coach is coaching the team. I told my players they play this long ball but you don't play that. You play Brazilian style passing game.'

I replied by saying, 'Well that's the way I like to play football and these are the players I've got to play that way.' It's strange that foreign coaches have always come up to me and said that my teams never played the 'traditional English style' (route-one football). There has always been a stigma attached to English football coaches that they play only one way but that's not true at all. Still to this day, foreigners keep on about route-one football, and to me it's a total fallacy. The aim of the game has always been to score more goals than the opposition and whether it takes one pass or 20 passes, it's never really mattered how we played as long as we scored more goals.

Following the end of the 1998/99 English Premier League season, we played Arsenal, who had finished runners-up in the league. The game was held in the Rajamangala Stadium in front of 50,000 football-mad Thais. Being an Englishman, the Thais thought I'd be supporting Arsenal, even though I was the Thailand head coach, so I had to point out to them that I was supporting my team – Thailand. I don't think they understood my philosophy of being 'Thai' (even though I was English) while I was living and working in their country. I thought it was quite simple really – as long as I was working for the Football Association of Thailand, I supported Thailand. Furthermore, I promised to give 100 per cent to beat any team we faced, including any English team. I think the locals found it very difficult to admit that a 'farang' could be on their side, as it were, and helping their cause. It was obvious they needed the help of foreigners and football was the number one passion in Thailand.

My position as head coach was high profile and, therefore, my philosophy was hard for the locals to accept. Arsène Wenger fielded a very strong side which included the likes of Seaman, Adams, Keown, Viera, Petit, Anelka, Kanu and Overmars and it was an indicator of how far we had come as a football team. We fielded two newcomers in Tananchai Boriban and Anurak Srikerd in midfield, and we managed to pull off a shock 4–3 win against a strong Arsenal side.

The most striking thing I noticed during that Arsenal game was that most of the crowd were wearing Arsenal shirts and not Thailand shirts; however, I do remember when we were winning, some of the fans changed out of their Arsenal shirts and put Thailand shirts on. People didn't tend to buy the national kit because of the cost, but they chose to buy 'cheaper' versions of Premier League kits (fakes). During my stay in Thailand, our shirts were made by a Singapore company called FBT Products and sold at a reasonable price for Thai standards, and I couldn't understand why more fans weren't buying the shirts. I thought being successful would enhance the reputation of the team and more people would buy the shirt, but from looking at the crowd that wasn't the case. Something had to be done about it, so I told the FA the shirts had to be cheaper and made more accessible to Thai people. I even went as far as going public in the media, asking people to be patriotic and to support their team by buying a Thailand shirt – even I wore a Thailand shirt everywhere I went. After a while, I think my point was made and more and more people bought the Thailand shirt.

We also gave the players another taste of English football when we travelled to Liverpool for a few days to train with the academy lads out near Kirby. The trip coincided with a Liverpool home game, so we took the lads to a weekend game at Anfield. They were in their element, looking round the club shop, and with a few quid in their pockets some of them bought some gear – but some of the lads were even more curious to make sure the replica shirts were originals and not fake. Once they saw the label inside the shirts they put them back on the rail because they saw they were 'Made in Thailand.' They thought the shirts were fakes but I assured them that everything they saw in the shop was original – even if the shirts were made in Thailand. Apparently, some Premier League clubs at the time had their shirts made in Thailand as it was cheaper to produce them there, but for every 1,000 shirts made and sent to Anfield, another 1,000 were sold on the streets of Bangkok and other Thai cities because they had no labels inside. The Thai authorities tried to clamp down on forgeries and the manufacturers sent people over from their head offices to check out the quality of their shirts, but that sort of thing happened all the time in Thailand.

About two years into my stay in Thailand, the minor cultural changes I had made were starting to become second nature. It was a case of me, a foreign coach, getting used to the team's ways, and them – both the FA and the players – getting to know my way of doing things. One change I made was to the procedure followed when the team won a trophy or received medals. I had noticed early on that the manager, assistant manager and head coach went up before the players to receive their medals or trophy. That was the opposite of the protocol we have always had in Europe, where the captain leads his players up to receive the award. I noticed it when we received our medals for the Asian Games and I asked Thawatchai why the players had to receive their medals last. He was a good listener and took in everything I told him, so I explained that it wasn't right to my way of thinking, because the players had earned the right to go up first, not the coaching staff. The very next time we went up to collect medals or a trophy, the players went up first.

During my stay in Thailand I found the Thai players were really quite humble as people and didn't misuse their new-found fame in the way that some European footballers did. During my spell as head coach, they had become more recognisable to the general public – I suppose the success had made them more famous. Moreover, there was a 6ft 2in white fella who stuck out from the rest, and I tended to get a lot of attention from the fans and the media. The one thing I couldn't change, though, were the politics around being the head coach of Thailand. There was an occasion when I was in a press conference with my captain, Zico, thinking it was going to be about the forthcoming game, but as it turned out the media wanted to talk about something completely different.

The first question fired at me was, 'What do you think about Zico?' I didn't understand the question so I asked the reporter to expand and he repeated the question, 'What do you think of him going to play in England?'

It took me aback a bit and came as a shock to hear someone from the media tell me my captain was moving to England and I didn't know about it.

I soon learned that was the way things were done in Thailand. I'd switched off and lost interest in the rest of the press conference, as it was obvious it was all about Zico and not about the game. Afterwards, I pulled Zico to one side and asked him what was going on.

'Oh, yeah, the president arranged for me to go to England to have trials.'

By that time I was getting a bit annoyed. 'Don't you think you should have asked someone who really knows what it's like to play in England?' However, before Zico could answer the question he was ushered away. I then approached the FA president and asked him who'd arranged for Zico to go to England but he just ignored my question and brushed me to the side. I didn't bother to question any further and just let it pass by. I didn't think Zico would have made it in England anyway, not because of his ability, but because of the differences in the style of football we played. If they had come to me and asked for my opinion, I would have advised for someone else to go with him, for support. I anticipated problems with the language, food and, of course, the weather, but they all ignored my worries.

As it turned out Zico went to Middlesbrough (on his own) and he encountered all the problems I had highlighted. He was left to his own devices and struggled. He found training hard to take because the English way was to shout at someone who'd made a mistake, while the Thais weren't used to that and he couldn't take it. Ironically, he moved to Huddersfield Town, managed by Steve Bruce and his assistant, Lou Macari, at the time. I went to see them training during one of my trips home and it was cold, wet and snowy. I saw Zico and he was wearing about three layers of clothing, a woolly hat and gloves. I asked him how it was going and he told me it was hard and he couldn't understand all the screaming and shouting the manager and his staff did. Zico didn't last long in England and returned home shortly afterwards.

I found Bangkok to be a full-on, 24/7 city where there was never any let-up, whatever the time of day. It's the kind of city you have to get out of from time to time. When it got too much, we would retreat to a beautiful place called Hua Hin, a beach resort town in the southern part of Thailand, some 200km south of Bangkok. The King of Thailand and the royal family had a summer palatial residence there. Every time we went to Hua Hin we always stayed at the luxury Dusit Resort. Kathy and I got to know the manager, a Thai fella called Victor, and his assistant, an Aussie called John Gill. In fact we got to know them so well we'd always be put up in the best suite in the resort and it became almost like a 'home-from-home.' We'd sometimes take the players there just to get out of Bangkok and train in different surroundings. It was an ideal place to go and chill out, play golf and enjoy the lovely food, and it made a change for the players not to train in the spotlight of the city. John and Victor allowed us to train on the huge pitch they had near the complex and we'd very often play practice matches against local teams at the resort just to bring a competitive edge to the training. The hotel couldn't do any wrong accommodating us, because every time we brought the team down there the media would be filming or taking shots with the resort as the backdrop, so in a way it provided them some free advertising.

Being a keen golfer, I joined the golf society that was run by an ex-pat, who just happened to be a Wolves fan. They hated me because I tended to win every tournament. Not only that but every time Jason and Gareth came out they'd always clean up so the Withe name became infamous amongst the golfing fraternity out there. One New Year we were invited to the Dusit Resort as special guests of John and Victor and as Gareth was visiting us he wanted to join us for the event as well. They put on an extravaganza like no other – it had Victor's name all over it. Victor was a flamboyant and colourful character who liked to do things out of the ordinary. For instance, his suit for that evening was a stunning lime green and only someone like Victor could have pulled it off. In fact it was so bright that it had sequins sown into the suit that lit up like a christmas tree – it was amazing but not something I'd wear myself. The resort itself had fabulous grounds, and for the occasion they erected a huge stage and hundreds of tables that were decorated with colourful flowers. The best part of the evening was the food – it was to die for, and it was everywhere! There was non-stop entertainment. The whole occasion was one of the best we've ever experienced and the best New Year party Kathy and I have ever been to. Gareth, too, said it was a great occasion and he would not have missed it for the world.

The Tiger Cup started on 6 November 2000 and it was being hosted by Thailand. We won the group consisting of Indonesia, Myanmar and the Philippines convincingly with three wins out of three and scoring nine goals in the process. In the semi-final, we faced Malaysia in the Rajamangala Stadium and saw them off with a 2–0 victory. Zico was in hot form, scoring four goals in the four games. In the final, we played Indonesia again, and beat them 4–1, which was the same scoreline as in the group stages, with Worrawoot Srimaka scoring a hat-trick to secure the second Tiger Cup title for Thailand.

It was my second regional title, following the gold medal in the Southeast Asian Games but all was not well, it seemed. In three years of being employed (and paid) by the English FA to coach the Thailand national side, I'd achieved great success for the nation. However, I got wind of the fact that the FA of Thailand couldn't afford to keep me on. According to some media reports, the FA 'weren't happy with my current performance' and they also suggested I hadn't introduced enough fresh talent into the squad. The latter was a load of rubbish because I'd travelled all over Thailand to watch football matches and kept an eye on certain young players. In fact, while I was head coach I'd actually changed the whole team around so the reports were way off.

While all the speculation about my future was being played out in the media, I'd been going to Singapore to report on the English Premier League for ESPN, working with John Dykes. I loved the work and giving my opinion on the games; the only problem was the time difference – I was working at 3am. I'd worked for Sky, the BBC and other media agencies before I took up the post in Thailand, so I was asked if I would consider working for ESPN full-time and had numerous meetings with George Greene at VP Productions. He made me an offer that included Championship football amongst other things. At one stage I actually agreed to an offer from ESPN in Singapore as a co-commentator, similar to what Andy Gray was doing at Sky at that time.

To be honest, I was looking to leave my position in Thailand anyway, and it got to the stage where we started looking at apartments in Singapore and we weighed up the pros and cons of moving. The deal was virtually done with George at ESPN and I just had to go through the formalities of signing the paperwork on a three-year contract and getting the appropriate working visas sorted. While we were in Singapore viewing apartments, I received a phone call from a friend of mine, Colin Dunjohn who worked for IMG, the global sports management group. He asked me if I'd signed a contract with ESPN. I told Colin the situation and he advised me to hold fire and fly back to Bangkok as soon as possible. Colin explained that there was a new sponsor (Channel 7) for the FA of Thailand to replace Channel 3 for the following two years – but it would only happen if I stayed on as head coach and the whole deal to sponsor the national side relied on me still being in position.

Surang Prempree (or Khun Daeng as she was nicknamed) was the lady who owned Channel 7 and was the person behind the deal. She couldn't understand why the Thai FA were trying to get rid of me, but she was willing to offer me any package I wanted in terms of salary to stay on. Things were moving fast and I wasn't too sure if I wanted to stay another two years in Thailand. Colin asked me to give him an indication of what sort of salary I would be looking for if I did decide to stay, so I went away and thought about it for a few days.

I talked it over with Kathy and thought about it overnight, and put a package together to include salary, accommodation and expenses then presented it to Colin. We didn't really want to go back to be honest as I felt I'd achieved what I set out to achieve in terms of moving the team forward, without really getting the credit I deserved. However, I was intrigued by the new sponsorship deal.

They say a week is a long time in football, and a few days later I'd signed a new two-year contract with the salary I'd asked for, and walked away from my offer from ESPN. To say ESPN weren't very happy was an understatement, but they never contacted me after that. I suppose I had only agreed in principle to the contract, and in the end I'd had second thoughts about whether I really wanted to sit in a studio commentating on games. Looking back, there was something nagging me about the ESPN contract. There was a clause that stated they could call me at short notice to work on a game. I felt they could effectively ask me to come in seven days a week if they wanted me to, so I wasn't happy about that for a start – I didn't want to work seven days a week that was for sure! I would have got ESPN to change that clause if I had taken up the contract on a permanent basis – but it wasn't necessary in the end. I'd have missed the day-to-day involvement of coaching, that's for sure. I loved coaching, and I was back as Thailand's head coach for another two years.

The next competition to prepare for was the 2002 Asian Games, which were being staged in Busan, South Korea. The format had changed from the previous tournament in Bangkok in 1998 in that we had to field our under-23 team with a maximum of four overage players. We were in a group with Vietnam, Yemen and Roy Hodgson's UAE and, in the battle of the English coaches we managed to win the game 3–1. We got through the first stages finishing top of the group, and that meant we were in the quarter-final again where we were drawn against North Korea. I'd already watched North Korea and seen they were a physically stronger side than us. After our last game, my captain, Zico, was ruled out due to suspension, so I plotted how we were going to get past North Korea. I changed the formation for that game. I decided to play one up front and flooded the midfield. It was a gamble but it paid off as we beat them 1–0, and the lad who played up front on his own, Manit Noywech, scored the winner. We were in the semi-finals again and had to face a strong Japanese side, who were one of the tournament favourites. We were beaten that time 3–0. In the third-place play-off we played one of the other favourites, South Korea and we lost that 3–0 too, so we ended up fourth again. If you consider we had competed against teams that had qualified for the World Cup in the past, it wasn't a bad effort.

The fourth-place finish in the Asian Cup was considered to be a success by the Thai FA, and shortly after that game they asked me to take charge of the Olympic qualifier against UAE, which pitted me against Roy Hodgson again. I was told that the Thailand team historically lost to the UAE. We had beaten them in the Asian Games with our first team but the game on 10 September 2003 in Dubai was at under-23 level and we lost that 4–1. We drew 1–1 in the home tie but should have beaten them as one of our lads missed a penalty. We didn't qualify for the Olympics.

It was around that time I came under increasing pressure because of an unlikely fashion faux pas I'd apparently (and not knowingly) made. It was a fuss about nothing but it all boiled down to me wearing shorts during matches. Despite all the success we'd had, the president of the FA of Thailand, Vijit Getkaew, told me before the UAE home game that I 'should be wearing a suit, not shorts during matches.' The very fact that I knew him and we got on quite well, as he was a keen golfer like I was, made it even more bizarre. The only time you'd see me in a suit would be if I'd been invited to an audience with the King of Thailand, the British Embassy or to meet the Thai Prime Minister. I was very disappointed in Vijit making an issue where there wasn't one, and more so for going to the press about it. The temperature in Bangkok was normally in the 40s (Celsius) – why would I want to wear a suit in that heat? I wasn't being stubborn about it, but the fact was it was too bloody hot to wear a suit on the touchline! I later explained to Vijit and the FA that my job was coaching the team so I chose to wear suitable and appropriate clothes for the job. Eventually, Vijit advised me to wear a tracksuit at all times, which again I wasn't comfortable with, but I went along with it as a compromise.

We were preparing to play in the 2002 Tiger Cup hosted by Singapore and Indonesia, and ten days before the start of the tournament, I told my players I was imposing a drinking ban until after the final. The Thai lads liked a tipple, so the ban included all the staff (and me as well). I told the lads, 'If we win this I'll buy you all anything. You can have whisky, anything you want – but wait until after we win.' The players agreed with the deal.

The tournament ran from 18 December 2002 until 29 December 2002 and if we made the final there'd be no Christmas for the Withe family that year. We'd been put into a group consisting of Singapore, Malaysia and Laos but our preparation wasn't the best. We won the opening game 5–1 against Laos, but lost the next 3–1 to Malaysia. As we had a better goal difference to Singapore, a draw would have been enough going into the final group game against the hosts. I knew we were getting better with each game and we ended up drawing 1–1, which was enough for us to reach the semi-final in Jakarta.

As we had come second, we had to play the winners of the other group, Vietnam, who hadn't lost a game all tournament. The game was to be played at the Gelora Bung Karno Stadium in Jakarta on the 27 December and I had a good feeling about it and was really looking forward to the occasion. I knew that their coach, Henrique Calisto wanted to beat us and make the final so it was going to be quite an occasion.

We didn't disappoint either because we came away with a comfortable 4–0 victory. After the game I stayed inside the stadium and watched the second semi-final, Indonesia vs. Malaysia so I could get a heads up on the final opponents. I somehow had a feeling we were going to face Indonesia in the final and I proved to be right.

In the final in Jakarta, with a partisan crowd of 100,000 we started the game well enough and Chuciat, our centre-half-come-midfielder scored in the 26th minute. By the 38th minute we were 2–0 up through Therdsak. The game didn't go all our way, because Chuciat got himself sent off in the second half and we had to try to hang on with ten men, but they scored twice to take the tie to extra time. Neither side could break the deadlock during the 30 minutes of extra-time so it all hinged on the dreaded penalty shoot-out. The one player who you would bet your house on to score was my captain, Zico, but he missed the first penalty while, their captain, Bambang, scored. As with most penalty shoot-outs it was pretty exciting stuff and it went down to the last penalty, which was taken by our left-back, Dusit. He had a sweet left foot and when he went up to take his kick he decided to run up and chip the goalkeeper. We won the shoot-out 4–2 and our bench went berserk – I'd won the Tiger Cup for the second time.

When we got back to the hotel the players remembered my offer and took full advantage of it. They never stopped drinking until we flew back to Bangkok nearly 24 hours after we'd won the final! If I remember rightly, one of the management team bought a gallon of whisky and we all sat round the pool drinking, and some of the lads were still there long after I went to bed.

I didn't begrudge them that because I said they could have anything they wanted if they won, and they did.

In the five years I was head coach everything had gone really well (better than expected, in fact) but I'd already told Kathy before the two-leg tie against UAE that I was ready for a break and I didn't want to continue as Thailand head coach after the Tiger Cup had finished. I was at Bangkok Airport waiting to board a flight to Perth, where we have a house, when the phone rang. It was a Thai reporter who asked me, in broken English, 'What do you think, you don't have team now?' He sounded a bit embarrassed to ask the question but I had no idea what he was talking about so asked him to repeat the question. He asked me again, 'Haven't you heard? You've been relieved and they've given the job to Carlos Roberto de Carvalho.' The reporter went on and told me that the Thai FA had suspended me. I was stunned – they never had the decency to actually tell me to my face that I'd been sacked! The reporter asked me if I had any comment and I responded curtly that I had not.

All I said to him was, 'It was nice of them to tell me ...' and left it at that. The phone must have rung about ten times after that. I was expecting a call from Virach, my assistant, but he didn't ring so I didn't answer.

I eventually arrived in Perth and told Kathy what had happened. I think I said something like, 'What would you think if you were talking to the ex-national coach of Thailand?' Kathy jumped up for joy and let out a cheer. Normally, when you tell your wife you've been sacked from a job you expect a slightly different reaction, but the news had actually made her day. I knew Kathy always felt I'd worked my butt off to get the team to where they were, and I wasn't getting the recognition for the achievements that I deserved, so she couldn't wait for us to leave Thailand.

However, my stay in Perth was short-lived. Virach eventually contacted me within a day of arriving in Australia, and told me to go back to Thailand immediately. He did confirm the news I was expecting, that I was no longer the national coach. While all this was going on and as I was in transit back to Bangkok, the Thai FA were saying to the media that they were finding other work for me. I still had 12 months left on my contract, so they either had to officially sack me and pay the remainder of my contract or find me 'other work.' When I asked Virach about what this 'other work' was, even though I had no intention of doing it, I immediately told him they could 'stick it.'

When I got back to Thailand I found out that Carvalho had already brought in his own fitness coach, goalkeeper coach and physio – all the jobs I had done myself.

I had no pre-warning and there was no explanation of my sacking. It wasn't so much getting sacked that hurt me, but the fact I found out from a reporter – and the statement they made to the media that they were 'finding him other work,' upset me a deal. Add to that the fact they had installed Carvalho to replace me behind my back and while I was still under contract and out of the country, that wound me up the most. That was like a red rag to a bull to me – the touchpaper had been well and truly lit.

I later found out that the unofficial reason for my sacking was that I'd refused to wear a suit during matches. I'd heard some rumblings beforehand, but it hadn't been thrown out into the open until the story made front-page news, and they linked it to my sacking, which was a load of rubbish anyway. It was just their way of getting rid of me.

The strange thing about the whole situation was that nobody ever confronted me when I'd done something wrong, so I was oblivious that by wearing shorts at a football match I could be causing offence, until it was too late. It was only then that the Thai FA and the media decided to make a big thing about it. However, I think the official reason for my sacking was more likely the fact that we'd lost to the UAE and failed to qualify for the 2004 Olympic Games in Athens – but I can't confirm that.

However trivial the row sounded at the time (and still does to this day) a decision had been made which effectively ended our time in Thailand. I asked the Thai FA to pay up my contract as I wasn't going to do the other work they wanted from me, and that's when the shit hit the fan and a dispute over my contract began. I knew I'd signed a three-year contract but I hadn't got a copy of it – and neither had the Thai FA (nor had the agent from IMG). At the time I really couldn't be bothered with it all and didn't want the hassle of a long-winded dispute with the Thai FA, so I settled for three months' salary to be paid and called it a day. After I'd been paid up I refused to do any media articles – I had nothing to hide but I just wanted to get as far away from Thailand as possible.

Since I left in 2002, Thailand have had ten coaches, including Bryan Robson and Peter Reid. Clearly the decision to sack me backfired on them!

Incidentally, I still remain the longest-serving and most successful head coach in the recent history of the Thailand national team. Not bad for a 'farang'.

17

The Rock & Roll 'Timnas' Coach

"There's been a disaster. There was an earthquake overnight near Aceh and now a tsunami's hit."

****

I was out of work after five happy years in Thailand – a country and a people I had grown very fond of. Having said that, it was nice to get away from football for the first time in five years with the sole intention of recharging my batteries and spending more time with Kathy. We decided to take a break and move on again to a place of Kathy's choosing. We ended up in Perth, Western Australia, where we already had a house. Kathy had always been there for me, when and wherever I'd needed to go for the last 30 years, so I thought it was time we lived somewhere she wanted to.

Kathy's brother and sister lived in Perth, but I hadn't been there before the year 2000. It was around that time that we decided we wanted to buy a property there, but because we hadn't got a visa at the time, we had to buy a brand new house, what they called 'approved' houses. So we began looking for an approved house on a golf course complex. However, we saw another plot that was literally on the ocean, just a few miles from Perth, so we made an appointment to see the show house. There was only one house on the estate at the time and the idea was to get the developer to build the same house wherever we wanted it. The show house was enormous, and after about five minutes Kathy said, 'I want this house.'

My reply was, 'Yeah, right ...' I didn't think for a minute it was Kathy's type of house and I knew she would soon change her mind. For me, the house was far too big – you needed to take a walkie-talkie around with you, it was that big.

Very often when you see something you initially think is going to be right for you, it can turn out quite the opposite; but that house had everything. We decided it was the one we wanted and tried to buy the house, but the builders didn't want to sell their show house. That suited us because we weren't in a rush to buy, so we negotiated a deal which saw it being used as a show house for two years, even though we legally owned it. At the time I was still contracted by the Thai FA, but I always intended to take a break from football at some stage in the future.

About 18 months later, after I was released from my contract with Thailand, we moved into the show house after all – even though it was too big for just the two of us!

Some people used to say that Perth was a quiet city and there was nothing to do (although things have changed in recent years) but we really enjoyed living there; the weather was great and generally speaking we loved everything about the place. The only problem was that there were times when Kathy was left alone and we had no neighbours nearby because the estate was still being built. There wasn't much to do in the immediate area and when I was away, Kathy quickly reached the point where she didn't want to leave the house. So we decided to put it on the market and once we sold up we bought a four-bedroomed place on a golf course in the area – where we had originally wanted to buy.

I'd been out of work for nearly 18 months when my ex-assistant manager, Virach contacted me out of the blue and told me the Vietnam and the Indonesian national teams were looking for new coaches and were trying to contact me. I was interested in the Vietnam job and decided to go there for a week to incorporate a meeting that had been organised with their FA. I knew a little bit about the team; they were a strong outfit and were always pushing Thailand every time we played them. I was considering the job, so much so that we started looking for apartments in Hanoi; however, I also had an offer of an interview with the Indonesian FA, so I couldn't make a decision until I'd spoken with them. Shortly after returning from Hanoi we flew to Jakarta and were entertained for a week by various delegates from the Indonesian FA.

After returning from a lovely week in Jakarta I had a big decision to make – Vietnam or Indonesia. There wasn't much in it really and in the end it came down to the proximity to Perth, which was our base. Perth was four hours from Jakarta but 13 hours from Vietnam and there were no direct flights from Perth to Vietnam either. The decision was easy to make on that basis – it had to be Indonesia.

Indonesia was a huge country and had a population of 220 million, so I expected there to be a huge pool of talented players there. Physically the Indonesians were big and powerful, not unlike a typical African player, certainly more powerful than most Asian players. For prospective employers such as the Indonesian Soccer Association (PSSI), the starkest endorsement of my abilities was the damage I did to Indonesia's Southeast Asian soccer credentials when I was Thailand head coach, after we'd beaten them in the finals of both the 2000 and the 2002 Tiger Cups. My success had led to a few national team offers before Indonesia came knocking, but in the end I looked at the 220 million people living in Indonesia and thought if we could get it right there, then we could really challenge for silverware on all fronts in Southeast Asia.

It's normal practice for a new manager to have a contract drawn up by the club or the FA but I decided to have a legal contract drawn up myself. It wasn't long before we were involved in contract negotiations, and amendments were made on both sides, but after a few weeks of travelling to and from Jakarta I agreed to sign to be head coach of the Indonesian national soccer team (Timnas).

A few days later I went back to Jakarta to put pen to paper but when I got there they wanted me to go straight into a press conference and sign in front of the media. I hadn't read the small print so I stopped the press conference before it got started. I knew the details in the contract had changed several times so I wanted to make sure all of my requests had been met before I actually signed. It was a good job I did because it didn't take me long to see things in the small print that I'd asked to have removed. I refused to sign the contract in front of the media but the Indonesian FA wanted me to make out I was signing it, just to give the press some pictures. I'd learned my lesson from previous contract negotiations, even though the circumstances were different; there WAS a contract in front of me – but the bloody wrong one! I left the press conference and went to locate a computer. I'd brought a disk with me that contained a copy of the correct contract so I printed two copies off. The president of the Indonesian FA then started to panic, but he read through it and we both signed the contracts.

I had another gripe with the Indonesian FA. They wanted me to sign for six years; I only wanted two years maximum but they insisted on a longer deal. I compromised on four years.

I didn't know at the time I signed my contract that they already had a head coach in place, a Bulgarian coach called Ivan Kolev. His contract was running out in four months and the Indonesian FA were not going to renew it, hence my appointment. I asked why they couldn't wait until his contract had ended but they didn't have an answer – I would have taken the Vietnam job if I had known that sooner. I called their bluff a bit and told them I couldn't wait for four months. They said I could take the under-19 team until Kolev left, as they wanted me to help prepare them for an under-19 tournament. It seemed like a bit of a game, but I agreed.

The contract they asked me to sign stated the position as 'technical director' but they told me that would change to 'head coach' after Kolev left. I went along with that as well, even though I wasn't entirely happy at not being able to take the job I'd applied for for another four months. In the end, I didn't think we were good enough to win the under-19 tournament (and we didn't win it) but it was a good starting point, it gave me an insight into how the national teams prepared and helped me spot some players for the future.

Kolev's contract (unsurprisingly) wasn't renewed and he left his position as head coach, leaving me to fill the gap immediately after the under-19 tournament had finished. It was all very bizarre and seemed a bit cloak and dagger, but I suppose I was used to the way the Asian countries worked.

The Indonesian FA wanted me to 'wear many soccer hats', just like I did in Thailand. I did everything from training sessions to preparing the senior team, the U-23s, the U-21s and the U-19s. People don't realise how big these national jobs in developing countries actually are. Basically, the football association wanted to use my experience as much as possible. I had two assistant coaches and despite having learnt little of the Indonesian language, I still managed to get my message across to the players. Unlike the British set-up where you have a head coach or a manager at the head of the team together with one or more coaches or assistants, in Asia they have a head coach AND a manager, plus a number of coaches. My manager was a guy called Muhammed Zen and he was the one who I negotiated my contract with – he was effectively my right-hand man.

I wanted to stamp my authority on the set-up and instil my mentality into the players. It was very different to the Thai football set-up, where I used to go and watch games on a Friday, Saturday or Sunday and very often there would be two games on each of those days. I'd end up watching most of the clubs in the Thai league over a typical weekend because most of the teams were based in Bangkok. Indonesian football was totally different because they had teams all over the country. I quickly found out I'd be doing a lot of travelling if I wanted to watch league football in Indonesia, as the country was so large – travelling from the furthest north to the furthest east you'd pass through three time-zones. When you work in a different country as a coach, you often take inspiration from what you already know works. I wanted to take the team to train in different places which would require lots of travelling, as I thought it would be good for the team to experience more of their own country.

I quickly found out that the training facilities for the Indonesian players in Jakarta were very poor to say the least. We had one pitch, and it wasn't even up to Sunday-league standard. Even though the Gelora Bung Karno Stadium looked fabulous from the outside, the inside was horrendous. There were quite a few brand new stadia in Indonesia that were built for a particular tournament, but they were built in the middle of nowhere and had never been used (or had only been used on rare occasions). I thought it was a ridiculous situation, and that was another reason why I decided to take the players around the country. It seemed the logical thing to do, as it would be a chance for the players to meet the supporters in each city we went to.

I soon found out there were a lot of technically gifted players in Indonesia but it was also full of players who were professional in name only. Everything they did appeared to be in slow motion; there was no pride when they played; everyone walked with a slouch and most couldn't care less. I had to try to communicate what playing for their country should mean to them. That was a challenge to say the least. I had to change their mentality to get them to focus more during training sessions. I'd always been brought up with the view that playing for your country was the highest honour you could possibly achieve as a footballer and I wanted to find out what their thoughts were. I knew that the Thai players I'd managed wanted to play for their country mainly because they wanted to play for the King, but I needed to know what it meant to the Indonesian lads. One day, I asked my captain to question the players to give me an indication of their motivation when playing for their country. I gave them three options: Are you playing for the national side for your own pride? Are you playing for your family? Are you playing for money? The captain went away and asked every single one of the 30 players, individually, those three questions. The feedback wasn't a surprise (to me anyway) but it was shocking just the same. All 30 players said they were doing it for the money. That told me what I had to do next, and with that in mind, I went to see the manager. I told him the answer I had got to my questions and he was shocked. I said that the Indonesian FA needed to get some sort of bonus payment scheme in place as soon as possible – they needed to get the money in place to reward the players as an incentive, otherwise I'd be wasting my time.

As a coach you have to find out what motivates your players and that's exactly what I did. All footballers these days play for the money because the stakes are so high, but I'd have thought most of them also harbour an ambition to play for their country, to win things and generally do well. In my day, I would say 75–80 per cent of players would have played even if they hadn't have been paid. That's probably the main difference between modern-day players and players of my era. The only thing we could have done to change the mentality of my players was to give them bonuses – on top of their appearance money. The fact that those players were paid more than the Thai players indicated to me that something was wrong with the game in Indonesia.

It wasn't long after my player survey that the bonus incentive scheme was brought in by the Indonesian FA. Just before one particular game I remember my manager telling the players that they would earn a bonus of US$200 if they won the game. I was infuriated and pulled him to one side and said, 'I know I told you they need bonuses, but don't tell them about them just before a game. You need to tell them just before a tournament starts that they will get a bonus, or if you want to do it after the game instead, then that's fine too – but don't do it before the game starts!' I didn't want the players thinking about the money when they went out on to the pitch.

The role of striker was one I knew inside out — having scored 193 goals across my career, some at the highest levels of club soccer. In Indonesia though, given the number of foreign players occupying striker positions at club level, I soon found a quality 'Timnas' (Tim Nasional Sepak Bola Indonesia) striker was hard to find. I had to scour the entire country looking for new talent, especially in the striker department. At first, I looked to see if I could bring in players of Dutch descent eligible to play for Indonesia, but my efforts were stonewalled by the country's rigid citizenship rules. Those rules must have since been relaxed, incidentally, given the inclusion of Nigerian-born Greg Nwokolo and Victor Igbonefo, as well as Dutch-born Sergio van Dijk, Irfan Bachdim and Raphael Maitimo in the side. However, I was able to bring the aging striker, Kurniawan Dwi Yulianto back into the national fold to plug the gap, alongside the legendary striker, Bambang Pamungkas, who went on to become Indonesia's all-time top scorer with 37 goals. I could see Bambang was a talent because, even though he was small, he had a gymnast's body that gave him tremendous spring, and he was technically brilliant at striking a football.

It was my philosophy to talk directly to the players regarding the decisions I'd made and I think they appreciated that approach. I used to tell the players to believe in their own abilities and that led to the team playing with a lot more confidence. I remember dropping Bambang once and he took it well. I'd always tell Bambang never to be afraid to take decisions in front of goal and play with freedom. All I wanted my players to do was to give 100 per cent on the pitch. Apart from Bambang, perhaps the real gem unearthed from my scouting exploits came in the form of Ilham Jaya Kesuma. No one had heard of Ilham but I went to watch him play and I saw something really special, and from relative obscurity, Ilham was catapulted to national fame.

Unlike the previous regimes, I'd often play players who nobody else would give a game to, mainly because of their age or their image. One such player was a Papuan lad called Boaz Solossa, who was known for his dribbling technique, his crossing accuracy and short passing with his left foot. He was a talent for sure, and had represented Indonesia at all levels except the full team before I arrived as head coach. I brought him into the side in 2004 and he came to the forefront for a while and became a bit of a cult hero. However, like most of his teammates Boaz had a different mentality to most modern European players in that he liked to have a drink. Even after I had secured him a contract with Adidas (who I was contracted to as well) and some other leading brands he went off the rails big time. Boaz was unable to perform for his club for almost six months due to an incident where he and his teammates assaulted a referee, and during the time he was out of action, many considered his skills dropped and his prospects wasted. It resulted in me dropping him from the national team in 2006.

Not only did I unearth some real talent in Indonesia, I also instilled a philosophy not dissimilar to present-day Barcelona's, rather than the traditional long-ball game of English football. We looked to get the ball down and play it, always looking for the pass. When we had the opportunity to press teams, even if it was a strong side like Japan or South Korea, we wanted to get the ball on the ground. We looked to put teams under pressure with exciting soccer that people could enjoy, and even to this day I still get messages from Indonesian supporters saying the way the team played back then is the way they want to see the team play today.

Nutrition was also on the coach's agenda. We had to improve their fitness levels starting with changing their diets, just like I did with Thailand. They found it difficult to press for the whole 90 minutes of a game, as they didn't have enough of the right carbohydrates in their bodies. It was a case of telling them, 'If you eat rice and noodles, you're only going to last for 70 minutes, but if you eat pasta and potatoes, you'll last for the whole match.'

After a few months, Kathy and I decided to look for a permanent place to live and we came across a fabulous apartment block called the Four Seasons. Everything about it was right for us, but when I told the Indonesian FA about it they said it was (not surprisingly) too expensive, and we wouldn't be able to move there. However, we later found out that when you rented properties in Indonesia you could get a discount according to the length of your employment contract. In other words, because my contract was for four years I was entitled to a large reduction in rent – but I was expected to pay the four years' rent up front. The Indonesian FA didn't want to pay a fortune for four years' rent in one lump sum, so they advised us to find somewhere cheaper. We carried on looking at apartments all over Jakarta, but couldn't find anywhere as good as the Four Seasons. Some weeks later we were told about an apartment block that was in the Golden Triangle, which sounded dodgy but was situated in the central business district and accessible for the stadium and training ground. Naturally, we thought it was an excellent location – at least until we experienced our first weekend there. Nobody had warned us when we signed the contract that the weekends would be reminiscent of hell on earth. During the week the area was largely quiet – just like any other business district it was busy during the day but quiet at night. However, the weekend was another matter: the main road the apartment was on turned into a racetrack for motorbikes and it began at midnight and went on throughout the night. It was unbearable! It was obvious the police knew what was going on but appeared not to care, so the residents were forced to put up with terrible noise pollution and were helpless to change it.

After several months of getting used to life in a new city, we started to build up a network of friends and contacts just as we did in Bangkok. On one occasion, just after one of our training sessions at the national stadium a guy approached me and said his boss, sitting in the car, wanted to talk to me. When I asked the guy where his boss was he said he wouldn't get out of his car unless I agreed to talk to him, as he didn't want to lose face. Eventually the boss got out of his car and introduced himself, and told me his family owned a company that did a lot of work in the oil business – one part of the family's business shipped people to and from the rigs by helicopter and the other part owned oil rigs and lots of related elements. It was all very mysterious, but he said he'd like to meet me for lunch to explain a proposition he had for me. I agreed to meet him later that day in a restaurant near to where he lived.

'The boss' was a Chinese-Indonesian guy and seemed to come from a very wealthy background. He told me about his life and his family, and after some small talk, he spoke about his proposition for me; he wanted me to coach 15 kids all belonging to his family. I thought it was very odd and what he was asking took me aback a bit, so I replied, 'Look, I'm not being funny but I can't do it ...'

He interrupted and said, '... and money's no object ...'

I explained, 'I'd love to do it but my commitments to the national team prevent me from doing anything else.' However, I suddenly had a brainwave, '... but I know someone who can. I've got a son who's a coach – he'll do it.'

He agreed and I told him Gareth could start the following weekend. I knew Gareth would love the job and fit in with the kids because he had that sort of personality – the job was made for him. After our lunch, I rang Gareth, who had just split up from his girlfriend at the time and was feeling sorry for himself. He was already a qualified coach back then and he was a good coach and used to help me when I did soccer schools back in the UK. I asked Gareth how he felt about the offer of coming to Jakarta to take up the coaching role, just to see how it went, and maybe extending his stay if he got on OK. Not surprisingly, he jumped at the chance as he was at a loose end, and said he'd fly to Jakarta straight away. They asked me to arrange for Gareth to come out to work with the children for a long weekend and see if they liked him and if all went well, he would be offered the job.

Gareth arrived in Jakarta less than 24 hours later and spent the first weekend with us before we went to visit his new boss at his house. When we arrived at the house we noticed there were six cars on the drive and, the house was enormous. Gareth had a weekend coaching the children and, as I thought, they all loved him, so Gareth was offered the job. We talked about what was required of Gareth. He was told he'd have to live nearby in a place called Glabagady. As they were building a new house, it was suggested that Gareth should stay in the old house. The new house was lovely and was nearing completion – it sounded too good to be true if I'm honest, and Kathy and I jokingly said we'd like to live there as well. I then sat down with the guy and sorted out Gareth's contract and the details of the job. I negotiated a terrific contract for Gareth – a two-year deal, a car with a driver, the accommodation together with live-in maid and his salary. All Gareth had to pay for was his food and living expenses. Gareth's previous job back in Solihull was a customer services job, answering queries in a call centre, but suddenly he had been landed a live-in coaching job with a multimillionaire. He was such a lucky boy.

Within a matter of weeks, Gareth's life had completely turned around and he loved it – who wouldn't? He was in his element, coaching football skills to 15 kids. After several weeks, his boss bought an indoor sports centre and he asked Gareth to run it for him. Life couldn't have been better for Gareth – but it was about to get even sweeter. One day, we were all invited to a function and, to cut a long story short, Gareth was introduced to his future wife, Jennifer. In fact, meeting Jennifer was the springboard Gareth wanted to move his career forward.

There was an occasion, just before the 2004 Tiger Cup, when my manager, Muhammed Zin told me there was a problem with the chairman of the Indonesian FA, Nurdin Halid. It was an odd situation because the police had apparently arrested him that day and he'd appeared in court. Nurdin had pending charges against him after he was named as a suspect in a case of illegally importing 73,520 tons of sugar and he'd been put in prison. On that particular day he bizarrely wanted the team to meet with him at his prison cell. I was just coming to terms with the size of the job at hand and its eccentricities when I was suddenly faced with taking the team to visit my boss behind bars, and that took it to a different level. When we arrived at the prison he gave a speech to the players and also gave everyone a gift – US$100 per player and US$200 to me. It was all very strange. After the visit I remained pragmatic and soon got back to the training pitch – we had to put the visit to the prison to the back of our minds and get on with playing football.

The Tiger Cup is always played during the month of December and involved those countries from Southeast Asia who don't celebrate Christmas. There were ten teams and two groups of five in the group stages of the 2004 Tiger Cup and we emerged as the Group A winners with ten points, 17 goals scored and none conceded. We soon became hot favourites to win the tournament outright after bundling out the hosts, Vietnam, with an unexpected 3–0 victory. At 6am on 26 December 2004, I was on the training ground, putting the team through its paces. We always trained very early in the morning, due to the extreme heat and humidity during the day. The training field wasn't the best in the world but it was all we had. I observed the players, praising them and offering advice as I always did. I'd only been in the job for a few months, but with decades of experience as a player, coach, manager and scout, I knew what to look for in the players I had at my disposal. I was watching to see which of the players were ready for the test to come – a test of national pride, as we readied to face our rivals and co-hosts Malaysia in the semi-finals at the Gelora Bung Karno Stadium on 28 December.

I've lived through a lot of strange events in my time but nothing, and I mean *nothing*, could have prepared me for what happened next.

I don't know why, but I had this eerie feeling something was going to happen that particular day. Call it a sixth-sense, I don't know, I just knew something wasn't quite right out there on that training pitch. I looked around at all the fans and officials watching the squad train and all of a sudden I sensed a jolt of activity throughout the crowd and it seemed everyone was suddenly talking amongst themselves about something or other. The talking got louder and louder and I decided to stop the session for a drinks break. I walked over so I could speak with my manager who wanted to tell me something.

'There's been a disaster. Someone's told me there's been a tsunami. There was an earthquake overnight near Aceh and now a tsunami's hit.'

Suddenly, the thought of playing football seemed insignificant.

During the break in training we discovered that the epicentre of the earthquake was at the northernmost point of the Sumatra region, about 1,500km from Jakarta, where we were training. The earthquake hadn't affected the area around Jakarta and I had no idea before the training session had started that one had struck in the Indian Ocean just after midnight on Boxing Day. The earthquake had recorded 9.1 on the Richter scale, the third-largest earthquake ever recorded; creating a tsunami that devastated the Aceh province. We heard later that at least 130,000 Indonesians had been killed in the aftermath of the tsunami.

How can anyone think about playing football after that?

All that was on my mind at that time were the players in my team and how they must have been feeling. I was trying frantically to get information about which of my players were from the region affected and I soon found out that six of them came from Aceh and had family there. As soon as I had that confirmed I halted the training session to let the players find out information about their families.

It was a strange day; it brought back memories of the day my own father died while I was in Malaysia watching my team playing in the Asian Cup 2000 qualifiers and how I reacted on hearing the news. We had played one game against North Korea on the 25 March (my son Gareth's birthday) and we drew 1–1. Kathy rang to tell me to ring my mother urgently and she informed me my father had passed away at 18:10 on 26 March 2000 at the age of 75. My father was a footballer and he'd have wanted me to carry on regardless – and so I did, for him.

I then thought about the current situation we were facing and asked myself, 'What would I want if I was in that situation?'

We still had to play our arch-rivals, Malaysia, and preparing the team for that game was difficult to say the least. The support for that game was magnificent but, unfortunately, we lost 2–1. I suppose a lot of people, not only in Indonesia but in other countries around the world, had also been affected by what had happened.

After that defeat, everyone started to write us off for the second leg, which was being played in Malaysia; however, I had other thoughts and put the first game down to many players being affected by the tsunami. I'd been thinking about the first leg and what we had to do to win the return tie. I decided to hold a meeting, first with the management team and then with the players. I knew the nation was in a state of severe mourning and I explained to the players that we had an opportunity to change the country's mindset; the nation needed to be lifted and taken away from the doom and gloom of the disaster. I held the meeting in a state of high emotion, and as I came to the end of my speech, I began to shed a few tears. Even though it wasn't my country, I felt quite emotional about the whole thing, as I was part of it, just the same as anyone else in the country was. My speech was meant to rally the players in the face of adversity and I explained that we needed to carry on training. My team-talk was so passionate that my interpreter broke down in tears, unable to convey my thoughts to the players who couldn't speak English. It was hard for them to think about football, but I told them it was a chance to unite the nation. It wasn't much, but what else could we do in that situation?

I asked the management to contact the media immediately and make them aware we were going to carry on. The players would need to put on brave faces and do interviews, to address the nation in front of the media. Indonesia was a football crazy nation. At every home game there would be 100,000 passionate fans cheering the team on – no matter who the opposition may be. The Indonesian FA were talking about calling the game off in the light of the disaster but I advised them the game should go ahead because it would have been a little bit disrespectful to the nation for them to be grieving for two or three weeks. I felt it was up to us as a football team to lift the nation's spirits. The Indonesian FA reluctantly agreed.

As a player, I had faced some of the best footballers to have ever graced the game: Michel Platini, Paolo Rossi, Karl-Heinz Rummenigge and even Pelé, considered by many to be the greatest the game has ever seen. Now, as manager of the Indonesian national team, I faced a test of a different magnitude: how to lift an entire nation in mourning and how to motivate the players of a squad, some of whom had family and friends in Aceh, for one of the biggest games of their careers – the semi-final of the Tiger Cup.

The game went ahead as scheduled just days after the worst disaster in the country's history. In the bowels of Gelora Bung Karno Stadium, 100,000 Indonesian fans were screaming, stomping their feet and igniting flares into the air as if nothing had happened. I got the players together and told them about a piece of psychology I'd always used in such situations. I said to them once they'd crossed that white line on to the pitch, it didn't matter what was going on in their lives. For 90 minutes, they were going to try to win a game of football – not for money but for their country. I was well aware of the role football was playing in respect of the situation the country was facing so I arranged for two giant screens to be placed outside the ground so the thousands of fans who were locked out could still see the match. It was only a game, but to the people of Indonesia it was more than that – it was a release from all the suffering. I don't know anyone personally that died in the tragedy, but almost every team member knew someone who had been affected. My assistant coach, Fachri Husaini and one of my players, Ismed Sofyan, were both from Aceh and were still waiting to hear from missing relatives at that time – it had struck that close to home.

In the second leg in Kuala Lumpur a week later I decided to bring back Boaz Solossa for the game, and I told him he was going to be our linchpin because he had pace and he was strong – even if he was tall and gangly. We had gone 1–0 down in the first half hour, but after I made some crucial decisions to change the game, the team rallied to beat Malaysia 4–1. It was an astonishing turnaround that saw us reach the final at our rival's expense.

Those few weeks were some of the saddest I've ever seen in football, but I do think we lifted a nation during the game in Kuala Lumpur. Everyone thought we were finished after the first-leg defeat, but suddenly we turned it around and people saw what my team was really about – it was very gratifying. I'd like to think the players gave something back to the nation, but I'd also like to think I led the players well, not only by my tactical changes during the second leg but also because of the speech I'd made just after the earthquake had struck on Boxing Day. I think it's important when a disaster like that happens, to say the right things at the right time, and that was one of them.

We had reached the final of the Tiger Cup – my third final as an international coach and my third Tiger Cup Final in consecutive tournaments. Before the first leg against Singapore at the Gelora Bung Karno Stadium in Jakarta, I visited Nurdin Halid in prison again and explained to him what my thoughts were for the game. He was 100 per cent with me. However, it all proved too much for us and we fell short in the end – maybe the weight of expectancy was too much for the players to handle as we lost 5–2 over the two legs. The fact that we'd had four players who lost immediate family in the tsunami finally took its toll. It was disappointing; however, national pride had been maintained just when the country needed it. I didn't blame the players for the defeat – how could I?

By the time the next tournament started in January and February 2007 I was over halfway through my four-year contract. There wasn't a 2006 Tiger Cup competition because the sponsors had pulled out, so the competition was renamed the 2007 AFF Championship. While I prepared the players for the tournament, Nurdin Halid unexpectedly started saying some unsavoury stuff to the media, in particular that my job was on the line if I didn't get the team to the semi-final of the new tournament at least. It was surprising and uncalled for and the last thing I needed, but I carried on regardless. I'd faced this kind of thing before in Thailand, so he wasn't going to upset me with his loose talk.

The championship was held in Thailand and Singapore and we were based in Singapore for our rounds. We were in a group with Singapore, Laos and Vietnam but we failed to reach the semi-finals on goal difference, with three sides finishing the group on five points. We didn't lose a game in the championship and we played well, but sometimes in tournament soccer you don't get what you deserve. After the press conferences following the group games it all kicked off big time, and all because of what Nurdin Halid had said before the tournament – that my job was on the line.

Shortly after returning from Singapore, someone from the Indonesian FA approached me and asked about a certain clause in my contract – something that was in every manager's contract worldwide. It was a clause that stated if a manager broke the law then that would lead to instant dismissal. I was shocked and amazed that the Indonesian FA were asking me about that particular clause and it was then that alarm bells started to ring in my head. I immediately contacted Jason, who was helping me with the coaching and told him what the Indonesian FA were asking me about and advised him to get out of the country. In my mind, it all signalled to them trying to get me out of the contract. I was trying to think what I'd done wrong, but deep down I knew I had done nothing wrong whatsoever. I also knew that it was all a game to them, a plan to get rid of me because my team hadn't performed well enough in their view.

Hours later the media reported that my contract had been terminated after the Indonesian FA had a meeting with the team in Jakarta. Yes, that's right. I'd been dismissed behind my back and my players had been told but I hadn't. To make matters worse, they said I had accepted it (which wasn't true). When I heard the news via the media I immediately contacted the Indonesian FA and tried to resolve the situation – but I failed. I think to a certain degree, Nurdin was forced into making that statement, but at the end of the day he'd said what he said and he had to follow through with it, no matter how well we'd played. He was left with no other option than to relieve me of my position, however cruel it seemed to me. I felt he wasn't strong enough to say to me face-to-face something like, 'Let's see what happens after the tournament ...' so he made the statement in the media and couldn't go back on it. I spoke to him after he'd made that statement to the media and I asked him if he realised what he'd done at the time. I said to him he'd actually put the pressure on the players to qualify for the semi-finals – but I don't think he understood that one bit.

From my perspective, I hadn't finished my job with Indonesia and still to this day I see it as unfinished business. When I look back at my time there, I felt we were making steady progress; but my tenure had been cut short and I couldn't do anything about it. As it turned out, Nurdin Halid was released from prison (for the second time) in November 2008 after being convicted for corruption on the distribution of cooking oil funds in September 2007. Nurdin was effectively running the Indonesian FA from behind bars – and was still in charge after his release.

Obviously I was upset about my sacking and the way it had been handled but it was at that point I decided to contact FIFA to make a complaint against the Indonesian FA. I didn't want the case to go to FIFA (as it wasn't cheap) but it was evident that my contract had been breached – and FIFA were backing my case against them. I compiled my case and I had all the press cuttings to do with the case in a scrapbook, and sent lots of documentation and my contract to the FIFA complaints department.

After liaising with the Indonesian FA, I vacated the apartment and quickly left the country to join Kathy in Perth.

In any contract complaint case, FIFA write to you for information, you send it to them and they also write to the other party (i.e. the Indonesian FA) asking for information, giving them deadlines to keep. However, even though I met every deadline, the Indonesian FA never replied to FIFA, delaying any decision being made for nearly two years. A final deadline was given to the Indonesian FA and they were given ten days to respond, otherwise the case would go to a hearing. Not surprisingly, they didn't respond. A hearing was eventually held (after two years of the enquiry) in front of a committee at FIFA HQ in Zurich where all the evidence was heard and a decision was made in my favour. Of course, the Indonesian FA had no evidence as they refused to respond to any of the FIFA questions and had no representation at the hearing, so it was a foregone conclusion in the end – it was just a matter of agreeing a compensation package. FIFA had to look at what I was entitled to in the contract, which included six business class flights to the UK a year for both Kathy and I. They came back to me with a figure and I agreed without hesitation because I just wanted an end to it. I just wanted to move on – I was so angry that they had dragged it out for so long.

Just when I'd thought the whole episode was over I received a message from the Indonesian FA asking if they could make the payments over a 12-month period. I was furious and sent the letter to FIFA and replied to the Indonesian FA declining their offer. Then they came back reducing the amount of time to pay to six months. Again, I sent their letter to FIFA and declined the offer a second time. FIFA told me it was up to me what action I took next regarding the payments; they would back any decision I made. I wrote back to the Indonesian FA and gave them four dates to make the payments on and made FIFA aware of my deadlines. It was dragging on again, and at that point FIFA stepped in and wrote to the Indonesian FA giving them two weeks to pay me, otherwise they would ban Indonesia from playing football in any international competition. Considering it was at a time when one of the Asian tournaments was coming up, it would have had maximum impact. FIFA had the power to stop, not only the national side from playing football, but also to stop any league in the world from operating. The threat resolved the situation and they ended up paying me within the FIFA deadline. I knew I hadn't done anything wrong and I just wanted to clear my name. For me, FIFA were worth their weight in gold just when I needed them.

With the FIFA case dragging on for two years I wasn't legally able to work but did get a chance to get on with other things in life. However, I did have to turn down a couple of jobs because of the impending case. One of the jobs was head coach of Perth Glory FC in Western Australia. I informed FIFA I wanted to apply for the job but they advised it may jeopardise my case and may reduce my compensation package if I got it. The club were going through a bad patch and I needed to do something, so I offered to help them out. It wasn't a well-paid job anyway, but as it turned out, I never got an interview. I think I applied for the job three times over the course of a few weeks and I even offered to do the job for free at one stage, but they never responded to me for some reason.

The owner of Perth Glory was a Brit called Tony Sage. He had financed and managed mining and exploration companies in Australia and overseas. I did some research into the type of people he employed at Perth Glory and I found out some of them were friends of mine from the past, so not being considered for an interview was a bit of a let-down. Coincidentally, Perth Glory did contact me sometime after – but not about the coaching position. One pre-season, Wolves went out to Australia and had a fixture against Perth Glory. The club obviously knew I lived in Perth and they found out I had played for Wolves in my past career, so I had a call from the commercial department offering me entry to the game if I did a pre-match speech and a guided tour for them. Normally I'd charge around £700 for something like that but on that occasion I did it for free as a one-off, although I insisted on a VIP ticket for the game. I thought it would give me an opportunity to see some people I hadn't seen for years, including my old Villa mate Tony Daley, who was part of the Wolves coaching staff.

I went to the game with a friend of mine, but as part of the deal I had to get on stage to deliver a speech about my time at Wolves to the members of the club – something similar to what happens before every Premier League game. Tony Sage was standing with someone else watching me deliver this speech, but apparently he didn't recognise me. After the game I was asked to do some local radio interviews and was ushered into a room where several other people were being interviewed. The girl who led me into the interview room didn't know who else was being interviewed, but she pointed towards a fella with his back to me. I immediately recognised the figure and as I approached him he turned round and asked, 'I know you from somewhere?'

I said, 'Yeah, yeah, I know you too. I know you because you played for two teams I played for. You played for Birmingham City and Nottingham Forest. You were born in Tamworth and you were a Welsh international.' He asked me how I knew all that but I carried on, 'You joined Nottingham Forest then you joined Derby County. You had a manager we both know.' He still hadn't clicked who I was until his son said, 'It's Peter Withe, dad.' His name was Terry Hennessey.

Time went by following my FIFA case with the Indonesian FA, and I spent a lot of time playing golf and enjoying the lifestyle in Perth, but you can only do that for so long. I wanted to keep busy and started to get itchy feet – I wanted to prove I could still coach at the top level. I'd been out of work for over two years and it's easier to find work when you're in a job.

I'd had enough of chilling out but I had no idea where my boots would take me next.

18

What Next?

"I don't know the players. Once I've coached them and been with them for a while I'll tell you what system I'll play."

****

With all the kids back in the UK, Kathy was beginning to feel the need to return home. Suddenly, out of the blue Jason sent me a message saying someone called Ian Seddon had been trying to get hold of me. He said I used to play with his father a long time ago and it was his father's 60th birthday. I remembered I played with a Ben Seddon at Southport and we were very good friends back in the 1970s but I hadn't seen him since then. I thought it was a bit random but it was a pleasant surprise to get the message, nonetheless. I contacted Ian and he explained that his father always talked about me in conversation and about all the fond memories he had of us playing together. After a few telephone conversations Ian asked me if I could come to the party. As I was still in Perth and didn't know exactly when I'd be back in the UK I told Ian it would be impossible for me to attend. Ian then asked me if I could record a video for his father so he could show it on the night so I thought about it for a few seconds and agreed to record a video.

As it happened, Kathy and I returned to the UK before the party was due to take place, and while I was visiting my mother in Liverpool I received another message from Ian to meet him at his friend's office in Hunt's Cross, a suburb at the southern edge of Liverpool. When I arrived at the office, a Sky Sports camera crew were waiting for me.

It was all a bit surreal to be honest. I asked Ian what he wanted me to say and he asked me to just talk about his father and the times we'd spent together at Southport.

The cameraman prepared me for the filming and asked me how many takes I needed, to which I replied, 'What do you mean? How many takes for what?'

The cameraman must have been used to recording take after take and asked me, 'How many takes for the filming?'

I replied, '... err, I only need one! I only need one take.' The cameraman asked what about if I got it wrong and I responded confidently, 'Well, I won't get it wrong.' The camera rolled and I spoke for about seven minutes about Ben. Not surprisingly, I only needed one take.

That was the first time I'd met Ian in person and he casually asked me why I wasn't working. Ian had done his research on me and knew my football and subsequent managerial career inside out and it was at that point he asked me straight up, 'Do you want to work back in the UK?' I think he'd put some thought into the question – it didn't appear to be a wild stab in the dark.

I told him the family were back in the UK and replied, 'Yes, I probably do,' so the seed was planted there and then. Ian mooted the idea of him being my agent, to which my reaction was a bit cool at first but I then said, 'If you want to be my agent that's fine – it's up to you.' I wasn't particularly bothered about having an agent to be honest – I'd never really had one before. Ian had a number of different offices and had a solicitor working for him, so he was not actually a football agent at the time. However, he subsequently became my first and only football advisor.

Ian and I kept in contact over the months that followed until, out of the blue he phoned to tell me he'd found a club who were looking for a coach and I fitted their bill. They were a non-league club called Woodley Sports based in Stockport. They had a vision for the future and were mad keen to see me. Ian sold me the package and I agreed to meet them. I later spoke to Kathy about it but she wasn't that keen – the money wasn't good to be perfectly honest but I needed to start getting back into the game. Part of me was thinking I must have been bloody mad to even think about it. In the end I decided to do it.

In April 2012 I became the head coach of Woodley Sports FC, who played in the North West Counties Football League Premier Division (and that's a mouthful in itself). The club were going through a transition and were about to change their name to Stockport Sports FC, and the new management team had what looked like a forward-thinking vision for the club. My initial task was to get some players in from the lower leagues. The owner was an Aussie businessman called Neil Baird but he didn't know anything about football, let alone non-league football; he was a businessman first and foremost and a 'silent' partner in the football club, although he seemed to pull all the strings. When I first met him I immediately recognised traits in him I'd come across before. He seemed full of himself and very self-assured, almost arrogant. He seemed like the type of person who would tread on anyone to get what they wanted. I'd come across a few people like him in the past and I was uneasy about him from day one, but I went along with it.

We went through the pre-season to the 2012/13 season and signed up some players. Everything started off quite well, considering the small budget we had. I didn't know the non-league scene so I got other people in to help find the players we needed. At the start I didn't have an assistant manager, until I was called into a meeting with Neil Baird, the other board members and another guy called Joey Dunne. We were chatting away, and about ten minutes into the meeting it became apparent to me the chairman had appointed Joey as my assistant without even asking me my opinion first. I looked Neil straight in the eyes and said, '... so what you're telling me is that you have now asked him (pointing at Joey) to be my assistant manager without speaking to me about it?' I then looked at Joey and he shrugged his shoulders and looked as surprised as I was. I said to Neil, 'What needs to happen now is for you lot to leave this room and I need to sit with him (pointing at Joey again) – so get out!'

I was left alone to talk to Joey in private and it became apparent that he thought I'd been told by Neil Baird that he was to be my assistant and that everything had been agreed. I told Joey I hadn't got a problem with him being my assistant – just with the way it had been done. I didn't know Joey but I thought if I could talk to him for ten minutes I'd soon know his character, know what he was all about and if I could work with him.

Joey was actually a fellow Scouser (and an Evertonian) who worked as a full-time psychiatric nurse and had played and managed in football for years. His knowledge was primarily non-league football so he was actually my ideal assistant as he knew the players that would fit into the club. On the downside, he had never coached, which was good in a way because I enjoyed coaching and he had been used to managing. I explained that the brief for him was to look after the paperwork and help me to manage the team, and I would get on with coaching the players. I asked him to go away and find the players who I could coach to improve and he agreed to my brief.

Stockport Sports had a small academy where kids from all over the world could come and be coached by a professional. It was meant to be a money-making exercise and although I wasn't entirely against it, that wasn't the reason why I joined. I hadn't come to coach kids – I had done that in the past and I felt I was beyond that stage in my life. Even though I was employed as first-team manager, Neil would say things like, 'I want you to take the academy team tomorrow ...' and in reply I told him it wasn't in my brief.

'You employed me to manage Stockport Sports – I'm not the youth-team coach. I haven't come all the way from Australia to be a youth-team coach, Neil. You should have people in place to do that.' He suggested he'd pay me to coach the academy lads as well, which was a joke because he wasn't even paying me a decent wage to manage the first team. We had a bit of a falling out about it and the idea of me coaching the youth team wasn't discussed again.

Kathy and I were living back in the West Midlands so it was a long day, getting up at 6am, driving up the M6 to Stockport to do morning and afternoon coaching sessions. On top of that, there were the added problems associated with being a manager of a football club, both on and off the field. Firstly, we had problems with the training pitches every day. There were also problems because some of the players worked full-time and the training hours didn't suit them. Then came the classic 'how to piss everyone off' stunt. Neil actually decided to install a clocking-in machine in the home changing room – yes, a clocking-in machine! I thought it was rather strange, the owner wanting all the staff, including me and the players to clock in and to clock out. When I first saw the clocking-in machine I immediately went to see him and asked him if the machine was a joke. Neil asked if there was a problem and I went ballistic, 'Yeah, there's a problem. I ain't clocking in and I ain't clocking out! My job is manager. What happens when we play away? How do I clock in then?' He didn't have an answer and said it was irrelevant anyway. The guy just didn't have a clue – he didn't understand football or football people. He just couldn't comprehend what I was telling him.

Because of the distance between Birmingham and Stockport, I tended to stay up there for a few nights a week, either with friends in the area or in a hotel. Neil offered to get me a car to use but it turned out to be the smallest Toyota on the road. After a couple of weeks, I noticed there was a problem with one of the tyres so I took it to my nephew, who was a car mechanic in Liverpool. After asking me how fast I drove the car, he told me the tyres were remoulds and could blow at any time if I drove them over 80 mph. The car was a 'ticking time bomb,' he said. When I got back to the club the next day, I immediately went to see Neil and told him what my nephew, Michael, had told me and to 'stick the car up your arse.' His reply wasn't very complimentary to say the least.

In the end I bought a second-hand Mercedes through an auction house and through a contact of Ian, Bob Woosey. However, I was driving up the M6 on the way to a game one day and the car broke down. Fortunately, I was quite close to Sandbach service station and I managed to pull in. I rang one of the lads at the club and told him the problem and he immediately said he'd come out and pick me up and take me to the game. I then rang Michael in Liverpool so he could come to pick the car up on a truck. I eventually got to the game, late, but fortunately someone took the warm-up for me. Neil saw me arrive late and came over to me and said, 'It's a bit bloody disrespectful that, you calling someone at the club to come and fetch you.'

By that time my blood was boiling, 'Listen, you're going somewhere you don't really want to go with this ...'

Neil, being his normal cocky self, carried on, '... having someone come and pick you up because your car breaks down ...'

I'd had enough of him by then but I took a deep breath and told him to leave it until the end of the game and told him I had a job to do.

Fortunately, Ian Seddon was at the ground so after the game I told him what Neil had said to me. We both walked over to speak to Neil again and took the discussion further.

"... hang on a minute, you're supposed to have supplied a car and you gave me a shit car in the first place. I go and buy my own car and it breaks down. You never had a car breakdown before? Listen, you're just a prat ....'

He tried to mumble something but I carried on.

'... well, just don't come too close to my face. The fact is he offered to pick me up in the first place. I would have got to the game somehow even if he'd have said no.'

From that day on, my relationship with Neil Baird deteriorated, until one day he came over to me during a training session.

'You know those players we've signed, well can you go back to them and ask them if they will take a drop in their wages?'

As you can imagine, I was furious. In essence, Joey Dunne had recruited the lads and Neil had authorised the signings and the deals, but Neil was asking me to get them to agree to a cut in their wages all of a sudden. I ended up having to negotiate with five of the players; one player out of the five didn't agree to the new terms and not surprisingly left the club. The others weren't happy but they wanted to stay. It wasn't as if the players could afford to take a pay cut – most, if not all, were part-time players and had another job.

It was evident that my initial perception of Neil Baird was the correct one. He was arrogant and always seemed to talk down to people – and it didn't matter who you were. He used to talk about people (players) who didn't perform, saying things like, 'Let's just fuck him off ...'

That was his attitude to everything, though. You can't act like that in business but that's the way he was. When I heard him speak like that, I kept telling him, 'That's why people don't want to come and play for your football club.'

We were a few months into the season when I first had second thoughts about my future at the club. Things were getting out of hand and when I spoke to Kathy about the situation she asked me why I spent so much of my time travelling up and down the motorway, taking training and dealing with Neil's crap, all for peanuts. I thought I did the right thing at first by taking the job but I began to struggle with the situation. It finally came to a head during a training session when Joey came up to me and told me he'd been sacked. Joey offered me his hand to shake and he said, 'He hasn't got a budget for me.' I couldn't believe that Neil hadn't had the decency to inform me that my assistant had been released but I guess that was par for the course. I immediately rang Ian and told him the story, and drove straight home after the session.

To add insult to injury, one Monday when I drove up to Stockport to take training as normal I arrived to find we couldn't get on to the training pitches. The club hadn't paid the rent and the groundsman wouldn't let us through the gates. Eventually, after a few phone calls, we were allowed onto the pitches to train; however, after the session, I sat in the car eating my lunch and rang Ian to tell him I'd had enough. I was fed up with Neil chipping away at me and making my life harder than it should have been and I decided there and then that enough was enough. I asked Ian to sort it out, and quickly. Ian mentioned something about constructive dismissal and he wouldn't let it lie and I pondered on that while I drove home. While I was on the motorway, the club secretary rang and asked me what was going on, and I told him I wouldn't be coming back.

I'd signed a two-year contract in the April and only five months into it, I'd already had enough. Besides, I hadn't been paid for the previous month. The days went by and the discussions carried on between Ian and Neil. I didn't really want to go to court over it, and Ian managed to arrange a meeting with Neil and Wayne Ashworth, the club chairman, to discuss my contract. I had planned to use the meeting to give Neil both barrels but before I could get going, Neil went on the attack and it was at that point that Ian stepped in and went into courtroom mode and gave them both a pasting – he absolutely took them to the cleaners. Ian knew exactly what to say and when not to overstep the mark. Neil accused me of walking free of my contract but we were taking the line of constructive dismissal. Ian knew all the right moves.

In the end I asked Ian to forget it and chalked it all down to experience. People often asked me why I was working for Neil, but for me it was something I wanted to try in order to get myself noticed back in England. Unfortunately it didn't work out. In the end, Kathy and I had come back from Australia for what we thought was two years at Stockport Sports but ended up being five months of hell.

It was time I looked at other things again – wherever it may be.

19

Never Say Never

"When we have the ball we're an attacking team but when we don't have the ball we're a defensive team."

****

I was finding it hard to get back into work in England but I was determined not to give up or retire. While I was looking for something, I got myself back into the media spotlight by doing some work for a local radio station in the West Midlands, and some national TV and radio interviews. I also did some FA refresher courses.

Even at 61 years old, I still had a point to prove.

Although I did get a few interviews with non-league clubs, including one with Luton Town and some false promises of jobs, nothing really materialised. As with so many clubs, much of it came down to finances. I even told Ian I'd work for nothing as a way of getting into a club and proving I could do a job – I was at a stage in my life where I just wanted to work. It was around that time that I introduced Brian Little to Ian, as he was also finding it difficult to get back into work. Ian was a good agent and I trusted him to find me and Brian some work.

It occurred to me that, because I'd been abroad for such a long time before I'd got the Stockport Sports job, people may have forgotten who I was. I was getting messages back from English clubs I'd applied to saying that I was 'too old' and 'the game [had] moved on in England.' My answer to that was, when I was 16 years old, the game was moving on and throughout my career the game has moved on, and now, I'm also moving on with the game. I didn't understand their logic. There's a perception that people who are in their 50s or 60s should just pack up football and retire. Well, I wasn't ready to retire.

When I was a player I was influenced by some of the best managers in the game and I can honestly say I took some of their skills and ideas into my own management style. Brian Clough, for one, taught me a lot about man-management, understanding players and about getting the best out of them. I could never emulate Brian because he was a one-off and totally different to me (or anyone else for that matter). As I progressed throughout my career I developed my own philosophy on how I wanted my teams to play. In the two years I had under Brian, I learned so much, like the importance of not suffering fools lightly and making sure the players knew who was in charge. When I was a coach I told my players not to be influenced by other people, especially in Asian football where it was pretty prevalent. I learned from some of the European game's most well-known motivators so I always tried to improve my players' skills as well as their mindsets. I tried to change things by giving the players a positive example and also by putting in the hours off the training pitch. I was a very hands-on coach.

To me, football is a simple game, a philosophy I shared with Brian Clough: 'You're a goalkeeper – you make a save; you're a full-back – you defend; you're a striker – you score a goal.' Football now seems to be full of complicated tactics, but as a coach, I always liked to keep it simple and logical. In my career, I've probably had about 25 different managers, and I learned something different from each and every one of them. I was often asked when I was working abroad, 'What system do you play – what's your style of play ...?' to which I would reply, 'I don't know the players. Once I've coached them and been with them for a while I'll tell you what system I'll play.' Ideally, I'd play 4-4-2, but that might have changed if we didn't have the team for it. My basic philosophy was always the same: we'd have 11 players defending when we'd not got the ball and we'd have 11 players attacking when we had the ball. It's quite simple really, but some people couldn't grasp the concept, that there are 11 people on the field who could score a goal and the same 11 people who could stop a goal. Most people in Thailand and Indonesia had never heard football described like that and were baffled by it. Another question I was asked was, 'Do you play attacking football?' to which I would reply, 'Well, yes when we have the ball we're an attacking team but when we don't have the ball we're a defensive team.' That was only effective if we had the best players and were organised. It wasn't rocket science.

It was during the winter of 2012 when I decided to take a break and go back to Perth for a few weeks, stopping off in Thailand for a week or so. I wanted to see a few people in Bangkok and tie up a few loose ends there – I also wanted to go to watch a few games. One of the first games I went to watch was Muangthong United and as soon as some of their fans saw me I got mobbed – there were supporters everywhere. I walked into the stadium wearing my trademark baseball cap and shorts and instantly got recognised by thousands of fans who all wanted their picture taken with the most successful coach of the Thailand national team. People never forgot me there. Even small kids, who wouldn't have known who I was, came up to me asking for pictures or autographs, saying their father remembered me.

I ended up spending three weeks in Bangkok. It was like turning the clock back because everywhere I went, everyone recognised me, even after ten years. It was very humbling. Once the media got wind I was in town I was doing local and national TV and radio interviews. Once my face was seen on national TV my phone never stopped ringing. I even had a call from the chairman of the Thai FA who persuaded me not to go back to Perth but to stay in town a week longer than I'd planned to meet with him. I agreed to stay, we had a meeting and he proposed that I consider returning to my role as Thai national coach as they were struggling at the time. The fact was they had been struggling since I left in 2002.

A few days later, the chairman called again and said he thought he had secured me a job if I wanted it. Without giving me any details he told me he'd organised a car to pick me up at 5pm for a meeting. I thought the meeting was going to be at the Thai FA headquarters but the car took me to the main office of one of the biggest (if not the biggest) companies in Thailand. I met the chairman of the club (PTT Rayong), who was also head of PTT, a Thai state-owned SET-listed oil and gas company, formerly known as the Petroleum Authority of Thailand; it owned extensive submarine gas pipelines in the Gulf of Thailand. It was a huge company and very wealthy.

The board knew what I'd done for the national team but they wanted to know what I could do for their Premier League team. I don't think they had any reservations about me because they asked me if I could start the next day. It took me aback a bit and I explained I had to go back to Australia before I could agree to anything. They insisted I cut my stay in Perth short to a weekend and I left the meeting and flew to Perth as planned – but decided to stay a week as a compromise.

My week in Perth went by quickly and I returned to Rayong and agreed to start work with my new team. The situation was that they had changed the regime prior to my meeting and sacked everyone from the chairman to the manager, and they wanted me as their new head coach. The club had been promoted from the first division to the Premier League by the skin of their teeth only the season before I arrived. They had a lovely stadium, not a huge one but it was fairly new and compact, with a capacity of 20,000. There was talk in the media that they wanted to sign some big names and Alessandro Del Piero had been widely linked, so I got to thinking I'd come to a progressive club. When I asked the chairman if we were signing Del Piero he shrugged it off as mere paper talk. I knew there couldn't have been much truth in the story as it was fact that Del Piero was getting around AUD$1m playing for Sydney FC in Australia. PTT was linked with several other high-profile players but (not surprisingly) none of them materialised.

Once I'd settled in, I began to realise there was no way PTT could ever afford anyone of Del Piero's stature, as the maximum salary for a player there was around US$10,000 a month. Compare that to Jay Bothroyd, who only a few years on (2014) signed for Muangthong United in a £5m deal over two years – tax free – and you can see the budget for the football club wasn't that great back then. There were four or five teams in the Thai Premier League who had unlimited resources, and PTT Rayong weren't one of them.

After being in Thailand for four years with the national team I'd watched lots of Thai Premier League football. The league, in my opinion, was at the equivalent level of the English League One, although some teams would probably hold their own in the Championship. There wasn't a lot of difference between the Thai Premier League and the Thai first division, although the better foreign players tended to go to the top Premier League teams.

I joined my team a few days after I returned from Perth and we got stuck into pre-season training. Early on in pre-season, I was wondering what I was doing wrong as our injury list was growing at a rate of knots. We had ten injured first-team players and with the season about to start, that was a worry. We started the season with a series of draws, a couple of wins and some defeats mixed in and we couldn't get any sort of momentum going. I told the players to be patient; things would improve once we got our injured players back. As with all the teams I've managed, I encouraged good football, but we couldn't string a good run together and we remained in the bottom three of the table.

The people who run football clubs in Thailand (and Asia in general) tend not to discuss the manager's future with you in person, but usually go to the media and say things like, '... if he doesn't get six points in the next three games he's finished ...' And that's exactly what happened after just six months of the season at PTT Rayong. It may have been normal for them to 'talk to me' (or talk about me, more like) via the media, but it wasn't my style, so I met with the board and explained it would be better if they discussed my future with me in person in future. I told them it was my job to take the pressure off the players, but they had now put the pressure back on the team by coming out with that sort of statement in the media.

The next time I saw the players I advised them to ignore what they read in the media, to go out and play football, and dispel any uncertainty there was over my future. However, talk was cheap and we lost the next game 1–0 at home. After the game I was called into a meeting with the board. The chairman was late for the meeting so I talked to the rest of board members about how the season was going and the style of football the team was playing. I took the small-talk as a positive that they discussed the team with me. That was until the chairman came in, sat down and the first thing he said was, 'OK, we'll give you a month's money ...'

I looked at the others sat around the table and said, 'So, what we've just discussed about the team, we shouldn't have bothered with that really? We should have just waited for him to say what he said?'

I didn't hang around; I thanked them, confirmed with the chairman that he was dismissing me and started to walk out of the room.

The chairman then stood up and said to me, 'What do you think then?'

I was just about to walk out of the door for the last time, turned back and said, 'Well, I came here because it was a two-year project and you knew that and now you're calling it a day after six months. I'm not happy!'

The chairman stalled for a few seconds and said, 'I'll give you two months' pay.'

I dismissed his second offer there and then but he came back and offered me three months' compensation. I thought he was clutching at straws a bit and I told him, 'I'll tell you what, you go away and think about it and I'll go back and discuss it with my wife.'

I agreed to meet the board the following day, and said to them, 'Right, I've gone away and had a think about it and discussed it with my wife. I've come here, given up everything in England, given up my apartment and thought we'd be here for two years and it's ended after six months.' Then I put my cards on the table. 'This is what I'll agree to, and it's not negotiable. This is what I want and if you don't agree to it, I'll go to FIFA.' I told them I wanted to see out my two-year contract with the club. I left it with them to think about over the weekend, saying I would wait until the Monday for their response, but by the Thursday they still hadn't contacted me. I phoned my assistant manager and he said openly that they weren't interested in my offer, so that was that.

I went to watch the next game from the stands and spoke to my assistant manager after the game. He indicated that the chairman wanted to speak to me. When I met the chairman he asked me if the situation could be resolved – I'd already told them how to resolve it during the previous meeting but obviously they hadn't taken any notice. He mumbled something under his breath and I came up with another offer.

'I'll tell you what and we'll shake hands over it here and now but if it doesn't happen now and you don't shake on it, I'll go to FIFA.'

I knew they wouldn't give me my job back so I asked them for six months' money as a way out of my contract, to keep the car for two months and to keep the phone.

In the end, the money was paid along with an invoice to return the car, computer and phone. I was running out of patience so I went back to them saying I was keeping the car for another two months. I'd had enough of negotiating – it was time for hardball.

I felt let down by the chairman and it was a big inconvenience to me and Kathy personally. We had just found a suitable apartment in the area after living in a hotel for a few months. However, while I was still in dispute with PTT I received a call from one of my ex-players who was coaching a Thai first division team called Nakhon Pathom United, who were based in the Nakhon Pathom province, about 30 miles west of Bangkok.

'Coach, can you help me? My team needs help. Can you come and help us?'

I wasn't working so I thought I'd go to meet him and have a look at the team, who were playing a match near Bangkok. After the game I was introduced to the manager and the owner and I explained I was in dispute with PTT but agreed to help the team and take a week of training sessions with him and the players. From what I saw, the team needed organising more than anything, which was right up my street. I told them I'd sit in the stands during the next game and they won that, so my influence must have worked, I guess. During the next couple of weeks I didn't do anything with the team as I was still in negotiations with PTT but out of the blue I got a call from the Nakhon Pathom chairman asking me to go to play golf with him.

As I'd still got the car, I drove from Rayong to the golf club only to find the chairman had an entourage of about ten buggies following him. I wondered what was going on but I soon realised the spotlight was on the chairman's wife, Tanika Aum (nicknamed 'The Madam'), who was a local media darling and didn't shun the limelight. After nine holes, the media who were following me, the chairman and his wife in the entourage took pictures of us all together. More pictures were taken after 18 holes and then, all of a sudden, pictures began to appear on Facebook and Twitter, with stories saying I'd agreed a contract with the club. This was strange because I hadn't even discussed money or any kind of terms with the chairman. When I found out the stories had appeared on social media I told them I needed to discuss things with Kathy before I decided on anything.

The owner of the club was only 37 years old and he said he remembered me managing the national side all those years ago and admired me as a coach.

He spoke very good English as he was educated in New Zealand, but his wife didn't. Tanika was around the same age and was the focal point of the club – wherever she went, the media followed and she loved being photographed.

I eventually agreed a deal until the end of that season – which ended in the November — so there were only four or five months left. The money wasn't great, but it was pocket money to be honest, given I'd just agreed to six months' salary from PTT as compensation for my sacking. The team was in the relegation zone and I was needed to turn things round and keep them in the division. I agreed to review the situation after the session had finished.

Nakhon Pathom FC were a new, family-run club formed in 1999. It was quite a contrast going from PTT, where I couldn't get a straight answer from anyone to Nakhon Pathom, where they couldn't do enough for me. It was to the extreme though; once I'd walked through the door in the morning I wasn't allowed to buy anything or do anything for myself. I had to sneak out discreetly if I wanted to go shopping. I think the instruction from the chairman (nicknamed 'The Boss') was, 'keep him happy, look after him and make sure anything he wants, he gets (up to a point).'

I had to release the apartment in Rayong, and as we'd already got an apartment in Bangkok we were on the lookout for something more local to the club. Kathy wasn't bothered about finding another place to live but she liked how we were being treated, so we found a house nearby. The club treated Kathy like a princess and, much like me, she wasn't allowed to buy or do anything once she stepped into the club. We both felt uneasy with all the fuss as we were used to paying our way. As the weeks went on it got to the stage where we were constantly in the limelight and being photographed – it was a bit embarrassing really.

On the field, I had to try to work with the players we had – I couldn't buy new players as there wasn't a budget, so I had to turn a team who kept losing into winners and pick them up from the bottom of the table. I think they went beyond their budget to get me to sign up as head coach as it was – even though they paid me peanuts. I was there to change the philosophy of the players and change the way the team played in order to keep them in the division. Relegation would have been a disaster for a club with so little funding. At the start, we were losing games we should have won and those games were all shown on live TV. I did a press conference after one game and said I was pleased with the way we played, even though we lost. In my own mind I knew what to do to change things and I assured the fans we'd be fine. I wanted to convince the fans watching that the better team lost the game because we didn't take our chances.

I had a meeting with my bosses and told them what we needed to do to stay in the division. We needed three more wins, and I promised them I'd get those victories. The next game we played a team well above us in the league and won the game 1–0, but the following game we were leading another high-flying team 2–1 until the 94th minute, when they equalised. That win would have made us safe. Two more back-to-back wins gave us a chance until the last game of the season and safety was in our own destiny. I picked an attacking side and it paid off because we won 5–1, even though it took us 25 minutes to score the first goal. After the game, the owners were all in tears and everyone was really emotional. I'd achieved the goal – we were safe.

The season had ended and I went away to think about my future, even though the owners had convinced themselves I would stay on for another season. The club gave me a contract to sign for the 2014/15 season and I signed it, even though I wasn't sure if I wanted to be in charge. Kathy and I had to fly to Perth, then on to Houston to see Gareth and the family for a few weeks at the end of the Thai season, but before we went I sat down with my son, Jason, and the owner to discuss the situation. I didn't feel I could give 100 per cent commitment for the next campaign so I suggested they took Jason as head coach for the next season. Jason knew the way I played and what they were getting was someone who could dedicate his time to the job. The owner agreed and Kathy and I flew back to Perth for a break.

What actually happened wasn't planned. Jason couldn't take pre-season training because his brother-in-law was ill and he had to be somewhere else, so Kathy and I cut our stay in Perth short and I ended up taking pre-season training. The owners obviously got the wrong message and thought I'd changed my mind and was going to carry on as head coach for the new season, so I had to explain the situation to them yet again. I had to spell it out to them that I wasn't staying and I was only doing it until Jason got back to Thailand. I promised to organise the team for the start of the season and Jason would then take over the reins.

As it turned out, the situation with Jason's brother-in-law worsened and he had to stay in the UK for the funeral, early in January 2015, so our stay in Thailand was extended until mid-January – a few weeks before the start of the new Thai season. I must have raised the owner's hopes that I would stay for the whole season, so I put them straight again after explaining Jason's situation. I hadn't said anything to the players about my future before the pre-season friendly game against Chonburi, who had finished 2nd in the previous Thai Premier League season – I thought that was the right thing to do. We were 2–0 down at half-time so I gave the team some tactical pointers during my team talk and it did the trick because we won the game 5–3. It was another feather in my cap and everyone at the club was made up that we had beaten a team far superior to our own. After the game I decided the time was right to tell the players that I wasn't taking the team for the new season.

'You didn't know, but it is my last game. I didn't want to say anything as I wanted you to concentrate on your football. This is my last game – I'm leaving and I'll be leaving the country next week. My son Jason will be taking over.'

The players were a bit shell-shocked but I shook every one of their hands and thanked them. I quickly packed up my stuff and walked out of the dressing room to leave the stadium after telling the players I was quitting and I was greeted by all the staff including the owners were lined up waiting for me. They all had tears in their eyes and were very emotional to see me leave but it was a decision I had made.

Our Thai adventure was over, and we were heading back home again, leaving Jason in charge of the team. The decision was made based on several things. We could have stayed in Thailand for four or five more years quite easily. It was a very cheap country to live in and the weather suited us, but I was 63 years old and not getting any younger. We were grandparents and our second granddaughter had just been born in Houston, Texas and there would have been limited chances to see them if I'd carried on as a coach in Thailand. I hadn't seen my mother (who was 85) for 18 months and we were also trying to sell properties in Solihull and in Perth, so there were a lot of domestic matters for us to deal with. There just wasn't the time or opportunity to do that while I was working.

I loved coaching but during the last pre-season I thought to myself, 'What am I doing this for? Am I doing this for the money?' The answer to that was no, because the salary at Nakhon Pathom (and at Stockport for that matter) wasn't anything like what Rayong paid me, and I was doing the job as a favour really. Even though I always got up early and sometimes drove long distances to the training ground, once I was on the field I loved it. But just like when you come to the end of your playing career, you just know the right time to pack up coaching. I was fortunate enough to play until the age of 39, and the time to throw in the towel had come.

****

During the summer of 2015, something very special happened – I was reunited with my 1982 European Cup winning shirt – the one I had swapped with Klaus Augenthaler. Apparently, it had been stored in the Bayern Munich museum for some years and my son Stephen contacted them and we arranged to meet up to exchange shirts. I travelled to Germany and spent a few days there and met up with Klaus, and I finally gave him his red Bayern shirt back. Unfortunately, he had signed the front of my shirt in black ink – but it was still really nice to have my shirt back after 33 years. I really thought I'd never see it again.

Also during 2015 I was sounded out by an agent to coach in India, but that would have only been a short-term thing and I'd never spend more than four or five months there, even though the money on offer was phenomenal. When you're my age, four or five months would go in no time but when you're young you tend to wish your time away, so it was a no to India.

It was during the summer of 2015 – while Kathy and I were staying with Gareth and seeing our granddaughter, Cara, for the first time in Houston, Texas – that I received an unexpected phone call from one of the old Portland Timbers players, Mick Hoban. He informed me the club were celebrating their 40th year (even though the team in its current form was only formed in 2009), winning the Western Division, and getting to the play-off final in 1975. I was the only player in that 1975 team who hadn't been back to Portland since. Mick told me the club were having a reunion and I was invited.

The club couldn't believe I hadn't been back in 40 years – they were extremely pleased to hear that I was in America at that very time and had accepted the invite. I agreed to stay in Portland for a week and the club put me in a very nice hotel. They wanted me to do some PR work in the run-up to the celebrations, so one morning I went to the training ground and addressed the players. As it happened, I knew one of the players, Liam Ridgewell, who used to play for Villa. The training ground was new and it was fitted out like a typical modern football facility. After I watched the lads train, the American coach, Caleb Porter, introduced me to the squad and then turned to me and asked if I wanted to say a few words. Obviously, I hadn't rehearsed anything, so he put me on the spot a bit, but I stepped up and said a few words. I'd done my homework and said to the players:

'It just so happens that back in 1975, no one had ever played soccer in Portland. We put soccer on the map and still to this day Portland is called 'Soccer City USA' – we started that. We went into the schools and everywhere to promote the sport in the area. When we left a year later, a million children were playing soccer. Now, this is what's good about America – I've been finding out that you guys have been doing the same thing, going out into the community and carrying on what we started. I think that's a tremendous achievement. They don't do this in the UK any more so I'm proud you're carrying on the tradition.'

I think they were quite touched by my words.

It was nice to go back to Portland, and I managed to hook up with some people we hadn't seen for 40 years. Roger Goldingay, one of only three Amercians in the 1975 side, invited all the ex-players for drinks at his apartment before (and after) the game and function at the Timbers Stadium. Before the game, we were led out on to the pitch and presented to the crowd, holding our Portland shirts – mine had '9 WITHE' on the back. It was a great week and there was a good turnout of ex-players, probably six or seven of us, reminiscing about old times.

****

Ever since I left Villa back in the early 1990s, people at the club have always said I was welcome to come to the Bodymoor Heath training ground any time I wanted, but I'd never been officially asked, as such, until Steve Bruce became Villa manager in October 2016. I actually think the invitations had been made in passing, but I'd had no firm offer to come.

In fact, there was one time I offered my services to an ex-Villa manager for free. I approached Villa and told them I could improve the first-team strikers by coaching them. Can you imagine – an ex-professional top-class striker coaching young, up-and-coming players how to be a top goalscorer? That offer has been open to the club ever since. I'd love the chance to teach the current Villa strikers – not many clubs can boast that their current strikers are coached explicitly in the art of scoring by their ex-strikers, I doubt! With that in mind, I met up with Steve early into his Villa tenureship and he actually invited me to watch the lads train. Brian Little took me round Bodymoor Heath and we watched a training session, and I explained why I hadn't been before. To cut a long story short, Steve extended the offer and said I could come any time I wanted so that was nice.

Personally, I think the art of being a good striker is slowly dying out. It's not difficult – it's just a case of getting in the right positions at the right time in order to score goals. I know that there were players at Villa who would have improved if I had coached them the right way. It's a sad indictment of Villa that I was the last Villa player (in 1981) to have scored 20 league goals in a season. Jonathan Kodjia came close at the end of the 2016/17 season when he scored 19, but he also missed chances. Dwight Yorke, David Platt and Christian Benteke also came close, but never managed to reach the magic 20-goal mark. I looked at Kodjia and thought if I had coached him during that season I could have got him past 20 goals, simply by making an improvement in his game of say 20 per cent. It's a travesty to a club like Aston Villa that my offer was never taken up, and one of the reasons why the club hasn't been as successful as it should have been in the last 35 years.

On one occasion I went up to Bodymoor Heath and there was a film crew there. The club asked me and Brian to do a slot for a video reel they were making where ex-Villa players said a few words about what it was like to play for Aston Villa. One of the things that always impressed me about Steve Bruce was that he wanted his players to understand the history of the club. He reckoned most of his squad probably didn't know who I was and that's something he wanted to change, which I found refreshing. For many years, the team who won the league and European Cup were almost forgotten and all reminders of them had been removed from inside the stadium – there were no pictures of those great years. Steve changed that. Both the training ground and Villa Park are now filled with reminders of the past and that gives the current players an insight into how big Aston Villa were (and still are) and what they should strive towards.

During my travels, I've always kept one thing in mind; whenever one thing ends, something else begins. Having travelled a lot since 2014 when I left my job at Nakhon Pathom, I have frequently been asked whether I am finished in football. The simple answer to that is you're never finished in football, no matter how old you are, and you've only got to look at the likes of Harry Redknapp and Roy Hodgson to justify that.

I'm now at an age where I watch a lot of football, live or on TV, do some commentating, and enjoy watching the way that the game evolves, which is great ... but I would still love to continue coaching and if a job came up that I thought was right for me, I'd consider taking it.

I've always said I would 'never say never' because there's always something round the corner, so we'll see what unfolds in the next chapter of my life.

Testimonials

The author would like to thank everyone who has contributed to this section with their fabulous stories of Peter and their times with him throughout the years.

****

Mick Martin

Former Newcastle United captain

Peter was signed by Bill McGarry at the start of the 1978/79 season from Brian Clough's great Nottingham Forest team, just before I joined Newcastle in the Christmas period of 1978. I didn't know a lot about Peter apart from seeing him play for Forest and, as a midfielder myself, I wouldn't have come into much contact with him being a striker but I'd imagine if I was a centre-half up against him it would have been a physical encounter, that's for sure.

Withey was a good player and a top-class centre-forward; a strong, physical type of player with a bit of pace about him. He was an aggressive sort of player, a typical old-fashioned centre-forward. He would have been in your face all the time because that's the way he played. That doesn't mean his game was purely about being physical; he also had a good touch and was good in the air and an all-round decent player. I enjoyed playing with him and made a few goals for him. I think we would have won the league (Division Two) the following season, prior to his move to Villa. Unfortunately, I got a bad injury in that season and that set us back a fair bit and we finished 9th.

As Newcastle captain, I was also an aggressive player, vocal in the dressing room and would point the finger if a player wasn't doing his job. Peter was a bit like that too. If things weren't going to plan, Withey would make players aware of the situation on the pitch and in the dressing room too. He was a big influence in the dressing room and would say his bit and get away with it, which was a good thing. I always thought it was best to be aggressive in the dressing room and on the field.

Off the pitch we'd socialise a bit – we'd go out into town with the wives after games and have a few drinks. It was the done thing back then – probably modern-day players don't socialise like that now. Very often, we'd arrange to play golf up at Gosforth, where Peter lived, or another venue in the area after training during the week. I remember just before Peter left for Villa the two of us played in Ray Clemence's testimonial golf match at Skegness Golf Club and we travelled down there together. They were great days.

Gordon Cowans

Former Aston Villa and England midfielder

As a target man, Peter was as good as anyone around at the time. He was always there making himself available for the ball, holding the ball up and bringing other players into the game. He would always get into the box whenever the wide players like Tony Morley and Des Bremner got on the ball, waiting for the ball to drop to his feet. He was also very good in the air. He was just very easy to play with. I played with Peter for England as well, which was nice as we knew each other's game which helped form a great partnership. He was a real top, top striker.

In the dressing room, Peter was very influential and always had his say. He had loads of passion for the game and when he spoke up he'd always say it how it was. Peter was to the point and he didn't mince his words. Some of the younger lads may have thought he was being abrupt but he wasn't – he was just telling the truth.

Something which I didn't know about at the time was that Peter and some of the other lads went in to see Ron Saunders to have a chat about the game or about football in general, on the odd occasion. That's not a bad thing as it showed the sort of open relationship we had with the manager.

Off the field, most of the lads liked their golf and socialised afterwards with a few drinks – sometimes it got a bit messy too, which was pretty normal in those days.

Ron Saunders

Former Aston Villa manager 1974–1982

I didn't know anything about Peter before I signed him but I did send three or four scouts to watch him, mainly to see how fit he was. Luckily, Peter kept himself very fit and I signed him for Villa in 1980. He was a credit to himself as he was a very fit lad indeed.

When I first met Peter he looked about seven foot seven and he came to the interview wearing a tracksuit as he had been doing some exercises, which really didn't impress me an awful lot to be honest. Apart from that, from my first impression of Peter, everything about him was professional.

Peter was the final piece of the jigsaw for that Villa team – he was all we wanted from a striker. One of the things that I noticed in his first game for us was that he never stopped yelling at our players and the opposition's players, which in itself was a tremendous asset to the team. From that first game, I saw him as a future manager.

It was a credit, firstly, having him at the football club and, secondly, having him in the first team. Peter was also a credit to himself because he always spared time helping the younger players at the club. Just having him around gave the kids a lift. Just about every apprentice admired Peter as much, if not more than anyone else at the club.

I'd like to think Peter listened to me when I gave out instructions but who knows if he did?

Ken McNaught

Former Aston Villa centre-half

Everyone would say Peter was always full of energy and that was his greatest asset, together with his enthusiasm. His work rate was phenomenal and he played a major part in what we did at Villa.

I knew Peter as a player before he came to Villa as I think I played against him when he was at Southport, all those years before, as I was coming through the Everton ranks. In those days there wasn't such a thing as a 'development squad.' I remember Everton had about five teams back then; I started off playing for the 'A' team (the third team) and we played the likes of Southport Reserves and as a 16-year-old kid that was part of your development, playing against grown men. Later on in my career, I played against Peter when he was at Wolves, Blues and at Forest but I can't remember specific times as it was too long ago. When I left Villa I moved to West Bromwich Albion and, low and behold, my first game was against Villa at Villa Park, so I played against Peter then and Villa beat us 4–3. In those days, it was a case of give and take – there were never any complaints from either of us so we'd just battle on and whoever won on the day took the credit.

Ron Saunders always made sure we'd give nothing less than 100 per cent, even in the five-a-sides in training. He expected us to work hard at all times and if you didn't he made it clear but as long as you did it on a Saturday he didn't take it further. The training was always quality, short and sharp drills throughout the week.

Like Peter, I love my golf. At Everton, we weren't allowed to play golf full stop but at Villa, the unwritten rule was you weren't supposed to play golf after Wednesdays. I'm sure Ron knew we sneaked off every Thursday after training to play 9 holes of golf at Whittington Barracks, but he never once mentioned it. Well, he never mentioned it to the older lads anyway – he might have mentioned it to the younger lads like Gordon Cowans and Colin Gibson.

When Peter moved to Villa we became good friends, mainly because he moved over to the Solihull side of Birmingham where I lived. We soon started to socialise, along with some of the other lads like Kenny Swain who lived in the area. It didn't take long for the wives and families to get together, especially when we were away playing. Sometimes after games, Jimmy Rimmer and Gordon Cowans, who lived on the other side of Birmingham, would come over with their wives. At that time we had a magnificent group of players who didn't just play well together but socialised well together.

Viv Anderson MBE

Former Nottingham Forest and England defender

When Peter came to Forest from Birmingham City you knew straight away he was a fit guy and any sort of running we were asked to do would demonstrate that he was the fittest player in the club at the time. You knew when you went out on to the football field he'd always give you 100 per cent – even 110 per cent – in every aspect of the game, whether it was chasing a ball, heading, trying to score or helping his teammates out. In my view, he was always a really first-class team player. It was testament to Brian really, for picking Peter. Brian was good at choosing which players to sign – Peter Taylor should take a lot of credit for that as well to be honest. Combined, they knew what they wanted. They knew what sort of player they wanted and what sort of characters they needed for the team, and obviously Peter fell into that category. It was a good choice, signing Peter.

We didn't really do much training as such with Cloughie – it was all about days off, Saturday afternoons and matchdays, when you were judged, but Peter was always keeping his fitness up and was probably training when the rest of the lads were off. He was that sort of lad and wanted to be extra fit to give 100 per cent come matchday.

I always remember he could eat for fun. One time at Forest we were having a function and Peter said he could eat all the chocolate eclairs on the plate – there must have been 50 or 60 (or more). He was always a right comedian and was always cracking jokes, but Peter had a wager with all the lads that he could eat the lot. Everyone put money in a jar betting against him and I said, 'No chance, Withey, can you eat all them.' There was a right tidy few bob in the jar in the end and guess what? Withey ate the whole lot!

When we were at the 1982 World Cup in Spain, Withey was always the first one down for breakfast and would dish the papers out to the lads. Peter was a jovial lad and was always a happy-go-lucky sort of person. He was a nice lad.

Peter was the catalyst for the team that went on to win two European Cups and everything else, so Nottingham Forest should take a lot of credit for signing Peter Withe and for what he did for the club at that time.

I met up with him many years later in Thailand and we shared a drink or two together. I know Peter has done really well as a coach in Thailand and proved very popular in that country but I honestly didn't see anything in him when he was at Forest which would tell me he'd become a coach or a manager in the future. Peter was always thinking about the day and getting on with his training and he very much focused on his family but didn't really look too far ahead of himself. Peter was the last person I'd have imagined who would have gone into management but he proved me wrong.

Steve Daley
Former Wolverhampton Wanderers winger

When Derek Dougan came back to Wolves from South Africa he'd noticed a certain person called Peter Withe who was playing out there for Arcadia Shepherds and didn't hesitate to tell Wolves manager, Bill McGarry, about him. It wasn't long after that Peter signed for Wolves. I thought at the time that it showed a great determination, strength of character and self-belief to become a footballer by going out to South Africa to resurrect his career. I know Peter wanted to come to Wolves to show people he had made it as a professional footballer. On top of that, he could play – he was a bloody good player.

I remember the first time Peter turned up for training at Wolves and everyone took the piss out of him because he had long hair and a beard. It wasn't long before Bill McGarry told him to get a haircut and have a shave – he didn't stand for any of that nonsense from his players.

From those early days as a 21-year-old to when he played for Villa I don't think Peter had changed much as a player. Obviously, he had persevered and gained a lot more experience over the years but he knew what he could do and he always played to his strengths. Peter was everything you'd want from a striker: he was big, aggressive, had good control, great determination and he was the fittest footballer I'd ever seen, without any shadow of a doubt. Whether it was pre-season training or training during the season, Peter's fitness levels were phenomenal – he'd outrun anybody in terms of stamina. He was also great in the air; he could shield the ball; he could score goals and he took a lot of battering and bad tackles during games but he always just got on with it. Peter could give as much as he took from the centre-halves. He was a strong character and a strong player. I'd guess that if you asked all the centre-halves of that era who was the hardest forward they played against I bet quite a few would have said Peter Withe.

Peter was never put down by his teammates but he'd always speak up for himself. He'd tell you on the park if you'd played a poor pass or hadn't crossed a proper ball into the box. He'd let you know about it there and then. He'd also tell you if you'd delivered a good one and it went into the back of the net.

Bill McGarry gave Peter that chance to prove himself, even though his chances at Wolves were limited, with the likes of Alan Sunderland, John Richards, Steve Kinden and Jimmy Curran in front of him as strikers but Peter would always give 100 per cent every time he put the shirt on. Bill also gave Peter an opportunity to pursue a career in the US with Portland Timbers, along with some of my other Wolves teammates. Sadly, Bill wouldn't release me so I didn't go with Peter.

I have so much respect and praise for the guy because what he did in the game was absolutely fantastic. He proved it at Birmingham City and at Nottingham Forest under one of the greatest managers ever in Brian Clough; he proved it at Newcastle and then at Villa where he won the European Cup. When England came calling, he proved it on the international front too and took his chance.

I didn't think Peter would become a coach or a manager back then but he worked under some great managers in his playing days and I think he took on certain aspects of the game from all of them. He put his own style into operation to become a coach in his own right and became a great success in Thailand.

When we were both at Wolves we would socialise together with the wives as we both lived in the Fordhouses area. We had a great friendship from the start and that friendship is still there today. We were and still are great mates.

John McGovern

Former Nottingham Forest midfielder and captain

The first thing you should do when you come into a new football club is to try to impress the guys you're playing with, and it was his determination and effort that helped Peter settle in very quickly. For Peter, it was a very smooth transition to move to Forest as he relocated straight away and that helped him and his family settle. Most players who move to a club with good players who want to do well will also do well, because you get energy from the help they give you when they're out there on the field. If you get transferred from one club to another and the club's struggling then you might struggle yourself. Peter came into a good, well-disciplined, hard-working side and that suited his work ethic, so it was a marriage made in heaven. By Peter joining Nottingham Forest, he benefited and we all benefited from his presence and ability to get goals and to provide service to the other striker. Peter was not only a goalscorer, he also laid on balls for the other players to score goals.

For Brian Clough and Peter Taylor to bring Peter to the club he must have had a lot of attributes and he was privileged just like the other players they brought into the club were. It was a privilege to work for them because they were both so good at what they did and I think Peter appreciated that also. If you've got a manager hungry for success and a player also hungry for success then you'll have a pretty smooth transition into a new club. The only difficulty you have is to try to stay in the side.

Peter came to Forest and did a great job as a target man. He was one of the most dedicated players in the side and had so much energy and always made a contribution on the football field. He was very easy to get on with and he had no problems settling in, mainly because he wanted to do well and had pride in what he was doing. He enjoyed it because he was well-supported by the other players when he went out there as the striker. The role of the striker is to get the goals but you need some kind of service. We ended up playing with people like John Robertson who was a winger and provided some great aerial service to Peter, who was very good in the air.

As a striker, you have a role to play to make yourself available so the other players can get the ball to you, and you also have to challenge and get yourself goals, which is the ultimate aim for a striker. Peter was capable of fitting in with the good side we had at Forest and obviously he was a successful part of that side from the goals he got and the industry he showed when he went out to play over 90 minutes.

As a group of players, we all listened to Brian Clough (most of the time) because what he said to us made good common sense and made good football sense, so when we went out on to the field we found out that if we put into practise his philosophy it was good for us as individuals and good for the team as well. Peter had no problem fitting in with a bunch of lads who wanted to do well. We were all decent players too. Brian had this unique ability for making each player 'comfortable' once you stepped over that white line and players felt that – they felt comfortable walking over the white line.

We are talking about a time here when players weren't allowed to talk to the media without permission and, at Nottingham Forest, Clough did all the talking for us because the media wanted him to. After all, he was better than anyone else, so apart from the odd comment from a player (when he was allowed to) the philosophy of the manager was very, very strong and singularly aimed at the players, the media and the public as well. Anybody that makes you feel 'comfortable' doing what you're doing, which was what Clough did, then if you've got ability you're going to succeed in what you're doing. It was that unique approach and the simplicity of the philosophy that he preached to his players that meant they became more successful than they were before they had met him. He had a knack of somehow bringing out the ability in all the players under his tutelage.

As a player, if you don't learn and improve under a manager who was considered a genius as Brian was, you'll never improve and certainly Peter improved as a player after spending two years at Nottingham Forest – as all the players did. Clough told us what to do, how to play and we went out there and did it. When Brian Clough joined Nottingham Forest, he had quality players like Martin O'Neill, Ian Bowyer, Tony Woodcock and John Robertson there and they were struggling against relegation. That's why managers get these jobs. Those same players that were struggling to avoid being relegated from Division Two in the 1974/75 season went on to win the European Cup (twice) a few years later. They all certainly became better players and all became internationals because of Brian Clough.

If there was ever a time when Clough would give us a few days off, more than likely Peter would go and do some training to keep himself in shape. Clough gave us a lot of time off and I'd have done some training if I thought

I needed it but Peter was so dedicated and exceptionally fit. Peter had an appetite of about three players, probably because he needed the intake of food with the work he did. Peter was a decent guy in the dressing room, a dressing room full of leaders and I don't think we felt anything other than pleasure for what we were doing as a group.

Brian Little

Former Aston Villa forward (1970–1980) and manager (1994–1998)

Peter often tells me he had a choice between Villa and Everton but when he spoke to Ron Saunders he wanted to Peter play alongside myself and he was enthused by that, and also by the fact we had some really good players at the club at that time, so Peter chose to come to Villa.

My early recollections of Peter were more of disappointment than anything else, not from Peter but when this big centre-forward came along I never got an opportunity to play with him and get to know him as a player. The irony of that was I got injured a lot and the only time I ever played alongside Peter was in my own testimonial against an England XI. I was really gutted I didn't have any other opportunities to play with him. However, in that game, a warm-up to the 1982 World Cup, I scored two goals but Peter keeps telling me I scored a hat-trick. I only played about half the game as my knee was sore but everyone was saying there wasn't anything wrong with me as I'd scored a few goals. Having said that, to play alongside Peter that day was brilliant.

Peter was certainly a character – a great and honest character who was (and still is) larger than life. What you see is what you get with Peter, that's for sure. There's no in-between, which was brilliant and I was like that but in a different way. Peter was a bit louder than me where I would be a bit more tactful. I would disagree with someone if I needed to but Peter would certainly be more vocal about it, let's put it that way. Neither of us liked to see people do things wrong so we're similar in that respect but I would probably put my point over in a different way.

Peter's always been a grafter, which I liked, and Gary Shaw got full benefit from working alongside him – and he was a good goalscorer as well. I got to learn more about Peter as time went on. When I went back to the club as a youth-team coach and watched him at close quarters, he'd train longer and harder than most players at the club, so I was always impressed with that side of him.

At the time we had Dennis (Mortimer) as our captain and were all inspired by the way he played. For me, Dennis was the best player I have ever seen not to be capped for England. Whereas Dennis was a leader in a quiet way, leading by example and getting on with his job, Peter was a leader on the pitch and was more vocal than Dennis. You could say Peter was a leader without the captain's armband in some respects. In a way, I'm a bit surprised Peter was never made a captain but to be honest Peter didn't need a captain's armband to be influential.

If I was managing him I'd tell everyone in the team to follow him. I'd have encouraged Peter to be himself on the pitch; however, I'd have kept a check on him as he had a bit of the devil in him as well – he was a cheeky character. He'd always make sure he won his particular battles on the pitch – not that he ever went looking for a battle. That's a leader for you. He never shirked any sort of challenge – in fact, the bigger the challenge the more he knuckled down to it. The old-fashioned centre-half shoving the centre-forward all the time has gone out of the modern game somewhat. Players want to play into spaces and to drift around these days but I think there's still room for a centre-forward to 'pin' the centre-half down, just like Peter did. Peter was an absolute expert at making sure the centre-half was 'in a game.' He would lead the team from the front. People talk about centre-halves being leaders on the football field but a centre-forward who leads a team is a mammoth figure in football and, for me, Peter was one of the best.

Later on, when Peter had retired from playing, he did do some scouting for me at Villa and I loved going to games with him because he'd have everything organised and knew exactly where he wanted to go and who he wanted to see. From working with Peter for that short space of time I could see how he went into management abroad and did well at that because he had great patience and always wanted to get his point across, but he was never angry at getting his word across – he was dominant but always very patient. Just like when he was playing, he would never give in to anything, even if he was working with someone who was nowhere near good enough, and he would always encourage that person to become better – that's just his personality.

I think Peter is a top bloke in all respects.

Barry Lynch
Former Portland Timbers full-back

As it happened, I knew a bit about soccer in America as I'd been there before with Atlanta Chiefs but Peter and the other lads I travelled there with didn't know anything about the NASL. Although the standard of football wasn't that good compared with our own leagues at the time, there were a lot of players from other countries over there so that improved the quality a little bit, although some players were past their best and seeing their days out; however, we were just young lads learning our trade.

Portland Timbers were originally formed in 1975 and I went over there with Peter, along with about four other players from Wolves, right at the start. I was playing for Villa at the time and I think Peter was at Wolves. I remember the other lads included Barry Powell, Jimmy Kelly, Chris Dangerfield and Donald Gardner. Vic Crowe, the former Villa manager was with us as well, managing the Timbers. We all travelled over there together from Birmingham to Portland.

From what I can remember, Peter was well-built and with his Scouse accent he stood out a bit. On the pitch he was always very vocal and was the focus of the team, with him playing centre-forward. Peter seemed to keep the team together and encouraged everyone around him, and he was also 'one of the lads.' Peter always played hard and wanted the team to do well, and wanted to do well for himself while he was at Portland. I remember in one of our early games we played against Seattle Sounders and Mike England was playing for them as centre-half. Mike was a great player in his day but he was past his sell-by date by then, but Peter turned him inside out that game. It was that game that made me realise that Peter could become a great forward in the future.

Ron Atkinson

Former Aston Villa manager (1991–1994)

Certain clubs have a revered position: at Manchester United it is the number 7 shirt and you've had legendary figures like Best, Robson, Cantona and Beckham wear it, but at Aston Villa it has always been the centre-forward – the number 9. Going back through the years you had people like Trevor Ford, Gerry Hitchens, Andy Lochhead, Andy Gray, and Peter Withe goes in that category – that's how highly rated he was. My father always said the best player to play for Villa was 'Pongo' Waring before the war and he set the standard and all those players I've mentioned come into that absolute 'legend' category. The number 9 has always been the 'hero' of the Villa side as long as I can remember and Peter Withe fits into that status.

I'm sure Peter made his debut for Wolves in a pre-season friendly while I was managing Kettering Town all those years ago. However, the irony of it all was that I once wanted to sign him when I was West Brom manager. I spoke to one of his former managers (Sammy Chung) and he was a little bit derogatory about Peter as he questioned his commitment. Anyway, I went to see him play for Forest in a game against QPR and he dived full-length in the mud and almost got his head kicked in but scored the goal. I thought, 'There's not too much wrong with this lad's commitment.' I didn't sign him (or anyone for that matter) but maybe I should have taken my own advice rather than listening to other people. I think Peter went to Newcastle from Forest.

It had been rumoured that Jo Venglos, when he was appointed Villa manager was told about Peter being a club legend striker and then apparently looked through some record books and confirmed Peter to be his assistant. Peter had been brought back to Villa from Huddersfield to work with Jo and when I replaced him, Peter and Jim Walker were the only two of the existing staff that I kept on. Peter looked after the reserves for me and he came in and just got on with his job, was very conscientious and did very well in that position. During the time he was working with me he was offered the Wimbledon job and took it.

Dean Holdsworth

Former Wimbledon and Bolton Wanderers striker

There were a quite few top British strikers in the late 1970s and early 1980s – Joe Jordan, Mark Hateley, Bob Latchford and Peter Withe. They were real target men in their day – proper number 9s. Aston Villa, in their glory days, with Peter Withe, Gary Shaw and Tony Morley were a force to be reckoned with and Peter, in particular, was highly respected by a lot of people because of the way he played the game.

I was about 14 years old at the time, and growing up I always wanted to play football. Peter was the player I wanted to emulate, as I wanted to be a striker just like him. Although I have never met Peter, my experience of him was second-hand if you like because my football coach would always refer to other players and every time we practised heading, he'd say to us, 'If you can head the ball like Peter Withe, then you're going to do well in the game.' He couldn't speak any more highly of Peter because he was at the top of his game. From then on, I would (as we all probably did) commentate to myself whenever I went up to head the ball during practice matches, 'Here comes Peter Withe and he scores ...' I would then take time to watch Peter on *Match of the Day* and watch how he headed the ball and how he scored his goals. Every time I saw him score on TV I smiled because he was my football 'manual', if you like.

Significantly, the biggest compliment I can give Peter is that later on in my life I tried to emulate the way he headed the ball and how he attacked the ball when I became a professional player myself. When I played for Wimbledon we played Liverpool at Anfield and the BBC Radio Five Live commentator interviewing me after the game said, I 'rose and attacked the ball like Peter Withe.' I instantly smiled because it drew me back to my younger days and how I'd emulate Peter. In fact I congratulated the commentator on his knowledge of players who could head the ball in the right way. It was that interview which made me think that all those days practising heading the ball were worth all the headaches I got from them.

Unfortunately, I didn't wear the wristbands Peter wore – they wouldn't have suited me.

For me, Peter's head was as good, if not better than his feet, because when he headed the ball it went where he wanted it to go and that was always about the technique of eyes open, using your neck muscles and knowing where the ball's going to go.

Incidentally, I joined Wimbledon just after Peter left the club as manager in 1992. It was a great shame because I could have talked to the man and learned a lot about technique and delivery from my boyhood hero – that would have been quite something.

Dave Watson

Former Everton and England defender

I was a young kid when I played for England with Peter – I think he was nine years older than me. Peter was a really good character around the camp and being a fellow Scouser and Evertonian, we hit it off and he was always great company. Being a youngster, he always made sure I was alright.

Even though I was at Everton for 14 years, it was actually when I played for Norwich that I first played against Peter (when he was at Villa). Peter and Gary Shaw were the superstars of the day for Aston Villa. One year we got to the latter rounds of the FA Cup and played Villa at Carrow Road, and within the first ten minutes Villa had a corner and Peter challenged me for the ball and I ended up concussed and got taken off. Villa went on to win the tie. That was my introduction to Peter Withe. However, it was never, ever intentional.

In those days, Peter and Gary Shaw were unstoppable – Peter either scored the goals or would lay the ball on for Gary to score. They were always tough to play against. I remember Peter always wore sweatbands – which was supposed to have stopped him sweating. No, seriously, Peter always got a good sweat on and put in a good shift every game. On the pitch, Peter was a hard player, but off it we were mates and he was always a proper gentleman. However, as soon as he crossed that white line, he would change completely – he was a frigging nuisance, always charging into people and causing problems. He would have this stare that would frighten any young player – including me. It was a great experience for me, looking back, but at the time I didn't think it was so much. Peter was dominant in the air and we gave each other as much as we received – it was toe-to-toe stuff. Peter had the experience where I didn't – he knew where to put his body and when to hold me off. I was just like a raw kid at the time and, more often or not, Peter won the battles with me. As the years went on, I learned from people like Peter and improved my own defensive game.

Peter always had his experience over me, and was a tried and tested centre-forward. He would very often climb above me and smash me on the head but I certainly learned an awful lot from playing against him – he really was one of the top strikers in the country. If he wasn't scoring himself, he was knocking balls down for someone else to score.

I first joined the full England squad in 1984 when I was selected to be a substitute against Scotland. All I can remember is Peter being loud in the England dressing room. Just as I joined the squad I think Peter must have left it around that time.

I've caught up with Peter several times recently and it's always good to see him – he's got a great sense of humour about him. He's a top lad.

Gary Mabbutt

Former Tottenham Hotspur and England defender

As a youngster at Bristol Rovers, I always remember watching Peter on TV when he played for Forest and they won the league and League Cup. Prior to meeting up with him on England duty in 1982 I'd never met Peter before, as he's a 'tad' older than me – by a decade or so.

I've always seen Peter as a 'gentle giant' – a very friendly guy and a great teammate of the England set-up in the early 1980s. Peter got into the England side before I joined up but it was always a pleasure to work alongside him. Of course, on the other side of the fence, playing against him he was always a formidable opponent. In the England dressing room, Peter was quite vocal at times – he certainly wasn't one of the quietest in the camp. He was an important member of the squad and probably fulfilled the same role for England as he did for his club sides.

I'd say the best thing about Peter was that he was a hard but always fair player. I never had any problem with him. We had some great battles, great tackles and some great challenges but I think we were both not considered to be 'dirty' players. Peter was big and a 'man-mountain' to play against but it was never anything else other than him trying to do his best for his team.

I've met up with Peter numerous times since and he's still the same decent guy as he always was back when we were playing for England.

Steve Stride

Former secretary and operations director of Aston Villa FC

I was appointed club secretary in 1979, just before Peter joined us a year later. The first time I met Peter was on a pre-season tour to Germany. Peter joined us in Düsseldorf if I remember rightly, just after he had signed for the club in 1980. Peter and I have been friends since that day and have remained very good friends ever since.

I've been following Villa for over 50 years and Peter, to me, was the best centre-forward I've seen in my lifetime, with Andy Gray a close second. Peter was the ultimate and had everything; he could play it on the ground; he could head the ball; he could pass the ball; he could shield the ball and he could hold the ball up and play others into the play. He also had a fantastic rapport with the Villa supporters and very often threw his sweatbands into the crowd after a game. Sometimes he would also give a bag of sweets to a lucky fan.

Peter was the final piece of the jigsaw for Ron Saunders's 1980–82 team who won the league championship and European Cup. It was special for me because I was around the same age as Peter and, in those days, most players had a rapport with the backroom staff and we used to go out socially with the players. Very often, our wives would join us, usually visiting a local restaurant after a Saturday home game. We were a very close-knit group. They were a great bunch of lads and we were all in it together.

I can recall a funny story involving Peter. I went on holiday one year, I think it was around 1982, and I booked ten nights in Cala Millor in Spain through the club's travel agency. When I got to Birmingham Airport I bumped into Peter and his family. I asked him where they were going and he said Cala Millor so I said it was a coincidence and we agreed to meet up. When we got to Cala Millor, Peter and his family were waiting in the reception of the apartment we were staying at. It was only a very small block of apartments and, low and behold, Peter and his family were located next door to my wife and me.

The thing that struck me about Peter was even when we had gone out at night, had a few drinks and a late night, he would get up early and be out on the beach running for an hour whereas I'd still be in bed with a hang-over. He was a fitness fanatic and even in the close-season you'd find him in his shorts doing some exercises on the beach. I also remember on that holiday, we both bumped into Brian Clough and he came and joined us for a chat.

In the dressing room, Peter was a big personality and an influence on the younger lads in the team. He always talked to the young lads and tried to help them improve their game. Peter was loud in the dressing room but at the same time he made everyone relax – he was a calming influence on the team. Peter was a lot of fun as well. I used to travel on the team coach to away games and Peter had a knack of impersonating a trimphone. Ron Saunders and I used to sit at the front of the coach and we would have to sit and listen to Peter impersonate this sound all through the journey and it got on our bloody nerves.

In my view, Peter would have made a good leader (if there wasn't Dennis Mortimer) as he'd always give 100 per cent on the pitch and you'd always see him throwing his fists at his teammates to gee them up and would rough-up their hair, making himself a nuisance. He was always going to make a good manager with those attributes. When Jo Venglos was looking for an assistant manager, Doug Ellis recommended Peter to him and Jo read up on Peter in a book of Villa greats before appointing him.

One story which sums up Peter was when he went to the World Cup in Spain (1982) he brought me back one of his red England shirts (which I still have to this day). He brought it into the office one day and in typical Peter style, threw it at me and said, 'Here you are.'

Tom Ross

Former Head of Sport at Free Radio (Birmingham) and Talksport commentator

Peter and I developed a special relationship that stemmed from his times at Birmingham City. I started off as a PA announcer at St Andrews and had already interviewed Peter a few times. When I became a reporter for BRMB Radio working for George Gavin it was my job to go to the training ground and go to the games to interview some of the players and the manager. The players in the 1970s and 1980s were much better than they are now in terms of dealing with the media and the fans. For me, Withey was always, always prepared to talk to the media – win, lose or draw he'd talk to anyone. Peter was always laughing as well – he had a smile on his face, maybe not on the pitch but definitely off it. I've got to say, Peter was one of the few football people I've ever felt was telling the truth. Peter was never loud and aggressive off the pitch – on the pitch it was a different matter. On the pitch he was ferocious. My first impression of Peter was that he a nice guy – and he was.

Whatever Brian Clough saw in Peter, he definitely got the best out of him because he became a great, great player. At Villa, Peter had a special relationship with the Holte End, throwing his wristbands into the crowd and giving out bags of sweets. Players these days kiss the badge and it's all PR rubbish but with Peter, when I talked to him about it he always made me feel he believed it. I think only him and Ian Taylor made me think it really meant something to them to play for Aston Villa. For Withey, I think it was because he'd had a lot of clubs before he joined Villa but when Ron Saunders signed him it was like he'd come home. He must have thought his glory days were behind him and suddenly he was playing for Villa and I don't think he believed his luck. Peter was universally loved by the Villa fans and to win the league and then score the winning goal in the European Cup Final he must have been in heaven.

On hearing the news Peter was picked to play for England in 1982, in the same month he'd scored that famous goal in the European Cup, I went to Bodymoor Heath and spoke to him about it and he really couldn't believe it. I'll never forget what he said to me, 'I don't care what happens – I'm just going to love it.' And he did. I think he'd thought his chances of playing for

England had gone but when he'd got picked he must have said to himself he was going to make the most of the opportunity.

When Peter quit playing, I became really good friends with him and Kathy and we'd go out socially and Peter was always great company. I don't know if it was his humble Liverpool upbringing, but what you see is what you get with Peter. For someone who had won the league, the European Cup and had played for England, there was nothing to him – no two sides to him, no 'big time Charlie' about him. Compared to some of today's players who have won nothing but think they are 'big time Charlies', Peter was a different class. To be fair, Peter can teach 99 per cent of modern-day players how to be a superstar and still be humble. He'd always have a laugh with us – Peter was and still is 'top drawer'. However, tongue-in-cheek, Peter is the tightest man I've ever met. He threatened to buy me a drink one day. Joking aside, it's an absolute dream to be in his company and to sum him up in two words – he's a proper bloke.

Gary Newbon

Sky Sports television sports presenter and executive

I first came across Peter when I covered Nottingham Forest for ATV in the Midlands. Peter was a very approachable guy, very media-friendly and a super fella. He definitely had something about him as a person and a player. That's probably why he's still in football management. As a player, he was terrific; strong as an ox and powerful in the air. I thought he was very underestimated and when he hit the headlines in that famous European Cup win he almost missed the ball but, fortunately, it came off his shin, hit the post and went in.

I was very close to Brian Clough, professionally, during the 1970s and 1980s and I remember a Forest game I covered for ATV against Ipswich when they were going for the championship. Forest won 4–0 and Peter scored all four. The story goes that Peter wanted the match ball but Brian Clough seized the ball off Peter at the end and shot off to his office. Apparently, Peter ran down the tunnel, got changed quickly and knocked on Brian's office door and Cloughie said, 'What do you want?'

Peter said, 'I want the match ball.'

In usual Cloughie style, the manager replied, 'You'll get it when you learn to play with it.'

Brian Clough was co-commentating with Brian Moore for ITV for the 1982 European Cup Final, and I was a reporter on the touchline that night. UEFA stitched me up by saying I couldn't get any interviews until one hour after the end of the game. That was no good to me because we were due to go off air shortly after the final whistle. However, before the game, I asked Villa manager, Tony Barton if I could 'dress up' as a substitute and sit on the bench with a hidden microphone. No word of a lie, I sat on the bench that night with Pat Heard on one side of me and Nigel Spink on the other. I was probably the only substitute in a European Cup Final not to be on the teamsheet.

Peter scored the winning goal so after the game the obvious target for an interview was Peter. However, the soundman hadn't given me a long enough cord so I stood up to go to interview Peter but I couldn't get very far because of the short lead and I started to yell at Peter, but he couldn't hear me. I was desperate to get a message to Peter but the only player who heard me was Allan Evans.

Peter White

Journalist and long-time friend of Peter

I was chief sports writer on the *Sports Argus* newspaper in Birmingham before and during Villa's pomp when they won the league and European Cup. When Peter first came to Villa, everyone got our names mixed up, being so alike and he always joked about it. In fact, most foreign stadium announcers when calling the teams out said, 'Number 9, Peter White ...'

Peter would always rib me about this, saying, 'Whitey, you're playing again, tonight. Get your boots on.'

I wasn't actually working during the European Cup Final but I went over to Rotterdam as a fan. I went on a coach and told the driver not to wait for me if

Villa won, as I'd make my own way back home. After the game, I was in the dressing room within ten minutes of the end of the game. If I remember, Brendan Ormsby got me in. I also managed to get on the team coach back to the hotel in Amsterdam, as I was the only journalist to be invited to the after-game celebration – even though I was off-duty. During that journey, I asked one of the players where the cup was as I couldn't see it on board the coach. Apparently, Peter had hidden the European Cup in the toilet, making people believe it had been nicked. Peter was a great joker and always played tricks like that.

I was also on the team plane back to East Midlands airport the next day and sat next to Dennis Mortimer. It was Peter who even suggested dropping me back off at Villa Park from the airport. Those few days could never be replicated. I had a special relationship with the players and the backroom staff; we all worked together and we all socialised together.

In those days, the players could take the European Cup anywhere they wanted so very often Peter would take the cup home in the boot of his car. One day we all went out to a pub in Hockley Heath, near Solihull, and Peter took the cup out of the boot of the car and stood it on the end of the bar inside the pub. Some people didn't believe it was the real thing – they thought it was a replica at first until they saw Peter sitting down with us having a pint.

On another foreign trip, a pre-season tour of Italy, I actually roomed with Peter. He made a point of saying he could sleep through anything; however, after the first night, Peter told me he'd never heard anyone snore so loudly as I did. That was the sort of friendship we had.

Peter was not only a good player, he was always great company and good fun to be around and we still speak now. He has never changed as a person, well maybe except when he was assistant to Jo Venglos. He adopted a strict discipline with the players and with the journos. It was always carte blanche at the training ground (Bodymoor Heath) where us journos had an almost 'open house' to the players. One day, I was walking round Bodymoor and Withey said to me, 'You know you shouldn't be round here don't you? You should be waiting in there (pointing to the press room) for us to finish training.' Talking about Jo Venglos, I asked him once why he chose Peter as his assistant. Jo replied and said he read about Peter in a 'Villa greats' book.

Golf was another social activity most of the players participated in. After training, you'd very often see the lads at The Belfry having a round on the Brabazon course.

They were unbelievable times.

Roger Fewtrell

Businessman and long-time friend of Peter's

I first met Peter when he came to Villa in 1980. I used to go down the Villa to see my other pal, John Gidman, and all the other lads by going into the players' lounge. They used to come back to my nightclub, Boogies, after the games for a drink or two.

I think Peter was a great player – very strong and had lots of courage in the box. He could take as well as give. We have been friends ever since I was best man at Jason's wedding. The team at that time was brilliant and went on to win the European Cup (as it was known in those days).

I still see Peter today. His career has been excellent and he was also very successful as a manager in Thailand, where I now live. I don't think Peter has changed in all the years I've known him and football is still in his blood. We sometimes go out to dinner and lunches and we are still good friends.

The one story I can tell you about Peter was at the European Cup Final in Rotterdam when Villa played Bayern Munich. Peter scored the winning goal in that 1982 final and Villa won the cup. We were all staying at the same hotel in Amsterdam after the game and there were lots of celebrations in the dining room. I filled the cup up with champagne – it took lots and lots of bottles for all the team to have a drink out of the cup. As Peter scored the winning goal he was first to have a drink – well you can imagine the cup was very heavy with all the champagne. When he tried to lift it up to have a drink the motion of the cup was like a bath of water going backwards and forwards and as he tipped it too drink from it he got covered from head to toe with the champagne. The lads had a fit of laughter at Peter's expense – but a very good night was had by all.

Professional Playing Career

Domestic Playing Record (league only)			
Period	Club	Appearances	Goals
1971	Southport	3	0
1971–72	Barrow	1	0
1972–73	Port Elizabeth City (South Africa)	0	0
1973	Arcadia Shepherds (South Africa)	26	16
1973–75	Wolverhampton Wanderers	17	3
1975	Portland Timbers (USA)	22	17
1975–76	Birmingham City	35	9
1976–78	Nottingham Forest	75	28
1978–80	Newcastle United	76	25
1980–85	Aston Villa	182	74
1985–89	Sheffield United	74	18
1987	Birmingham City (on loan)	8	2
1989	Huddersfield Town	38	1
1989	Power Dynamoes (Zambia)	0	0

International Playing Record			
Period	Country	Appearances	Goals
1981–84	England	11	1

Management Record		
Period	Club	Position
1989	Huddersfield Town	Assistant Manager
1989	Power Dynamos	Sabbatical Loan
1991	Aston Villa	Assistant Manager
1991	Wimbledon	Assistant Manager
1992–98	Aston Villa	Youth Development and Chief Scout
1998–2002	Thailand national team	Head Coach
2004–07	Indonesia national team	Head Coach
2012	Stockport Sports	Head Coach
2012–13	PTT Rayong	Head Coach
2014–15	Nakhon Pathom	Head Coach

Playing Honours & Management Achievements

Playing Career Honours

1975	Western Division Champions	Portland Timbers (USA)
1976	Anglo-Scottish Cup Winners	Nottingham Forest
1976/77	Promotion to Division 1	Nottingham Forest
1977	League Cup Winners	Nottingham Forest
1977/78	League Division 1 Champions	Nottingham Forest
1978	FA Charity Shield Winners	Nottingham Forest
1980/81	League Division 1 Champions	Aston Villa
1981	FA Charity Shield Winners	Aston Villa
1982	UEFA European Cup Winners	Aston Villa
1982	FIFA World Club Runners-up	Aston Villa
1983	UEFA European Super Cup Winners	Aston Villa

England Playing Career

Career Record

Played:	11 (2 Sub)
Won:	5
Drew:	3
Lost:	3
Goals:	1

England Caps 1981–1984

12/05/1981	v	Brazil	(H)	Lost	1 – 0	Friendly
20/05/1981	v	Wales	(H)	Drew	0 – 0	Home International
23/05/1981	v	Scotland	(H)	Lost	1 – 0	Home International
09/09/1981	v	Norway	(A)	Lost	2 – 1	World Cup Qualifier (Sub)
27/04/1982	v	Wales	(A)	Won	1 – 0	Home International
02/06/1982	v	Iceland	(A)	Drew	1 – 1	Friendly
27/04/1983	v	Hungary	(H)	Won	2 – 0	Euro Qualifier (1 goal)
28/05/1983	v	N Ireland	(A)	Drew	0 – 0	Home International
01/06/1983	v	Scotland	(H)	Won	2 – 0	Home International
02/10/1983	v	Hungary	(A)	Won	3 – 0	Euro Qualifier (Sub)
14/11/1984	v	Turkey	(A)	Won	8 – 0	World Cup Qualifier

Management Achievements

National Team – Indonesia

2004	Silver Medal in the Tiger Cup

National Team – Thailand

1998	4th place in the Asian Games
1999	3rd place in the King's Cup
1999	Gold Medal Winners in the Southeast Asian Games
2000	King's Cup Winners
2000	Thailand qualified for the Asian Cup in Lebanon
2000	Gold Medal Winners in the Tiger Cup
2001	Thailand qualified for the World Cup – Asia stages
2001	Runner-up for Asia Coach of the Year
2002	Runners-up in the King's Cup
2002	4th place in the Asian Games
2002	Gold Medal Winners in the Tiger Cup

Professional Management & Coaching Qualifications

1982	English FA Preliminary Coaching Award
1984	English FA Full Licence Coaching Award
1987	English FA Football Management
1992	UEFA 'A' Full Licence
2003	English FA Pro-Licence Diploma
2003	UEFA Pro-Licence Diploma
2013	Refresher of Pro-Licence